Psychoanalysis and Holoca
Testimony

Psychoanalytic work with socially traumatized patients is an increasingly popular vocation, but remains extremely demanding and little covered in the literature. In *Psychoanalysis and Holocaust Testimony*, a range of contributors draw upon their own clinical work, and on research findings from work with seriously disturbed Holocaust survivors, to illuminate how best to conduct clinical work with such patients in order to maximize the chances of a positive outcome, and to reflect transferred trauma for the clinician.

Psychoanalysis and Holocaust Testimony closely examines the phenomenology of destruction inherent in the discourse of extreme traumatization, focusing on a particular case study: the recording of video testimonies from a group of extremely traumatized, chronically hospitalized Holocaust survivors in psychiatric institutions in Israel. This case study demonstrates how society reacts to unwanted memories, in media, history, and psychoanalysis—but it also shows how psychotherapists and researchers try to approach the buried memories of the survivors, through being receptive to shattered life narratives.

Questions of bearing witness, testimony, the role of denial, and the impact of traumatic narrative on society and subsequent generations are explored. A central thread of this book is the unconscious countertransference resistance to the trauma discourse, which manifests itself in arenas that are widely apart, such as genocide denial, and the "disappearance" of the hospitalized Holocaust survivors and of their life stories, mishearing their testimonies, and ultimately refusing them the diagnosis of "traumatic psychosis."

Psychoanalysis and Holocaust Testimony provides an essential, multidisciplinary guide to working psychoanalytically with severely traumatized patients. It will appeal to psychoanalysts, psychoanalytic psychotherapists, and trauma studies therapists.

Dori Laub, MD, himself a child survivor of the Holocaust, is Clinical Professor of Psychiatry at the Yale University School of Medicine and a psychoanalyst in private practice. He has worked for decades with victims of genocidal, childhood sexual abuse, and combat trauma. Laub is a cofounder of the Fortunoff video archive for Holocaust testimonies at Yale and has written extensively on the topic of testimony and bearing witness, and on the relationship between testimony and psychoanalysis. Working with the testimonies of chronically hospitalized survivors in Israeli psychiatric institutions is a pioneering step in that direction.

Andreas Hamburger is Professor of Clinical Psychology at the International Psychoanalytic University of Berlin, Germany.

The Relational Perspectives Book Series (RPBS) publishes books that grow out of or contribute to the relational tradition in contemporary psychoanalysis. The term *relational psychoanalysis* was first used by Greenberg and Mitchell to bridge the traditions of interpersonal relations, as developed within interpersonal psychoanalysis and object relations, as developed within contemporary British theory. But, under the seminal work of the late Stephen A. Mitchell, the term *relational psychoanalysis* grew and began to accrue to itself many other influences and developments. Various tributaries—interpersonal psychoanalysis, object relations theory, self psychology, empirical infancy research, and elements of contemporary Freudian and Kleinian thought—flow into this tradition, which understands relational configurations between self and others, both real and fantasied, as the primary subject of psychoanalytic investigation.

We refer to the relational tradition, rather than to a relational school, to highlight that we are identifying a trend, a tendency within contemporary psychoanalysis, not a more formally organized or coherent school or system of beliefs. Our use of the term *relational* signifies a dimension of theory and practice that has become salient across the wide spectrum of contemporary psychoanalysis. Now under the editorial supervision of Lewis Aron and Adrienne Harris, with the assistance of Associate Editors Steven Kuchuck and Eyal Rozmarin, the Relational Perspectives Book Series originated in 1990 under the editorial eye of the late Stephen A. Mitchell. Mitchell was the most prolific and influential of the originators of the relational tradition. Committed to dialogue among psychoanalysts, he abhorred the authoritarianism that dictated adherence to a rigid set of beliefs or technical restrictions. He championed open discussion, comparative and integrative approaches, and promoted new voices across the generations.

Included in the Relational Perspectives Book Series are authors and works that come from within the relational tradition, extend and develop that tradition, as well as works that critique relational approaches or compare and contrast it with alternative points of view. The series includes our most distinguished senior psychoanalysts, along with younger contributors who bring fresh vision. A full list of titles in this series is available at https://www.routledge.com/series/LEARPBS.

Psychoanalysis and Holocaust Testimony

Unwanted Memories of Social Trauma

Edited by Dori Laub and Andreas Hamburger

Routledge
Taylor & Francis Group

LONDON AND NEW YORK

First published 2017
by Routledge

2 Park Square, Milton Park, Abingdon, Oxon OX14 4RN
and by Routledge
711 Third Avenue, New York, NY 10017

Routledge is an imprint of the Taylor & Francis Group, an informa business

© 2017 selection and editorial matter, Dori Laub and Andreas Hamburger;
individual chapters, the contributors

British Library Cataloguing in Publication Data
A catalogue record for this book is available from the British Library

Library of Congress Cataloging in Publication Data
Names: Laub, Dori, editor. | Hamburger, Andreas, editor.
Title: Psychoanalysis and holocaust testimony : unwanted memories of
    social trauma / edited by Dori Laub and Andreas Hamburger.
Other titles: Relational perspectives book series ; v. 79.Description:
    London ; New York : Routledge, 2017. |
Series: Relational perspectives book series ; v. 79 | Includes bibliographical
    references.
Identifiers: LCCN 2016006774| ISBN 9781138859203 (hardback) |
    ISBN 9781138859210 (pbk.) | ISBN 9781315717456 (ebook)
Subjects: | MESH: Stress Disorders, Post-Traumatic—psychology |
    Holocaust—psychology | Psychoanalytic Therapy
Classification: LCC RC552.P67 | NLM WM 172.5 | DDC 616.85/21—dc23
LC record available at http://lccn.loc.gov/2016006774

ISBN: 978-1-138-85920-3 (hbk)
ISBN: 978-1-138-85921-0 (pbk)
ISBN: 978-1-315-71745-6 (ebk)

Typeset in Times New Roman
by Swales & Willis Ltd, Exeter, Devon, UK

Printed and bound in Great Britain by
TJ International Ltd, Padstow, Cornwall

To Johanna Bodenstab PhD 1961–2015

Contents

List of contributors   x

Introduction   1
DORI LAUB AND ANDREAS HAMBURGER

PART I
Social trauma in psychoanalytic practice and
research: media and history   17

1 Treatment, trauma, and catastrophic reality:
   a double understanding of the "too much" experience
   and its implications for treatment   19
   WERNER BOHLEBER

2 Knowing and not knowing: forms of traumatic memory   32
   DORI LAUB AND NANETTE AUERHAHN

3 Traumatic shutdown of narrative and symbolization:
   a failed empathy derivative. Implications for
   therapeutic interventions   43
   DORI LAUB

4 Genocidal trauma: individual and social consequences of
   assault on the mental and physical life of a group   66
   ANDREAS HAMBURGER

5 The psychoanalysis of psychosis at the crossroads of
   individual stories and of history   92
   FRANCOISE DAVOINE AND JEAN-MAX GAUDILLIÈRE

6 The developmental psychology of social trauma
   and violence: the case of the Rwandan genocide   104
   SUZANNE KAPLAN AND ANDREAS HAMBURGER

PART II
Perspectives on testimony 125

7 The question of my German heritage 127
JOHANNA BODENSTAB

8 Visible witness: watching the footprints of trauma 133
DANIEL DAYAN

9 Reflections of voice and countenance in historiography:
methodological considerations on clinical video testimonies
of traumatized Holocaust survivors in historical research 150
SONJA KNOPP

10 Scenic-narrative microanalysis: controlled psychoanalytic
assessment of session videos or transcripts as a transparent
qualitative research instrument 166
ANDREAS HAMBURGER

PART III
Exploration in the social void: the Israel
video testimony project 183

11 The psychiatrically hospitalized survivors in Israel:
a historical overview 185
RAKEFET ZALASHIK

12 The Israel project story 195
DORI LAUB

13 The Israel story: my story 202
IRIT FELSEN

14 Video testimony of long-term hospitalized psychiatrically
ill Holocaust survivors 209
RAEL STROUS

15 The institutional experience: patients and staff responding
to the testimony project 217
BARUCH N. GREENWALD

16 Traumatic psychosis: narrative forms of the muted witness 228
DORI LAUB AND IRIT FELSEN

17 Counter-testimony, counter-archive 242
AMIT PINCHEVSKI

PART IV
Manifestations of extreme traumatization in the testimonial narration of hospitalized and non-hospitalized Holocaust survivors: two case studies   255

18 Introduction   257
DORI LAUB

19 Parapraxis in mother–daughter testimony:
unconscious fantasy and maternal function   260
JOHANNA BODENSTAB

20 Narrative fissures, historical context: when traumatic
memory is compromised   270
SONJA KNOPP

21 Refracted attunement, affective resonance: scenic-narrative
microanalysis of entangled presences in a Holocaust
survivor's video testimony   279
ANDREAS HAMBURGER

22 Discussion of Bodenstab, Knopp, and Hamburger   298
DORI LAUB

PART V
Conclusions   303

23 Unwanted memory: an open-ended conclusion   305
DORI LAUB AND ANDREAS HAMBURGER

24 Epilogue   314
DONALD MOSS

Index   316

Contributors

Nanette Auerhahn, PhD, is a clinical psychologist and psychoanalyst in private practice in Cleveland, OH. She is a child of Holocaust survivors. Dr Auerhahn received her BA from Barnard College and her PhD from Yale University and did post-doctoral training at Stanford University. She has taught at a number of universities including Yale, Stanford, Case Western Reserve, and the California School of Professional Psychology in Berkeley. Dr Auerhahn has worked in various clinical settings including hospitals, mental health centers and residential treatment centers. She specializes in the treatment of personality disorders and posttraumatic stress disorder and has written extensively on trauma and the therapeutic process. Dr Auerhahn has received fellowships from the National Science Foundation, the Mark Kanzer Fund, the Stanford Humanities Center, and Stanford's Center for Research on Women and Gender. Her writings have been awarded the 2012 and 2017 Cleveland Psychoanalytic Center Essay Prizes.

Johanna Bodenstab (1961–2015) was a journalist, author, translator and independent researcher. She held an MA in German literature and theater from Freie Universität Berlin. She was a graduate of the "Psychoanalysis for Scholars" program at Western New England Society for Psychoanalysis in New Haven, CT. She defended her doctoral dissertation on mother–daughter relationships during the Holocaust at Kassel University in 2015.

Werner Bohleber, PhD, Psychoanalyst in Frankfurt am Main, training analyst, German Psychoanalytic Association (DPV), and president DPV 2000–2002. He has been editor of the leading German psychoanalytic journal *Psyche-Zeitschrift für Psychoanalyse* since 1997 and was recipient of the Mary S. Sigourney Award in 2007. His research is concerned with the theory and history of psychoanalysis, adolescence and identity, the psychoanalytic history of the Nazi regime, xenophobia and anti-semitism, and trauma and terrorism. His recent books include *Transgenerationale Weitergabe kriegsbelasteter Kindheiten: Interdisziplinäre Studien zur Nachhaltigkeit historischer Erfahrungen über vier Generationen* (co-edited with Hartmut Radebold, and Jürgen Zinnecker, 2008), and *Was Psychoanalyse heute leistet. Identität und Intersubjektivität, Trauma und Therapie, Gewalt und Gesellschaft* (2012) and *Destructiveness, intersubjectivity, and trauma: The identity crisis of modern psychoanalysis* (2012).

Françoise Davoine, agrégée de Lettres Classiques, PhD in Sociology, is a retired professor from the Ecole des Hautes Etudes en Sciences Sociales in Paris, where for 40 years, until his death in 2015, she held a weekly seminar on "Madness and the Social Link" with Jean Max Gaudillière. She was a member of the Ecole Freudienne de Paris, founded by Jacques Lacan, until its dissolution in 1981. She has worked as a psychoanalyst in private practice, in public mental hospitals and also as a consultant for some 30 years. She is a member of the International Society for Psychological and Social Approaches to Psychosis (ISPS), USA, and an Erickson Scholar in the Erickson Institute of Research at the Austen Riggs Center in Stockbridge, Massachusetts. She has attended regular conferences in Europe, Latin America, and the USA, mainly on the psychoanalysis of psychosis and trauma, at the crossroads of particular stories and Big History. Her publications include, *Crazy Mother* (1998) (made into a film directed by Mieke Bal (2011)), *History beyond Trauma* (2004), *Wittgenstein's Folly* (2012), and *Fighting Melancholia: Don Quixote's Teaching* (2016).

Daniel Dayan is a fellow of the Marcel Mauss Institute, Paris (CNRS,EHESS). He was educated at the Sorbonne, Stanford University, and École des Hautes Études en Sciences Sociales. Dayan holds degrees in Anthropology, Comparative Literature, and Film Studies. He received a PhD in Aesthetics under Roland Barthes and an habilitation in Sociology. Dayan has been a professor at Centre National de la Recherche Scientifique, and the Institut d'Études Politiques, Paris. He has also been a lecturer and visiting professor of Film and Media Theory at the universities of Oslo, Jerusalem, Tel Aviv, Moscow-RGGU, Bergen, Geneva,

Milano, the University of Southern California, Stanford University, the University of Pennsylvania, and the New School for Social Research. Dayan has been a translator, journal editor, and media commentator in print and on screen. He has taken part in three documentaries and contributed chapters and papers to about one hundred books or journals. His most recent books are *La Terreur spectacle: Terrorisme et Télévision*, 2006; *Owning the Olympics: Narratives of the New China* (with Monroe Price, 2009); *Televisao, Das Audiencias aos Publicos* (with J.C. Abrantes 2010). In 1975–76, Dayan was invited to join The American Film Institute (Research and Publications committee) and the Columbia University Seminar on Film. From 1999 to 2004 he was a member of the European Science Foundation, Media Research program. In 2000 he was a resident of the Rockefeller Foundation, Bellagio. In 2001 he served as a foreign expert on media studies for the British Research Assessment Exercise. In 2005 he was invited as a resident fellow at the Institute for Advanced Studies, Hebrew University, and as an Annenberg Scholar at the University of Pennsylvania. In 2006 he was the Free Speech visiting professor at the University of Bergen. In 2010 he received the ICA Fellows classic books Award for his book *Media Events*, written in collaboration with Elihu Katz. In 2012 he was appointed to the Jury of the Bernheim Prize for the Social Sciences. In 2013 he gave the William Phillips lecture (*Partisan Review*, New York). Dayan's work is available in 13 languages.

Irit Felsen, PhD, is a clinical psychologist specializing in the treatment of trauma and traumatic loss. She was born in Israel, the daughter of two Holocaust survivors. She completed her MA degree in clinical psychology at the Hebrew University of Jerusalem and her PhD in psychology at the University of Hamburg, Germany, followed by post-doctoral training at Yale University in the USA. Dr Felsen is an Adjunct Professor at Yeshiva University in New York. Dr Felsen maintains a private psychotherapy practice in Mountain Lakes and in Englewood, NJ, where she works with individuals, couples, families, and groups. Additionally, Dr Felsen serves on an emergency response team for the delivery of clinical services following critical incidents, she is a member of the NGO committee on Mental Health in Consultative relationship with the United Nations, and a researcher with the Yale University Trauma Study Group, Genocide Studies Program.

Jean-Max Gaudillière (1943–2015) graduated from the École Normale Supérieure in Classical Literature, French, Latin, and Greek. He was a professor at the L'École des hautes études en sciences sociales, part of the Center of Studies of Social Movements directed by Alain Touraine, the École Freudienne of Jacques Lacan, and Erikson Scholar at Austen Riggs Center and other training institutions. He worked as a psychoanalyst in private practice in Paris. For 40 years he led, together with Francoise Davoine, a famous weekly seminar at EHESS on "Madness and the Social Link" dealing with madness, trauma, refugees, patients, and abused women and children. His main books, published with Francoise Davoine, are *History beyond Trauma* (2013) and *A World to the Wise* (forthcoming).

Baruch Greenwald (M.S.W., The Hebrew University of Jerusalem 1993), a certified Cognitive-Behavioral Therapist, has worked in the Mental Health division of the Israeli Ministry of Health since 1994, where he opened and directed the Holocaust Survivor Home in Beer Yaacov from 2000 to 2008. His last position before retiring from the Ministry was as director of a regional department for social work in mental health. Baruch has taught at the Ariel University, the Sheinbraun School of Academic Nursing, and the Psagot Institute, and has presented at various international and local conferences including the EABCT in Geneva and the International Conference on Cultural Psychiatry in Tel-Aviv.

Andreas Hamburger, PhD, Psychologist, Psychoanalyst (DPG), and Training Analyst (DGPT, BLÄK), graduated in psychology and German literature. He is Professor of clinical psychology, International Psychoanalytic University, Berlin; Senior Lecturer (Privatdozent), Kassel University, Fellow Researcher, Sigmund Freud Institut, Frankfurt am Main; Training Analyst and Supervisor, Akademie für Psychoanalyse und Psychotherapie, Munich. His current research is concerned with video analysis of Holocaust survivors' testimonies, psychoanalytic supervision, and film psychoanalysis. His principal publications have been on dreams, literature and film analysis, time, language development, and psychoanalytic supervision. He is the editor of *La Belle et la Bête: Women and Male Images in the Movies* (2016) and *Trauma, Trust, and Memory* (forthcoming).

Suzanne Kaplan is Associate Professor of Education and researcher at the Hugo Valentin Centre/Holocaust and Genocide Studies, Uppsala University, Sweden. She was the coordinator in Sweden for USC Shoah Foundation Institute for Visual History and Education and coordinated 330 interviews in 1996–99. She used the archive testimonies as a point of departure for her genocide studies. Postdoctoral studies were carried out in Rwanda. She is a psychologist and child and training psychoanalyst, and a recipient of the Hayman Prize for published work pertaining to traumatized children and adults (2001 and 2007). Her publications include *Children in Genocide: Extreme Traumatization and Affect Regulation* (2008), and *Revenge: On the Dynamics of a Frightening Urge and Its Taming* (with Tomas Böhm, 2011).

Sonja Knopp, MA, is a PhD-candidate in history at Freie Universität Berlin. The working title of her dissertation thesis is History Without Memory: Video Testimony of Traumatized Holocaust Survivors and Their Meaning for the Historiography of the Persecution and Extermination of Romanian-Bessarabian Jewry. Her research brought her to Yale University as a Research Fellow at the Genocide Studies Program and to Yad Vashem in Jerusalem. Currently, she is a Fellow of the Fondation pour la Mémoir de la Shoah Paris.

Dori Laub was born in Cernauti, Romania on June 8, 1937. He is currently a practicing psychoanalyst in Connecticut and works primarily with victims of massive psychic trauma and with their children. He is a Clinical Professor of Psychiatry at the Yale University School of Medicine and Co-Founder of the Fortunoff Video Archive for Holocaust Testimonies. He obtained his MD at the Hadassah Medical School at Hebrew University in Jerusalem, Israel and his MA in Clinical Psychology at the Bar Ilan University in Ramat Gan, Israel. He was Acting Director of the Genocide Study Program (GSP) in 2000 and 2003. Since 2001, he has served as the Deputy Director for Trauma Studies for the GSP.

Donald Moss is a faculty member of the Institute for Psychoanalytic Education, NYU Medical Center. He has served on the editorial boards of *International Journal of Psychoanalysis, Journal of the American Psychoanalytic Association*, and *Psychoanalytic Quarterly*; and is author of *Hating in the First Person Plural* (2003), *Thirteen Ways of Looking at a Man* (2012), and *At War with the Obvious* (in press). He has published more than 50 articles in the past 25 years.

Amit Pinchevski is a Senior Lecturer in the Department of Communication and Journalism at the Hebrew University. His research and publications focus on philosophy of communication, communication ethics, witnessing, and media and collective memory. He is the author of *By Way of Interruption: Levinas and the Ethics of Communication* (2005), and coeditor, with Paul Frosh, of *Media Witnessing: Testimony in the Age of Mass Communication* (2009).

Rael Strous MD, MHA is the Director of the Inpatient Psychiatry Department at the Maayenei Hayeshua Medical Center and full professor of psychiatry at the Sackler Faculty of Medicine, Tel Aviv University. He previously served as the Director of the Ambulatory Service and Deputy Hospital Director of the Beer Yaakov Mental Health Center. He completed his training in psychiatry at the Albert Einstein College of Medicine in New York followed by a clinical research fellowship in psychopharmacology at the Massachusetts Mental Health Center, Harvard Medical School. His research interests are in the fields of psychopharmacology, genetics, neuro-imaging, neurosteroids, epidemiology and ethics. He is the current Editor of the *Israel Journal of Psychiatry*.

Rakefet Zalashik is a historian of medicine and the author of two books on the history of psychiatry in Israel: *Ad Nafesh: Refugees, Immigrants, Newcomers and the Israeli Psychiatric Establishment* (2008 [in Hebrew]), and *Das unselige Erbe: Die Geschichte der Psychiatrie in Palästina und Israel* (2012). Her work has also appeared in journals, such as *Science in Context, The Journal for the History of Psychiatry*, and *Korot: The Israel Journal of the History of Medicine and Science*.

Introduction

Dori Laub and Andreas Hamburger

This book is an inquiry, from a psychoanalytic perspective, into the staggering topic of the sequelae of genocide and extreme social traumatization. It demonstrates how the consequences of social brutality continue to operate latently in the deepest layers of survivors' minds, as well as in the emotional atmosphere surrounding them, where they take the form of, in effect, a conspiracy of silence and denial. We have also attempted to capture the phenomenology of extreme traumatization and tried to identify and highlight its core elements, or 'markers.'

Our study draws on decades of observations made during our clinical work with Holocaust survivors and their offspring (Laub & Felman, 1992; Laub, 1998, 2005), as well as on numerous video testimonies taken from survivors. Some of the subjects of these video testimonies lived regular lives, with families and careers; others had spent decades hospitalized in psychiatric institutions in Israel. The latter represent a deeply traumatized and re-traumatized population, to whom we have dedicated substantial and systematic testimonial and analytic effort (Laub, 2005; Strous et al., 2005).

The phenomena we observed can be thought of as a series of concentric circles, rippling outward from the verbal content of survivors' accounts to other modes of remembering such as their body language, facial demeanor, parapraxes, and transference. The dialectic of remembering and forgetting, the rhythm with which memories came back, at what time and in what form, with what syntax, and what composition: all carried the unique imprint of traumatization and were, in fact, themselves forms of remembering. Yet the survivors were not alone in this process of memory recovery. Even when silent, the therapist and interviewer were active contributors. Similarly, the context surrounding the testimonial event bore the impact of traumatic memories and resonated with their advent. This was particularly apparent in the study of the hospitalized patients. Without its ever being consciously admitted, contextual events triggered by the testimonial process were primarily responsible for the unbroken chain of obstacles we ran into, from the beginning of the project to when it came time to archive the tapes. However, it was the historical variation in societal attitudes towards traumatic memories that constituted perhaps the most decisive factor in blocking or facilitating the remembrance of the traumatization.

Extreme traumatization and denial

Historical events of extreme traumatization elicit powerful emotions on an individual and collective level. Every single genocide—the Armenian, the Jewish, the Cambodian, the Bosnian, the Rwandan—has been accompanied by steadfast denial, even though the facts have been readily available. Indeed, genocide scholars now consider denial to be one of the hallmarks of genocide (Smith, 2014). As clinicians, we shall attempt to understand such denial as an unconscious manifestation of countertransference resistance to extreme trauma—whether the latter has been perceived, imagined, or empathically known. Our own experiences confirmed the trauma literature that we consulted; together, they ripped apart any illusion that our patients were the only ones affected. We were confronted with the fact that trauma residues are not to be found solely in patients' symptoms, reenactments, and life trajectories; they also resonate powerfully in the countertransference responses of every single person who comes into contact with these extreme traumatic events. What remained was to explore our own modes of responding and to understand how such powerful events cast their shadow both on individual responses and on the collective life experience.

Why the Holocaust still?

From the very beginning, we were haunted by the following question: Why, when talking about extreme collective traumatization and its testimony, do we still start from the Holocaust? History has had to deplore many genocides since. Do the testimonies of Holocaust survivors, seventy years after the Nazis' defeat, still demand the focus of our attention? The answer, we think, is yes. The Holocaust is still the main and unique paradigm that not only subverted trust in the advance of civilization—or of what Freud (1939/1964b, 111) termed "intellectuality"—but also changed the writing of history, both utterly and irrevocably (LaCapra, 2014). Giving testimony to this barbarian regression in the midst of a highly developed society not only puts in question notions of progress and social development, but also, as Knopp (2017) argues in this volume (chapter nine), challenges the premises of historiography itself. Objective historiography carries with it the unexpressed conviction that the sequence and continuity of events is not just fortuitous, but reflects something like an evolving process—such as the unfolding of enlightenment, rationality, and socioeconomic growth. The collapse of civilization in the midst of civilization put this conviction deeply in doubt. Humanity may perfect its economic performance and machinery, but since the industrial genocide of Auschwitz we have to accept that progress itself might be as blind and cruel as nature—perhaps even more so.

Work on the testimonies of Holocaust survivors has been a seminal influence on important historical, political, and literary debates for decades. Authors like Cathy Caruth (1996) and Dominick LaCapra (1998) felt their work to have been inspired by Laub and Felman's (1992) *Testimony: Crises of witnessing in literature, psychoanalysis, and history*, even as others questioned the psychoanalytic approach to Holocaust testimony (Alexander, 2004; Trezise, 2008; cf. Laub, 2009). Notably, one fragment of a testimony reported by Laub (1992) in his chapter "Bearing Witness, or the Vicissitudes of Listening" in the aforementioned edited volume has become a steady point of reference in debates on how to represent memories of social trauma and their historical, cultural, and psychoanalytic meanings. It is a survivor's memory of four chimneys being blown up in the Auschwitz uprising, even though historical documents mention only one blown-up chimney. This quotation has attracted attention in the form of a huge controversy on the veridicality and/or 'otherness'—in Derrida's sense—of Holocaust memory (see Oliver, 2003; Delvaux, 2003; Bellamy, 2004; Hirsch & Spitzer, 2009; Prendergast, 2011; Pinchevski, 2012, among many others).

The unspeakability of the Holocaust

At the 2015 International Psychoanalytic congress in Boston, a public panel on *The Future of Holocaust Testimonies*, chaired by Anna Ornstein and featuring Clara Mucci, Andreas Hamburger, and Thomas Trezise, struggled its way through this volatile debate. Adopting a variety of interdisciplinary perspectives, it searched for a new language and a new way of approaching these testimonies so as to ensure their place in future societal discourse. An enterprise of this kind is always simultaneously at risk of seeing survivors too strictly as patients (and hence underestimating their coping potentials), and of seeing history from an overly subjective angle. It is in this context—the search for a mode of addressing this topic that would avoid the aforementioned biases—that we raise the question of a transparent psychoanalytic reading of the testimonies, and what it might add to the investigation of and reflection on historical fact. By explicating the intersubjective nature of memory, denial, and testimony, we can avoid projecting the unspeakable onto survivors as a kind of pathological mutedness, and accept responsibility for our own difficulties in listening.

The uniqueness or 'unspeakability' of the Holocaust is a much-discussed topic; taking such an interpersonal stance might make it easier to understand. The claim of historical uniqueness expresses both piety and a breach in culture; it establishes a kind of "negative sacralization" of the Holocaust (LaCapra, 2014). As social facts, denial and the awestruck feeling of the 'unspeakability' of the Holocaust mirror the difficulty faced by civilized language in trying to represent such acts of barbarism committed in the heart of civilization. Historians agree that memories of the Holocaust are 'unspeakable' not always in the sense of historical opacity—in fact, Nazi atrocities were well documented—but in the sense of a deeper 'inapprehensibility.' To listen to Holocaust testimonies, "one must listen to the silences or read between the lines, attentive to what impels and exceeds understanding" (Trezise, 2001, 62). Here, psychoanalysis, as the art and science of listening to the "unspeakable," may help provide a language to address the unaddressable. The Holocaust, to put the problem in a psychoanalytic key, was an event and an experience that annihilated the good object (humanity, God, the intimate other) in the internal world representation both of the individual and the collective. In its wake, customary forms of experiencing, remembering, and imagining were severely compromised, if not abolished. The processes of symbolization, mental representation, and narrative came to a halt at the nidus of the extreme traumatization. Yet they came to a halt not only, as traditional psychoanalytic trauma theory assumed, by bursting through the stimulus barrier that protects the psyche of the victim, but also—and primarily—by the social interplay between the act of traumatization itself and the mechanisms whereby it might be acknowledged or denied its place in social memory. Both in the event and in the memory of the Holocaust, there was a breakdown of intrapersonal and interpersonal communication. To address the catastrophe, defensive processes were set in motion side by side with patches of erasure or non-recognition of the experience. What emerged were 'shards of memory'—fragments at once of shattered experience and of the defensive operations attempting to contain them. These found their way into fragmented narratives, reenactments, re-experiencing, transference, and, most strikingly, an abundance of countertransference phenomena.

The Holocaust survivors in psychiatric hospitals

In order to examine closely the phenomenology of destruction inherent in the discourse of extreme traumatization, this book will center on a particular case study: the taking of video testimonies from a group of extremely traumatized Holocaust survivors undergoing long-term hospitalization in psychiatric institutions in Israel. This case study will be traced from its inception, when reports of these patients began appearing in public media and television, to the actual archiving of their testimonies at Yale University in 2013. Among the questions explored will be those of bearing witness, testimony, the role of denial, and the impact of traumatic narratives on society and subsequent generations. The central question, however, which has to be kept in mind, is that of the particular clinical state that has, for decades, kept these patients in psychiatric wards. There, they have undergone a plethora of treatment interventions, to which they only partially responded. For lack of a better definition, most of them were diagnosed as schizophrenic and hidden away in substandard private institutions. Only when a routine census of chronically hospitalized psychiatric patients (that is, patients who stayed in the hospital for longer than one year) was undertaken in the 1990s was it accidentally revealed that about 15 percent of the chronic-patient population in Israel were Holocaust survivors—a substantial group whose existence had been unknown, and whose identity remained very much in question. Their medical charts included very little information relating to the history of their Holocaust persecution. Were their traumatic biographies the source of this obscurity? Were they pushed out of awareness, their existence denied, because they were the undeniable evidence of the Holocaust experience and its devastating effects? Perhaps their histories speak to the refusal by Israeli society, by the medical profession, and by individuals to know and remember the extreme trauma that had affected so many of them.

A central thread of this book, which will be revisited time and again, is the unconscious countertransference resistance to trauma discourse, which manifests itself in such widely disparate arenas as genocide denial; the 'disappearance' of the hospitalized Holocaust survivors and their life stories; and practices such as not asking them about their Holocaust experiences, mishearing their testimonies, and ultimately refusing them the diagnosis of 'traumatic psychosis.'

We will examine how this project was conceived of, how it originated, how it unfolded, what the preliminary findings were, and what their implications are in a wide range of arenas, from clinical diagnostics to trauma theory, history, communication and media studies, and, ultimately, the video testimony project. In an era when testimonies were gathered all over the world by the tens of thousands, these were the survivors who were never asked to tell their stories—in spite of the fact that they were easy to find, living together in psychiatric units specifically designated for Holocaust survivors. Moreover, they were approaching the end of their lives, and there was not much time left to hear their stories.

Inasmuch as most of these patients had been diagnosed as schizophrenic and had been hospitalized for decades, the widely held opinion was that they could not be motivated to tell the story of their lives, or were incapable of doing so. It was believed that they had long ago withdrawn into their silent, private, and psychotic world, and had chosen to cease communicating. The door had been hermetically shut.

Having worked with testimonies, both listening to them and facilitating their being given, and having observed for decades the struggles and impediments involved in bearing witness to atrocity and tragedy, we knew these were exactly the survivors—those on the far end of the continuum of witnessing—that we wanted to approach. We had no idea how they would respond. We had no idea whether they would agree and whether they would be able to tell their stories, or what modifications we would have to make in our approach as interviewers, in order to make it possible for them to give testimony.

The communicative breakdowns at the heart of the traumatic experience

The most startling, salient, and impressive finding in a preliminary study of several of these testimonies was the abundance of parapraxes: mishearings, misunderstandings, and, accordingly, flawed responses. These miscommunications could occur on an intrapersonal and on an interpersonal level.

By intrapersonal we mean the internal communication between the survivor and herself. This was apparent when she drew a blank, when she could not find the word she was looking for and replaced it with another, could not elaborate or free associate, or created a metaphor that roughly approximated to but didn't quite say what she wanted to convey. Such intrapersonal parapraxes in survivors essentially reflect a trauma-induced absence to oneself, which precluded the symbolization of traumatic affect and experience. By interpersonal parapraxes we mean survivors testifying together and not accurately hearing each other's words, and interviewers not picking up on such dissonances or simply hearing something other than what the survivor said. Both forms of parapraxis demarcate a communicative breakdown, which we believe lies at the heart of the traumatic experience.

It takes a close reading of the testimonies to locate and comprehend such communicative breakdowns. When survivors who were hospitalized are compared to those who led a regular life, they overlap in form, but can also be very different. In hospitalized survivors whose ability to communicate internally and externally was much more compromised, there was a very high frequency of parapraxes. It was as though the traumatic memory was unformulated, immediate, and fragmenting. Both survivor and interviewer were under its spell. The affects of terror and loss were tangible, and a meaningful narrative was replaced by near stammering. The interviewer had to repeatedly intervene in order to maintain the narrative flow and provide it with cohesion. Yet the interviewer, too, frequently misheard and misunderstood, most likely due to his countertransference response to the omnipresence and immediacy of the traumatic experience. In the testimonies of the non-hospitalized survivors, the narrative flow was spontaneous, evolving, driven from inside, cohesive, and rich in affect and nuance. There were, however, moments of proximity to trauma in which it stalled, sputtered, and was at loss for words. At such times, the interviewer's intervention was needed to bring it back on track. Most noteworthy, however, were the sweeping parapraxes—including overlooked contradictions and incongruities—by both the survivor and the interviewer. It appeared as though, despite the seeming coherence of the narrative, the traumatic experience was only deceptively under control; at bottom, the communicative breakdown was all too present.

The findings described above will be presented in detail in the fourth part of this book dealing with the two testimonies. They also informed the book's writing. A central theme will be that of 'traumatic erasure.'

Communicative breakdowns of the kind just discussed destroy all form. Extreme trauma destroys the 'internal other,' leaving no one to communicate with. Therefore, nothing is communicated and there is a complete void in the internal world representation. Coming near it is like experiencing the proximity of an abyss. 'Traumatic erasure' will be an absence continuously present in this book.

The uniqueness of the hospitalized survivors' testimonies

Other questions were also of great interest to us. How did the hospitalized patients experience and/or remember their persecution differently from other survivors, and so end up with an unlived life? Why have they never stopped living in their unremitting psychotic state? Was their internal language different from that of non-hospitalized survivors? Metaphorically speaking, did it have a different grammar, a different syntax? How did their trauma narratives differ? What affects did they experience, and how did they experience those affects? Could one detect a peculiarity as to how trauma affected their narrative—a 'trauma signature,' so to speak—that was unique to them? We did not expect their survival experiences to be more horrendous than those of other survivors; our inquiry was rather into how similar experiences uniquely impacted their ways of knowing, remembering, retelling, and reliving them. Ours was an attempt at observing the workings of their minds when it came to thinking and talking about their traumatic experiences.

Another question was also close to our heart: What kind of factual history would these survivors be able to tell, as compared to historical information gleaned from written documents and from testimonies of non-hospitalized survivors? Could they contribute an important dimension to the historiography of the Holocaust?

The findings reported in this book do not provide answers to all the questions listed above, yet they do bring new information (some of it surprising) on many core issues related to this project. We would like to stress that the vast majority of the testimonial texts have not been analyzed yet, and we wholeheartedly hope that this volume will elicit interest leading to further research on this vast database. After all, these are the only archived testimonies of psychiatrically hospitalized Holocaust survivors in the world.

It is interesting to reflect on the fate of Holocaust testimony in general. A prevailing myth has it that survivors were not willing to talk, that it took them years before being ready. Evidence suggests otherwise, however. Between the years 1945 and 1950, about 20,000 written testimonies were collected. American psychologist David Boder even audiotaped over 100 testimonies in DP camps in Central Europe in the summer and fall of 1946. The flow dried up not because survivors were reluctant to talk, but because there was no one there to listen. It took a societal shift, a resurgence of interest and curiosity, for the major testimonial projects (Yale's Fortunoff Video Archive and Spielberg's Shoah Foundation) to take hold. This very lack of interest applies as well to the psychiatrically hospitalized Holocaust survivors, who ultimately remained the forgotten witnesses.

There is by now a vast literature on the intergenerational transmission of trauma. We offer examples of such transmission in chapters two and three of this book. Children unconsciously absorb the unconscious and conscious memories and feelings of their parents and proceed to experience and enact them in their own lives. In most instances they are clueless about it. They are more likely, however, to engage in psychoanalytic psychotherapy than are their parents, for whom the traumatic memory is all too close and too real. Hence the abundance of clinical vignettes from individuals of the second generation. Recent publications have also dealt with the transmission of Holocaust trauma to the grandchildren of survivors. We can choose to include these intergenerational transmissions in the broad category of countertransference phenomena; as such, they differ from the experiences of the traumatized victim. We prefer not to address those differences, however, because our concern is primarily with the ever wider repercussions of the traumatic experience, and not specifically with its intergenerational transmission.

Testimonies and psychoanalysis: theoretical considerations

We make generous use of video testimonies as the source of so-called 'clinical vignettes.' In order to clarify our position on this matter we shall now present some theoretical considerations on the relationship between testimony and psychoanalysis.

Testimony is a meeting-place for the mutual witnessing and repair of trauma-induced fragmented memories and psychic disruptions. The testimonial intervention is responsive to and addresses what has been left deeply wounded—that which has not found an opportunity to heal—in the trauma survivor. A psychoanalytic understanding of the relationship between interviewer and interviewee during the testimonial intervention can not only contribute vastly to our understanding of the traumatic damage, but also inform us as to the healing processes that need to be set in motion to repair it.

The uniqueness of the testimonial intervention lies in the fact that there is always an event, an experience—sometimes coextensive with the lifetime itself—that is known to be 'out there,' even if it has not hitherto been consciously formulated. It is thus information that has yet to be recorded or brought to an addressee, to a party interested in receiving it. Testimony is, therefore, a transmittal of information, and there is an internal unrelenting pressure to convey, as well as an external readiness and eagerness to receive it.

When such a transmission has been accomplished, the survivor no longer is or feels alone with the inexpressible extreme experience. She is less helplessly prey to its devastating impact. The internal cauldron of sensations and affects has been put into the frame of a sequential narrative. This narrative enables such sensations and affects to be remembered, transmitted, and, eventually, forgotten. Such a narrative is, however, never complete, and highly charged blank spots of the inexpressible (and almost unimaginable) experience persist, exerting their magnetic power on the survivor, who feels compelled endlessly to revisit them, even as she constantly flees their proximity.

It is these intense affect-laden voids of memory, which can obliterate the traumatic experience in its entirety, that constitute the power source driving testimony and exerting the pressure for its deliverance. This holds true for a broad range of experiences of extreme trauma. In more recent observations, cancer survivors, when feeling safe in the company of other survivors, are also driven to 'tell their story' of their encounters with death. The group of chronically hospitalized 'psychotic' Holocaust survivors, interviewed in Israel in recent years, experienced the same internal pressure to bear witness. Unfortunately, their capacity to symbolize, free associate, reflect, and verbalize has been so profoundly damaged by the chronic nature of their condition (which has lasted for decades), by their social isolation, and by their somatic treatments (insulin shock, ECT, and psychotropic medication), that they were able to create no more than a narrative that was constricted, static, and fragmented.

The goal of traditional psychoanalysis, on the other hand, is to allow for the emergence of the unconscious through the method of free association and the elucidation of the transference experience. There is no particular force, no inner compulsion that drives it, no story that reaches for words. It is, rather, a surrender to the wanderings of the mind, made possible while feeling protected by the analyst's nonjudgemental presence and neutrality. It has a rhythm set by the frequency of the sessions, and it lacks an endpoint in time. Dreams, parapraxes, transference experiences and enactments, and, last but not least, remembrances provide the latticework along which the analytic narrative unfolds. Although there is no explicit addressee in traditional analysis, the analyst's emotional presence implicitly fulfills that function, thus becoming the equivalent of the testimonial 'thou.'

The psychoanalytic literature is indeed replete with references to the internal good object, usually highlighting the infant's relationship with the mother. Beginning with Freud's (1929/1961) concept of the oceanic feeling, of being one with the universe, that arises from the oneness with the mother, a number of psychoanalytic concepts—from Winnicott's (1953) "transitional object" to Mahler's (1963) developmental phase of symbiosis, Henri Parens's (1969) "inner sustainment," Mahler, Pine and Bergman's (1975) "object constancy," and Kohut's (1971) "self object"—all deal with processes that are essential for internal representation and symbolization to occur. These latter are core components of the testimonial intervention.

Within the spectrum of psychoanalytically informed therapeutic interventions, the testimonial process possesses four unique elements: the internal pressure to transmit and tell, the real story that is 'there,' the yearning for a listener to receive it, and the presence of such a listener. On closer scrutiny, these four elements do not place testimony in a category that is separate from psychoanalysis. Testimony and psychoanalysis are both essentially dialogic. The analysand does not speak into a void, even if he speaks to himself. It is his own internal good object, projected onto the analyst, that he addresses in such a case. In both processes, the narrative deepens and branches out, taking turns that may come as a surprise to the narrator. Freud's (1933/1964a, 80) dictum, "where the id was, there the ego shall be," applies to both, although in the lengthier process of psychoanalysis this can go much further than in the single-session testimony. Furthermore, in both, there is set in motion a process that can continue on its own far beyond the timeframe of the psychoanalysis or testimonial event. This process includes, but is not limited to, symbolization, self-reflection, and remembering. While it is not a particular event that serves as an organizing principle like in testimony, psychoanalysis, too, leads to the recovery of memories that may emerge as organizing principles and thus become building blocks of the psychoanalytic narrative. The remaining basic difference between testimony and traditional psychoanalysis may be limited to the inner intense pressure to transmit and the experience of transmission itself, which are at the center of the testimonial intervention. The latter can, therefore, be seen as a piece of psychoanalytic work that is limited in scope and does not include work with parapraxes, transference, or dreams.

The testimonial momentum may also be operative, in traditional psychoanalysis, when traumatic experience is involved. At such a juncture it becomes the process that fuels the therapeutic action and provides the impetus for clinical movement and flow. It would be methodologically very difficult to isolate and study such momentum in the context of traditional psychoanalyses; therefore, the nontraditional modality of the testimonial intervention is needed in order to provide the most suitable research setting that can capture the testimonial momentum for in-depth investigation.

Psychoanalytic and interdisciplinary approaches to social trauma and testimony

The study of the Holocaust and of Holocaust testimony cannot be accomplished through the narrow lenses of a single academic discipline. Both event and experience happened in the past, yet they remain ever present. The events are so unsettling, radical, and multifaceted, the experiences so extreme, unimaginable, and multilayered, that it takes an interdisciplinary integration to begin to grasp them. This book is an example of one such attempt at integration. Psychiatry, psychoanalysis, history, media studies, and literature are represented in it.

The book is divided into four parts. Part I introduces the frame and substance of the trauma discourse—where it is positioned in the history and theoretical evolution of psychiatry and of psychoanalysis, and what phenomenology it addresses. Part II contains reflections on the process of giving video testimony and the methodology of its evaluation; represented are the perspectives of a media scholar, a historian, and a psychoanalyst. Part III describes the evolution and implementation of the Israel Project and its historical contextualization. Part IV presents discussion and comparison of two video excerpts, one from the testimony of a survivor who led an adaptive life, the other from a survivor who spent the last five decades in a psychiatric hospital.

Conclusion

To conclude this introduction, we would like to recapitulate some of the ideas central to this book. The murderous atmosphere of the camps, with its failure of human empathy, led to a traumatic shutdown of symbolization and of narrative. Communicative breakdowns ensued that manifested themselves in parapraxes of different kinds and in memories that were fragmented and ultimately brought about a traumatic erasure of the whole experience. The testimonial intervention, the resumption of dialog with an external and internal 'Thou,' sets the processes of memory (re)integration in motion and thereby can be considered as psychoanalytic work that is limited in scope. Careful methodological consideration is necessary to evaluate these testimonies of trauma; the scenic-narrative micro-analytic approach, by focusing in detail on the transferential moments of the testimony, was able to illustrate the above mentioned communicative breakdowns in all their richness and complexity. An interdisciplinary and intergenerational approach further enriches these findings, in particular those regarding the ubiquity of countertransference resistance. We have become convinced, from even our brief incursion into examining the phenomenology of trauma discourse in our case study, that countertransference plays a very central role; we recommend considering the whole evolution of this project as part of trauma discourse. In that sense, the unbroken chain of obstacles we ran into can be seen as countertransference resistance to knowing the reality of extreme traumatic experience, irrespective of the damage that comes in the wake of such refusal. The life of these patients, over the past four to five decades, was defined by such a refusal to know on the part of their caregivers. The majority were diagnosed as schizophrenic, treated by a plethora of biological interventions, and kept in chronic inpatient facilities. No matter what their symptoms, this diagnosis never changed. Out of the twenty-six we interviewed, we found no more than four who qualified, in our opinion, for that diagnosis, inasmuch as they experienced active delusional systems. The possibility that extreme traumatic experience could generate psychiatric symptoms, and perhaps even psychotic states, was never seriously entertained by those who treated them. This diagnostic refusal, or rather misdiagnosis, constitutes a clear indicator of unconscious countertransference resistance to the acknowledgement of trauma. History has repeatedly taught us what the consequences of such a refusal to know, when it occurs on the political and the societal level, can be.

There are many people to whom we would like to express our thanks for supporting this project. Marianne Leuzinger-Bohleber and Werner Bohleber discussed many aspects of the reanalysis of the Israel testimonies with us; the directors, medical staff, and staff of the Beer Yaakov Mental Health Center, doctors Moshe Kotler, Mordechai Weiss, Rael D. Strous and Baruch Greenwald, the Lev Hasharon Mental Health Center, and doctors Avraham Bleich, Yuval Melamed and Boris Finkel helped with the Israel project, as did the Department of Psychiatry, Yale University School of Medicine, New Haven, Connecticut. The study was supported by grants from the Institute for Social and Policy Studies, Yale University, the Conference on Jewish Material Claims Against Germany, Inc., and the International Psychoanalytic Association. We are very grateful to Jean-Jacques Petrucci, Susan Jones, and Paul Franz for editorial assistance.

No one, however, was so much a sustaining element for this book as Johanna Bodenstab, to whom we dedicate it in love and friendship. She was taken away from us before we reached the harbor. If humanity, as an emphatic concept, is something like the sea of all individual human beings' decisions to be human, then Johanna was a most beautiful wave in it.

References

Alexander, J. C. (2004). On the social construction of moral universals: The "Holocaust" from war crime to trauma drama. In J. C. Alexander, R. Eyerman, B. Giesen, N. J. Smelser, & P. Sztompka (Eds.), *Cultural trauma and collective identity* (pp. 196–263). Berkeley, CA: University of California Press.
Bellamy, E. J. (2004). "Laboratories" against holocaust denial: Or, the limits of postmodern theory. *Parallax, 10*(1), 88–99.
Caruth, C. (1996). *Unclaimed experience: Trauma, narrative, and history.* Baltimore, MD: Johns Hopkins University Press.
Delvaux, M. (2003). Dichtung und wahrheit: Jacques Derrida and the untranslatability of testimony. *Studies in Practical Philosophy, 3*(2), 40–56.

Freud, S. (1961). Letter from Sigmund Freud to Romain Rolland, July 14, 1929. In E. L. Freud, T. Stern, & J. Stern (Eds.), *Letters of Sigmund Freud 1873–1939* (p. 388). London: Hogarth Press. (Original work published 1929)

Freud, S. (1964a). New introductory lectures on Psycho-Analysis. *Standard Edition, 22*, 1–182. (Original work published 1933)

Freud, S. (1964b). Moses and Monotheism. *Standard Edition, 22*, 1–138. (Original work published 1939)

Hirsch, M., & Spitzer, L. (2009). The witness in the archive: Holocaust studies/ memory studies. *Memory Studies, 2*(2), 151–170.

Knopp, S. (2017). Reflections of voice and countenance in historiography: Methodological considerations on clinical video testimonies of traumatized Holocaust survivors in historical research. This volume, chapter 9.

Kohut, H. (1971). *The analysis of the self: A systematic approach to the psycho-analytic treatment of narcisstic personality disorders*. New York: International Universities Press.

LaCapra, D. (1998). *History and memory after Auschwitz*. Ithaca, NY: Cornell University Press.

Laub, D. (1992). Bearing witness, or the vicissitudes of listening. In D. Laub & S. Felman, *Testimony: Crises of witnessing in literature, psychoanalysis, and history* (pp. 57–74). Routledge: New York

Laub, D. (1998). The empty circle: Children of survivors and the limits of recon-struction. *Journal of the American Psychoanalytic Association, 46*(2), 507–529.

Laub, D. (2005). From speechlessness to narrative· The cases of holocaust histo-rians and of psychiatrically hospitalized survivors. *Literature and Medicine, 24*(2), 253–265.

Laub, D. (2009). On holocaust testimony and its "reception" within its own frame, as a process in its own right: A response to "Between history and psychoanalysis" by Thomas Trezise. *History & Memory, 21*(1), 127–150.

Laub, D., & Felman, S. (1992). *Testimony: Crises of witnessing in literature, psychoanalysis, and history*. Routledge: New York.

Mahler, M. (1963). Thoughts about development and individuation. *The Psycho-analytic Study of the Child, 15*, 307–324.

Mahler, M., Pine, F., & Bergman, A. (1975). *The psychological birth of the child*. New York: Basic Books.

Oliver, K. (2003). Subjectivity and subject position: The double meaning of witnessing. *Studies in Practical Philosophy, 3*(2), 132–143.

Parens, H. (1969). Inner sustainment: Metapsychological considerations. *The Psychoanalytic Quarterly, 39*(2), 223–239.

Pinchevski, A. (2012). The audiovisual unconscious: Media and trauma in the video archive for holocaust testimonies. *Critical Inquiry, 39*(1), 142–166.

Prendergast, J. (2011). Discontinuous narrative: The trace dance. *Current Narratives, 1*(3), 25–34.

Smith, R. W. (2014). Genocide denial and prevention. *Genocide Studies International, 8*(1), 102–109.

Strous, R., Weiss M., Felsen, I., Finkel B., Melamed Y., Bleich A., Kotler M., & Laub, D. (2005). Video testimony of long-term hospitalized psychiatrically ill holocaust survivors. *American Journal of Psychoanalysis, 162,* 2,287–2,294.

Trezise, T. (2001). Unspeakable. *The Yale Journal of Criticism, 14*(1), 39–66.

Trezise, T. (2008). Between history and psychoanalysis: A case study in the reception of Holocaust survivor testimony. *History & Memory, 20*(1), 7–47.

Winnicott, Donald W. (1953). Transitional objects and transitional phenomena. *International Journal of Psychoanalysis, 34,* 89–97.

Part I

Social trauma in psychoanalytic practice and research
Media and history

The first section of the book addresses the basic concept of social trauma from a psychoanalytical perspective. It comprises six chapters. The first, by Werner Bohleber, charts the history of the interest of psychiatry and psychoanalysis in traumatization and the political and social events that led to research in this area. Bohleber examines the difficulties psychoanalysis initially faced in conceptualizing traumatic phenomena and the various theories it drew on. He emphasizes how crucial it is to recognize that a real event has occurred and to keep such historicity present in the treatment. Next, Dori Laub and Nannette Auerhahn present a spectrum of traumatic memories, organized on a continuum of 'knowing and not knowing,' each form progressively representing a consciously deeper and more integrated "level of knowing," and hence increasing integration and ownership of the memory. Both deficit and defense, ego capacity and the extremity of the trauma, its immediacy and distance, and, most importantly, its overwhelming nature, are at work in giving form to the traumatic memory. In a further chapter, Laub postulates a theory of object deficit. In his view, the absence of an internal dialogic 'thou' is the cause for the shutdown of the processes of narrative and symbolization, thus foreclosing the possibility of an internal representation of the traumatic experience. He attributes that absence to the complete failure of empathy in the external environment of the Holocaust. When there is no responsive 'other' on the outside, there is no longer a matrix of two people—the self and the resonating other—in one's internal world representation. Under such circumstances, faith in human communication dies. In light of the above assumptions, there follows an exploration of the principles of therapeutic intervention. In Chapter 4, Andreas Hamburger differentiates the broad DSM 5 diagnosis of PTSD from a socio-clinical perspective. He distinguishes between individual and social—especially genocidal—trauma. One of the main differences to be recognized here is that social traumatization targets whole groups, and thus affects the individual's immediate holding environment, cutting it off from important protective processes that foster resilience. Furthermore, social trauma is implemented in a societal context, thus involving the surrounding society in the traumatic process. Both conditions entail major consequences for the impact and prognosis of the resulting posttraumatic disorder. Special attention is devoted to social denial as perpetuating the posttraumatic condition. Next, Francoise Davoine and Jean-Max Gaudillière describe the connection between madness and denied trauma in two case examples, exemplifying the healing affect of a witnessing analyst. In the last chapter of this section, Suzanne Kaplan and Andreas Hamburger discuss the specificity of this kind of traumatization when children and adolescents are afflicted. They illustrate the argument of this chapter with findings from Kaplan's video testimony work with child survivors of the Rwandan genocide.

Chapter 1

Treatment, trauma, and catastrophic reality

A double understanding of the "too much" experience and its implications for treatment

Werner Bohleber

Introduction

For a long time, research on trauma was more or less a blank page in the theoretical and clinical psychoanalytical discourse. Although psychoanalysis had begun as a theory of trauma, and although Freud would return time and again to trauma (particularly during World War I), and despite the looming barbarism of National Socialism, psychoanalysis, as a whole, had not attributed the significance it ought to have done to political and social violence. While the psychic consequences of both world wars compelled one to focus on traumatization, interest therein paled and was extinguished altogether a short time thereafter. Given the multiple catastrophes and extreme experiences that people were exposed to and suffered from during the twentieth century, trauma ultimately became the signature mark of the entire century. Considerable time was to elapse, however, before psychoanalysis, psychiatry, and other human sciences took up this theme and made it a central theme of research. Only after the Vietnam War, once the diagnosis of PTSD became part of psychiatric nomenclature in 1980, did comprehensive research on traumatization get under way. In psychoanalysis, it was, above all, the survivors of the Holocaust who enforced a renewed and sustained pursuit of the theory and treatment of trauma. They confronted psychoanalysts with the effects of extreme experience, which were hitherto unknown. Through the feminist movement in the 1980s, a public debate was initiated on the subject of sexual abuse and its consequences, which then brought about a renewed pursuit of these within psychoanalysis. Taken as a whole, and in recent decades, trauma has experienced a huge boost in attention, so much so that in everyday communication, the concept has assumed an almost banal character. Today, trauma research is anchored in many disciplines, beginning with psychiatry through to literary studies.

That, for a considerable period of time, psychoanalysis experienced difficulties with the theoretical and clinical understanding of trauma, is a circumstance that goes back to its theoretical preferences. The field of psychoanalysis was the inner world of the human being—the unconscious, and unconscious phantasies. For many analysts, the adequate integration of external reality seemed like an intrusion on psychic reality and the meaning of the unconscious. As a consequence, research into and adequate treatment of traumatization lagged considerably behind. This is owing to the fact that trauma is not only the consequence of a shaking to the core of the psyche's structure, but also that the ego/self is abruptly overwhelmed and reacts with helplessness, fear of death and annihilation anxiety: the psychic processing mechanisms become paralyzed, and only emergency reactions are possible. This experience of massive psychic overwhelming then results in permanent change to the psyche's organization. Naturally, not every traumatic situation impacts upon everyone in the same way; predisposing factors also play a role. The normal functioning of psychic organization is, however, suspended. While the traumatic event and the experience thereof are registered, they are not psychically integrated by way of the associative formation of meaning. The attempt at integration is only subsequently set in motion, where the ego/self—challenged by repetition compulsion—attempts to process the consequences, and to integrate the trauma into its patterns of experience.

This description of traumatic processes remains relatively cursory, serving only to emphasize the psychically unbearable weight, the "too much" that characterizes external reality in the case of traumatization. Detailed consideration reveals, however, that the situation is more complex. The reason for addressing the topic here is to elucidate why, for a considerable period of time, analysts have had such great difficulties when it comes to appropriately conceptualizing traumatic phenomena.

Psychoanalytic models of the trauma

How do psychoanalysts describe the psychic reality of traumatic experiences today? For a psychoanalyst, it is not enough to study the affective-cognitive storage of traumatic memories; the aim is rather also to comprehend the horror, the pain, the abandonment, and the fear of death and annihilation which shattered the psychic equilibrium, and which then form the inner core of the traumatic experience. Before pursing this in greater detail, I would like first to give a brief presentation of two of the main models of trauma which we find in psychoanalytic theory. They also form the basis for the further discussion. The first is based on Freud's psycho-economic model, the second on Ferenczi's object-relations psychological approach.

Sigmund Freud's psycho-economic model of trauma

In *Beyond the Pleasure Principle* (1920/1955), Freud developed a model of trauma from a psycho-economic point of view. In the moment of traumatization, the excessive quantum of excitation cannot be psychically bound and overwhelms the ego, breaking through the protective shield. The force of the surging quantities of excitation is too great to be mastered. In order to accomplish the task of psychic binding, the psychic apparatus regresses to more primitive modes of response. Freud introduces the concept of the repetition compulsion in order to describe the special nature of this experience beyond the dynamics of the pleasure–unpleasure principle. Through the repetition compulsion, the traumatic experience is actualized in the hope of thereby psychically binding the excitation and setting the pleasure principle back in motion, as well as its associated forms of psychic response.

In *Inhibitions, Symptoms and Anxiety* (1926/1959), Freud connected the psycho-economic view of trauma with his theory of anxiety. He draws on the concept of automatic anxiety that he developed for the actual neuroses. The excessive quantity of excitation in the traumatic situation gives rise to a massive anxiety. It floods the ego, which is defenceless against this onslaught, and renders it absolutely helpless. Automatic anxiety has an indefinite quality and lacks an object. In a first attempt at mastery, the ego attempts to convert the automatic anxiety into signal anxiety, which makes it possible for the absolute helplessness to be transformed into an expectation. The ego thereby develops an inner activity and repeats the traumatic experience "actively in a weakened version, in the hope of being able itself to direct its course" (1926/1959, 167). The situation of external dangers is thereby internalized and acquires significance for the ego. The anxiety is symbolized and no longer remains indefinite and objectless. The trauma thus acquires a hermeneutic structure and becomes possible to overcome.

Baranger, Baranger, and Mom (1988) have rightly emphasized this economic aspect of automatic anxiety as a key element of the traumatic experience. They characterize the anxiety situation, with its psychic indeterminacy and objectlessness, as the "pure trauma." What the authors characterize as pure trauma, Freud conceptualized as absolute helplessness. The traumatized person attempts to control and alleviate the pure trauma by giving it a name and incorporating it into a comprehensible, causal system of behavior. The authors emphasize the paradox that the trauma— as something alien—is actually intrusive into the psychic organization; however, as long as it remains alien, it is revived and falls into repetitions without becoming comprehensible. Since human beings generally cannot live without explanations, they attempt to give the trauma an individual meaning and to historicize it. These retroactive historicizations are mainly screen memories. It is the task of the analytic process to recognize these screen memories as such, and to reconstruct the authentic history, whereby the task of historicizing, which means comprehending the trauma as a part of the past, is open-ended, basically endless.

In *Inhibitions, Symptoms and Anxiety*, Freud repeatedly described the helplessness experienced by the ego as the consequence of an object loss. This form of complete loss of internal protective objects constitutes the foundation of the second model of trauma.

The model of trauma in object-relations theory

With the development of object-relations theories, quantitative considerations concerning an intolerable mass of excitation that floods the ego were rejected. The paradigm for the model is no longer an isolated experience with a shock impact—such as an accident—but the object relationship itself. Ferenczi anticipated many insights of later research into trauma. Above all, his work on the "Confusion of the Tongues Between the Adults and the Child" (1933/1949) is an analysis of traumatic disorders that still remains modern today. Michael Balint (1969) was the first to follow him in this respect. He emphasized that the traumatogenic quality of a situation depends on whether an intensive relationship has developed between the child and the object. The object relationship itself thus acquires a traumatic quality. As later studies (Steele, 1994) confirmed, it is not primarily the child's injuries from physical force that produce a traumatic disorder; rather, the most intensely pathogenic element is mistreatment or abuse by the person whose protection and care is actually needed. This viewpoint broadens the understanding of psychic reality in a traumatic situation.

The greater the trauma, the more severe the damage to the internal object relationship, and the more severe the breakdown in the protective, stabilizing internal communication between self- and object-representations. This gives rise to isolated fragments of traumatic experience that are encapsulated and cut off from the internal communication.

The object-relations theory approach to trauma theory was further developed by research into the severe traumatization that was suffered during the Holocaust. A key psychic consequence of such experiences is the breakdown of the empathic process. The communicative dyad between the self and its good internal objects breaks down, resulting in absolute internal isolation and the most intense desolation. The internal good object becomes silent as an empathic mediator between self and environment, and the trust in the continual presence of good objects and the expectation of human empathy is destroyed (Cohen, 1985; Kirshner, 1993; Laub & Podell, 1995). This conception gives us a better understanding of the experiential core of severe traumatization. It consists of a domain of experience that is almost incommunicable: a catastrophic isolation, an inner abandonment that not only paralyzes the self and its possibilities of action, but also annihilates it, which is at the same time accompanied by mortal fear, hatred, shame, and despair.

Attachment research has also developed, in a similar way, a conception of an inner traumatic core which is almost incommunicable. An attachment trauma is generated by neglecting the child in the sense of leaving the child psychologically alone in the midst of emotional distress. Allen described this point with extreme simplicity: "the essence of traumatic experience is being afraid and alone" (Allen, 2013, 164). Being alone means that there is no one to help regulate the intense emotional distress. The traumatic experience is conceptualized as an unmentalized inner core of experience.

The conceptions in object relations theory represent a major advance in the understanding of trauma. We nevertheless require both the psycho-economic models and the models based on object relations theory in order to comprehensively cover the psychic processes of traumatization. Allow me to recapitulate how the different conceptualizations of trauma have described the intrusion of an excessive reality and its effect on the psychic organization. The psycho-economic models center on the violence and abruptness of the intrusion of an overwhelming outside reality into the psychic organization. Metaphorically speaking, the psychic texture cannot absorb or bind the stimuli because of their excessiveness of excitation.

Other concepts used in this context are 'automatic objectless anxiety,' 'pure trauma,' and an 'absolute helplessness of the ego.' The object relational models, however, center on the destruction of the empathic protective shield which is formed by the internalized primary objects; a destruction with absolute inner loneliness and the most extreme hopelessness as a consequence thereof. Other concepts used in this context are a quasi-autistic incommunicable region, an unmentalized foreign body, a rupture of the network of signifiers (Kirshner, 1994), a black hole (Kinston & Cohen, 1986). Seeing both models together, then, the object relational group of concepts are better suited to explain the psychic phenomena of loss of trust in the continuous presence of good objects, and the loss of trust in the shared symbolically mediated world by which we are preconsciously connected. They are also better suited to explain the traumatic breakdown of the very construction process by which we generate meanings. However, to explain the direct traumatizing force, which is a massive surplus, a 'too much' that ruptures the psychic structure, we also need the psycho-economic models.

After this review of psychoanalytic concepts of trauma, I would now like to turn our attention to some clinical problems in the treatment of traumatized patients.

Reconstruction, historicization, and mental integration of traumatic memories

The excessive arousal in a traumatic situation significantly alters the processes of encoding and storing of incoming information, thereby disrupting or prohibiting the subsequent consolidation of a memory. The integrative function of memory is overwhelmed and shuts down, as the self and its functions collapse, surrendering to the situation by numbing physical and emotional pain (Krystal, 1988). Consequently, this leads to the emergence of a dissociated self-state, as a result of the fact that the traumatic experience and the resulting memories have become encapsulated. Since the time Freud replaced it with repression, the concept of dissociation has long been absent from psychoanalytic theoretical and clinical discussion. Not until recently did the concept reclaim its place within the corpus of psychoanalytic theory. I cannot, however, go into this any further here. What strikes me as significant, however, is the way in which the mechanism of dissociation creates multiple discontinuous self-states. When activated, they cause the affected individual to enter into an altered state of consciousness.

Metaphorically, this had long been characterized as a 'foreign body' within the psychic matrix. This means that it cannot connect or exchange with the associative tissue of the psyche.

I must emphasize, however, that we should not think of this dissociative encapsulation as a complete isolation, but rather, as a matter of degree in the limitations it places on possible connections between thoughts. Seen in terms of neurobiology, Siegel (2006) considers an unprocessed trauma to be an interrupted cortical consolidation process, whereby the memory of the traumatic events cannot be transferred into permanent, explicit memory. Psychoanalysis enables us to depict this kind of process with greater nuance. The encapsulated material cannot be brought into a free exchange with other parts of the associative network of the mind. Depending on the severity of the trauma, this exchange is obstructed, yet not completely excluded from the associative stream of psychic material, or from any transformation of the material. Evidence of this is provided by empirical trauma research. A study by Guez et al. (2011) has shown that patients suffering from PTSD or Acute Stress Disorder exhibited a marked impairment in their associative memory for new information learned after the traumatizing event. In addition, a tendency to falsely associate unrelated stimuli to the traumatic material was also identified. This implies, for example, that the traumatic affect may associatively attach itself to previously experienced reactions, which were hitherto not related to the traumatizing event. They can now erupt as negative memories with a similar force and abruptness like the traumatic memory itself. This should consequently be born in mind when, during therapy, intrusive phenomena are encountered.

In addition, what we discover again and again in therapeutic work with traumatized persons are certain typical psychic transformations in traumatic memories.

1   The traumatic experience confronts the ego with a "fait accompli" (Furst, 1978). The ego's reactions are too late in coming. They do not come in response to an impending danger, but only after the event, and once the ego has been passively subjected to the shock of trauma. The collapse of the self in the traumatic situation can cause long pre-existing, threatening, and repressed fantasies to break into consciousness. Internal archaic convictions can then present themselves as having become true, just as central, frightening images can also become almost insolubly fused with the experience of the traumatic situation.

2   Another type of transformation can occur after the traumatic event. This is because the trauma suffered tends to be revived, and to repeat itself in flashbacks, in nightmares and through symptoms. The repetition has the character of something intrusive and not comprehended, but at the same time it is also the ego's attempt to master the incomprehensible. The traumatized person attempts to tame and attenuate the pure trauma, in that he seeks to integrate it into a comprehensible causal processing system. These subsequent attempts at historicization are predominantly screen memories. One typical form of subsequent processing following the traumatic experience prompts some victims of trauma to attempt to escape from this ensuing sense of passivity—of being completely at another's mercy—by blaming themselves for what happened in order to create the semblance of activity induced by themselves. This consequently gives rise to guilt feelings, split-off convictions, and screen memories.

3   The paralyzed psychic activity of the traumatized self freezes the mental sense of time, producing an internal, temporal standstill. Post-traumatic states are often described as the sensation that a part of the self has been left behind, more or less remaining the same (i.e., as it was when it was left behind) because it can no longer be exposed to life. It is also described in terms of 'standing aside' or as a 'darkened existence.' Others simply say that their inner clock stopped at the moment of traumatization.

4   Primarily in cases of massive traumatization, this utter helplessness causes inner objects, which were previously protective companions, to become silent. A catastrophic isolation arises, an absolute loneliness, accompanied at the same time by mortal fear, hatred, shame, and despair. The traumatizing other, the perpetrator, then becomes the sole object to which the self can turn for help in the traumatic situation. Unconsciously, the object of the perpetrator assumes the function of the primary object. In many cases, the core of the traumatic experience thereby becomes a self–object fusion that is difficult to resolve and persistently impairs the individual's sense of identity. Amati (1990) described this process with regard to torture victims: the torturer constantly occupies the patient's inner world. The malicious persecuting object takes the place of existing internal objects and determines inner dialog. The traumatized person later attempts to escape from this in order to put earlier, pre-traumatic objects back into their original place.

These are but a few examples, which I mention here in order to illustrate what is meant by the psychic transformation of traumatic memories. If we accept this process as a fact, then, in therapy, it will not suffice to simply make the encapsulated, dissociated memory of the trauma accessible again and to then integrate it into memory. The situation is rather more complex, and I would now like to describe the main issues in this regard.

1   Discovering the reality of the trauma and its associated affects– namely its historicization, however fragmentary or approximate—is only the first step or the first prerequisite for elucidating and comprehending the trauma's transformation (by secondary revision) as effected by unconscious phantasies and meanings, and resulting, for example, in feelings of guilt and punitive impulses. Fantasy and traumatic reality are thereby disentangled and the ego acquires an alleviating context of understanding. Historicization also involves recognizing the traumatic fact and understanding the individual experience, as well as the emerging long-term consequences resulting therefrom. When such a reconstructive interpretation succeeds, patients often speak of astonishing improvements in their condition. The sensation of psychic integration they report indicates that the self-organization is at work restructuring itself. In addition, the previously encapsulated traumatic entity can now become more associatively interconnected. Likewise, the past can be more clearly distinguished from the present. This does not, however, primarily involve a cognitive differentiation, but an altered affective regulation. A patient once described this as a sort of inner expansion that freed her from being bound up in anxiety. It was, she reported, as if deep inside a clamp had been loosened and finally released (Bohleber, 2010).

2   An inaccurate reconstruction of the traumatic event remains ineffective, however, no matter how meaningful it might appear. Why might this be? One of the underlying reasons is that a reconstruction must correspond with the reality of the patient's trauma, while also grasping the reality of the event that caused the traumatization. Likewise, the interpretation has to account for the additional elements that were already set or inherent to the traumatic experience itself. From a neurobiological perspective, it is assumed that the implicit and explicit parts of a memory are usually associated. Traumatic experiences, however, generally lead to a dissociation of implicit and explicit memory.

There is now some evidence that in a reconstruction that captures the reality of the traumatic experience the explicit elements of the memory can be reconnected to their implicit counterparts (Siegel, 2006). Seen psychoanalytically, a reconstructive interpretation of the traumatic reality will not suffice; rather, the secondary transformation of meaning must be interpreted along with it. It is necessary to recognize what has been suffered, to articulate screen memories and split-off convictions, and then to understand and interpret them in connection with the traumatic events. This is not to say, however, that all aspects of experience can be verbalized. Dissociated contents are organized upon various levels of psychic representation. Further, a number of gaps have to be bridged by constructions. These constructions are based on, for example, the interpretation of somatic symptoms and repetitive dreams, or on external hints from others. In a reconstructive—that is, verbal—formulation of the traumatic event that had overwhelmed the patient, the self-state dissociated through the trauma can be reconnected to non-dissociated mental material. The narrative that emerges from this reconstruction both articulates and furthers an ongoing process of mental integration.

3   When a dissociated state is reactivated, the emerging therapeutic narrative also helps the patient to avoid relapsing into feeling completely passive and overwhelmed. Such a relapsing is often the case when the traumatized patient suffers from flashbacks or sudden intrusions of traumatic memories. Such intrusions—or following Freud, "repetition compulsions"—represent some of the most complex and difficult problems to overcome. Indeed, they represent something of a double-edged sword: while these intrusions can further mental integration and the discovery of meaning, they also threaten to become disruptive and overwhelming at the same time. In the latter case, recurring intrusions can have a re-traumatizing effect, rendering the individual passive once again, and leaving him helplessly at the mercy of the event. At the same time, however, they can also strengthen the ego, as mediated in therapy, by helping it to depart from the position of the powerless and the overwhelmed and thereby reconstituting itself as an active ego. A reinvigorated sense of self is then able to mitigate the pervasive and overwhelming force of traumatic fragments, which then guards against a recurring sense of helplessness and, in turn, also serves to strengthen the patient's sense of self.

4   Some final comments on historicization: central to the interpretation and narration of traumatic experience is that it be tied to an awareness that something *real* has in fact occurred, no matter how fragmentary its reconstruction might have been. This knowledge can provide patients with a sense of truth and security which they can then use to understand their traumatic transformations of the self, of their object relationships and affects, instead of simply processing them in terms of guilt. The reconstruction of the historical truth of the traumatic experience is most notably at stake here. Therefore, it does not get to the heart of the matter to only construct a meaningful narrative and to integrate the dissociated mental material. I am convinced that it is entirely insufficient, in therapy, to analyze the transference and countertransference of traumatized patient solely in the here-and-now of the analytic situation, as this can give rise to meaningful narratives that however lack any reconstruction of the traumatic reality that caused them. Such narratives are in danger of failing to distinguish between fantasy and reality, and—in the worst case—threaten to re-traumatize the patient.

Man-made disasters: individual and collective memory

Regarding disasters that are defined as man-made, such as the Holocaust, war, and political and ethnic persecution, as well as other social catastrophes, it lies beyond the individual's capacities to integrate such traumatic experiences in a narrative context, on an idiosyncratic basis. In many of these disasters, a conspiracy of silence prevailed in the period that followed them. To some extent this was politically motivated, having to do with the denial of guilt and with the acceptance of one's own responsibility on the side of the perpetrators. Another reason had to do with the fact that there was a strong reluctance among people to listen to the narratives and experiences of the victims. The consequence was that they simply became silent. To be able to talk, a social discourse is required regarding the historical truth of the traumatic events, as well as the uncovering of its denial and defensive repudiation. In this sort of man-made disaster, only historical explanation and social recognition of causation and guilt are able to restore the interpersonal context, and thus the possibility of discovering what actually happened at the time in an uncensored manner. This is the only way in which the shattered understanding of the traumatized self and the world can be regenerated. If defensive impulses predominate in society, or if rules of silence persist, traumatized survivors are left alone with their experiences. Instead of drawing support from other people's understanding, they are often dominated by their own guilt, then serving as an explanatory principle. A current example of this can be seen in Russian society, where the lack of public debate concerning the Stalinist terror still continues to exist (Solojed, 2006; Figes, 2007). As a collective framework for discussion is lacking, and as structures and reference-points that could give people a sense of security in this discussion are also lacking, many victims still believe in their own guilt and still cannot understand, for example, the significance of the Stalinist purges and their politics. With respect to its significance, then, the catastrophic quality of the experience of historic events and of their consequences remains—both for the individual as well as for the collective society involved—either underexposed or even silent, and thus damages the subsequent generation's sense of reality.

References

Allen, J. (2013). *Mentalizing in the development and treatment of attachment trauma.* London: Karnac.

Amati, S. (1990). Die Rückgewinnung des Schamgefühls. *Psyche, Zeitschrift für Psychoanalyse und ihre Anwendungen, 44*, 724–740.

Balint, M. (1969). Trauma and object relationship. *International Journal of Psychoanalysis, 50*, 429–436.

Baranger, M., Baranger, W., & Mom, J. M. (1988). The infantile psychic trauma from us to Freud: Pure trauma, retroactivity and reconstruction. *International Journal of Psychoanalysis, 69*, 113–128.

Bohleber, W. (2010). *Destructiveness, intersubjectivity, and trauma: The identity crisis of modern psychoanalysis.* London: Karnac.

Cohen, J. (1985). Trauma and repression. *Psychoanalytic Inquiry, 5*, 163–189.

Ferenczi, S. (1949). Confusion of the tongues between the adults and the child. *International Journal of Psychoanalysis, 30*, 225–230. (Original work published 1933)

Figes, O. (2007). *The Whisperers: Private life in Stalin's Russia.* London: Penguin.

Freud, S. (1955). Beyond the pleasure principle. *Standard Edition, 18*, 7–64. (Original work published 1920)

Freud, S. (1959). Inhibitions, symptoms and anxiety. *Standard Edition, 20*, 77–174. (Original work published 1926)

Furst, S. (1978). The stimulus barrier and the pathogenicity of trauma. *International Journal of Psychoanalysis, 59*, 345–352.

Guez, J., Naveh-Benjamin, M., Yankovsky, Y., Cohen, J., Shiber, A., & Shalev, H. (2011). Traumatic stress is linked to a deficit in associative episodic memory. *Journal of Traumatic Stress, 24*(3), 260–267.

Kinston, W., & Cohen, J. (1986). Primal repression: Clinical and theoretical aspects. *International Journal of Psychoanalysis, 67*, 337–355.

Kirshner, L. (1994). Trauma, the good object and the symbolic: A theoretical integration. *International Journal of Psychoanalysis, 75*, 235–242.

Krystal, H. (1988). *Integration and self-healing: Affect, trauma, alexithymia.* Hillsdale, NJ: Analytic Press.

Laub, D., & Podell, D. (1995). Art and trauma. *International Journal of Psychoanalysis, 76*, 991–1,005.

Siegel, D. (2006). Entwicklungspsychologische: Interpersonelle und neurobiologische Dimensionen des Gedächtnisses. Ein Überblick. In H. Welzer & H. Markowitsch (Eds.), *Warum Menschen sich erinnern können: Fortschritte in der interdisziplinären Gedächtnisforschung* (pp. 19–49). Stuttgart: Klett-Cotta.

Solojed, K. (2006). Psychische Traumatisierung in den Familien von Opfern des Stalinismus. *Psyche- Zeitschrift für Psychoanalyse und ihre Anwendungen, 60*, 587–624.

Steele, B. F. (1994). Psychoanalysis and the maltreatment of children. *Journal of the American Psychoanalytic Association, 42*, 1,001–1,025.

Chapter 2

Knowing and not knowing

Forms of traumatic memory[1]

Dori Laub and Nanette Auerhahn

We all hover, at different distances, between knowing and not knowing about massive psychic trauma, caught between the compulsion to complete the process of knowing and the inablility or fear of doing so. It is the nature of such trauma to elude our knowledge, both because of defense and because of deficit. To protect ourselves from affect, we must, at times, defend against knowledge. Trauma also overwhelms and defeats our capacity to organize it: facing real acts of massive aggression, our psychological abilities are rendered ineffective.

And yet in spite of the difficulties around and the struggle against knowing, the reality of traumatic events is so compelling that knowledge prevails nevertheless, despite its absence to consciousness and its incompleteness. In this chapter, we examine various forms of knowing massive psychic trauma and the circumstances under which they arise. We have organized the different forms of knowing along a continuum according to the distance from the traumatic experience. The following list sets forth these forms of knowing according to the progression we shall follow. Movement from the top to the bottom of the list indicates increasing distance from the trauma, and hence increasing integration and ownership of memory:

- Not knowing
- Fugue states
- Fragments
- Transference phenomena
- Overpowering narratives
- Life themes
- Witnessed narratives
- Metaphors.

It must be noted that these various forms of knowing are not mutually exclusive, and that several forms may, to a greater or lesser degree, coexist in any particular individual at any given point in time.

Not knowing

Massive psychic trauma breaks through the stimulus barrier and defies the individual's ability to formulate experience. Erecting barriers against knowing is often the first response to such trauma. An adult facing severe trauma re-experiences infantile remnants of primary traumatization while at the same time attempting to ward them off by primitive mechanisms of defense—for example, denial, splitting, amnesia, derealization, and depersonalization. These early defense mechanisms result in a non-receptivity to the experience and, in varying degrees, the splitting off of reality. Years later, acknowledgement and the lack thereof continue to exist simultaneously, without integration. This double state of knowing and not knowing leaves the survivor in grief not only for his dead loved ones but also for his lost memories. The lack of knowledge prevents the revival of despair that would accompany memory, but leaves the survivor alone and unknown to himself.

Fugue states

While the previous form is characterized by the disappearance of content or of a connection to an experiencing 'I,' other forms are marked instead by the intrusive appearance of split off, fragmented behaviors, cognitions, and affect. At its most extreme, fragments are 'recalled' without the individual knowing that the 'I' or subject who experienced the event is different from the one who recalls it—there is a collapse of the two at the moment of 'recall,' with no reflective self present. The experience simply happens—without any subject whatsoever.

This second form of knowing trauma actually involves reliving (rather than remembering). Blank (1985) gives examples of one type of flashback experienced by Vietnam veterans, in which combat experiences were relived in highly dissociated, dream- or fugue-like states, with little or no ability to communicate them in words. This form of reliving often involves the experience of vivid imagery, usually (but not always) visual in nature.

This form of traumatic memory contrasts with the previous one in that what is known in fugue states is kept separate from the conscious self in such a way as to preserve the latter intact. The ego's protective mechanisms, however pathological, are still operative.

Fragments

A third form involves the retention of parts of a lived experience in such a way that they are decontextualized and no longer meaningful. The individual has an image, sensation, or isolated thought but does not know what it is connected with, what it means, or what to do with it.

A., a man in his mid-forties, consulted a psychoanalyst with a very specific wish: he wanted to recapture an elusive memory which seemed to be haunting him. He was aware of bewildering states of unusual intensity, for which he sought a link in a forgotten memory. A. felt that things had been going badly over the last fifteen years, since he had broken off a ten-year relationship. He had tried relentlessly to reconnect with the woman, but she did not respond. The click of the phone when she hung up on him elicited a sense of dread and a vague recollection, perhaps of a cocked revolver. There were also psychosomatic complaints that bordered on the delusional—electricity running through his body, ringing in the ears, and a particular sensitivity to noise, especially sirens. If ever he found himself at the scene of an accident, he felt compelled to speak to the injured person, to apologize for not being able to save his or her life. And he could not bring himself to touch a pistol, despite having liked playing with pistols as a young child.

A. had been born in 1938, to a Christian family in a little town in Eastern Germany. The war was on and his father worked away from home. During that time the mother took in lovers—German soldiers who were on leave from the front line. When he was six, A. was hospitalized for a mysterious disease, later diagnosed as typhoid or meningitis. The most important and enigmatic figure in his recollections of this period was a Jewish female doctor from the nearby concentration camp, Buchenwald. Her help in the hospital was needed because of the shortage of medical personnel. The boy and this doctor created a special relationship, and she would spend hours talking to him. Growing up in the Nazi atmosphere and then being befriended by a Jewish doctor must have created a very difficult conflict for a small child.

Toward the end of the second month of therapy, the patient confided that he felt he was close to the secret: the Jewish doctor had been killed, executed, and he was somehow responsible for that. He saw her lying down, her face covered with blood; a shot had been fired. In sessions that followed, the memory emerged more fully with an unusual intensity of affect. A. recalled an air raid, with everyone taking cover in the basement. After the air raid most of the people returned upstairs. Only he and the doctor remained, sitting side by side. The doctor turned to him, said she would come back shortly, and left, but did not return. He walked into the adjacent room where she had gone, only to find her hanging from the ceiling. In panic he grabbed her body, trying to pull her down, screaming, "Auntie doctor, auntie doctor, please come down!" Perhaps this had been the final blow to her life, because in pulling he might have choked her even more. Continuing to scream, eventually he did tear her loose. Other personnel came running. One of the SS officers pulled out his pistol and shot her—perhaps she had still been alive? The little boy screamed and cursed this SS man, and had to be restrained. The image of sirens returned to him, together with images of being in an ambulance, and of electric shocks. The analyst hypothesized that the electric shocks might have been administered in order to help him forget.

Following this breakthrough, something began to change in A.'s life. He took a job caring for an old man, spending nights in the hospital, and attempted to address the man's depression. Fearing that the man might commit suicide, A. removed the latter's pistol, touching a pistol for the first time since childhood.

This successful attempt at saving somebody's life represented a movement beyond the fragments of behavior in which he would apologize to those killed in accidents. Having recovered the memory he lost, its intrusive fragments no longer blocked A. from pursuing his life.

Transference phenomena

When unintegrated fragments from the past are enacted on the level of object relations, the survivor's 'knowledge' is in the form of transference experiences. This form of knowing involves the grafting of isolated fragments of the past onto current relationships and life situations which become colored by these 'memories.' The fragmentary quality of these transplants is responsible for the resulting absurdity, inappropriateness, and distortions in present experience. Transference reactions vary in intensity from the psychotic delusional state to the mini-psychotic episode to more classical neurotic transferences that involve retention of the observing ego. Thus even if the survivor recognizes the irrationality of traumatic grafts, the fragments can continue to exert their influence, distorting reality according to past scripts.

Survivors may, at times, lead their lives in resonance with such transferences. For example, self-discipline was often a necessary (if not sufficient) condition for survival in the Nazi concentration camps, where a shoelace tied incorrectly might mean death. Accordingly, obligations in the present at times may continue to be experienced as life and death matters, with resulting consequences for superego functioning. Likewise, separations continue to be experienced as final. This is a continuation of the inmates' attempts to stay together as a means of survival and human support under conditions where neither was possible.

Overpowering narratives

A fifth form of 'holding' a traumatic experience does not involve derivatives that are enacted, but rather memories for which there is a more conscious knowing. The memory can be described and the event narrated. There is an 'I' present—an internal witness who holds the experience together and synthesizes it into a narrative. The moment the fragment comes to mind, however, it breaks away from the narrator, obliterating or at the very least obscuring the rest of current reality. He may stop such images in their tracks when pursuing his daily life activities, so that they do not interfere. At night, however, they assume a life of their own, appearing in regularly recurring nightmares which affectively color the day that follows.

For instance, many Holocaust survivors retain fantasies of the last moments of those from whom they were separated and who were later killed. Often survivors will shift to the present tense while narrating these memories. Particularly gruesome events have such staying power that they can obliterate the survivor's sense of living in the present. *Sophie's Choice* (Styron, 1979) is an example in point. Sophie could not bring the moment in which she had relinquished her child to memory, neither in dialog with another nor with herself. When she finally did, she killed herself.

These unintegratable memories endure as a split-off part, a cleavage, in the ego. Ever greater amounts of energy are required to maintain ego functions, until real life becomes a fringe phenomenon around the nucleus of the trauma. Some survivors of massive psychic trauma show a great deal of achievement in their professional lives, amassing wealth, substantial personal acclaim, and social status. But they experience it all as insubstantial. If one talks with them, one finds that there is no sense of enjoyment, no full sense of living. They are absorbed in the nightmare which they find at the center of it all.

Life themes

A sixth form of knowing is that of living out life themes. Memory, in the form of an overpowering narrative, is transformed to the level of life themes when a degree of distance from the traumatic event is established and when there is less immersion in the concrete details of the trauma. This form of traumatic memory involves an interpretation, a distillation of a message or moral from an overpowering narrative that, like the overpowering narrative, has a life of its own. While all these processes may be unconscious or at best fleetingly acknowledged—in particular in their linkages to the underlying memory—they nevertheless constitute a greater differentiation and distance from the actuality of the experience itself.

As opposed to the multiplicity of different transferences that might occur from fragments, a life theme tends to be unitary, an organizing principle that becomes the center of an individual's personality. The individual limits and shapes his internal and interpersonal life according to the life theme, which is often not only played out in relationships (as are transferences) but also can become a cognitive style. Thus, life themes involve a unique personality configuration, deriving from the particular way that individual perceived and distilled his traumatic legacy.

Life themes enacted in close relationships are often found in children of Holocaust survivors. An example of an adaptive life theme is the tendency of children of survivors to become mental health workers—they have an interest in secrets, and a need to decode them and help those who suffer from them. An example of a negative life theme is the sense of futility involving human relationships in general and verbal communication in particular that characterizes some second generation individuals.

For these people the events of the Holocaust could never be fully articulated or shared and therefore there could be no hope of ever achieving real intimacy.

Witnessed narratives

A seventh form of traumatic memory involves witnessing, in which the observing ego remains present as a witness. On this level, knowing takes the form of true memory. When the individual narrates on this level, there is a distance, a perspective retained by the observing ego. The ego is present and understands itself to be continuous with the remembered subject, but currently at a different stage. The memory is very vivid but not immediate. The following example is an excerpt from the videotaped testimony of a survivor of labor camps and death camps who describes his arrival in one such place.

> These are some of the episodes, I probably don't recall all of them, but these are some that stand out in my mind . . . We went through Skarzysko-Kamienna, where we were working in an ammunition factory. This was quite an experience. As usual when the transport arrived we had to get out in double time and run through a gauntlet of SS people who beat us with their rifle butts, clubs. We were somehow arbitrarily divided into three groups . . . One was called Work A, another Work B and the third Work C. My group went to Work C. This is something really nightmarish. I can probably describe something for somebody who hasn't seen it but who has seen the film *Apocalypse Now*. We came at night and were surrounded by a group of people with yellow faces, begging for scraps of bread, covered with blankets. Typical musulmans. As we found out the following day, Work C was fabricating chemicals, mainly picrine, to fill the shells . . . Working with that chemical, your life span is only three months. Your skin turns yellow, you shrivel, and these were the "picrinaires" that surrounded us. Now I was fortunate enough that I knew some carpentry and they needed some carpenters for Work A, and therefore I only stayed there one night.
>
> The following day when they asked for people with carpentry skills I raised my hand and together with a group of twenty or thirty other inmates I was taken to Work A. I remember like today the guard who

was escorting us, the German guard who said, "You don't know how lucky you are. You have to thank God that you are going to Work A." I had some friends who stayed in the other group; they didn't survive. ("Leon," 1980)

Trauma as metaphor and more

An eighth level of knowing trauma is the use of the imagery and language of massive psychic trauma as metaphor and vehicle for developmental conflict. This form of traumatic memory parallels the witnessed narrative to the extent that the distance between event and witness is preserved, yet goes beyond (but paradoxically never reaches) the previous level of knowing in that an element of play vis-à-vis the event enters, enabling the event's use as a metaphor that has some latitude. The imagery of trauma readily appears in associations, and does not have to be inferred or drawn out from ingrained silent modes of action. The individual chooses only those aspects of the event that reverberate with his or her internal conflict. The motive for this form of traumatic memory comes more from a need to organize internal experience than, as with the previous forms, from a need to organize the external, historical reality. Nevertheless, traumatic imagery is not without its impact on how developmental conflict resolves as well as how psychic structure emerges. The following case example is presented to illustrate not only the use of the Holocaust as metaphor, but especially the manner in which such use may organize the intrapsychic life of an individual.

D., an American born Jew in his early thirties, persistently acted out Oedipal guilt feelings by assuming a downhill course in his life and his career. He had repeatedly alluded, during a certain period of the analysis, to a movie he had seen about a Nazi criminal fleeing justice. This criminal would kill his opponents by slashing their abdomens in a single punch with a jack-knife secretly attached to his wrist. D. was fascinated with this murderous act.

Eventually it came to be understood as a variation of his continuously recurring savage primal scene fantasies (or observations), which made any contact with a real woman extremely unsafe. As a young boy, D. had identified with Hitler, through learning and reciting his speeches to family and friends. How could he now detach the savagery of his fascinating sexual fantasies from the reality of the atrocity events that occurred?

D. lived like a lonely, monastic ghost, convinced only of his criminality and dedicating his life to the abstinence and obedience that would atone for it—but which he still did not trust as genuine, sensing the murderousness behind it all.

To what extent did the reality of the aggression D. identified with (Hitler, the Nazis, war criminals) render his link to it more persuasive and the atonement more essential? Our patient never committed the real murder, but merely borrowing the Holocaust metaphor lent an inextricably grisly quality to the bond he had thus created. The question is whether such themes went beyond providing appropriate content to time-honored developmental conflicts—whether the metaphor acquired a life of its own, subtly changing the actual objects and processes it stood for and producing structural changes. Can external reality change the contemporary unconscious, even while that unconscious makes use of reality to deal with its own conflicts? (Appy, 1988)

Conclusion

Our focus in this chapter has been on what kind of knowledge of trauma is possible. There are many levels of remembering and preserving the horror of atrocity, all of which range along a continuum of differences in the degree of presence of an observing ego and its synthetic functions.

Although none of the various forms of traumatic memory is mutually exclusive, and several may, to a greater or lesser degree, co-exist in any particular individual at any given point in time, it is generally true that victims know mostly through retention of unintegrated memories or by reliving such memories in transference phenomena. Children of victims tend to know through particular themes which prove central to their identities and characters, while those not directly affected by massive psychic trauma know of it through experiencing their own conflicts and predicaments in its language and imagery.

Understanding the level of traumatic memory is crucial in knowing where therapeutic intervention must focus. For the survivor who is bombarded by unintegrated percepts of the past, deficit is more prominently active than defense, and thus concerns around cohesion of the self and fragmentation anxiety take precedence over conflict. Elucidation of split-off and diffusely re enacted memory fragments is essential in order to facilitate reconstruction of the 'unknown' traumatic event and comprehension of its meaning. Thus reconstruction of the event, construction of a narrative, and abstraction of a theme are all necessary if the fragment—the symptom—is to lose its power and be properly integrated into memory.

For the victim's child in whom the traumatic wound has been transformed due to the intergenerational dialog that is neither necessarily verbal nor conscious, life themes exist but the events and narratives that were their starting point must be reconstructed. The child must connect his cognitive styles and life choices with a memory and story that are not his alone and that he only very hazily recalls—a memory and overpowering narrative that nevertheless affect his personality.

Finally, in the individual who uses traumatic metaphors, defense predominates over deficit, for knowing on this level is the product of the transference of a fantasy rather than of a lived experience. This form of knowing allows the individual to be aware of, but not responsible for, impulses and thoughts. He places them in a past, external reality, making them not his own. For such individuals, traumatic imagery and language must be taken out of the past and placed into the present, especially into their fantasy. Unlike the survivor and his child who must place their aggressive and sexual impulses back into the traumatic context to make them part of reality and thus free up fantasy life, the non-victim who uses trauma as a metaphor must undergo the opposite process: he must own the imagery as originating not in the event but in himself.

Whether the traumatic experience is lived or fantasized, there is, inevitably, a disruption of the transmission and evolution of memory within a single individual, or between one generation and another, that results in symptoms. The connections and movements between traumatic event, memory, meaning, interpretation, and character structure are inevitably obscured. They must be reinstated and articulated if trauma's impact in the mosaic of forces that determine development and character formation is to be clarified. Simply put, therapy with those impacted by trauma involves, in part, the reinstatement of the relationship between event, memory, and personality.

Note

1 First published as Knowing and not knowing in massive psychic trauma: Forms of traumatic memory, *The International Journal of Psychoanalysis, 17* (1993). Reprinted by permission of John Wiley & Sons, Inc.

References

Appy, G. (1988). The meaning of "Auschwitz" today: Clinical reflections about the depletion of a destructive symbol. Paper presented at the Fourth Conference of the Sigmund Freud Center of the Hebrew University of Jerusalem, Jerusalem, Israel.

Blank, A. S. (1985). The unconscious flashback to the war in Viet Nam veterans: Clinical mystery, legal defense, and community problem. In S. M. Sonneberg, A. S. Blank, & J. A. Talbott (Eds.), *The trauma of war: Stress and recovery of Vietnam veterans*. Washington, DC: American Psychiatric Press.

"Leon" (1980). *Video recording of Leon S.* Holocaust Video Testimony HVT-45. Fortunoff Video Archive. Yale University, New Haven, CT/USA.

Styron, W. (1979). *Sophie's Choice*. New York, NY: Random House.

Chapter 3

Traumatic shutdown of narrative and symbolization

A failed empathy derivative. Implications for therapeutic interventions[1]

Dori Laub

The massive failure of the holocaust environment to satisfy one's most basic needs undermines the individual's internal representation of the mediating content and deconstructs the internal link between self and other. The existence of empathy, human communications, and unfortunately one's own connected humanity is thrown into question. A sense of aloneness, vulnerability, and fragmentation in the internal world representation ensues. These themes will be depicted in survivor's dreams, reenactments, and conscious attitudes, as well as in transference and countertransference phenomena. Implications for therapeutic interventions will be explored.

A case of countertransference blindness

The analyst was a candidate in psychoanalytic training and this was his first control patient. He himself was a child survivor who had spent two years between the ages of five and seven in a Nazi concentration camp during World War II. Before he started working with this patient, the analyst's immigration status in the United States was in question and threatened to interrupt his psychoanalytic training. He was advised by the institute that if he could not assure his stay in the US for a sufficient length of time, he could neither start his first control case nor could he proceed with his classes. He felt he was about to be deported again, exiled from the country in which he lived and worked, and banished, or at least not protected, by the institute in which he was training. An unexpected change in US immigration law allowed for a resolution of this crisis, and he was referred his first control patient.

The supervisor of the case was an eminent psychoanalyst, also a refugee from Nazi-occupied Europe. He was known and admired for his flexibility and tolerance and for his original writings on the new object relation experience psychoanalysis offered, which would allow reexamination of damaging object relationships in early childhood, thus setting a healing process in motion.

The candidate's control case was a woman in her late twenties, single, working as a teacher. She was the older of two children, with a brother five years younger of whom she was intensely jealous, because she regarded him as the parents' favorite. Aside from working, her life was pretty empty. She had very few friends and no social life to speak of. She had never had a relationship with a man, and had never fallen in love. Her symptoms were episodes of depression, hopelessness, and panic attacks, one of which landed her in the emergency room.

Once on the couch, she became very suspicious of the analyst, reading all kinds of feelings into his abstinence. She felt that from the moment she came into his office, he treated her with contempt, put her down, and was cold and always critical. She likened him to her mother, whom she thought of as distant and very harsh. Transference interpretations, however, did not change the situation. She had frequent angry outbursts, yelling in such a loud voice that the analyst next door, a colleague, humorously asked the candidate what he was doing to this patient. Was he torturing her? Upon reflection years later, the analyst thought that the question might have been relevant.

From past history, obtained in interviews, it emerged that the patient was born shortly before World War II and her father was drafted soon thereafter. He served in the Pacific theater. As early as 1942, he disappeared, and his fate was unknown. He was considered missing in action. The mother regarded him as dead. The analyst could imagine a little girl with a depressed, grieving mother, who was perhaps unavailable to her. Reconstructions of this kind, however, made no difference.

Many of the feelings the analyst harbored in the supervisory setting and toward the institute that nearly interrupted his training were permeated by his childhood persecution experiences and inhibited his creativity and his analytic freedom to explore. As things were not going well in the analysis, the supervisor suggested that the candidate sit the patient up and speak to her face to face. The candidate was afraid that he was going to lose the credit he needed for the completion of his analytic training if he followed this advice. He was also afraid that he would be asked to leave his training, as almost half of his class had been, because of unsatisfactory progress. The threat of near deportation that had preceded the work with his patient was also very much on his mind.

Further details from the history of the patient showed that the father miraculously returned at the end of the war and was decorated with the Silver Star. There was still no information, nor were there any questions by the analyst or by the supervisor, as to the whereabouts of the father during his several years' absence. Neither registered surprise that would have led to inquiries. The analytic process was stalemated. The patient's angry outbursts occurred again and again. After nearly four years of rather barren work, the analyst told the patient that he could not see how he could further help her and that another therapist might.

All this happened between 1969 and 1973. Shortly after the interruption of the analysis, the analyst served as a psychiatrist with the IDF forces in the Yom Kippur October War in 1973. He was stationed in a treatment facility in Northern Israel, which received casualties from the Syrian front. To everybody's surprise, the proportion of the psychiatric casualties was staggering. Reservists had been called up from synagogues, thrown into makeshift units and sent into the battlefield to stem the Syrian advance. The abruptness of the transition into combat, the absence of a familiar social support network with the comrades in arms from their regular unit, with whom they trained and served, the enormity of losses, dead and wounded, and above all, the level of violence they were exposed to, led to the psychological decompensation of many.

What the analyst observed was that the most severe and least treatable casualties were children of the Holocaust survivors. One such case arrived in a deep depressive stupor. He had no name, no family, no memory. Spending hours upon hours in a dimly lit tent with him and gently prodding him, the analyst gradually learned that he had been a radio operator on the front line, who saw tank crews stop on their way to the battlefield and then listened to their voices on the radio. He heard their last messages before they went silent. They were out of ammunition and surrounded by Syrian tanks. To him, it strongly resonated with the images of many family members who had been murdered in the Holocaust and whose names were mentioned, but little was said about them. They were, nevertheless, ubiquitously present to him in their very absence, in their silence. Gradually, as he was making this connection, he emerged from his stupor, remembered his name, and recognized his wife, who was about to give birth to a baby. The baby, a son, was named after one of the fallen tank commanders.

Another example was a soldier who came to the analyst in a state of psychotic agitation. His utterances made no sense; his affect and his behavior were severely out of control. He was a military policeman whose duty was to prevent civilians from reaching the front line. He had failed to stop a car with two men in it, only to find it later destroyed with two mangled bodies inside. He proceeded to boot a Syrian POW officer in the head. In his ramblings, he told of his father's stories of SS men smashing the heads of Jewish children into a wall. The front line brutalities triggered the memory of the tales of brutalities he grew up with and that was more than he could contain. His mental state did not improve in spite of robust pharmaco- and psychotherapeutic interventions, and he had to be transferred to a chronic facility.

The familial exposure to Holocaust violence in these patients increased their vulnerability to the violence on the battlefield. Whereas other soldiers would better insulate themselves from it by using the customary defenses against traumatic experiences, such as dissociation, derealization, depersonalization, and others, for them, such defenses no longer worked. Extremes of violence had for them a personal-historical context that was continuously present and, therefore, could not be pushed aside.

In the years that followed these experiences, the analyst became very much involved with clinical work with PTSD and the transgenerational transmission of trauma. Reflecting on his analytic case, described earlier, he began to piece things together in a new and different way. It dawned on him that a very likely explanation for the father's absence for several years was that he had been detained in a Japanese POW camp. The analyst had read of the severe treatment of American POWs by the Japanese and could now better understand why the father had been awarded the Silver Star. Did he possibly undergo torture, and did that experience intrude itself into the analytic space?

The analyst realized that after the father's return, the joyful couple celebrated the occasion by having a new baby. The patient, appropriately, was excluded from this celebration. It was imaginable that the father, after years spent in a POW camp, could have been suffering from PTSD symptoms and some of his traumatic experiences might have been transmitted to his daughter. The analyst suddenly felt that he understood the patient's terror, helplessness, and resultant rage, but unfortunately it had not occurred to him to ask the question that would have enlightened him about the father's whereabouts during the war or his symptomatology after he came back. Belatedly, he could only guess that the father might have suffered from nightmares for years. In addition, the father's PTSD symptoms might have been the cause for an emotional withdrawl from his little daughter, which was repeated in the transference and in the patient's relationships with men.

In retrospect, what is striking here is the absence of such curiosity, the lack of creative speculation, and the question of whether the analyst's own childhood camp experience had defensively blinded him to the possibility that the patient might have encountered trauma in her own childhood. It was as though the analyst himself experienced a shutdown of reflection and self-reflection that led to a lack of curiosity about something that was very close to the surface, if not obvious. He failed to notice that he did not know the reason for the father's absence and his whereabouts during that absence. What is also striking is that the supervisor, who was known for his open-mindedness and clinical sensitivity, had not asked this question either. Was he too, perhaps, unaware of the effect of his own traumatic experience? Did the suppressed memory of his own persecution exert a force that blinded him to the possibility that a similar event might have happened in the patient's family? Years later, the analyst wondered whether this was a case of double-countertransference blindness—his own, and that of his supervisor.

What is striking in this vignette is the inexplicable absence, or rather shutdown, in both analyst and supervisor, of the processes of analytic hearing, associating, integrating, and ultimately comprehending, through the processes of symbolization, exactly what the patient experienced and reenacted in the analytic setting. The father's disappearance and the implications of his return, which lay clearly in front of their eyes, had not been acknowledged or explored. How can we explain this? Is it possible that the patient's transgenerationally received traumatic experience reverberated with echoes of the massive life trauma that both analyst and analytic supervisor had experienced? Is that what stopped the analytic process in its track, allowing for no empathic inquiry, for no associative linkages to be formed and thus keeping the three traumata discrete and frozen in their place?

The nature of the traumatic experience

Clinicians and scholars (Laub & Auerhahn, 1993; Caruth, 1996; Oliner, 1996) describe trauma as occurring 'out there,' not as an event related to an experiencing subject, the 'I.' It is likened to an external event dissociated from the narrator who has gone through it. Often, survivors emphasize that they indeed live in two separate worlds, that of their traumatic memories (which is self-contained, ongoing, and ever-present) and that of the present. Very often they do not wish, or are completely unable, to reconcile these two different worlds. The memory is thus timeless, the experience is frozen. It is automatic and purposeless, bereft of meaning. Caruth (1996) states, "Traumatic experience . . . suggests a certain paradox: that the most direct seeing of a violent event may occur as an absolute inability to know it" (pp. 91–92). Elsewhere, Caruth tells us, "It is not simply, that is, the literal threatening of bodily life but the fact that the threat is recognized as such by the mind one moment too late. The shock of the mind's relation to the threat of death is thus not the direct experience of the threat, but precisely the missing of this experience, the fact that, not being experienced in time, it has not yet been fully known" (p. 62).

Yet in spite of, and perhaps because of, their separateness, their having a life of their own, the power the memories of trauma exert on the continuance of life is immeasurable. Van der Kolk, McFarlane, and Weisaeth (1996) state, "Terrifying events may be remembered with extreme vividness or maybe totally resist integration . . . Trauma can lead to extremes of retention and forgetting" (p. 282). These memories remain intense, yet frozen, immutable, and unaltered by the passage of time. They are not subject to assimilation or to evolutionary change through integration in the associative network. They remain discrete, retaining their magnetic power in their contradictory detailed and persistent clarity on the one hand and in the concomitant dense yet absorbing opaqueness that enshrouds them on the other. They are qualitatively different from ordinary memories.

Attempting to understand the absences

How are we to understand these 'absences,' these 'blanks' in our experience and the framing, distancing strategies put in place when atrocities penetrate our consciousness? To come to know something is to process new information, to assimilate and integrate an experience into one's own inner world representation. It is essentially to build a new construct inside ourselves. Richard Moore (1999) defines memories of trauma as "new constructions of a previously constructed reality which was originally based on some particular direct experience" (p. 167). These, in fact, can even be someone else's experiences.

That which might otherwise be constructed overwhelms the construction process and therefore the constructor . . . We know this
has occurred only when others are able to supply a narrative. The
traumatized person lacks the ability or the opportunity, or both, to
initiate, create or integrate this interaction. Potential reality over-
flows the capacity to construct it, and the result is not a reality created
by one's experience, but the loss of one's capacity to participate in
it at all. (Moore, 1999, 168)

What specifically overwhelms the process of construction and therefore the
constructor himself, resulting in a total loss of one's capacity to participate
in one's own reality?

To process information, to make it our own, we employ the process
of symbolization. In "Symbol Formation in Ego Development," Melanie
Klein (1930) states, "not only does symbolism come to be the foundation
of all fantasy and sublimation, but more than that, it is the basis of the
subject's relation to the outside world and to reality in general" (p. 221).
Therefore, to perceive, grasp, or participate in reality, the process of symbolization needs to be in place. "Symbol formation," according to Hannah
Segal (1951, 395), "governs the capacity to communicate, since all communication is made by means of symbols." She proceeds, "Symbols are
needed not only in communication with the external world, but also in
internal communication": that is, with oneself (p. 396). "The capacity
to communicate with oneself by using symbols is, I think, the basis of
verbal thinking, which is the capacity to communicate with oneself by
means of words" (pp. 395–96). Freud (1891/1953) himself, in one of his
earliest works, postulated an internal psychic event, a 'thing' representation, which came to be linked to another psychic event, a psychological
word representation. A linkage between the two psychic events created
the symbol—the psychological word. "All object representations that are
linked to a word are a symbol. To speak then is to symbolize in words, the
representations of a bodily mind" (Rizzuto, 1993, 124). Rizzuto emphasizes that for Freud, listening was an active process. "It requires a certain
inner speech to ourselves. The word we understand is the combined word
of the person who spoke and the inner word we spoke to ourselves. This
inner word has a psychic history already. Listening, therefore, means associating external words to inner words, and in the end, we hear ourselves
internally" (p. 124). In other words, Freud saw the formation of the

symbol as occurring in the context of such internal communicative processes. Such an understanding of symbolization is based on an internal dialogic process. One comes to know one's story only by telling it to oneself, to one's internal 'thou.'

Reality, therefore, can be grasped only in a condition of affective attunement with oneself. Massive psychic trauma, however, is a deadly assault, both on the external and the internal 'other,' the 'thou' of every dialogic relationship. The executioner does not heed the victim's plea for life, and relentlessly proceeds with the execution. The 'other,' the 'thou,' who is empathically in tune and responsive to one's needs, ceases to exist, and faith in the possibility of communication itself dies. There is no longer a 'thou,' either outside or inside oneself, a thou whom one can address. An empathic dyad no longer exists in one's internal world representation. There is no one to turn to, even inside oneself. It is an utterly desolate landscape, totally void of life and humanity, permeated by the terror of the state of objectlessness.

Kirshner (1994) emphasizes that "the good object—and here I refer explicitly to an internalized sense of goodness in its most symbolic sense—is essential to the capacity for emotional participation in the world of others and perhaps for psychic survival" (p. 238). In summarizing the work of other psychoanalytic theoreticians, he states: "I argue that what is fundamentally at stake across the theories of trauma of Ferenczi, Klein, Winnicott and Lacan (and the list could be expanded) is the constant threat of destruction or loss of 'the good object' and that the therapeutic efficacy of psychoanalysis is, therefore, closely connected with its function of maintaining or restoring this symbolic object" (p. 239).

I would add that it is the very presence of this good object that enables and safeguards the communicative process of symbolization, the dialog with the internal 'thou' that names, enhances meaning, and creates narrative. Trauma, by abolishing the good object, precipitously (or gradually) shuts this process down.

Conscious memory is the first casualty of the abolition of the internal good object. Furthermore, erasure of traumatically lost objects, and of the traumatic experience itself, may lead the survivor to complete oblivion, or to doubt the veracity and the authenticity of his own experiences. His sense of identity and continuity may be compromised; his ability to invest in intimate relationships may be severely impaired, leading to a life with a sense of doomed aloneness. In the absence of an internal responsive 'thou,' there is no attachment to nor cathexis of the object.

To follow Andre Green's (1996) line of thought, with the loss of the good object (the dead mother complex), the primary ego, which is melded with the object, relentlessly relives its loss and becomes "as disinterested in itself as in the object, leaving only a yearning to vanish, to be drawn towards death and nothingness" (p. 13). Later, Green even more eloquently points out that when "the lost object becomes an inaccessible good object, we come to deal with nothingness [the blank psychosis] . . . characterized by blocking of thought processes, the inhibition of the function of representation . . . The final result is paralysis of thought . . . a hole in mental activity [and an] inability to concentrate, to remember, etc." (pp. 40–41).

Although I find the formulation just described both compelling and accurate, the limits the author sets on its applicability render it incomplete, in my opinion. Green (1996) limits this phenomenon to the understanding of "failures" of favorable evolution. The infant, when growing up with an "emotionally dead" mother, instead of separating into an individual invested in himself, ends up narcissistically depleted in a "deathly deserted universe" (p. 167). He buries part of his ego in the "maternal necropolis."

At this point I want to underscore how my view differs from Andre Green's. I believe that the same dynamics and a comparable phenomenology hold true not only for the infantile symbolic maternal loss, but also for the traumatic loss of the good internal object at any age. The analytic candidate in the vignette that opens this essay made the same mistake Green makes. He related the patient's empty life and the reenactment of the bad object in the analytic transference to maternal deprivation—or to put it in Green's (1996) words, to the "dead mother complex." He did not entertain (nor did his supervisor) the possibility that it was the father's likely severe traumatic experiences in a Japanese POW camp (father's loss of the good object through his possible torture experience) which, through intergenerational transmission, introduced the bad object into the analytic space.

Failed empathy: fragmentation and the loss of the link to the internal 'other'

> Trust in the world includes . . . the certainty that the other person will spare me . . . that he will respect my physical and metaphysical being. The expectation of help . . . is . . . one of the fundamental experiences of human beings . . . But with the first blow . . . against which there can be no defense and which no helping hand will ward off . . . [one] can no longer feel at home in the world (Amery, 1966/1980, 28–29, 40)

The link between self and other is predicated on the possibility and the expectation of empathy, which are to some degree taken for granted. In the concentration camps, the sadistic, bureaucratic killing disproved this basic expectation. An empathic response was absent not only from the Nazis, but from fellow citizens and Allies as well (i.e., from society at large). When people prove malignant on such a massive scale, the survivor retains the memory of a basic deficit—of a compromise in the empathic dyad. When their vital needs are neither heeded nor responded to by others, individuals lose the expectation that their needs will be met. Faith in the possibility of communication dies and intrapsychically there may no longer be a matrix of two people—self and resonating other. Accordingly, we propose that an essential feature of the trauma suffered by a survivor of a genocide is the victim's feeling of inability to affect the environment interpersonally so as to elicit a sense of mutuality. The victim feels that there is "no longer anyone on whom to count" (Wiesel, 1968/1970, 229), as the link between self and other has been effaced by the failure of empathy (Auerhahn & Laub, 1987).

By the failure of empathy, we mean a massive failure of the interpersonal environment to mediate needs. Neither wishes that are an integral part of the individual's existence and generally need not be expressed (e.g., wishes for food, protection, sleep, warmth, companionship), nor wishes that are within reason and are expressed, elicit an understanding, appropriate responsiveness from another human being. It is as if the victim's messages were sent into outer space. Such lack of receptivity can only occur when the person experiencing and expressing the wish is not regarded as equally human. The Nazi belief system defined the Jewish race as a different species; it sanctioned the radical and sadistic negation of the other. Nazism was founded on the victory of a delusion that subverted the normal generational boundaries within which adults take care of the young, the weak, and the helpless. The Nazis' subversion of normal boundaries was total, so that the Jews were deprived of any response to them as humans.

For the targets of Nazi ideology, the human ambience in which they were living was instantaneously destroyed. Such an experience, when prolonged, will throw into question the existence of empathy, human communication, and ultimately one's own humanity, for which no mirroring, confirming experience exists. The natural outcome is a lonesomeness in one's internal world representation: "in the Lager . . . everyone is desperately and ferociously alone" (Levi, 1958/1978, 80).

The failure of empathy not only destroys hope of communicating with others in the external world and expectation of resonance with the internal other in the inner world, it also diminishes the victims' ability to be in contact and in tune with themselves, to feel that they have a self. Survivors' desperate attempts to find lost families after the war, their hope against hope for years that loved ones are still alive, as well as the urgency with which they established new bonds and families can be understood as stemming from their need to find themselves again. We quote Amery (1966/1980): After the Holocaust, "I was a person who could no longer say 'we' and who therefore said 'I' merely out of habit, but not with the feeling of full possession of myself" (p. 44).

Living on borrowed time

We realize that the survivor experience is not a uniform one and that no two testimonies are alike. We do, however, postulate a generic survivor experience, common to all those who were directly affected by the Nazi persecution, whether in hiding, ghettos, labor camps, or extermination camps. This generic survivor experience is linked to the sense of living under a death sentence put into effect by the policy of genocide.

The dread of annihilation, consciously experienced as feelings of being sentenced to death, finds its way into survivors' relationships, attitudes, symptoms, and transference phenomena. We have been impressed by the ubiquitous presence of execution fantasies, imagery, and dreams among survivors and their children. The sentenced-to-death feeling is manifestly expressed in unrelenting screen memories of having witnessed an execution or in dreams of facing a firing squad, being pursued, and running. It is as if the brutal and sudden enactment of their deaths, decided and willed by another, were imminent and unavoidable. More frequently, survivors have a vague yet compelling sense (often only hinted at) that they are living on borrowed time in a state of suspended execution. Every minor error or oversight intensifies the survivor's fearful expectancy.

Real events often pave the way for the internal representation of the breakdown of empathy. For example, one survivor recalls his grandmother requesting help getting onto a wagon and a German soldier responding by promising help, yet proceeding to kill her. "The inhumanity of someone asking for help and the help . . . being expressed as a killing action" (Auerhahn & Laub, 1984, 339) has a hold on the survivor's memory by virtue of epitomizing the failure of responsiveness and the subversion of the normal ways people relate. Such events become the template for future fantasies, dreams, and the expectation of execution. The same survivor reports, "I have nightmares—being followed by somebody, being chased by somebody . . . Sometimes I am facing a firing squad."

Another survivor reports a recurring nightmare that eventually boiled down to a surrealistic, abstract representation of a feeling of helplessness. "It was like a conveyer belt on which I was moving toward a press which was rolling; there was no power whatsoever to stop it. I couldn't move; I was just rolling closer . . . I would wake up totally disoriented, crying my head off, screaming, sweaty, and shaking."

Loneliness and desolation

The sense of being alone in the world is apparent in dreams of disconnected or depersonalized human encounters. One survivor had numerous dreams involving not having the right passports or papers. In these dreams, as in Kafka's stories, formality was important; the letter, rather than the spirit, of the laws governing all requests was dominant. Much of the same loneliness pervades the work of Wiesel (1958/1960) who wrote, "I was alone— terribly alone in a world without God and without man" (pp. 73–74). In the void left by Holocaust, the sense of abandonment by God is, at times, the most painful. Whereas the manifest content of the survivor's accusation is often the issue of justice, the latent content is the question of God's presence and involvement. The issue of the unempathic other is frequently projected onto theological and legal planes. Accordingly, Wiesel (1982) characterized the anguish of the solitary individual—not as an unjust punishment by God, but as abandonment by God. God did not know about him or her—God was uninvolved with His creation.

Considering the survivors' utter desolation in a "world which has lost its center, a world abandoned by God and filled with the corpse of His worshipers" (Ezrahi 1980, 146), we may understand their use of the words 'I' and 'we.' The word 'we' is frequently found in survivors' narratives. It is possible that its use sometimes reflects a high degree of social bonding (to both the dead and the living; Des Pres, 1976/1978), but often 'we' is a defense against saying 'I' with any feeling. For survivors to use 'I' feelingly is to acknowledge the profoundness of their sense of abandonment and lonesomeness: it can lead to despair and surrender.

One survivor we interviewed poignantly summarized the sense of loneliness that has suffused his life since the war:

> In Auschwitz I still had the feeling of protectiveness as long as my father was standing behind me in the same commando. And there was suddenly an emptiness there once he was gone . . . We were a big family, perhaps 60 people . . . wherever we went there were relatives. There is nothing there . . . an . . . emptiness. No more the home one had before . . . And there is no longer the connection . . . the linkage is gone. I live now in a Jewish community with all the Jewish traditions—but nevertheless I live in an exile, estranged . . . As if from one day to the next a chasm opened into which everything fell . . . a wall of fog remained, through which I cannot penetrate . . . I have no true friends. One can talk of everything with one's wife in a good marriage and I have a good marriage . . . and the wife tries to be there in my loneliness and in my sadness . . . but this cannot quite work because one still has a corner in the depth of one's heart where another cannot come close, not even one's wife . . . because this violent ending of one's youth, this violent extinguishing of a whole period that still lies before one's eyes, cannot be replaced—not even by one's own wife . . . The absolute worst that happened to the one that survived is the feeling that he is totally isolated in this world. He stands totally alone. He has nobody—nobody near him in the good days and not in bad days . . . when I talk about it I do not feel understood although I recognize the effort of those who try to understand me . . . I can never feel protected enough to feel as a child again . . . feel unburdened enough to feel close . . . This joy, this uninhibited joy, I must say I have no more. (Klein, 1993)

The form of other people is present, but the inner connection has been and is difficult to experience.

We have repeatedly witnessed survivors' attempts to evade this inner sense of desolation by searching for and by imagining the existence of human responsiveness in the most absurd circumstances (i.e., from the executioners). The 'good Nazi,' an SS man or camp guard who, through a glance, gesture, unintentional oversight, or even, simply, by a failure to kill, conveyed a sense of compassion, is more prevalent in survivors' accounts than is the compassionate fellow inmate. Such stories represent projection of empathy and attempts to humanize the recipient of the projection. One survivor described his hours of endless waiting in a block of selectees for gassing at Auschwitz: An SS man came by to take a head count, and the prisoner thought that he detected a "big tear rolling down the SS man's cheek."

Loss of structure and fragmentation

The mind is severed from its forms (Lifton, 1981) in the absence of a primary object. Specifically, when the world of people proves malignant on a massive scale, the internal representation of the need-mediating context is destroyed, the individual loses the capacity for wish-organized symbolic functioning (Cohen, 1985), and wishes regress to being dangerous biological needs. Recuperative psychological processes of symbolization and sublimation are compromised, when bereft of a reliable interhuman environment, on which they depend.

The tenuousness of victims' interpersonal ties results in a sense of internal fragmentation, of being unable to put things together. Metapsychologically, the observer of survivors can speak of destructuring; phenomenologically, the victim experiences a sense of fragmentation. As memories of the traumatic past break through into conscious awareness, the survivor experiences a decompensation in his or her ego; he or she can neither absorb nor organize such experience. Discussing the past usually feels like reliving raw impressions. Formulation would require a sense of contact with a good other who could hold things together and compensate for the disruption in the survivor's self-observer (Auerhahn & Laub, 1987).

Holocaust survivors remember their experiences through a prism of fragmentation and usually recount them only in fragments. Asked to describe a whole day in the camps, one survivor said, "There weren't whole days. Everything had been broken to pieces, since 1938." Another admitted, "One couldn't deal with the total of what is happening. It was what happened this morning, tonight." Indeed, how can there "be a logic of composition when one's theme is the irruption of the irrational" (Gray, 1962, 5).

We have become aware of survivors' sense of internal fragmentation through their transmission of it to their listeners. For the listener, the survivor-narrator often seems not part of the narrative; what is spontaneously recounted seems to be fragmented percepts, entrenched in the survivor's mind like foreign bodies that never became an integral part of a whole human experience. We believe that the listener's recall reflects survivors' recall of their own experience as disjointed, fragmented, belonging neither to a whole nor to themselves in a particular place and time, even though it nevertheless continues to lead its intense and excruciating existence in their minds. Rendition of their stories in the form of fragments is not healing for survivors; instead it can further traumatize them.

While turning such fragments into a cohesively narrated personal history is not sufficient for healing to occur, it nevertheless constitutes an essential step in the process of healing. Narrative must be rebuilt in order to reach beyond the fragmenting barriers of the traumatic event and renew linkage with the lost pretraumatic past. For this building process to occur, a certain degree of disengagement from externalities must take place, whereby survivors are with and within themselves, introspective and attuned to their inner lives. Paradoxically, individuals' capacities to be sufficiently alone so as to discover that inner life are dependent on the presence of a reliable 'good object' in their psychic reality (Winnicott, 1958/1965). For the survivors of genocide, who have sustained physical and psychological assaults that have torn down their good internal objects, that state of being alone with themselves—that is, separate from external objects—has become too painful to bear. To protect themselves from pain, they may relinquish all contact with their inner real, yet fragmented selves, their memories, and their yearnings, and focus on the external only, guided by what seems right, appropriate, and useful to others, a "pathological alternative [that] is a false life built on reactions to external stimuli" (Winnicott, 1958/1965, 34). Hence the crucial importance of a holding presence that would make it possible for survivors to be alone ("that is to say in the presence of someone," Winnicott, 1958/1965, 34) in order to restore their inner worlds and resurrect empathic ties by turning inward to pretraumatic memories, for that is "the only place . . . [they know] of where a whole, hale world exists" (Beissner, 1962, 23).

What underlies the restoration of a responsive environment is the resurrection of infantile, parental figures, more specifically, the maternal presence. The turning inward is toward the mother, for the internal other who must be present "is equated ultimately and unconsciously with the mother" by virtue of the fact that it is she "who, in the early days and weeks was temporarily identified with her infant, and for the time being was interested in nothing else but the care of her own infant" (Winnicott, 1958/1965, 36). By the term mother, we mean mothering figure—that other who consistently and empathically provides a stimulating, structuring, and responsive environment for the growing child. For the victim of the Holocaust, there has been a disruption of the synthesizing, predictable, internal mother because of the malignancy of internalized objects. Reality has broken the protective empathic shield of (m)other, whose continuity is no longer guaranteed.

The turning to mother is overdetermined. Flight to gratification and mother arose, too, from an inability to rely on order—on justice being victorious. The paternal order failed to protect. That is, the murders wrought by the Nazis destroyed the predictability, structure, and regularity of existence. Father as guardian of order and hence, life, failed; mother as feeder of immediate supply might yet prevail. Indeed, during the Holocaust, life and survival were frequently linked to the bond between mother and child. Even when gone, the image of mother as present and powerful was preserved. A split is often detected in survivors' accounts between the image of mother as a protective, soothing guardian who had taught how normal people behaved and social relationships proceeded and that of father as a sad, helpless figure who awakened compassion and yearning but not much hope, vigor, or faith. Nor did his loss arouse the kind of consuming panic and death fear that mother's departure did. During the war, father often ceased to be a living psychological force and became a memorial to a world that was gone. In contrast, mother was often experienced as having the power over life and death; her loss meant the irreparable loss of the good internalized world.

Frequently, survivors will try to reestablish a sense of connectedness through their families and children, asking them to share in an illusion of togetherness and make a world that is complete again—a world that is familiar and known. Survivors often expect their children to be exquisitely sensitive to their needs, to know their minds, and to be a part of their selves, and children of survivors often are very sensitive to their parents' feelings, especially to their fears and sorrows. The survivor's need is to reestablish a responsive, nurturant relationship internally; the wish is to be parented through the child.

Survivors often make many different kinds of attempts to replace their lost worlds through intimate relationships. Sometimes the replacements are instantaneous, almost indiscriminate. Marriages were concluded in a hurry, new families were started up quickly, and new communities were embraced. But these substitutions, while providing temporary relief, ultimately fail, for the act of substitution, which is an exchange of something new for something that has been lost, precludes the gradual incremental process of mourning through which one frees oneself from ties to that which is lost. Substitution leaves those older ties intact, while the ongoing comparison between the new and the old underscores the sense of incompleteness and of things no longer being 'the same.'

The survivor's relationship to the substitute is not a true object relationship and the substitute is not an object in the psychological sense. The substitute is not loved for his or her own real attributes or actions (Brightman, 1984). Instead, the substitute is evaluated in terms of its ability to recreate a lost relationship and, specifically, to meet the survivor's need for a perfectly empathic 'mirroring other'; a quality of unreality there by pervades the substitution process. Ultimately, the survivor's inability to form new genuine ties only compounds his or her sense of lack of intimacy.

The greatest failing of substitutes is their failure to know. Having neither lived in the past nor gone through its destruction, they cannot know what the survivor is all about. Turning to substitutes, thus, not only does not alleviate survivors' loss and lonesomeness, it actually places them back where they mostly fear to be; it replicates the lack of recognition, abandonment, and failed empathy of the original persecution.

It is in the context of our thesis that psychic structure is relational and trauma is deconstructive that we present the following narrative of a Holocaust survivor. This woman was married at the age of 16 in the Warsaw ghetto and subsequently lost her entire family except for her husband:

> A lot of people got married in the ghetto . . . You wanted to attach yourself to someone; you wanted to have some connections to someone else . . . [After the war, I found my husband alive.] The man I married and the man he was after the war wasn't the same person. And . . . I was not the same person either . . . But . . . we had a need for each other because he knew who I was and I knew who he was . . . You feel like you come from nothing, you are nothing. Nobody knows you. You need some contact; you need some connection.

Implications for therapy

Given the desolation and the destruction of the traumatic landscape, how can we as analysts restore life to it? How can we mobilize libidinal forces that can be put to use to counteract traumatic erasure?

The character structures of many survivors show a surprising mosaic of areas of high level psychological functioning coexisting with the potential for severe regression. It is as though we see 'black holes' in an otherwise throbbing, pulsating, and alive galaxy. A recurring memory, nightmare, or even fantasy can totally eclipse the well-functioning survivor's experience of present day reality, causing an affective blackout of the present—its color, shades, details, and subtleties. In such moments of affective blackout of the present, loneliness and desolation are total; and execution is experienced as imminent. Fully living in all its continuity, creativity, and connectedness stops at such moments, for the synthetic functions of the ego are as paralyzed as they were in the traumatic moment of absence of the empathic other.

There are several implications from the foregoing for therapy with survivors. The first involves the integrating work the therapist must do. A narrative of the trauma is as yet nonexistent; its emergence via joint reviewing and witnessing is part of the therapeutic task (Wilson, 1985). However, the therapist cannot expect the elements of a narrative to fall into place via a synthetic process which is based on earlier internalized integrations. With survivors, the therapist must take the integrative step and lead the reconstructive process more actively than he or she would normally do. Trauma cannot be integrated by the survivor alone; neither the internal good other nor the benevolence of the therapeutic situation nor the essential goodness of the therapist is sufficiently taken for granted to allow the synthetic process to proceed.

A second therapeutic implication involves the therapist's style of intervention and appropriate distance when listening to survivors. The survivor's impaired perception of the other sustains the belief that "the world being faced is the same as existed during the time of traumatization" (Cohen, 1985, 183), while the inability to represent the trauma turns memory into repetition. Affect storms marked by terror, cognitive disturbances, and blocked functioning can characterize the return of traumatic percepts. The survivor may experience analytic neutrality toward the re-emergence of traumatic memories as actively malignant if it is felt to represent a repetition of the negation of his or her selfhood by victimizers. Neutrality can also arouse echoes of a silent world by representing a failure to take a stance in what the survivor may experience as a life and death matter, recalling those who "countenanced the Holocaust by pretending to ignore it" (Langer, 1982, 168). The analytic setting itself can thereby become the very focus of reenactment of the traumatic event, which according to Simitis

(1984, 17) has a desymbolizing effect. Thus neutrality, which often accentuates the survivor's periodic feeling of terror, is not helpful during affect storms. During these moments, contact with the historical, therapeutic, and everyday reality is required; only through such contact can the survivor's sense of danger be relocated from the present to her memory.

Finally, because the traumatic state cannot be represented, it is unmodifiable by interpretation. The traumatic state "can only be modified by interactions with need-mediating objects" (Cohen, 1985, 180). Stated differently: What is required initially in the therapy is not elucidation of psychic conflict but restructuring of the internal relationship between self and other. The link between self and other must be rebuilt. The task of the therapist working with a traumatized individual is to re-establish relations which would result in the reinstatement of symbolization and wishing. It is in this context that "the meaning and function of the analyst as a true primary object can be realized" (p. 184). As Moore (1999) put it,

> Recovery from trauma apparently requires an experience, probably not dissimilar from that originally shared with a parent in whose arms shared constructions were first initiated . . . The infant in the mother's arms cannot ask if the mother believes her; it is the mootest of points. Correspondingly, for the severely traumatized person, the issue is not whether rape occurred or whether Auschwitz existed. There is no clinical point in involving theory to qualify such powerful and painfully established realities. The point is that such experiences be shared, constructed and reconstructed in a manner that mobilizes and repairs the constructive process itself, until a narrative that integrates the traumatic experience in the deepest and most unifying way is established. (pp. 169–170)

"The Analyst," Kirshner (1994) states, "now realizes that the establishment of a condition of relative safety which I've defined in terms of maintenance of the good object in its capacity to represent the symbolic order, is a pre-condition for a clinically useful transference repetition of trauma . . . It must be said that more active measures seem to be necessary to provide an atmosphere of safety and confidence required for analytic work to be sustained. I refer here to overt expressions of interest and concern, willingness to participate in discussions about 'external reality' as experienced by the patient, and attention to empathic contact" (p. 240).

The genuine experience of surprise in analyst and patient at the totality of a large blind spot, not seeing the self-evident, may in itself be re-libidinizing, especially if such surprise is spontaneous and mutually shared. The therapeutic alliance, Kohut's self-object, and Winnicott's "holding environment" are useful concepts in understanding how the re-libidinization of the self and object and the connection between the two occurs. Auerhahn, Laub, and Peskin (1993) state, "It is only when survivors remember with someone, when a narrative is created in the presence of a passionate listener, that the connection between an 'I' and a 'you' is remade" (p. 436). Andre Green notes the new meanings that are constructed once symbolization resumes.

I end this essay with a clinical vignette from the training analysis of the candidate whose blind spots I described at the beginning. It is presented in the first person, because he himself is the reporter. It illustrates the approach of his own training analyst, who is not only a step ahead of his analysand, but offers him at a certain moment an item of historical information that is compellingly relevant to the aforementioned blind spots.

> As a child, I was deported to Transnistria, the part of Ukraine occupied by the Romanian army, who were allies of the Germans. What I remembered for years was sitting with a little girl on the bank of the River Bug, the demarcation line between the German and the Romanian occupation territory. It was a beautiful summer day; there were green meadows and rolling green hills and a winding blue river. It was like a summer camp. We were having a debate at age five, arguing whether you could or could not eat grass. I recounted this memory in my second week of analysis in 1969 and luckily enough, my analyst was Swedish. His response was, "I have to tell you something. It was the Swedish Red Cross that liberated Theresienstadt and took depositions from women inmates in the camp. Under oath some of these women declared that conditions in the camp were so good that they received each morning breakfast in bed brought by SS officers." There could not have been a more powerful interpretation of my denial. I stopped talking about young girls, green meadows, and blue rivers and started remembering other things, my own experiences of trauma.

Conclusion

The inevitable conclusion of this chapter is that in cases of massive psychic trauma, it is necessary to establish a setting "which allows the birth and development of an object relationship" in which the analyst participates in the construction of "a meaning which has never been created before the analytic relationship began . . . the analyst forms an absent meaning" (Green, 1996, 47–48). This is so because the survivor, in solitude, continuously faces the horrendously difficult task of dealing with his own inner voids, as well as with whatever he has fabricated or taken in to fend off the terror of these inner voids. In the last mentioned vignette, this was the fairy tale of the "summer camp" on the banks of the river Bug, a "pseudonarrative" at best. In addition, societal processes may pose formidable barriers that prevent traumatic experience from being heard and being known. A lot of resistance had to be overcome to recognize and address these voids. Such resistance is illustrated in the first vignette as operating in all three persons involved—patient, analyst, and supervisor.

The contribution of Green's concept of 'The Dead Mother Complex' is of greatest value. As I mentioned earlier, his error lies in limiting its relevance to the absence of maternal care. I find that it applies to all cases of massive psychic trauma where the internal 'good object' has been destroyed. The mistake the analyst made in the first vignette was believing what Green believes, that maternal deprivation alone was at the root of his patient's difficulties, thus not allowing for the possibility of the destruction of the good internal object through the traumatic experience that her father is assumed to have suffered.

Note

1 First published as Traumatic shutdown of narrative and symbolization. *Contemporary Psychoanalysis, 41*(2) (2005). Reprinted by permission of Taylor & Francis, LLC.

References

Amery, J. (1980). *At the mind's limits: Contemplation by a survivor on Auschwitz and its realities.* Bloomington, IN: Indiana University Press. (Original work published 1966)

Auerhahn, N., Laub, D., & Peskin, H. (1993). Psychotherapy with Holocaust survivors. *Psychotherapy: Theory, Research, Practice, Training, 30*, 434–442.

Auerhahn, N. C. & Laub, D. (1984). Annihilation and restoration: Post-traumatic memory as pathway and obstacle to recovery. *International Review of Psycho-Analysis, 11*, 327–344.

Auerhahn, N. C. & Laub, D. (1987). Play and playfulness in Holocaust survivors. *Psychoanalytic Study of the Child, 42*, 45–58.

Beissner, F. (1962). Kafka the artist. In R. Gray (Ed.), *Kafka* (pp. 15–31). Englewood Cliffs, NJ: Prentice-Hall.

Brightman, B. K. (1984). Narcissistic issues in the training experience of the psychotherapist. *International Journal of Psychoanalytic Psychotherapy, 10*, 293–317.

Caruth, C. (1996). *Unclaimed experience: Trauma narrative and history.* Baltimore, MD: Johns Hopkins University Press.

Cohen, J. (1985). Trauma and repression. *Psychoanalytic Inquiry, 5*, 164–189.

Des Pres, T. (1978). *The survivor.* New York: Oxford University Press. (Original work published 1976)

Ezrahi, S. D. (1980). *By words alone.* Chicago: University of Chicago Press.

Felman, S. & Laub, D. (1992). *Testimony: Crises of witnessing in literature, psychoanalysis and history.* New York: Routledge.

Freud, S. (1953). *On aphasia: A critical study* (E. Stengel, Trans.). New York: International University Press. (Original work published 1891)

Freud, S. (1961). Civilization and its discontents. *Standard Edition, 221*, 59–145. (Original work published 1930)

Gray, R. (Ed.). (1962). *Kafka.* Englewood Cliffs, NJ: Prentice-Hall.

Green, A. (1996). *On private madness.* London: Rebuz Press.

Hilberg, R. (1973). *The destruction of the European Jews.* New York: First Viewpoint.

Kirshner, L. (1994). Trauma, the good object and the symbolic: A theoretical integration. *International Journal of Psychoanalysis, 75*, 235.

Klein, H. (1993). *Interviews with Holocaust survivors in Frankfurt.* Unpublished document, Sigmund Freud Institut, Frankfurt, Germany.

Klein, M. (1930). The importance of symbol formation in the development of the ego. *International Journal of Psychoanalysis, 11*, 221.

Klein, M. (1975). *Love, guilt, and reparation and other works, 1921–1945.* New York: Delacorte Press/Seymour Lawrence.

Langer, L. L. (1982). *Versions of survival.* Albany, NY: State University of New York Press.

Laub, D., & Auerhahn, N. (1993). Knowing and not knowing: Forms of traumatic memory. *International Journal of Psychoanalysis, 74*, 287–302.

Levi, P. (1978). *Survival in Auschwitz: The Nazi assault on humanity.* New York: Collier. (Original work published in 1958)

Lifton, R. J. (1981). *Toward a theory of traumatization and survival*. Paper presented at Holocaust Trauma: A Working Conference, Yale University, New Haven, CT.

Moore, R. (1999). *The creation of reality in psychoanalysis*. Hillsdale, NJ: The Analytic Press.

Oliner, M. (1996). External reality: The elusive dimensions of psychoanalysis. *Psychoanalysis Quarterly, 65*, 267–300.

Rizzuto, A. M. (1993). Freud's speech apparatus and spontaneous speech. *International Journal of Psychoanalysis, 74*, 113–127.

Segal, H. (1951). Notes on symbol formation. *International Journal of Psychoanalysis, 38*, 391–397.

Simitis, I. (1984). Vom Konkretismus zur Metaphorik. *Psyche-Zeitschrift für Psychoanalyse und ihre Anwendungen, 38*, 1–28.

Van der Kolk, B., McFarlane, A., & Weisaeth, L. (1996). *Traumatic stress: The effects of overwhelming experience on mind, body, and society*. New York: Guilford Press.

Weiner, B., Russell, D., and Lerman, D. (1979). The cognitive emotion process in achievement-related contexts. *Journal of Personality and Social Psychology, 37*, 1,211–1,220.

Wiesel, E. (1960). *Night* (S. Rodway, Trans.). New York: Hill & Wang. (Original work published 1958)

Wiesel, E. (1970). *Legends of our time*. New York: Avon. (Original work published 1968)

Wiesel, E. (1982). *Attitudes toward suffering*. Seminar taught at Yale University.

Wilden, A. (1968). *The language of the self*. Baltimore, MD: Johns Hopkins Press.

Wilson, A. (1985). On silence and the Holocaust: A contribution to clinical theory. *Psychoanalytic Inquiry, 5*, 63–84.

Wilson, J., and Lindy, J. (1994). *Countertransference in the treatment of PTSD*. New York: Guilford Press.

Winkler, R. (1985). *Torturers*. Unpublished manuscript.

Winkler, R. O. C. (1962). The novels. In R. Gray (Ed.), *Kafka* (pp. 45–51). Englewood Cliffs, NJ: Prentice-Hall. (Original work published 1938)

Winnicott, D. W. (1965). *The maturational processes and the facilitating environment*. London: The Hogarth Press and the Institute of Psycho-Analysis. (Original work published 1958)

Winnicott, D. W. (1975). *Through paediatrics to psycho-analysis*. New York: Basic Books. (Original work published 1951)

Chapter 4

Genocidal trauma

Individual and social consequences of assault on the mental and physical life of a group

Andreas Hamburger

What is trauma? Definitions usually begin with the word's meaning as 'lesion,' which is sufficiently clear in the realm of physical trauma. It does not make much difference for the surgeon whether a leg was broken in an accidental fall from a roof or during torture. However, when it comes to psychological trauma, it does matter. A mental trauma or 'lesion' is a metaphor, which compares a psychological reaction to physical damage caused by an external event. In psychology, the term indicates a specific class of exposure-reactive mental disorders, differentiated from those caused by inner conflicts or structural deficits. Thus, when in the aftermath of the Vietnam War PTSD was introduced to DSM-III (1980) as the only etiology-based diagnosis, it was linked to a wide definition of a traumatic event that would cause "significant symptoms of distress in almost anyone." This first definition was felt to be too broad, so the first revision (DSM-IIIR, 1987) added that the event was "outside the range of usual human experience." Both definitions, however, left the necessary assessments of 'significant,' 'anyone,' and 'usual' to the clinician. This open definition of the 'stressor' seemed to work well in clinical reality (at least, no complaints about it being too vague were published by clinicians). However, it proved unsatisfying for research. As a consequence, DSM-IV (APA 1994, text revision DSM-IV TR, 2000) undertook a more conclusive definition of traumatic stress:

> a traumatic event in which both of the following have been present:
> (1) the person experienced, witnessed, or was confronted with an event or events that involved actual or threatened death or serious injury, or a threat to the physical integrity of self or others (2) the person's response involved intense fear, helplessness, or horror. (Note: In children, this may be expressed instead by disorganized or agitated behavior.)

This narrow definition, however, turned out to be all too narrow, since the only objective reasons for being traumatized were now physical threats. As a result of the introduction of the A2 criterion (emotional reaction), a greater variety of stressors were included (Breslau & Kessler, 2001), while others were clearly excluded, such as "cumulative prolonged exposure to harassment, abandonment, incest and most kinds of sexual abuse, as well as historical collective identity traumas such as genocide and holocaust that go beyond the threat to the individual's physical integrity" (Kira et al., 2008, 62).

The classification of posttraumatic disorders

In accordance with the medical, 'lesion'-oriented trauma concept, literature on psychic trauma and its consequences tends to concentrate on posttraumatic clinical symptomatology, regardless of the type of trauma exposure. Only a minority of studies either draws on stressor-specific psychological symptoms or calls for a taxonomy of traumatic experiences (e.g., Briere, Elliott, Harris, & Cotman, 1995; Kira et al., 2008; cf. Kirmayer, Kienzler, Afana, & Pedersen, 2010; Santiago et al., 2013). However, the dilemma remains of defining a mental disorder by an external event while at the same time avoiding any definition of the event. Thus, despite extensive research, the nosological classification of posttraumatic disorders has never attained a univocal definition. To take the ongoing discussion into account, new sources of psychological trauma were unanimously regarded as specific stressors. DSM-5 (APA, 2013) added sexual violence, hence introducing a mental and/or social aspect to the hitherto physically oriented definition of traumatic stress. However, the clinical relevance of the revision was immediately placed in doubt (Elklit, Hyland, & Shevlin, 2014). ICD-11 (expected to be issued in 2017) will most probably address the existing, clinically unsatisfying definitions by renaming the former category F62.0 from "enduring personality change after catastrophic experience" to "complex posttraumatic stress disorder" (CPTSD), and possibly also by moving it from personality disorders to a parent category of stress-related disorders (Cloitre, Garvert, Brewin, Bryand, & Maercker, 2013). CPTSD will be a supplemental diagnosis to PTSD with additional, not necessarily trauma-triggered effects upon self-concept, affect, and relations (ibid.). This revision resolves the long-existing discussion as to whether the specific posttraumatic symptoms found in cases of severe social and early-onset traumatization should be classified together with the vast range of traumatic experiences to be encountered in ordinary life (Streeck-Fischer, 2006).

> Complex PTSD is a new disorder category describing a symptom profile that can arise after exposure to a single traumatic stressor, but that typically follows severe stressors of a prolonged nature or multiple or repeated adverse events from which separation is not possible (e.g., exposure to genocide campaigns, childhood sexual abuse, child soldiering, severe domestic violence, torture, or slavery). (Maercker et al., 2013, 201)

Clinical reality demands that psychic trauma not be defined solely by typical symptoms examined independent of the situations which had traumatic impact. There are strong arguments which justify reticence when it comes to classifying situations and specificities of traumatic impact. Abstracting from the specific, exposure-related suffering of the victims may deprive such suffering of acknowledgement—which in cases of social trauma might even lead to re-traumatization, since the lack of acknowledgement lies at the very core of the trauma and of its perpetuation. The 'broken leg' of the genocide survivor is a broken memory, and the harm done to the person was precisely that of disregard for his human individuality and dignity.

Furthermore, consideration of the precise situation and circumstances of trauma exposure is necessary for understanding the etiology. Social and social-cognitive factors play a role in any psychotraumatic experience, but in social trauma they play a decisive role in coping with the experience in the peritraumatic situation, as well as in the course of posttraumatic life. Neither the traumatogenic situation itself nor its impact or its recollection are isolated, individual-psychological items, as they proceed within frames of social relations, and thus the analysis of these frames is necessary for understanding and treatment. The 'broken leg,' to refer to the metaphor again, is not a part of the body, not even part of the isolated individual's mental or 'inner' life—it extends to a breach in his social relations. Therefore, purposeful violence, socially accepted by the perpetrator's own social group, causes damage not only to the victim, but also to the perpetrator and to society overall. Genocidal disregard of humanity endangers humanity. This is why genocide is also engraved in the collective memory— sometimes by historical traces like "chosen trauma" (Volkan, 1997, 1999), sometimes by the significant absence of such traces, as if in a social void. Mental disorder classifications, on the other hand, keep attempting an ever more subtle assessment of the fracture, thereby disregarding the interactivity and complexity of the 'broken leg' and its social nature.

The step towards objectivization of symptom descriptions, strongly suggested by international classifications and taken by most researchers, is at the same time accompanied by a tendency to objectivize the posttraumatic experience itself. Recent studies tend to investigate the neurobiological more than the social conditions of PTSD, and therapeutic efforts are prone to concentrate on coping with trauma rather than addressing and understanding it (Kar, 2011).

The main symptom which has caused discussion in the field of disorder classification is chronic permanence of some of the lead symptoms of PTSD under certain circumstances. Furthermore, research on 'Disorders of Extreme Stress Not Otherwise Specified' (DESNOS) (or, as it will be referred to in ICD-11, 'Complex Posttraumatic Stress Disorder,' CPTSD) emphasizes the early onset of trauma, where stress exposure and immature psychic development come together and compound one another. Due to the trauma's ongoing and multiple impact on psychological development, a multiplicity of consequences has been observed: psychopathological symptoms such as dissociation, affect dysregulation, and problems in interpersonal relationships, as well as social deviation in such forms as violent or auto-aggressive behavior. Neurophysiological changes in long-term posttraumatic conditions have been discussed, such as an aberrant amygdala response to emotional conflict (Dannlowski et al., 2012), hampering the automatic affect regulation (Marusak, Martin, Etkin, & Thomason, 2015). Clinical observation, by contrast, suggests linking long-lasting forms of PTSD to an underlying context of severe, human-induced trauma, especially if the onset of such a trauma lies in childhood (Strous, 2017). Strous points out that in cases where children were victims of traumatic experiences during the Holocaust, support structures such as families were often unavailable. These children could not speak about their experience, neither immediately after their exposure to trauma nor later on—due to disbelief and denial of such experience in their social environment, and as a consequence of the "general mood by some that one should 'move on' and not focus on the past, no matter how distressing" (ibid.).

Man-made traumatizations often affecting great parts of the population—caused, for instance, by genocide, war, and dictatorship with racist, ethnic, and political persecution—have a special position. The involvement of the social environment in the traumatization (through victimization) of an entire group, and a 'perpetratorization' (to coin this term by analogy) of another group or nation causes severe traumatic consequences visible on an interactive level. Denial of acknowledgement, a conspiracy of silence, institutional rejection, breakdown of successful myth construction, and, moreover, of historical elucidation, are among the social symptoms perpetuating social trauma—and they backfire on the traumatized individual who, in a scarred and sometimes hostile environment, is then deprived of major resilience factors necessary for a successful coping process (see Bonanno, 2004; McAfee, 2008; Karstoft, Armour, Elkit, & Solomon, 2013; Bohleber, 2017).

Notions of trauma

In order to widen the scope of the trauma concept, which appears to be confined within the classifications provided by medicine and clinical psychology, it is worth having a look at the notion of trauma as used in various other discourses such as sociology, gender studies, literature, and political science. What we will find is a view that goes beyond individual pathology—but is perhaps also quite distanced from human suffering. The constructivist approach may prove to be another way of seeking mental distance from genocide.

In the social and cultural sciences, the concept of trauma addresses a shock to cultural identity, such as war experiences, especially if they are unexpected atrocities that violate limits; but it also refers to changes in technology and political culture, which can in turn lead to traumatic changes in societies.

In her book *Unclaimed Experience: Trauma, Narrative, and History*, the influential literary scholar Cathy Caruth (1996) re-reads the psychoanalytic trauma discourse from Freud's Moses (1939/1964) to Lacan, showing how closely the psychoanalytic experience in sharing the subjectivity of the traumatically shattered mind parallels the way in which social trauma is addressed in literature and the arts.

> Trauma is not locatable in the simple violent or original event in an individual's past, but rather in the way its very unassimilated nature—the way it was precisely not known in the first instance—returns to haunt

the survivor later on [. . .] trauma seems to be much more than a pathology, or the simple illness of a wounded psyche: it is always the story of a wound that cries out, that addresses us in the attempt to tell us of a reality or truth that is not otherwise available. (Caruth, 1996, 3–4)

In their frequently cited book on 'cultural trauma,' Alexander, Eyerman, Giesen, Smelser, and Sztompka (2004) relativize this psychoanalytically inspired concept of trauma as the unsymbolized 'wound' from the perspective of a sociological theory of trauma. In this view, social trauma is not a reaction to a historical cause, but a collective construction. Thus, the Holocaust can be seen as "the traumatic reference of German national identity" (Giesen, 2004) or as the subject of changing historical narratives (Alexander, 2004); slavery can be seen as an identity-granting reference point for the formation of African-American identity (Eyerman, 2004), just as communism can be seen as doing so for post-communist society (Sztompka, 2004).

The sociological approach to trauma draws upon the everyday, ordinary-language use of the term. People (increasingly) call traumatic what they experience as unsupportable, horrifying, or overwhelming. Trauma as an intuitively understood term is a social fact in itself, and it points to some underlying social experience which can be sociologically reflected. In the common-sense understanding of trauma, something akin to a natural force is assumed. Socially traumatic events—metaphorically speaking—are experienced as quasi-earthquakes, even if their man-made nature is obvious.

However, sociological reflection demonstrates that naturalistic approaches in ordinary language as well as in scholarly concepts of social trauma—prominently including psychoanalytic ones—are, each in their own way, naive. For the sociologist, social facts are not causes, but attributions:

First and foremost, we maintain that events do not, in and of themselves, create trauma. Events are not inherently traumatic. Trauma is a socially mediated attribution. The attribution may be made in real time, as an event unfolds; it may also be made before the event occurs, as an adumbration, or after the event has concluded, as a post-hoc reconstruction. Sometimes, in fact, events that are deeply traumatizing may not actually have occurred at all; such imagined events, however, can be as traumatizing as events that have actually occurred. (Alexander, 2004, 8)

In this perspective, the impact of trauma on society is not so much defined by the trauma itself, but by the society in which the traumatic experience is fostered. Traumatic events are reference points of memory and/or re-projection of societies, situated at the core of the century-long stabilization of their group identity. Jewish identity is deeply rooted in the Exodus, and Christian identity is deeply rooted in the Crucifixion. Serbian identity draws on the historical Battle of Kosovo (1389) against the Ottomans, and postwar German identity on the Holocaust (Volkan, 1999; Volkan, Ast, & Greer 2002).

From a socio-clinical perspective, however, social trauma cannot be reduced to such a construct on the one hand, while nevertheless remaining brutal reality on the other. The mental and social 'legs' of our tortured and persecuted patients are broken in reality, and a theory of socially mediated attribution, sophisticated as it may be, simply falls short of the mark. Therapists and counsellors dealing with real survivors of social trauma, and also the growing literature on healing social trauma (e.g., Worthington & Aten, 2010; Delić et al., 2013), rely heavily on a "naturalistic" perspective, strongly underlining the indispensable acknowledgement of the reality of trauma. From the sociological perspective, these efforts may be regarded as just another segment of trauma culture, being part and parcel of cultural trauma identity construction; in the perspective of the survivors themselves, the notion of trauma as a mere construct could be construed as an obscenity. Analogous to the shift towards abstract, syndrome-based trauma concepts in the clinical field, the social sciences tend to keep a distanced stance to experienced reality.

But even given these reservations as seen from a clinical perspective on social and genocidal trauma over against an all too abstract constructivist sociological approach, we nevertheless cannot discard this approach. The haunting conclusion here is that we cannot return to naturalism. In fact, suffering in our immediate (Western) environment has widely become a media phenomenon. Our perception of the Holocaust, too, is influenced by its presentation in the media—and should we then meet a survivor in the flesh, we meet this person as a specimen of our medially formed pre-conceptions (Hamburger, 2016).

As an outcome of this short review of the very different notions and implications of the trauma concept in different discourses and paradigms, it can be stated that the specific nature of the traumatic situation seems to play a marginal role in clinical as well as in sociological discourse. While the former constructs psychological trauma as a symptom profile, regardless of the stressor, the latter depicts trauma as a construct, akin to other social facts. The nature of the specific type of experience is less important than its social communication and resonance.

The warning from the social sciences cannot be ignored: every medical or psychological approach to social trauma is embedded in a social frame. Some approaches to 'trauma healing' are criticized as serving the import of a Western concept of healing more than offering an adequate support to survivors (Meierhenrich, 2007).

As a countercurrent to this mainstream, modern psychoanalytic trauma concepts envisage the personal specificity and embrace a relational view of the traumatic experience. This is in line with literature and the arts, which, much like psychoanalysis, cannot do without individualizing the traumatic experience, and thus rendering it tangible.

Within the psychoanalytic trauma paradigm, however, a wide spectrum of approaches can be identified. While in the early years of psychoanalysis the concept of trauma was quite narrowly defined as an overriding of the protective shield due to sexual abuse (Zepf & Zepf, 2008; Bohleber, 2017), then adjusted by the idea of 'traumatic neurosis' to reflect the shell shock syndrome of soldiers in World War I, more recent concepts are characterized by an overgeneralization in two entirely different directions.

One tendency is to subjectivize trauma. In Heinz Kohut's self psychology, a prominent approach in the 1970s, traumatization was almost automatically equated with a lack of empathy (Cooper, 1986, 49). However, one of Kohut's prominent followers, Anna Ornstein (2013), explicitly opposes the general pathologizing of genocide survivors. On the other hand, in more socio-psychoanalytic discourse, the concept underwent an objectivistic overgeneralization (e.g., Hernández de Tubert, 2006, 151, defining social trauma as the sum of "unsuitable and damaging life conditions, originating in the social milieu"). The following discussion will use a much narrower definition of trauma, closer to Prager's (2011) critique of such overextended use of the concept.

As Bohleber (2017) points out, a revised psychoanalytic trauma theory based on object relations theory is much more suitable for the conceptualization of social trauma than the classical theory referring to overwhelming quantities of anxiety. What is more, this approach explains some of the cognitive symptoms, such as dissociation and the breakdown of symbolic functioning. Da Rocha Barros and da Rocha Barros (2011) highlight this breakdown as one of the central aspects of extreme traumatization. In a relational view, symbolic functioning is linked to a mutual enactment in the developmental matrix, as well as in the consulting room (Hamburger, 1995; Thomas, 2009).

Dori Laub's seminal work on genocidal trauma and genocide realizes an up-to-date concept of psychological trauma, close enough to the subjective experience of the survivor and yet systematic enough to embrace the subjective as well as the constructivist notion of trauma, while avoiding the pitfalls of either overgeneralization or disengagement. Extreme trauma, as he explains, is truly neither an 'objective' nor a 'subjective' entity. It is a hole in representation. As one of the pioneers of listening to contemporary witnesses of the Holocaust, he first had to face and overcome the reluctance of historiography towards using testimonial sources. Laub's reflective approach does not simply invoke the subjectivity of individual testimony to refute historical positivism. He does not claim that a well ordered 'story' exists in the survivor's autobiographical memory, complementing what cannot be grasped by the facticity of historical documents. On the contrary: psychoanalytic testimony acknowledges the disturbed autobiographical narrative and intentionally exposes itself to the uncertainty, the overwhelming fuzziness of memory, in which both the survivor and the testimonial witness find themselves. Testimony is cultural trauma construction, but different from ideology, since it does not construct—at least, not at the outset—an inhabitable past. It acknowledges and connects itself to the presence of the past as a contradictory, fragmented process, drenched in silence and parried by defensive maneuvers on both sides, by the survivor as well as the interviewer. As a result, but only when the unspeakable as such has had time to remain in the open after having been expressed, it sometimes happens—quite some time after the testimony— that a change may occur. Survivors as well as interviewers and staff may feel relieved, as if an unconscious "conspiracy of silence" had been broken (Laub, 2005a; Strous et al., 2005). This specificity of the testimonial process mirrors the structure of the survivor's memory, where "the traumatic event became an 'absent' experience because at the core of the executioner-victim interaction all human relatedness is undone. The internal other, the 'Thou' to whom one can address one's plea, tell one's story, no longer exists. Therefore the 'story' is never known, told, or remembered" (Laub, 2005a, 257).

The consequences of trauma are not enclosed in the individual psyche of the survivor. They are located in the mutual enactment between the survivor and his or her environment, including the testimonial witnesses. This re-enactment is especially forceful, since the splitting processes which occur in the fragmented biographical memories of Holocaust child survivors, as we have seen above, elicit strong complementary reactions on the part of the interviewer (Hamburger 2017b). Thus, in accord with a contemporary, relational psychoanalytic point of view, the dichotomy discussed above existing between 'objective' and 'subjective' trauma, 'stressor' and 'stress,' is neither accepted nor avoided. It is addressed.

Individual vs. social trauma

Proceeding from the theoretical insight that social trauma can neither be defined by a symptom profile, nor with an objective exposure scale, we shall now take a look at some more detailed arguments.

Epidemiological and clinical data

The epidemiologic evidence available does not yield a clear picture, but instead an overt tendency that points toward the specificity of social and genocidal trauma. Only a few studies have been conducted in order to differentiate social and individual trauma—but many studies conducted for other purposes can be consulted to support the impact of such a difference in trauma exposure. First of all, and most generally, evidence shows a statistical correlation between 'dose' and 'effect' of trauma: "All things being equal, extreme stressors are more likely to produce PTSD symptoms than are mild stressors" (McNally, 2004, 6). Despite the prevailing opinion that the type of exposure does not influence PTSD, Breslau et al. (1998) have demonstrated in the Detroit Survey (N = 2,181) that conditional risk of PTSD varied from 53.8 percent after being held captive or kidnapped, to 0.2 percent after having discovered a dead body—to name only the extreme cases. More refined than this simple dose-response model is a development-based model of cumulative trauma, designed and empirically supported by Kira, Fawzi, and Fawzi (2013), demonstrating that a pattern of different, underlying trauma profiles predicted different configurations of symptoms. Interestingly, in this sample collective-identity trauma predicted all mental health conditions, especially those related to annihilation anxiety, more strongly than did personal-identity trauma and all other types of trauma.

Moreover, there is epidemiological data indicating that the specific type of trauma impact rather than its severity predicts certain kinds and degrees of symptoms. Amir, Kaplan, and Kotler (1996) found that a battlefield-experienced group was more severely affected by PTSD than subjects that had experienced civilian terrorism or work and traffic accidents. In a study conducting structured clinical interviews with 157 children (aged 8–17) seeking help, Luthra et al. (2009) found that confrontation with traumatic news, witnessing domestic violence, experience of physical abuse and sexual abuse were significantly associated with PTSD, while witnessing a crime, being the victim of a crime, and exposure to accidents, fire, or disaster were not. A study by Heins et al. (2011) made the under-lying, exposure-specific mechanisms plausible: childhood abuse, but not childhood neglect, predicted later positive psychotic symptoms, even as compared to siblings. Ehring and Quack (2010) showed, in a large sample (N = 616), that difficulties in emotional regulation associated with PTSD in trauma survivors occurred significantly more often in survivors of early-onset chronic interpersonal trauma than survivors of single-event and/or late-onset trauma.

More generally, DiMauro, Carter, Folk, and Kashdan (2014) assert, in their systematic literature review of the historical trajectory of trauma-related diagnoses, that the heterogeneity of traumatic experiences grouped under the unified DSM-5 definition of PTSD should be differentiated by type of trauma. Interestingly enough, their analysis addresses only four types of trauma: combat, natural disaster, life-threatening accident, and sexual assault. Similarly, the five trauma type categories used by Utzon-Frank et al. in their meta-analysis on late-onset PTSD (2014) include only natural disaster, terrorism, accident, injury/disease, and military combat/deployment.

With regard to the specificity of genocidal traumatization and persecution of ethnic groups, there is much clinical, but relatively little epidemiological evidence.

One important study is a set of meta-analyses conducted by Barel, Van IJzendoorn, Sagi-Schwartz, and Bakermans-Kranenburg (2010). In 56 surveyed studies drawing on 71 samples with a total of 12,746 participants, comparing Holocaust survivors with groups that had no Holocaust background, three meta-analyses (one for each generation under examination) demonstrated that Holocaust survivors were less well adjusted, particularly showing substantially more posttraumatic stress symptoms than the non-exposed groups. Another finding was that the survivors also showed remarkable resilience. Since the underlying studies were not aimed at comparing different types of trauma exposure, but rather at comparing the effect of Holocaust exposure to non-exposure, this meta-analysis teaches us about the eminent long-term impact of the Holocaust, but it does not give a sufficient answer as to the specificity of genocidal trauma as compared with other types of trauma exposure. Attachment may be an important factor (Bar-On et al., 1998; see below for further discussion). Sagi-Schwartz et al. (2003) found, in their well-controlled study on attachment in female child survivors, that even 50 years after the Holocaust survivors showed more signs of traumatic stress and more often lack of resolution of trauma than did members of the comparison group.

In a study with school-going adolescents (N = 100), Kravić, Pajević, and Hasanović (2013) found that adolescents who had lived in Srebrenica during the siege—as compared to a group that had lived in the 'free territory'—had lived through a significantly higher number of traumatic experiences, but displayed no higher overall PTSD scores. Although there was no significant difference in the total score of posttraumatic stress reactions, single items (memories, sleep, coping with danger) revealed significant differences. Furthermore, Srebrenica adolescents had higher sociability levels. In a sample of Darfuri female university students (N = 123), Badri, Crutzen, and Van den Borne (2012) found a strong association between war-related trauma exposures and the full catalog of symptoms associated with PTSD. Neugebauer et al. (2014) assessed Tutsi children shortly after the Rwandan genocide and found that posttraumatic stress symptom (PTSS) did not show the expected decline of symptoms over time. However, a systematic comparison to normative data was not accomplished. Müller, Moeller, Hilger, and Sperling (2015) compared two groups of victim/witness trauma sufferers (general PTSD vs Holocaust-experience PTSD) and found that the latter showed substantially more specific PTSD symptoms and higher symptom-specific intensities. Despite some counterevidence (see Meierhenrich, 2007), these data indicate that the specificity of genocidal traumatization should be further explored.

Apart from specific genocidal traumatization, there is evidence in favor of a broader conception of the social ramifications of trauma exposure and coping. Brewin, Andrews, and Valentine (2000) showed, in a meta-analysis of risk factors for posttraumatic stress disorder in trauma-exposed adults, that factors operating during or after the trauma—such as trauma severity, lack of social support, and additional life stress—had somewhat stronger effects than pre-trauma factors. Priebe et al. (2010) assessed 3,313 persons from war-affected community samples in former Yugoslavia with the Mini–International Neuropsychiatric Interview. Multivariable analyses across countries showed that having more potentially traumatic experiences during and after the war was associated with higher rates of mood and anxiety disorders. Stefanović-Stanojević and Nedeljković (2009) measured attachment patterns in three samples of adolescents (N = 247) who had grown up under different war impact conditions in towns of former Yugoslavia (Banja Luka, Nis, Skopje). Results showed significant differences in attachment style as related to types of war exposure, deserving further exploration. Again, it becomes clear that further research and meta-analysis has to be done in order to differentiate between different types of exposure.

As a conclusion, we might say that epidemiological data from various, hardly comparable studies point towards the specificity of social and genocidal trauma. Meta-analytic and epidemiological research remains to be done in order to clarify this issue.

Qualitative evidence

There is more than quantitative proof, however, for the specificity. Qualitative research efforts have been undertaken to delineate the characteristics we encounter in working with survivors. Apart from epidemiological evidence, clinical experience and assessment as well as qualitative research indicate a specificity of social and genocidal trauma (Blum, 2007). As mentioned above, seminal descriptions of this type of trauma have been provided by Laub (1998, 2000, 2003, 2005a, 2005b; Laub & Auerhahn, 2017). Condensed clinical experience in testimonial interviews with Holocaust survivors (Strous et al., 2005; Strous, 2017), with slave laborers (Laub & Bodenstab, 2010), and with survivors of the genocide in Rwanda (Laub, 2005a; Kaplan, 2006, 2013) demonstrates typical cognitive and emotional symptoms. Moreover, these symptoms are not only individual ones, but are mirrored in specific countertransference reactions of the interviewer (Grünberg & Markert, 2012; Grünberg, 2013; Hamburger, 2017a, 2017b), characterized by Laub (2017) as "traumatic shutdown." Among these symptoms are, most prominently, that survivors do not have a life history in the form of a coherent autobiographical narrative and that they display an erasure of feelings of sorts, comprising a massive denial and/or disavowal of trauma, extreme ambiguity, speechlessness, psychotic or seemingly psychotic delusions, and other psychotic and psychosomatic symptoms, replacement of repressed or split-off memories by screen memories, frequent nightmares, flashback memories, as well as daydreams of persecution (Laub & Auerhahn, 2016; Laub, 2017).

These symptoms are connected to the interactional field; even the traumatic memory failures themselves only become visible once patients are asked to recount their life stories, as in the case of the testimonial process. Apart from this active type of investigation, patients otherwise often withdraw from all social contacts and avoid talking about their former life.

The damage in social communication is also addressed by Varvin (in Rosnick, 2013, 1,201), who describes the symptoms of extreme trauma as centered around the loss of the individuals' narrative capacity, turning their lives into a prolonged dissociative state. In particular, "persistent attacks against one's religious or ethnic or racial identity can disrupt the traumatized individual's capacity to restore intrapsychic cohesion through membership in their group" (ibid.) with consequent damage to the social and cultural context (cf. Varvin, 2003, 2006). This socio-environmental damage is compared by many of the psychoanalytic authors (Laub, 2017; Gerson, 2009) to Andre Green's (1983) concept of the "Dead Mother," the internalized remnant of the experience of being with a depressed mother. Testimonial work with survivors of extreme and genocidal persecution demonstrates that this loss of the empathic dyad is the main symptom (Bodenstab, 2015, 2017).

Kaplan (2006) summarizes the result of extreme trauma as a specific failure of affect regulation in her concept of "perforating"—namely, as a "puncture in the psychic shield," experienced as recurring, invasive bodily panic, a loss of the sense of time, and dissociation in the sense of memory being stored as isolated fragments, sensory perceptions, affective states, or behavioral re-enactments (Kaplan, 2013, 94). These findings are consistent with the symptoms described for survivors of early childhood abuse (Van der Kolk & Fisler, 1994). Again, the importance of the social environment is underlined: "the individual has a safe psychic space in which to reflect about the fear and destructive fantasies that may follow the traumatic experience" (Kaplan, 2013; cf. Böhm & Kaplan, 2011).

This short outline of the rich qualitative and clinical findings makes clear that all the authors refer to interactive aspects of extreme and especially of genocidal traumatization. The findings, however, are not entirely consistent; comparative studies would be required to connect the clinical concepts and epidemiological findings. However, the studies seem to indicate differences between social/genocidal trauma and individual trauma.

Conceptual differences

Summarizing our findings on epidemiological differences and qualitative specificities of social and genocidal trauma, and in order to prepare for future research in both fields, in the following section the notions of social and individual trauma will be conceptually discussed. Of course, both diagnoses are not strictly disjunctive. Social trauma is not limited to war and genocide; but it requires a relevant involvement of the social environment. Thus, a trauma can be individual and social at the same time, since individual traumatic events may contain a social factor. Rape, for example, if committed in private (and not, for example, as rape committed in the midst of war or as part of mass violence), would be regarded as an individual trauma—however, and as the occurrence of rape crimes in society is related to the particular society's values on bodily autonomy and sexual self-determination, it may, at the same time, also be a social trauma insofar as through the act of rape women as a group are injured in their dignity. Even earthquakes or traffic disasters may have a social component, should they reflect poor management of security issues in a society, as directed against less privileged classes. However, the main issue and the core phenomenon of social trauma reveal themselves when the whole of the social environment is under threat of persecution or actually experiencing persecution; in the case of genocidal trauma, it must be remembered that the threat is a deadly one.

Many psychoanalytic theories could be quoted here to explain the specificity of traumatogenic experience involving severe social persecution and/or genocide. To take just one example, the impact of collective persecution can be analyzed in terms of mentalization theory (Fonagy, Gergely, Jurist, & Target, 2004), which offers a strong explanatory model for the psychopathology of childhood trauma (Fonagy, 2010). One of the basic mechanisms responsible for mentalization is "reflective functioning" as an unconscious, automatic, implicit procedure to regulate emotions and behavior according to a basic understanding of reciprocal influences between feelings and behavior of the self in relation to others. This reflective functioning is developed in emotionally charged relations with caregivers and peers, where the infant can internalize the image of himself in the caregiver's mind by reading the caregiver's intentions. Situations in which the caregiver shows 'marked affects' in exchange with the infant help to advance from equivalent mode, where the difference between imagination and reality is not yet established, to pretend mode, where an inner world can be established, uncoupled from outer perception. Pretend play is one of the important junctures on the path from pretend mode to proper mentalization, where the developing individual can shift between perception and imagination of his own feelings to the empathic perception of the other's feelings and intentions. These achievements may be hampered under conditions of childhood trauma—when, for example, in family abuse the role of trusted attachment figure and abuser are commingled (Fonagy 2010). By building a bridge from the model of mentalization to the social psychology of genocide and persecution, group traumatization can be addressed in a more specific way: it damages mentalization through a different mechanism, since it systematically affects the mentalizing capacity and playfulness of the caregiving environment. When caregivers themselves are under threat of persecution in reality, they cannot provide the security necessary for the child to perceive the difference between outer and inner fears, experienced in equivalence mode as outer threats. To put it in the words of Bion (1957), the parents lose their reassuring, containing capacity. Thus, the parental sheltering space is turned into a poisoned, danger-laden horizon. The mental container, otherwise available for the individual to metabolize its individual traumatic experiences, is itself perverted into an equivalence mode.

The same effect holds for the wider environment. Everyday narratives of a social group grant it its coherence. Addressing actual experiences and reworking them with recourse to social narratives takes on the function of pretend play. The story of the hero, the story of the enemy, and the story of the trauma—all of these convey meaning and structure to hardly containable experiences, such as war and persecution exposure. More generally, culturally relevant narrative or "ideology" convey meaning to life experiences, giving them a communicative matrix.

But what happens if the narrative fails? What if the experiences are too overwhelming to be successfully played through, mentalized in the pretend play of the narrative? The failure of the narrating function has been widely discussed in survivor studies from different angles (Felman &

Laub, 1992; Laub, 1998). The mentalizing capacity of the social narrative is more likely to be overburdened if the subject is too young to narrate and mentalize, or if the social environment—the resonance body for narrative exchange—is damaged. This is specifically the case when an entire group has been expelled and eradicated by a society of which it had previously been an important part of, as in the Shoah and in the ethnic cleansings and war rapes in the Ex-Yugoslavian War (Priebe et al., 2010; Hasanović, 2011, 2012). Unlike persecution during war by an external enemy, the expulsion by one's own surrounding society leads to the annihilation of a reparative social network (Laub, 2003, 2005a; Varvin, 2003; Kaplan, 2005, 2006; Böhm & Kaplan, 2011). Groups persecuted in war can provide psychic repair by mythogenesis, collective hate, and revenge feelings (as well as a literature of hatred and revenge), while genocide results in a breakdown of reparative communicative mechanisms. The traumatic parts of collective experience, excluded from discourse and insulated by the 'conspiracy of silence,' correspond to the dynamic unconscious, or—to put it in Bion's terms—the Beta elements of society.

Therefore, both social and genocidal trauma are not one-person phenomena, but social processes. Besides the act of persecution itself, the damage done to memory building by the extinction of the cultural environment as a resonance body is their distinctive feature, and as this leads to long-term denial of the trauma and its consequences, it can be regarded as a permanent re-traumatization. This ongoing 'infectiveness' of social trauma can be demonstrated by a detailed description of the countertransference reactions in testimonial interviews—a kind of undertow, dragging the interviewer (and researchers) into the fragmented psychic world of the survivor (Hamburger, 2017a, 2017b). Posttraumatic and dissociative disorders in cases of social traumatization are not only man-made, they are man-perpetuated, since the environment is part and parcel of the disaster. Social trauma is not a just a consequence of a historical crime committed there-and-then. It is a shared state of mind, which tends to perpetuate the conditions of de-symbolization as long as the countertransference entanglement is not reflected in the here-and-now.

Institutional rejection

A special aggravating factor in socially embedded trauma is the fact that the public regularly fails to acknowledge or even actively denies the social trauma. This has been observed in cases of mass persecution and genocide all over the world; famously the rejection of concentration camp survivors by German psychiatry led to a fierce debate after World War II. Many survivors of German concentration camps were denied compensation, with reference to supposed previous mental vulnerability. In this debate, Eissler (1963) published a paper whose title polemically exposed the impudence implicit in this psychiatric practice: "Die Ermordung von wievielen seiner Kinder muss ein Mensch symptomfrei ertragen können, um eine normale Konstitution zu haben? [The murder of how many of his children must a person be able to endure symptom-free in order to be considered normal?]" (Eissler, 1963; see also Eissler, 1967). Strangely enough, the neglect of social trauma also occurred in post-war psychiatry in Israel, as the case of the 'forgotten survivors' described in this book demonstrates (Greenwald, 2017; Hamburger, 2017b; Knopp, 2017; Laub & Felsen, 2017; Strous, 2017; Zalashik, 2017). If trauma research can be regarded as an institution as well, we should take great care not to be swept along by the undertow of social neglect.

Conclusion

Posttraumatic Stress Disorder was introduced into the diagnostic classificatory systems as the only category of mental illness defined by an external event. Since then, however, clinical and epidemiological research has shown a tendency to concentrate more on the differentiation of symptomatology than on the typology of trauma exposure. From a sociologically informed clinical perspective, it can be argued that such a concentration on symptoms tends to neglect important specificities of genocidal trauma, which may affect its immediate experience as well as its aftermath. The main difference between individual and social or genocidal trauma is that the latter is strongly embedded in a social matrix. Genocidal acts are directed at an entire group, therefore affecting not only the individual victim, but also his social environment. The traumatic consequences will not necessarily, but may possibly be influenced by this group-relatedness— a fact that is frequently overlooked in clinical treatment and research. Moreover, social and genocidal traumatization not only targets a group, it is also committed by a social group. Both groups, victims and perpetrators, are frequently part of the same overarching society. This double social character of the traumatic event affects the persistence of its results. In a society where victims as well as perpetrators are prone to shame-driven denial or lack of acknowledgement, psychosocial repair mechanisms—such as the exchange of autobiographical narratives, in which memory can be verbalized and acknowledgement can be experienced—are hampered to the extent that a 'conspiracy of silence' seems to rule.

References

Alexander, J. C. (2004). On the social construction of moral universals: The "Holocaust" from war crime to trauma drama. In J. C. Alexander, R. Eyerman, B. Giesen, N. J. Smelser, & P. Sztompka (Eds.), *Cultural trauma and collective identity* (pp. 196–263). Berkeley, CA: University of California Press.

Alexander, J. C., Eyerman, R., Giesen, B., Smelser, N. J., & Sztompka, P. (2004). *Cultural trauma and collective identity*. Berkeley, CA: University of California Press.

American Psychiatric Association (1994). *Diagnostic and statistical manual of mental disorders* (4th ed.). Washington, DC: American Psychiatric Association.

American Psychiatric Association (2013). *Diagnostic and Statistical Manual of Mental Disorders* (5th ed.). Arlington, VA: American Psychiatric Publishing.

Amir, M., Kaplan, Z., & Kotler, M. (1996). Type of trauma, severity of posttraumatic stress disorder core symptoms, and associated features. *The Journal of General Psychology, 123*(4), 341–351.

Badri, A., Crutzen, R., & Van den Borne, H. W. (2012). Exposures to war-related traumatic events and post-traumatic stress disorder symptoms among displaced Darfuri female university students: An exploratory study. *BMC Public Health, 12*. Retrieved December 12, 2016, from https://www.ncbi.nlm.nih.gov/pubmed/22863107.

Barel, E., Van IJzendoorn, M. H., Sagi-Schwartz, A., & Bakermans-Kranenburg, M. J. (2010). Surviving the Holocaust: A meta-analysis of the long-term sequelae of a genocide. *Psychological Bulletin, 136*, 677–698.

Bar-On, D., Eland, J., Kleber, R. J., Krell, R., Moore, Y., Sagi, A., Soriano, E., Suedfeld, P., Van der Velden, P., & Van IJzendoorn, M. H. (1998). Multigenerational perspectives on coping with the Holocaust experience: An attachment perspective for understanding the developmental sequelae of trauma across generations. *International Journal of Behavioral Development, 22*(2), 315–338.

Blum, H. P. (2007). Holocaust trauma reconstructed: Individual, familial, and social trauma. *Psychoanalytic Psychology, 24*(1), 63–73.

Bodenstab, J. (2015). *Dramen der Verlorenheit: Mutter-Tochter-Beziehungen in der Shoah: Zur Rezeption und zur narrativen Gestalt traumatischer Erfahrungen in Videozeugnissen.* Göttingen: Vandenhoeck & Ruprecht.

Bodenstab, J. (2017). Parapraxis in mother–daughter testimony: Unconscious fantasy and maternal function. This volume, chapter 19.

Bohleber, W. (2017). Treatment, trauma, and catastrophic reality: A double understanding of the "too much" experience and its implications for treatment. This volume, chapter 1.

Böhm, T. and Kaplan, S. (2011). *Revenge: On the dynamics of a frightening urge and its taming*. London: Karnac Books.

Bonanno, G. A. (2004). Loss, trauma, and human resilience: Have we underestimated the human capacity to thrive after extremely aversive events? *American Psychologist, 59*(1), 20–28.

Breslau, N. & Kessler, R. C. (2001). The stressor criterion in DSM-IV posttraumatic stress disorder: An empirical investigation. *Biological Psychiatry, 50*, 699–704.

Breslau, N., Kessler, R. C., Chilcoat, H. D., Schultz, L. R., Davis, G. C., & Andreski, P. (1998). Trauma and posttraumatic stress disorder in the community: The 1996 Detroit Area Survey of Trauma. *Archives of General Psychiatry, 55*(7), 626–632.

Brewin, C. R., Andrews, B., & Valentine, J. D. (2000). Meta-analysis of risk factors for posttraumatic stress disorder in trauma-exposed adults. *Journal of Consulting and Clinical Psychology, 68*(5), 748–766.

Briere, J., Elliott, D. M., Harris, K., & Cotman, A. (1995). Trauma symptom inventory psychometrics and association with childhood and adult victimization in clinical samples. *Journal of Interpersonal Violence, 10*(4), 387–401.

Caruth, C. (1996). *Unclaimed experience: Trauma, narrative, and history*. Baltimore, MD: Johns Hopkins University Press.

Cloitre, M., Garvert, D. W., Brewin, C.R., Bryant, R. A., & Maercker, A. (2013). Evidence for proposed ICD-11 PTSD and complex PTSD: A latent profile analysis. *European Journal of Psychotraumatology, 4.* doi:10.3402/ejpt.v4i0.20706.

Cooper, A. M. (1986). Toward a limited definition of psychic trauma. In A. Rothstein (Eds.), *The reconstruction of trauma: Its significance in clinical work* (pp. 41–58). Madison, CT: International Universities Press.

Da Rocha Barros, E. M., & da Rocha Barros, E. L. (2011). Reflections on the clinical implications of symbolism. *International Journal of Psychoanalysis, 92*, 879–901.

Dannlowski, U., Stuhrmann, A., Beutelmann, V., Zwanzger, P., Lenzen, T., Grotegerd, D., Domschke, K., Hohoff, C., Ohrmann, P., Bauer, J., Lindner, C., Postert, C., Konrad, C., Arolt, V., Heindel, W., Suslow, Th., & Kugel, H. (2012). Limbic scars: Long-term consequences of childhood maltreatment revealed by functional and structural magnetic resonance imaging. *Biological Psychiatry, 71*(4), 286–293.

Delić, A., Hasanović, M., Avdibegović, E., Dimitrijević, A., Hancheva, C., Scher, C., Stefanović-Stanojević, T., Streeck-Fischer, A., & Hamburger, A. (2014). Academic model of trauma healing in postwar societies. *Acta Medica Academica, 43*(1), 76–80.

DiMauro, J., Carter, S., Folk, J. B., & Kashdan, T. B. (2014). A historical review of trauma-related diagnoses to reconsider the heterogeneity of PTSD. *Journal of Anxiety Disorders, 28,* 774–786.

Ehring, T., & Quack, D. (2010). Emotion regulation difficulties in trauma survivors: The role of trauma type and PTSD symptom severity. *Behavior Therapy, 41*(4), 587–598.

Eissler, K. R. (1963). Die Ermordung von wievielen seiner Kinder muss ein Mensch symptomfrei ertragen können, um eine normale Konstitution zu haben? *Psyche-Zeitschrift für Psychoanalyse und ihre Anwendungen, 17,* 241–291.

Eissler, K. R. (1967). Perverted Psychiatry? *American Journal of Psychiatry, 123*(11), 1,352–1,358.

Elklit, A., Hyland, P., & Shevlin, M. (2014). Evidence of symptom profiles consistent with posttraumatic stress disorder and complex posttraumatic stress disorder in different trauma samples. *European Journal of Psychotraumatology, 5.* doi.: 10.3402/ejpt.v5.24221.

Eyerman, R. (2004). Cultural trauma: Slavery and the formation of african american identity. In J. C. Alexander, R. Eyerman, B. Giesen, N. J. Smelser, & P. Sztompka (Eds.), *Cultural trauma and collective identity* (pp. 60–111). Berkeley, CA: University of California Press.

Felman, S. and Laub, D. (1992). *Testimony: Crises of witnessing in literature, psychoanalysis, and history.* New York: Routledge.

Fonagy, P. (2010). Attachment, trauma, and psychoanalysis: Where psychoanalysis meets neuroscience. In M. Leuzinger-Bohleber, J. Canestri, & M. Target (Eds.), *Early development and its disturbances: Clinical, conceptual and empirical research on ADHD and other psychopathologies and its epistemological reflections* (pp. 53–75). London: Karnac Books.

Fonagy, P., Gergely, G., Jurist, E. L., & Target, M. (2004). *Affect regulation, mentalization, and the development of the self.* New York: Other Press.

Freud, S. (1964). Moses and monotheism. *Standard Edition, 23,* 1–138. (Original work published 1939)

Giesen, B. (2004). The trauma of perpetrators: The holocaust as the traumatic reference of German national identity. In J. C. Alexander, R. Eyerman, B. Giesen, N. J. Smelser, & P. Sztompka (Eds.), *Cultural trauma and collective identity* (pp. 112–154). Berkeley, CA: University of California Press.

Green, A. (2001). *Life narcissism death narcissism* (A. Weller, Trans.). London: Free Association Books. (Original work published 1983)

Greenwald, B. N. (2017). The institutional experience: Patients and staff responding to the testimony project. This volume, chapter 15.

Grünberg, K. (2013). Scenic memory of the Shoah: "The adventuresome life of Alfred Silbermann". *The American Journal of Psychoanalysis, 73*, 30–42.

Grünberg, K., & Markert, F. (2012). A psychoanalytic grave walk: Scenic memory of the Shoah. On the transgenerational transmission of extreme trauma in Germany. *The American Journal of Psychoanalysis, 72*(3), 207–222.

Hamburger, A. (2016). Blick-Winkel. Psychoanalytische Reflexion in der Forschung mit Videozeugnissen. In S. Knopp, S. Schulze & K. Eusterschulte (Eds.), *Videographierte Zeugenschaft: Geisteswissenschaften im Dialog mit dem Zeugen* (pp. 218–255). Weilerswist-Metternich: Velbrück.

Hamburger, A. (2017a). Refracted attunement, affective resonance: Scenic-narrative microanalysis of entangled presences in a Holocaust survivor's video testimony. This volume, chapter 21.

Hamburger, A. (2017b). Scenic narrative microanalysis: Controlled psychoanalytic assessment of session videos or transcripts as a transparent qualitative research instrument. This volume, chapter 10.

Hansen, A. (1999). Human disaster, social trauma and community memory. In K. L. Rogers, S. Leydesdorff, & G. Dawson (Eds.), *Trauma and life stories: International perspectives* (pp. 220–231). New York: Routledge.

Hasanović, M. (2012). Posttraumatic stress disorder in Bosnian internally dislocated and refugee adolescents from three different regions after the 1992–1995 war in Bosnia and Herzegovina. *Paediatrics Today, 8*(1), 22–31.

Heins, M., Simons, C., Lataster, T., Pfeifer, S., Versmissen, D., Lardinois, M., & Myin-Germeys, I. (2011). Childhood trauma and psychosis: a case-control and case-sibling comparison across different levels of genetic liability, psychopathology, and type of trauma. *American Journal of Psychiatry, 168*(12), 1,286–1,294.

Hernández de Tubert, R. (2006). Social trauma: The pathogenic effects of untoward social conditions. *International Forum of Psychoanalysis, 15*(3), 151–156.

Kaplan, S. (2006). Children in genocide: Extreme traumatization and the "affect propeller." *International Journal of Psychoanalysis, 87*, 725–746.

Kaplan, S. (2008). *Children in genocide: Extreme traumatization and affect regulation.* London: International Psychoanalysis Library and Karnac Books.

Kar, N. (2011). Cognitive behavioral therapy for the treatment of post-traumatic stress disorder: A review. *Neuropsychiatric Disease and Treatment, 7*, 167–181.

Karstoft, K.I., Armour, C., Elklit, A., & Solomon, Z. (2013). Long-term trajectories of posttraumatic stress disorder in veterans: The role of social resources. *Journal of Clinical Psychiatry, 74*, 1,163–1,168.

Kira, I. A., Fawzi, M. H., & Fawzi, M. M. (2013). The dynamics of cumulative trauma and trauma types in adult patients with psychiatric disorders: Two cross-cultural studies. *Traumatology, 19*(3), 179–195.

Kira, I. A., Lewandowski, L., Templin, T., Ramaswamy, V., Ozkan, B., & Mohanesh, J. (2008). Measuring cumulative trauma dose, types, and profiles using a development-based taxonomy of traumas. *Traumatology: An International Journal, 14*(2), 62–87.

Kirmayer, L. A, Kienzler, H., Afana, A. H., & Pedersen, D. (2010). Trauma and disasters in social and cultural context. In C. Morgan and D. Bhugra (Eds.), *Principles of social psychiatry* (2nd ed., pp. 155–177). West Sussex: John Wiley.

Knopp, S. (2017). Reflections of voice and countenance in historiography: Methodological considerations on clinical video testimonies of traumatized Holocaust survivors in historical research. This volume, chapter 9.

Kravić, N., Pajević, I., & Hasanović, M. (2013). Surviving genocide in Srebrenica during the early childhood and adolescent personality. *Croatian Medical Journal, 54*(1), 55–64.

Laub, D. (1998). The empty circle: Children of survivors and the limits of reconstruction. *Journal of the American Psychoanalytic Association, 46*(2), 507–529.

Laub, D. (2000). Eros oder Thanatos? Der Kampf um die Erzählbarkeit des Traumas. *Psyche-Zeitschrift für Psychoanalyse und ihre Anwendungen, 54*(9–10), 860–894.

Laub, D. (2003). Kann die Psychoanalyse dazu beitragen, den Völkermord historisch besser zu verstehen? *Psyche-Zeitschrift für Psychoanalyse und ihre Anwendungen, 57*(9–10), 938–959.

Laub, D. (2005a). From speechlessness to narrative: The cases of Holocaust historians and of psychiatrically hospitalized survivors. *Literature and Medicine, 24*(2), 253–265.

Laub, D. (2005b). Der Genozid in Ruanda: Das Kaleidoskop der Diskurse aus psychoanalytischer Perspektive. *Psyche-Zeitschrift für Psychoanalyse und ihre Anwendungen, 59*(2), 106–124.

Laub, D. (2017). Traumatic shutdown of narrative and symbolization: A failed empathy derivative. implications for therapeutic interventions. This volume, chapter 3.

Laub, D., & Felsen, I. (2017). Traumatic psychosis: Narrative forms of the muted witness. This volume, chapter 16.

Laub, D., Auerhahn, N.C. (2017). Knowing and not knowing: Forms of traumatic memory. This volume, chapter 3.

Laub, D. and Bodenstab, J. (2010). Forced and slave labour in the context of the Jewish Holocaust experience. In A. von Plato, A. Leh, & C. Thonfeld (Eds.),

Hitler's slaves: Life stories of forced labourers in Nazi-occupied Europe (pp. 364–374). New York and Oxford: Berghahn Books.

Laub, D. and Felman, S. (1992). *Testimony: Crisis of witnessing in literature, psychoanalysis, and history.* New York: Routledge.

Luthra, R., Abramovitz, R., Greenberg, R., Schoor, A., Newcorn, J., Schmeidler, J., & Chemtob, C. M. (2009). The relationship between type of trauma exposure and posttraumatic stress disorder among urban children and adolescents. *Journal of Interpersonal Violence, 24*(11), 1,919–1,927.

Maercker, A., Brewin, C.R., Bryant, R.A., Cloitre, M., Van Ommeren, M., Jones, L.M., Humayan, A., Kagee, A., Liosa, A.E., Rousseau, C., Somasundara, D.J., Souza, R., Suzuki, Y., Weissbecker, I., Wessely, S.C., First, M.B., & Reed, G.M. (2013). Diagnosis and classification of disorders specifically associated with stress: Proposals for ICD-11. *World Psychiatry, 12*(3), 198–206.

Marusak, H. A., Martin, K. R., Etkin, A., & Thomason, M. E. (2015). Childhood trauma exposure disrupts the automatic regulation of emotional processing. *Neuropsychopharmacology, 40*(5), 1,250–1,258.

McAfee, N. (2008). *Democracy and the political unconscious.* New York: Columbia University Press.

McNally, R. J. (2004). Conceptual problems with the DSM-IV criteria for posttraumatic stress disorder. In G. M. Rosen (Ed.), *Posttraumatic stress disorder: Issues and controversies* (pp. 1–14). West Sussex: John Wiley.

Meierhenrich, J. (2007). The trauma of genocide. *Journal of Genocide Research, 9*(4), 549–573.

Müller, H. H., Moeller, S., Hilger, Y., & Sperling, W. (2015). Prognostic influence of witness/victim experiences and PTSD-specific symptoms on working and educational capacity: A comparison between two groups of individuals post-trauma. *Annals of General Psychiatry, 14*(5). Retrieved December 12, 2016, from https://annals-general-psychiatry.biomedcentral.com/articles/10.1186/s12991-015-0045-3.

Neugebauer, R., Turner, J. B., Fisher, P. W., Yamabe, S., Zhang, B., Neria, Y., Gameroff, M., Bolton, P. & Mack, R. (2014). Posttraumatic stress reactions among Rwandan youth in the second year after the genocide: Rising trajectory among girls. *Psychological Trauma: Theory, Research, Practice, and Policy, 6*(3), 269–279.

Ornstein, A. (2013). Trauma, memory, and psychic continuity. *Progress in Self Psychology, 10*, 131–146.

Prager, J. (2011). Danger and deformation: A social theory of trauma part I: Contemporary psychoanalysis, contemporary social theory, and healthy selves. *American Imago, 68*(3), 425–448.

Priebe, S., Bogic, M., Ajdukovic, D., Franciskovic, T., Galeazzi, G. M., Kucukalic, A., Lecic-Tosevski, D., Morina, N., Popovski, M., Wang, D., & Schutzwohl, M.

(2010). Mental disorders following war in the Balkans: A study in 5 countries. *Archives of General Psychiatry, 67*, 518–528.

Rosnick, P. (2013). Mental pain and social trauma. *The International Journal of Psychoanalysis, 94*(6), 1,200–1,202.

Sagi-Schwartz, A., Van IJzendoorn, M. H., Grossmann, K. E., Joels, T., Grossmann, K., Scharf, M., Koren-Karie, N., & Alkalay, S. (2003). Attachment and traumatic stress in female Holocaust child survivors and their daughters. *American Journal of Psychiatry, 160*, 1,086–1,092.

Santiago, P. N., Ursano, R. J., Gray, C. L., Pynoos, R. S., Spiegel, D., Lewis-Fernandez, R., Friedman, M. J., and Fullerton, C. S. (2013). A systematic review of PTSD prevalence and trajectories in DSM-5 defined trauma exposed populations: Intentional and non-intentional traumatic events. *PLoS One, 8*(4): e59236.

Stefanović Stanojević, T., & Nedeljković, J. (2009). Attachment in the students from the towns of the former SFRY. *Facta Universitatis Series: Philosophy, Sociology, Psychology and History, 8*(1), 93–104.

Streeck-Fischer, A. (2006). *Trauma und Entwicklung. Folgen früher Traumatisierungen in der Adoleszenz*. Stuttgart: Schattauer.

Strous, R. (2017). Video testimony of long-term hospitalized psychiatrically ill Holocaust survivors. This volume, chapter 14.

Strous, R.D., Weiss, M., Felsen, I., Finkel, B., Melamed, Y., Bleich, A., Kotler, M., & Laub, D. (2005). Video testimony of long-term hospitalized psychiatrically ill Holocaust survivors. *American Journal of Psychiatry, 162*, 2,287–2,294.

Sztompka, P. (2004). The trauma of social change: A case of postcommunist societies. In J. C. Alexander, R. Eyerman, B. Giesen, N. J. Smelser, & P. Sztompka (Eds.), *Cultural trauma and collective identity* (pp. 155–195). Berkeley, CA: University of California Press.

Thomas, N. K. (2009). Which horse do you ride? Trauma from a relational perspective. Discussion of Prince's "the self in pain." *American Journal of Psychoanalysis, 69*, 298–303.

Utzon-Frank, N., Breinegaard, N., Bertelsen, M., Borritz, M., Eller, N. H., Nordentoft, M., & Bonde, J. P. (2014). Occurrence of delayed-onset post-traumatic stress disorder: A systematic review and meta-analysis of prospective studies. *Scandinavian Journal of Work, Environment & Health, 40*(3), 215–229.

Van der Kolk, B. A., & Fisler, R. E. (1994). Childhood abuse and neglect and loss of self-regulation. *Bulletin of the Menninger Clinic 58*, 145–168.

Varvin, S. (2003). Extreme traumatisation: Strategies for mental survival. *Interntional Forum of Psychoanalysis, 12*, 5–16.

Varvin, S., & Beenen, F. (2006): Trauma und Dissoziation: Manifestationen in der Übertragung und Gegenübertragung. In M. Leuzinger-Bohleber, R. Haubl, &

M. Brumlik (Eds.), *Bindung, Trauma und soziale Gewalt. Psychoanalyse, Sozial- und Neurowissenschaften im Dialog* (pp. 197–220). Stuttgart: Vandenhoeck & Ruprecht.

Volkan, V. D. (1997). *Bloodlines: From ethnic pride to ethnic terrorism*. New York: Farrar, Straus, and Giroux.

Volkan, V. D. (1999). *Das Versagen der Diplomatie: Zur Psychoanalyse nationaler, ethnischer und religiöser Konflikte*. Giessen: Psychosozial-Verlag.

Volkan, V. D., Ast, G., & Greer, W. F., jr. (2002). *Third Reich in the unconscious: Transgenerational transmission and its consequences*. New York: Brunner-Routledge.

Worthington, E. L., Jr, & Aten, J. D. (2010). Forgiveness and reconciliation in social reconstruction after trauma. In E. Martz (Ed.), *Trauma rehabilitation after war and conflict: Community and individual perspectives* (pp. 55–71). New York: Springer.

Zalashik, R. (2017). The psychiatrically hospitalized survivors in Israel: A historical overview. This volume, chapter 11.

Zepf, S., & Zepf, F. D. (2008). Trauma and traumatic neurosis: Freud's concepts revisited. *International Journal of Psychoanalysis, 89*, 331–335.

Chapter 5

The psychoanalysis of psychosis at the crossroads of individual stories and of history

Francoise Davoine and Jean-Max Gaudillière

In our book *History Beyond Trauma* (Davoine & Gaudillière, 2004), we assumed that the psychoanalysis of psychosis started during World War I, stemming from the 'forward psychiatry' practiced among traumatized soldiers. But actual war experience was forgotten later on, when the war was over, during the 'long weekend' between two wars. For example, our training in the Lacanian school did not address the specific topic of transference in psychosis. This transference pertains to this very field of investigation of catastrophic areas, claiming the analyst, too, as a witness. As has been shown by the work of Cathy Caruth (1996), and Shoshana Felman and Dori Laub (1992), giving testimony takes a long time; it requires passing through a timeless dimension, and the sessions are constantly going back to square one. Examples will be taken from our clinical experience and from literature: healing the traumas of history is a very old story, as is demonstrated by the enduring popularity of Don Quixote.

Psychosis is assumed to be a fight against perversion, defined as the objectification of people: a fight led by modern Don Quixotes who struggle, after the fashion of their role model, to restore trust and faith in the given word (*la parole donnée*) and "defend maidens, protect widows, and come to the aid of orphans and those in need" (Grossman, 2004). If statistics are required, 100 percent of our psychotic patients have been raped or abused, or traumatized by some event. In each case these events were denied at the time, and were perhaps experienced directly only by previous generations. We regularly look for catastrophes in the lifetime of psychotic patients and their ancestors. In doing so, we follow the advice given to us in the 1980s, during my supervision with Gisela Pankow (1969), one of the few psychoanalysts working with psychosis in our country at that time.

For instance, one of the present authors had as a patient a Jewish lady, diagnosed as bipolar, who regularly suffered from severe mood swings, putting her through an infernal circle of ups and downs, which had jeopardized her life. She had been periodically hospitalized and came to see me as her last chance. When I met her, she was heavily medicated and looked very much like a wreck. To my surprise, at this first encounter, I mentally saw myself rising from my chair to stand at her side. This sensation was strong.

After some time, I asked her if some catastrophe had befallen her. She mentioned as a triviality—as the sort of thing that commonly happens— the burning of her family's home when she was a child in North Africa. I asked some further questions. It was difficult for me to picture, as her country was known to me only through tourist brochures. When did it happen? She did not know. What happened? There were people shouting in the street. She remembers only their flight to escape the fire. Immediately, without any reflection, the thought occurred to me that they had fled through the cellars; then, just as quickly, I forgot about it.

This image turned out later to have been wrong. Besides, I had entirely failed to connect it with the fact that cheese cellars had played a role in my early childhood as a place to take refuge, during World War II in the Alps. Our little town was constantly bombarded, and our house, a communal home for cheese makers in the mountains, was a meeting place for the underground. Those things, too, I considered trivial, since my own psychoanalysis had not focused on them.

As I followed her speech describing her violent mood swings, her ups and downs, I took seriously her use of words derived from combat. She felt alternately over-triumphant and desperately defeated, as if she were in an endless war without any enemy. I saw distinctly what she was showing, without words: terror during the down phases, spent motionless on her couch all day long, followed unexpectedly by a rush of euphoria and senseless overspending—which did not seem wrong to me when you've escaped death. How did I know that she had? After a period during which she kept coming and going in and out of the hospital, I told her, out of the blue: "This burning was a pogrom." I was sure and, at the same time, I was ashamed—for I had no clue about her birthplace.

Where did this knowledge come from? From a little delusion of mine dating from when I was eight or ten, which I had never told my very Lacanian analyst. He was more interested in signifiers than in what had really happened, and not at all curious about the war. On his account, this delusion had been put aside, though not at all rendered unconscious—until some patients, later on, triggered it out of its timeless state. "Who are you?" the survivors ask, as Dori Laub explains, speaking of video testimonies of the Holocaust. And we have to be answerable to that question. "How did I meet you?" asked the psychotic patients in the public psychiatric hospitals where I used to work. Speaking of time in psychosis, it took me more than fifty years to identify who was who in the following story.

I had imagined, though I believed it was half reality and half fantasy, that I had a lover who wore a blue uniform. Every Monday, week after week, while cycling to school, I told my dear school friend about our Sunday meetings. I believed that story while I was building it up, and perhaps escaped madness thanks to the presence of my companion.

Fifty years afterward, I happened to ask my father, who is now turning one hundred: "But actually—what did I do during the meetings of a group of the French Resistance at home, from the moment I was born until I was two years old?" (That is, between 1943 and 1945.) Until then, I had assumed I must have been too small to realize what was going on.

It is quite bewildering to hear people who have stayed silent on that topic for ages simply answer when you ask them questions: "Well, you kept quiet with a book, a children's coloring book featuring Don Quixote." Then he added, casually: "There was a man who loved you very much. He always took you on his lap. He must have had a child your age. He arrived separately from the others, together with someone else, who was taller. The others found them suspicious because they both wore a blue uniform. I was the only one to know he was spying on some Pétain organization. One day there was a roundup, and I was warned to hide—*quick, quick*—by a friend who said, 'You were right: he's been caught, he's with us.' The last time I saw him, I had been warned he would be at the train station, so I went. He stood between two Nazi soldiers. He had been horribly tortured, his face was like a piece of bloody meat. He looked at me. I met his gaze. I was the last one he saw, since they shot him soon after. Every day I see his eyes. He was Jewish; his name was Vitek."

My childhood delusion had made real the beloved man in the blue uniform who haunted my father. I believe that when, in my mind, I rose to stand at the side of this lady—and of others condemned as mentally inept, who lose their sense of identity under psychiatric diagnosis and heavy treatments—I recalled this man from beyond the looking glass, whose existence had been erased for me, and who came back in a child's real daydream.

It was Vitek, so to speak, who had prompted the insight that this lady had escaped from a pogrom. Now, I insisted again on asking her the date. She did not know; she had been two or perhaps eight or even older. One day, I resolutely took the historical dictionary from the shelf beside my chair and looked up the dates of Israeli wars during her youth. While I read history, she began to look amazingly calm, then stated, in the same casual tone, only now in the present tense: "For sure I am thirteen, during the Yom Kippur war. My home is attacked by the crowd. We flee across the street, through the hatred, toward a friend's house. We could have been killed. Holding my little brother's hand, I repeated to myself: *I am not afraid, I am not afraid*. Nobody ever spoke of that day again, at least not to the children. The adults used to whisper, and many left the country."

After that session, the oscillations of terror and elation diminished little by little. With a witness standing at her side, her madness receded, its task accomplished. The casual tone in both stories had become music that was suddenly in tune, for the place of a witness had been carved out. Why, she asked, was she the only crazy one in the family? I told her one is enough to do the job of recording an erased truth. She realized that her symptoms had also benefitted others. She had been nuts, poor thing, so they could feel good! From now on, though, she lifted her head, and used her astute intelligence to bring about her 'come back' on her own terms.

The other author tells the story of a man who came to him after several months in a public psychiatric hospital. This patient had broken his teeth with a screwdriver and hammer, because they contained microphones that spied on every word he uttered. He couldn't even speak freely when speaking to himself! He was convinced he was being spied on throughout the time of our sessions, and he identified me as an accomplice in the universal plot. But then, one day, all of a sudden, he ceased from his delusion, and startled me with the simple words: "Do you think I could go back to the psychiatric hospital?" The distance between this utterance and his delirium was incredible.

From that moment on, and in the precise conditions I describe in our last book (Davoine & Gaudillière, 2013), the ordinary world reinstated itself, with its imperfections and gaps, its dirtiness and pettiness—and with room for me as well. We parted a few months later by mutual agreement. He had needed more than two years, though without any deliberate plan, to lead me through our weekly appointments back to a time escaped from time, to the era of his father's business with the Germans, when he was eight years old, and when I had just been born.

His delusion constituted itself in the present (please note that delusion is often linked to the particular grammar of verbal conjugation), in the landscape and social relationships of the German occupation in Paris. His delusion worked on me like a dynamic process, and it was anyone's guess which of us was the more resistant. Afterwards, I was forced to conclude that he was trying to lead me back to times and places I had known as a baby, with a baby's special knowledge—primary impressions, impossible to fool. Yet for me, as for the majority of the French population, everything had since been covered over by the waves of historical revisionism, by the right-mindedness that follows any war.

As has been common knowledge for more than sixty years, back then, everyone was a *résistant*, united with the Allies against the enemy—until, that is, historians eventually proved that more than 90 percent of the population was in favor of Maréchal Pétain, or at least neutral. Time and embarrassment organized the erasure of horrors: our colleague and friend the historian Annette Becker (Becker, 2010), in a recent book entitled *Red Scars* (*Les cicatrices rouges*), disclosed the awful facts of the German occupation of the North of France during World War I, a rehearsal of the experience of World War II, including deportations.

The erasure of strong affects progressively dissolves into the desire for peace and the culpability of the survivors; we generously reserve for the poor Jewish people the task of crying about the innumerable procession of people having died in concentration camps, so that others need not be ashamed or even rigorous in their criticism of the political outcome of this gray era. Even the simplest words are progressively corrected. In France, the words 'enemy' and 'nation' are now suspect, no longer politically correct. That is the price of peace, they say. When the French celebrate the armistice between the allies and Germany on the 11th of November, they call out the names of the dead soldiers. Formerly, the ritual answer of the audience was: "Died for France" (*Mort pour la France*). This has been changed, and the people are asked to say, "Died for liberty," substituting this formula without any fuss—"without drum nor trumpet" (*sans tambour ni trompette*), as we say in French. Why? If there is no more France, then there is no more Germany; and so, there will be no more war, no more army, no more soldiers, no more dead. Maybe the same simplification means there will be no more liberty, either—but here we only have to recognize a positivist truth: dead people don't speak. What a tragic error to think that they could!

It had taken more than two years before this patient could entrust the mind of the analyst with the instrument of his delusion, including rather complicated graphological exercises, and could be led to reconstitute the political landscape of his birthplace. It appeared at last in a dream—a dream of the analyst. In my earliest memories, this little town in Burgundy had been quickly dressed in the fanfare, the torchlit drumbeats of Victory, Bastille Day, and the polls that quickly transform a few Resistance fighters and a lot of former collaborators—those not too marked by what happened—into the notables of today, all meeting together in the new centers of political and economic power.

This patient, after a painful struggle that had eaten up several decades of his life, succeeded in crossing my path. The dream he induced led me to stand in front of the memorial to those who died for France during the two world wars. It was in the time of my childhood, in that city where I had lived the first two years of my life under the heel of the Gestapo and the collaborationist militia: son of a father who fought and was taken prisoner in the Ardennes in 1940, yet who escaped in 1942; grandson of a Jewish woman openly named Levy who never wore the yellow star. Her daughter, my aunt, made false documents for Jewish people, and hid the nephew of my grandmother's close friend, a Jewish medical doctor, after the latter was assassinated by the militia not far from our apartment. My own mother helped protect this nephew; without their help, he would have been deported. I didn't know until that dream that I was a year and a half old when this happened; I thought all this tragedy had taken place before my birth. I pieced together as well that the so very nice and reconciled city of my birth had been in constant political, and eventually racist, division for years after the end of the war.

Naturally, I told that patient my dream—a dream of history that he had managed to build, with me as the dreamer. Clearly I was not the only owner of that dream. "Serendipity," as Americans say—but it became an analytical action, one by which he seemed at first a little surprised. Soon after, though, he brought me definitive proof of the truth of his delusion, in the form of a folded paper. We didn't open it that day—we had other things to talk about—and I put it by my phone. The next week, shortly before his arrival, I happened to remember the paper, but was completely unable to find it again, even in the little space of my office. Before I tried to make up an excuse, we discovered together that his delusion had disappeared, and that the paper was superfluous. The patient's delusion had been addressed to the analyst's experience of the war; it had found a resonance in the analyst's dream. It stopped because there was no longer need for further proof; because, as Dori Laub has written in his chapter "An Event Without a Witness" (Felman & Laub, 1992), a witness had been found for events without a witness.

Madness is a war against denial and perverted social links, waged in order to restore the given word and explore historical truths falsified for the sake of power games. This reference to war sounds politically incorrect: war is hell, everybody knows that. Nevertheless, since antiquity the battleground has been considered a psychological ground: a place of blood and death, but also a place of estrangement, where otherness is at stake. Why not take our patients' delusions seriously as testimonies to historical catastrophes? When these testimonies are considered anachronistic we condemn patients to total solitude.

The battleground is psychological, for it imposes the absolute necessity of the 'companion' for survival. *Therapōn* in Homer's *Iliad*—the root of 'psychotherapist,' the *therapōn* of the *psyche*—has two meanings: the attendant in combat, who cares for the mind and body of his companion, and the ritual double, who takes care of the funeral duties if he dies. Let us assume that the analyst's duty in the case of psychosis and trauma is to join the patient's total solitude and become the *therapōn*, part of a 'plural body' of survival amid psychic death. He can do this only at his own expense, by, as it were, giving away a piece of broken shard, more or less fitting the patient's broken narrative, so as to create a 'symbol' out of pure destruction. In Ancient Greek, the word *sumbolon* means exactly that process: the reuniting of two pieces of terra cotta broken long ago as a sign of hospitality, and given to the guest-friends' descendants. *Diaballein* ('to disperse')—as in the word 'diabolical'—is the opposite of *sumballein*.

Talking about transference in psychosis is therefore a therapeutic obligation. What does it take to become the ritual double, responsible for funeral duties? We often find ourselves in charge of the burial of disappeared people—that is, with the inscription of their names, since they have no graves and haunt their descendants. This duty is in contrast with the mottos of our younger mental-health professionals. The governing belief is either that "There is no transference in psychosis," or "Beware of massive transference in psychosis." Both justify the use of shocks, permanent medication, and occupational workshops, all of which solidify a so-called psychotic structure that is supposed to be irreversible. Who cares for recovery in cases of the reputed incurable?

How to stand, however, as a guarantor of truth and trust when this agency collapses with the subject of speech? Lacan himself did not explore transference in that field. He concluded his "On a Question Prior to Any Possible Treatment of Psychosis" (Lacan, 1958/2006) with his refusal to venture into it.

No wonder, for in those cases the Real is at stake. According to Lacan, the Real is what is impossible to name and to imagine, it can be addressed neither to what he calls the big Other, warrant of truth, nor to the little other, in a mirror-like relationship. Therefore, the transference cannot follow its orthodox definition. When the symbolic chain is broken, echoing repressed signifiers do not work. When the big Other of the given word, guarantor of truth and trust, has collapsed, the arrow of time does not point to the future, nor even to the past. We have to create otherness from scratch; we have to build a mirror for the unimaginable and start to link words, sounds, and sensorial images—those coming from "an event without a witness," as Dori Laub (1992) puts it.

We were taught to be neutral and we have to intervene—sometimes to say no, and even sometimes to give some advice. Shocking! We were taught to wait for free associations, but we anticipate the patients by giving historical clues. We were taught to stay silent when we are summoned by indiscreet questions, or triggered by body language. But then silence is equivalent to denial. We were taught to explore the past, and it is useful—but anamnesis seems to fail in catastrophic areas, for there, time stops, and all that counts is the here and now. So we are stuck in a stalemate, with periodic returns to square one. We feel stupid, and tend to think that psychoanalysis is not useful. Still, at that precise moment, as is shown by our examples, something new may occur, stemming from the unconscious on the analyst's side, triggered by the patient's investigation, at the crossroads of their respective stories and of history.

We call it an "entrenched, cut out unconscious," one different from the repressed unconscious. Returning to Freud, we find him mentioning "an unconscious which is not repressed" in some texts about ghosts, like his essay on *Gradiva* (Freud, 1907/1959), in his essay on *"The Uncanny"*

(Freud, 1919/1955), and in *Moses and Monotheism* (Freud, 1939/1964), written on the verge of the annihilation, when Hitler and Stalin were in the process of mass murdering 14 million civilian people between the beginning of the 1930s and 1945, across a swath of territory that a recent historian at Yale, Timothy Snyder (Snyder, 2010), has called *Bloodlands*.

This unconscious which is not repressed registers terror at the breakdown of the symbolic order. Usually described with a derogatory vocabulary naming objectively the lack of this or that in psychosis, this unconscious records, on the contrary, a huge energy that is deadly and vital ("radioactive," as Yolanda Gampel [1993a] calls it), one impossible to share, for no otherness is available—due to a case of "failed empathy," according to Laub and Auerhahn (1989). It impacts body and psyche as an excess impossible to filter, one shattering all mirrors, and unimaginable in that it has no reflection.

Indeed time stops, for time is measured by symbols. But still, this huge energy produces intense physical and psychical impressions, which express themselves through voices, images, visions, and signs impossible to validate except through this uncanny transference. There is a psychotic onset, like a traumatic revival, with the seismograph of the body registering a deadly danger, in a way similar to a soldier's bodily arousal while marching toward the threat of death. Your heart rate skyrockets; you sweat, stop eating, stop sleeping, become restless or immobile, hypersensitive or numb. Sounds become unbearable, or else are shut out completely; vision is blurred, or else focuses only on the vividness of futile details. Time slows down and stops on that experience (Grossman, 2004).

Of course, the diagnosis of trauma—like that of 'shell shock or war neurosis' for our grandfathers during World War I—is meant to tell soldiers that they are not mad. But this is also true the other way round. In the frame of that singular transference, we tell patients who go through their surrealistic experience that they are in the middle of a fight and we are there at their side. Then they get better and we are happy. But the fight has not begun. For when it starts, it is launched precisely against us, the analyst, in defiance of this possible 'thou.'

The *therapōn*—the combat attendant in Homer's *Iliad*—is also tested. This is especially so when the Real Other—the ruthless agency that transforms people into things, and the analyst into a wreck—appears unexpectedly and challenges our new link of trust. Usually, it happens when we are proud of some progress in the analysis. Suddenly time stops again; an ominous presence—the CIA, They, the Plot, the Devil, Death itself—threatens the analyst, who feels she is null, incapable, ready to give up.

"Time ambles," says Shakespeare. The problem, therefore, for the analyst, is to link ominous voices, visions, or fugue states together with withdrawal, by becoming their addressee. This is more easily said than done: this address can neither be offered artificially nor programmed, but only found by chance and under unpredictable coincidences, which escape the omnipotent agency. Slight details may hit, for instance, the analyst's suppressed stories, but also her favorite things: books, songs, and landscapes. This encounter brings relief, in both senses of the word: not only soothing, but also opening up a third dimension in the deadly flatness of dualistic ideologies and hollow discourses.

An area of catastrophe, says the mathematician René Thom (1991) in his "catastrophe theory"—originally conceived when he collapsed after winning the Fields Medal—occurs when the contrast between content and form is blurred, when predators and victims are no more distinct. The abused child is accused of being the guilty one, soldiers of being perpetrators, women of seducing their rapists, and the analyst of being the accomplice of soul murderers.

Some relief may happen when the analyst acknowledges that, through the transference, the roles may be reversed for a brief moment. The patient's gift for research and psychotherapy has hit some entrenched clue on the side of the analyst (such as Vitek was in one of our stories, or such as familial acts of resistance were in the other), and so undoing, on both sides, the falsification of historical truths. Then, a new social link may be created, a place where a witness may defeat denial. *Testimony* is at the core of this transference, as Shoshana Felman and Dori Laub (1992) have demonstrated in their powerful book.

Let us conclude with the training that psychosis imposes on us by quoting the philosopher Ludwig Wittgenstein, who changed his formula from the end of his *Tractatus Logico-Philosophicus* (1922/1961), largely written during World War I, while he fought on the Eastern Front: "Whereof one cannot speak, thereof one must be silent." Returning to Vienna from battles and captivity, he nearly became psychotic, abandoned philosophy for ten years, and came back to Cambridge at the end of the twenties with a new point of view: "Whereof one cannot speak, thereof one cannot help showing, exhibiting the unspoken" (Wittgenstein, 1953/1983). To whom must one give it? In this chapter, I answer: to the analyst, who may, in the proximity and immediacy of the sessions, say with expectancy: "Yes, recovery is possible. No, you are not that incurable case, a poor thing monitored by electric machines and biochemical treatments."

We have simply gathered here the four principles of Thomas Salmon, who formulated them in 1917 (Salmon, 1917), on the eve of the entry of American forces into World War I: Proximity, Immediacy, Expectancy, and Simplicity—no jargon—are at the root of the Forward Psychiatry then invented to debrief psychic casualties. They are also at the root of the handling of transference in the "forward psychoanalysis" of trauma and psychosis—the latter considered as an unclaimed trauma waiting, as Cathy Caruth (1996) says, in a frozen time across generations, until it can be claimed. What if the psychoanalysis of psychosis were a long patient-debriefing of disquieted ancestors whose memory has been betrayed by their own people's denial?

References

Becker, A. (2010). *Les cicatrices rouges, 14–18, France et Belgique occupées*. Paris: Fayard.

Caruth, C. (1996). *Unclaimed experience: Trauma, narrative and history*. Baltimore, MD: Johns Hopkins University Press.

Cervantes, M. (2003). *Don Quixote* (E. Grossman, Trans.). New York: HarperCollins.

Davoine, F., & Gaudillière, J.-M. (2004). *History beyond trauma* (S. Fairfield. Trans.). New York: Other Press.

Davoine, F., & Gaudillière, J.-M. (2013). *A bon entendeur salut! Face à la perversion, le retour de Don Quichotte*. Paris: Stock.

Davoine, F. (2016) *Fighting melancholia: Don Quixote's teaching*. London: Karnac.

Felman, S., & Laub, D. (1992). *Testimony*. New York and London: Routledge.

Freud, S. (1955). The "Uncanny." *Standard Edition, 17*, 217–256. (Original work published 1919)

Freud, S. (1959). Delusions and dreams in Jensen's Gradiva. *Standard Edition, 9*, 1–96. (Original work published 1907)

Freud, S. (1964). Moses and monotheism. *Standard Edition, 23*, 1–138. (Original work published 1939)

Gampel, Y. (1993a). From the thing in itself by modelling through transformation by narration in the therapeutic space. *British Journal of Psycotherapy, 9*(3), 280–290.

Grossman, D. (2004). *On combat*. Millstadt, IL: Warrior Science Publications.

Lacan, J. (2006). *On a question prior to any possible treatment of psychosis*. In J. Lacan, *Ecrits* (B. Fink, Trans., pp. 445–488). New York: W. W. Norton. (Original work published 1958)

Laub, D. (1992). An event without a witness: Truth, testimony, and survival. In D. Laub & S. Felman (Eds.), *Testimony: Crises of witnessing in literature, psychonanalysis, and history* (pp. 75–92). New York: Routledge.

Laub, D., & Auerhahn, N. C. (1989). Failed empathy: A central theme in the survivor's Holocaust experience. *Psychoanalytic Psychology, 6*(4), 337–400.

Pankow, G. (1969). *L'homme et sa psychose*. Paris: Aubier-Montaigne.

Salmon, T. W. (1917). *The care and treatment of mental diseases and war neuroses (shell shock) in the British army*. New York: War Work Committee of the National Committee for Mental Hygiene.

Snyder, T. (2010). *Bloodlands*. New York: Basic Books.

Thom, R. (1991). *Prédire n'est pas expliquer: Entretiens avec Emile Noël*. Paris: Eshel.

Wittgenstein, L. (1961). *Tractatus logico-philosophicus* (2nd ed.; D.F.Pears & B. F. McGuinness, Trans.). New York and London: Routledge. (Original work published 1922)

Wittgenstein, L. (1983). *Philosophical investigations* (G. E. M. Anscombe, Trans.). Oxford: Basil Blackwell. (Original work published 1953)

Chapter 6

The developmental psychology of social trauma and violence

The case of the Rwandan genocide

Suzanne Kaplan and Andreas Hamburger

When children become victims of violent or abusive maltreatment, the psychic consequences are, in many cases, much different than those observed in adults, as the specific vulnerability of the developing mind and body has the effect of making children less capable of coping with the resultant trauma. This is due to two main factors. The first is that a psychic structure still growing will react to unsupportable pain by changing the course of its growth, resulting in a multi-faceted developmental trauma affecting all fields of mental life. In a developed psychic structure, on the other hand, the traumatic impact will cause lesions or scars in already existing mental processes, such as affect regulation and memory. Moreover, a second factor applies: Since children's coping capabilities strongly depend on their family environment, the unfolding of the trauma is intertwined with recognition and containing within the primary relation. Often, those relations are the very reason for the trauma itself, so that here, the child finds itself in a trap between trauma and trust. Many case reports have confirmed the difficulties children experience in coping with traumatic experiences, but also show, at the same time, their readiness to resort to support wherever they find it, as well as to accept opportunities for healing (cf. Axline, 1964; Shengold, 1989; Streeck-Fischer, 1998; Kaplan, 2008). This will be demonstrated in detail through the experience of survivors of the Rwandan genocide. The case of the Rwanda child survivors will show that traumatic experience, even if genocidal in character, does not necessarily lead to severe psychopathology for the survivor. It depends on resilience factors, mainly occurring in the social environment, whether and how children cope with the traumatic experience.

Many children exposed to genocide do not survive without psychic damage, however. Among the many specific mental effects of childhood trauma, psychiatric disorders like complex posttraumatic stress disorder

(CPTSD), as well as maladaptive stress responses, are at the center of the symptomatology; there are also social consequences which result from being exposed to genocide, such as a tendency towards re-victimization. Furthermore, cognitive impairment, physical disabilities, and even early death have been reported (Gagnon & Hersen, 2000; Read, Os, Morrison, & Ross, 2005; Morgan & Fisher, 2007; Briere, Kaltman, & Green, 2008; Stessman et al., 2008; Acierno et al., 2010; Maschi, Baer, Morrissey, & Moreno, 2012).

From work with different populations of child survivors separated geographically and in time—namely, survivors of the Holocaust and the Rwandan genocide—Kaplan (2006) has concluded that severe traumatization resulting from genocide and other extreme events is experienced in similar ways, regardless of differing cultural environments. However, each individual's personal vulnerability, life history, and neighbor/ proximity status vis-à-vis the perpetrators have a bearing upon how he or she regulates anxiety in the aftermath of genocide and other extreme events. A central element here is the issue of revenge. Our aim is to show that the psychology of revenge has extensive applicability and that previous findings and conceptualizations (Kaplan, 2006, 2008) in extreme cases resonate with the more general everyday victim–perpetrator relationships in the realm of violence.

Developmental trauma

Trauma begins with events outside of the child. Once these have occurred, internal changes occur that may be lasting, often to the detriment of the young victim (Terr, 1991). Child survivors often show more and longer-lasting symptoms than those described in posttraumatic stress disorder (PTSD), especially if the trauma is not a single event, but an ongoing circumstance affecting the immediate social environment of the child such as, for example, family abuse. Herman (1992) therefore pleaded for taking this specificity into account, and consequently research was conducted on (the term used at the time) "Disorders of Extreme Stress Not Otherwise Specified (DESNOS)" (Roth, Newman, Pelcovitz, Van der Kolk, & Mandel, 1997; D'Andrea, Ford, Stolbach, Spinazzola, & Van der Kolk, 2012). Van der Kolk's (2005) description of Developmental Trauma Disorder (DTD) in childhood refers to the "significant disruptions of protective caregiving" that can cause persistent dysregulation, including emotional, somatic, behavioral, cognitive, and relational difficulties, such as distorted concepts of self and others. These difficulties tend to be generalized by the child and produce anticipatory defensive reactions. In order to allow for the adult consequences resulting from such childhood pathology, many of these symptoms have been grouped in the syndrome of complex posttraumatic stress disorder (CPTSD, Cloitre et al., 2009), which will be included in the forthcoming eleventh edition of the International Classification of Diseases (ICD-11, expected for 2017). The symptoms described are related to affect regulation (heightened emotional reactivity, violent outbursts, reckless or self-destructive behavior, dissociative states, emotional numbing, and joylessness), negative self-concepts (including worthlessness, shame or "survivor guilt"), and interpersonal disturbances including persistent avoidance, deriding, or breaking off of close relationships (for details see Ford, 2015).

Some of these consequences of childhood traumatization will now be discussed in the light of a psychoanalytic approach to childhood trauma, and specifically as related to genocide. We must bear in mind, however, that although trauma is a necessary pre-condition, it is not a sufficient reason or single cause for the pathology described, as many children display an amazing capacity for self-healing and for accepting assistance, and consequently survive without severe psychopathological consequences.

Memory

Memory, in state of the art psychology, is not simple storage; rather, it resembles a construction process, combining abstract engrammes with subjectively convincing mental images, resulting in what is experienced as a vivid recollection. It can be shaped through and co-constructed in communication (see Hamburger, 1998, for further discussion). Therefore, the impact of traumatic experience on memory is not so much on the level of content but rather on the level of function, whereby interactive processes play a major role. Tutté (2004) emphasizes the current view on memory in terms of separate multiple systems—the difference between declarative and non-declarative or procedural memory—and stresses that "there is no disputing today that there is a sharp difference between what can be thought of, represented in images or put into words and what is inscribed in terms of affect-charged procedures, or affect-motor schemes" (Davis, 2001, quoted in Tutté, 2004, 912). If children cannot translate traumatic experience into the developmental phase in which they find themselves, it remains unassimilated (Emde, 1999). The experience cannot be given any meaning and therefore cannot be contained by the individual. The probable consequence is a repetition in the next developmental phase. In summary then, there is, on the one hand, the repetition of intrusive memory fragments associated with bodily sensations/affects that may be triggered by clues in the present. And on the other hand, there is a process of remembering that builds on the traumatized person's having been able to verbalize in connection with the traumatic event (to symbolize) and in doing so, to assimilate and transform sensory perceptions into mental representations. This should be respectively compared to aspects of implicit procedural memory and declarative explicit semantic memory (see Tutté, above). The established term of "invading memory" thus becomes a contradiction; it must rather be a matter of "invading affects" (Kaplan, 2006).

Another more general model of trauma-related memory distortion underlines the fact that the human brain changes in a "use-dependent" fashion (Perry, Pollard, Blakely, Baker, & Vigilante, 1995). Memory is shaped through an interplay of cognitive, emotional, and motor-vestibular processes, and this interplay is strongly influenced by the momentary state of arousal. In the case of a traumatic experience, the influence of stress hormones and stress-related neurotransmitters affect the encoding and structural reshaping of traumatic memory, resulting in specific deficits in autobiographical memory (Van der Kolk, McFarlane, & Weisaeth, 1996). Firstly, memories associated with trauma can be over-consolidated and separated from later experience; secondly, they can remain in the implicit memory mode, emerging as flashbacks rather than as retrievable memory images. Moreover, the state of hyperarousal associated with traumatic situations may result in the modelling of a world-view characterized by unpredictability and permanent threat. Traumatized children tend towards hypervigilance, arousal, and persisting anxiety (ibid.). Children exposed to violence develop persistant fear-responses, with an interesting gender difference: Girls are more likely to dissociate, while boys tend to develop 'fight or flight' behavior (ibid.)

A third aspect of traumatic memory is connected to the fact that children are much more entangled in the social matrix of their caregiving environment than adults. They depend on physical and mental help, and they need assistance in order to develop an autonomous self and autonomous affect regulation. Affect regulation seems to be one of the central arenas where phantasmatic parent–child relatedness (Lebovici, 1988) intersects with the social consequences of trauma. As we will discuss later, affect regulation also plays a major role in the spiral of revenge. Moreover, affect regulation is directly connected to measurable posttraumatic changes in neurophysiological functioning. Recent fMRI-research shows that childhood trauma exposure is connected with an aberrant amygdala response to emotional conflict (Dannlowski et al., 2012), thus disrupting the automatic regulation of emotional processing (Marusak, Martin, Etkin, & Thomason, 2015). These individually observed neuropsychological effects should, however, be understood in connection with interactional aspects: A child with a psycho-biologically dysregulating parent who initiates but poorly repairs shame-associated misattunement has these failures stored in his or her memory, largely outside conscious awareness, as a prototype for all future interactions (Schore, 2003).

Attachment

Another important factor of traumatic childhood experience is the failure of early attachment, with a consequent series of effects on adolescent and adult mental life and behavior (Breidenstine, Bailey, Zeanah, & Larrieu, 2011; Allen, 2011; D'Andrea et al., 2012; Lowell, Renk, & Adgate, 2014; Dimitrijević & Hamburger, 2016). One important example is the unregulated shame affect, to which we shall return later in this chapter. In general, traumatic experience activates the security system, which in turn inhibits exploration (Bowlby, 1969). "We feel distressed, and we want to be hugged" (Fonagy, 2010, 58). This very mechanism, however, lies at the root of posttraumatic attachment disorders. In the early 1970s, Mary Main observed that a high percentage of the children showing unclassifiable behavior in the Strange Situation Test had been maltreated (Main & Weston, 1981)—an observation that gave birth to the seminal concept of the disorganized attachment style. Later studies confirmed that early childhood trauma predicts disorganized attachment style (Carlson, Cicchetti, Barnett, & Braunwald, 1989; Carlson, 1998), which in itself proved to be an important factor in all kinds of adolescent and adult psychopathology (Cassidy & Mohr, 2001).

The possible impact of early trauma on attachment development might also explain some of the mechanisms of intergenerational trauma transmission. Studies of life histories of Holocaust survivors and survivors from the Rwandan genocide have shown that pregnancy sometimes causes intense anxiety. Regression occurring at the beginning of pregnancy (which is, in fact, a regression in the service of the ego) and identification with the coming child combine to release a specific kind of signal anxiety: the anxiety of coming in contact with invading affects. Parents who themselves were child survivors and live in areas with ongoing political conflicts are more at risk of transferring trauma from one generation to the next via sudden interruptions in their natural web of emotions towards the infant (Kaplan, 2008). Schore (2003) stresses the effects of the caregiver's stress-regulating and dysregulating interactions on the infant's maturing coping systems. During Hutu power in Rwanda, sexual reproduction was attacked through rape, experiments, and torture. The resulting phenomena seemed to merge into an anxiety about childbearing and about being a parent.

However, it is not a necessary consequence of infantile trauma that it be handed down through the generations (cf. below). Fraiberg, Adelson, and Shapiro hypothesize that "morbidity in the parental history will not in itself predict the repetition of the past in the present." Only if parents "in the extremity of childhood terror formed a pathological identification with the dangerous and assaultive enemies of the ego" and split off the associated affective experience did they show a tendency to reenact the "ghosts in the nursery," while "access to childhood pain becomes a powerful deterrent against repetition in parenting" (Fraiberg, Adelson, & Shapiro, 1975, 419f.).

Mentalization

As a further consequence of attachment dysregulation, the child's capacity for mentalization can be affected (Fonagy, 2010). If so, children will experience difficulties in learning words for emotional experiences and will be unable to proceed from an equivalence mode, where inner and outer reality are inseparable, to a mode that distinguishes between an 'inner world' of phantasy and the outside world. As a consequence, when the child has become an adult suffering from a mentalization disorder, he or she may interpret traumatic flashbacks or trauma-related phantasms— projected in 'equivalence mode' onto the outer world—as threatening and as actual external dangers, perhaps even calling for an aggressive defense. When empathic dialog has been impaired in early childhood, when the framework of a traumatically disturbed attachment has not allowed the capacity for mentalization to grow, the surviving adolescent may display repeated loss of control, self-mutilation, or violent and revengeful behavior (Streeck-Fischer, 2006). "The most characteristic feature of traumatization is the oscillation between psychic equivalence and pretend mode of experiencing the internal world" (Fonagy, 2010, 57). Apart from this general theory of posttraumatic mentalization disorder and in addition to it, Hamburger (2017) points out that in genocidal conditions, the impairment of mentalization takes a specific course because not only the individual, but the complete social environment is under realistic mortal threat. Under these circumstances, a playful "pretend mode" (Fonagy & Target, 2007) is probably inhibited: where otherwise the child might learn to separate his phantasies from reality by simulating them in the frame of a secure, holding caregiver relationship, the child growing up in an ethnic group threatened with extinction will see his destructive phantasies confirmed, not put into perspective. However, there is the exception to the rule—case reports show how some children under extreme threat of persecution can nevertheless develop creative phantasies to survive (cf. the case of Jean, quoted below, who can overcome his revenge phantasy by imagining his future children).

Granted, impairment of the mentalizing capacity after childhood trauma can also work the other way around, as mediated by and through the disorganized attachment style. Instead of failing and giving up mentalization, the survivor displays the phenomenon of "hypermentalizing" in the sense of highly activated, but unsuccessful mentalizing tentatives (Bateman & Fonagy, 2004). This kind of hypervigilant monitoring of the environment can be observed in many survivors of childhood trauma (Boulanger, 2008).

The specificity of genocidal traumatization

In our previous discussion, we have mentioned some specific characteristics of genocidal childhood traumatization. This will now be discussed in more detail, drawing on the work of Kaplan and Böhm (Kaplan, 2006; 2008; Böhm & Kaplan, 2011). Genocide is characterized by its total and systematic nature. The persecution of Jews under Hitler proceeded from old and new prejudices via hateful propaganda to discrimination and segregation, and finally to the Holocaust. The central aim of the 1994 Rwandan genocide was also the extermination of an entire people, the Tutsis. Any possibility of a new generation was to be eliminated, and the perpetrators referred to the killing of women and children as the equivalent of pulling out the roots of bad weeds (Mamdani, 2001). Plans had been laid out years in advance, and Hutu extremists had prepared the ground with propaganda on ethnic hatred, spread mainly over the radio; social conditions including political upheaval and severe economic deterioration were also essential factors that set the genocidal process in motion.

In cases of societally or ethnically directed extermination of an entire societal subgroup—that is, under conditions of genocidal trauma (cf. Hamburger, 2017)—the consequences of such specific trauma on child victims are different than those resulting from childhood traumatization in an individual context. From her interviews with Rwandan child survivors, Kaplan (2006, 2008) was able to demonstrate that a *generational collapse* can occur, where a basic, common experience ensues to which most of the significant junctures or "clues" in the life histories of the survivors seem to be linked. It builds on two secondary concepts and the dynamics between them—namely, on *perforation* and *space creation* (ibid.). *Perforation* refers to a puncture in the psychic shield, resulting from the inconceivable cruelties and systematic persecution to which Nazis subjected Jews, and to which Hutu extremists subjected Tutsis. The perforating concept connects to theories of Anzieu (1989), who stresses Freud's (1920/1955) fruitful metaphor of a wound, a puncture in the psychic shield, with internal bleeding resulting from psychic trauma. The psychic membrane has figuratively been punched 'full of holes,' for example, by an invasive, frightening voice, by family members torn away, and by 'body markings.' These markings can be symbolic/fabricated racial differences (the Star of David on the clothes of Jews; a 'T' in the identity card of a Tutsi) or actual and real (the experience of abuse). Children only register what has happened through a panicky feeling in the body. 'You didn't think' is an comment often heard. A perceptual image or sound can be imprinted in the body, so that the event cannot be left behind as a memory in the way we normally think of memories. Instead, it remains as an inexpressible discomfort in the body (Scaer, 2014). *Space creation* is Kaplan's term for the inner psychic processes through which the persecuted can, in brief moments, create their own space for thinking and fantasizing. From various perspectives, theorists have addressed the development of thinking and its connection to the child's active search for a containing object (Bion, 1967), and have focused on the significance of the transition phenomenon (Winnicott, 1971). Symbolizing and mentalizing are understood as mental processes that transform bodily/ affective experiences into mental representations.

Phil[1] fantasized about a normal life, "having a permanent place that I would call my own with an address." He could thereby mentally "move himself" out of a terrifying situation and for a fleeting moment feel "alive"—fending off the fear of dying.

In studying the ways Rwandan interviewees expressed emotion, Kaplan (2006) became aware that *how* something was said, and the interviewees' voices, facial expressions, and body language were just as important for her understanding of what the victims had been through as *what* was said. She saw two directions of the psychic process: one of them being *trauma linking* whereby traumatic experiences are 'easily awakened' associatively as the interviewees give their testimonies and in conjunction with events of everyday life. This concept can be compared to the kind of symptoms described in the general literature on trauma as intrusions, flashbacks, and irritability. There is a constant fear that the perpetrators might show up. Dissociative symptoms, as described in PTSD, were found in the Rwandan child survivors as well.[2] A split in the self appears as a result of the difficulties in dealing with fear and anxiety in the aftermath—a compartmentalization of experience, which is stored in memory as isolated fragments.

The term 'linking' refers to the associative connections between affective states and major narrative elements. The second psychic process referred to above is *generational linking*, whereby subjects have their attention directed towards significant persons and objects in the past as well as in the present. This facilitates a feeling of living in a societal context with less anxiety—an aspect of reconciliation. The survivor feels freer in relation to the past. One could say that the trauma no longer exists as contained only in a closed part of the self, but also is integrated to a certain degree into a time perspective relating to the course of one's life. The framework for this analysis is the "affect propeller" (Kaplan, 2006), showing both the complexity and the regulation of trauma-related affect, which occurs as an oscillation between aspects of trauma linking and generational linking.

Violence and revenge

Revenge fantasy has been described as an essential element of the psychological interplay between victim and perpetrator. Thoughts about revenge arise from fear after having been put in an inferior position, that is, after a traumatic event defined by external violations and internal vulnerability (Böhm & Kaplan, 2011). It needs to be emphasized that the role and significance of humiliation in human-caused traumatic experiences have long been overlooked (Lindner, 2001). A Rwandan boy, Phil, asked: "How do you Europeans see us? As some kind of crazy animals?" People who have been forced to endure extreme traumatization often express feelings of shame. Wurmser (1981) speaks of the shame experience as a spectrum of emotions, from the mildest twinge of embarrassment to the searing pain of mortification. In Kaplan's recordings of testimonies of teenage boys in Rwanda who had lived as street children after the genocide, the enactment of feelings of humiliation in revenge fantasies became visible as a crucial factor in potential violence (Kaplan, 2013).

> Jean[3], aged 17, experienced the unbearably painful loss of his entire family. I asked: "What constantly comes back into your mind when you are alone?" Jean's face twisted in rage and he held his finger tips on his forehead as he said: "Whenever I thought about that man who had killed my sister . . . I felt like . . . I could hunt him down and kill him. I felt that, even if they found me out there and killed me, I would have been able to take revenge for my sister and that was what mattered." However, at the end of his testimony, after recalling elements of his restoration process, he suddenly looked considerably more relaxed and said, "I no longer think the way I used to because those who are dead can't come back to this life that we're living in. I just hope for a better future with a wife and children. I'll tell them about everything I have gone through."

The example of Jean shows a rapid fluctuation of emotions—from aspects of trauma linking to constructive generational linking.

After being traumatized, the individual first feels an intense, urgent need to regain control over life but lacks the capacity to cope with these intense feelings. To immerse oneself in hatred and concrete plans for revenge can be seen as a way of postponing the necessary mourning process. It is as if the psychic wound can be magically transferred to the perpetrator, and thereby eradicated from oneself. The border between fantasy and action—and also between victim and perpetrator—may be thin, and a destructive spiral of *revenge fantasies* may move into *revenge acts*, a way to avoid thinking and instead give rage free rein. Such behavior is destructive both for the one who is acted upon and for the purveyor of the action, even though the latter does not think in such terms. As soon as fantasies are turned into action, it is as though the one acting becomes "another person"—a perpetrator—and the revenge spiral escalates (Böhm & Kaplan, 2011). The victim attacks the other in order not to feel helpless and inferior. Also, one often puts an extra force into one's violence when paying back, in order to maintain the upper hand. People often have residues of cruel impulses, or pockets of cruelty (Igra, 2004), which can easily break through the thin border between cruelty and concern and which, without effective counterbalances, are not always manageable.

Some individuals encapsulate or withdraw. They may be afraid of their own very strong affects, which may lead to self-destructive behavior and even suicide. Survivors may identify with the dead or the injured, thus becoming lifeless or depressed, in order to escape the guilt of surviving. Freud underlines, in *Mourning and Melancholia* (1917/2003), the difference between mourning over a person whom one has lost and identifying with the lost person, as happens when someone is depressed. Resistance towards mourning, which is probably the most common reason for stagnation after a trauma, can be masked in several ways. Most often, people try to conceal such resistance by turning it into acts of revenge. Zulueta (2006), in writing about abused children, describes the process from pain to violence and stresses that the child can either be victim or victimizer, depending on the context. The internalized relationship between self and other, such as the mother–infant relationship, becomes a working model of the self in interactions with others. This explains the related tendency of abused persons to identify with the aggressor, a role that ensures them at least some control over events but also puts them at risk for revenge acts.

Ways out of the revenge spiral and onward to reparation, restoration, and reconciliation

There is a healthy aggression that protects one's integrity without harming the other, and provides a way out of the spiral—a possibility of refraining from revenge—through the person's own counter-abilities. In the best case, it is possible to attain a mental realm of reflection—a dialog, with the skills for compromising, and also for strengthening one's own integrity and dignity. The likelihood of surviving psychological damage and humiliation increases if there is a capacity for reflective functioning as a result of secure attachment during the first years of one's life (Fonagy, Gergely, Jurist, & Target, 2002). Mentalizing—the capacity for empathy, of trying to understand the feelings and perspectives of the other—is a prerequisite. To forgive is not possible, but the effort to (re)construct the historical narrative could mean the chance of being able to go on living, for example, in the same country. The perpetrator might, in the best-case scenario, experience strong guilt feelings. If the perpetrator moreover struggles with remorse, then something might happen in the meeting between perpetrator and victim that will make it somewhat easier to leave behind the frightening fantasy that 'it may happen again.' Suspicion and the risk of violence from both sides may subside (South African Truth Commissions; see Gobodo-Madikizela, 2013).

On an individual level, reparation processes focus on repairing and restoring self-esteem and human dignity, as well as on setting boundaries for one's integrity and protecting one's interests. Restoration requires a continued inner dialog to conquer or tame the impulse towards acts of revenge. In the words of Van der Kolk (1993, 222), "fear needs to be tamed before proper integration of experience can occur . . . so that people are able to think and be conscious of current needs." On the societal level, the next step is reconciliation, a process that requires mutual acknowledgement between victim and perpetrator and a "conflict ethos" (Bar-Tal, 2000).

In restoration and reconciliation work, professionals and other helpers can play a vital role as listeners. A special challenge for listeners is to be attentive to expressions of emotion when the words are not there (Laub & Auerhahn, 1989; Laub, 2017). The listener needs to be able to 'contain' the afflicted, to be a model for affect tolerance, and to show that it is possible to bear strong feelings without breaking apart. By picking up on themes associated with generational linking phenomena, and highlighting them—even when their presence is subtle and not obvious—the helper can support the individual's predilection for creativity and resilience. Symbolizing is needed to diminish anxiety-driven behavior and group regression (Kaplan, 2008).

Developmental trauma, as discussed above, is perpetuated by a psycho-social vicious circle. Shame and humiliation frequently accompany early childhood abuse and may serve as an interpersonal matrix for dissociated rage. If affect regulation is disturbed in children who have suffered early attachment damage, their untamed affects can develop into frustrated hatred and pronounced aggression after adolescence (Schore, 2003). In certain cases, children may suffer early attachment damage as well as even more serious later maltreatment by their parents or guardians, thus growing up with an ever-intensifying desire for revenge. Crimes are often committed by individuals with inadequate mentalizing capacities or lack of reflective function (Zulueta, 2006). We can easily understand how people with a background of child abuse might fit into this category. This vicious circle is specifically articulated in the case of genocidal trauma, since unresolved shame and humiliation persist in the social environment, too, inducing the potential perpetrator to hold the potential victim responsible for his own inner confusion.

When humiliation triggers affect invading that stems from early life, the individual who is spiraling into a perpetrator may easily project elements of himself that he experiences—elements experienced as shameful and degrading—onto others (Varvin, 2003): "I'm not the one who is inferior and violated; they're going get a taste of what they're trying to do to me!" Most shame-generated conflicts have traumatic origins, where the trauma or the defense against it, is repeated time and time again (Wurmser, 1981). In such a revenge spiral, the persecutory guilt grows. When these tormenting primitive emotions—in which the perpetrator perceives the victim as persecuting him from within—become too weighty to bear, they are projected onto the victim. The victim is hated for reprimanding the perpetrator for his earlier violent actions. The perpetrator perceives the people he attacks, and not his own acts of violence, as the cause of his inner discomfort. This faulty perception leads to increased violence, since it blocks regret, empathy, making amends, and reconciliation.

In a totalitarian and violent society or in a society at war, people have a heightened susceptibility to humiliation and to primitive revenge drives. We can move from seeing humiliation on the individual level of the abused child to the group level. It may be connected to poverty, inarticulacy or lack of influence, leading to compensatory narcissistic pride and difficulties with compromise and dialog. In Staub's (2011) description of the interplay between group identity and deprivation, a cycle of envy and idealization may arise. Those who feel deprived tend to put others on a pedestal, either those at whom their envy is directed or those whom they hope can lead them out of their humiliation (Böhm & Kaplan, 2011). In a society in which people have been accustomed to following strong authoritarian figures, the risk of mass violence will increase. Genocide often evolves from persistent conflict between groups (Staub, 2011).

Freud (1921/1955) compared the group's relationship to its leader with the individual's relationship to a hypnotist. Individuals turn over their critical powers to someone else and lose their awareness. Their thoughts and behavior are adapted to the group's attitudes. In such cases, the revenge spiral will continue if no external force brings it to a halt. People are changed in a destructive way by the revenge process itself. Orthodoxy takes hold, and people move towards a more and more radical and intolerant position with regard to others' beliefs (or supposed beliefs).

The Rwandan testimonies illustrate these dynamics. The Rwandan youths were initially reluctant to give their testimonies, showing how they had internalized their fear of group reprisals and how overwhelmed they were by their inconceivable losses. People like Jean, who struggle to survive psychologically, risk being picked up by political extremists, because belonging to a group gives them an opportunity to adopt a pseudo-identity. Group pressure and destructive leaders have the potential to push teenagers toward joining groups of potential perpetrators—which may also come as a result of individual and group regression to more primitive forms of affect regulation, such as 'black-and-white thinking.' Luckily for them, Jean and other youths were surrounded by good leaders, helpers, and a society working on restoration.

Throughout this account of trauma and violence, it is obvious that attachment, mentalization, and affect regulation play a key role. Recent findings on affect regulation come from neuroscientific studies of emotion and memory. The essential point is that all feelings—the awareness of affects—fulfill some form of regulatory function that benefits the individual (Damasio, 1999). Van der Hart, Nijenhuis, Steele, and Brows (2004) stress that when significant others deny trauma instead of assisting in the integration of painful experience, dissociative tendencies are enhanced. Loss of the ability to regulate the intensity of feelings and impulses is perhaps the most far-reaching effect of trauma and neglect (Van der Kolk & Fisler, 1994).

Concluding remarks

The specificity of childhood trauma as compared to adult trauma, and furthermore the specificity of childhood trauma in a genocidal context have been described. In the latter case, a socio-psychological vicious circle may

arise when important resilience resources of the child, such as the mentalizing and affect-regulatory capacity of the environment, are already damaged, and this damage is compounded by personal traumatic experiences.
One of the negative consequences of the post-genocidal situation has been
described in detail: the trauma-perpetuating spiral of revenge. Those who
succeed in extracting themselves from the revenge spiral have usually had
a good early attachment to their parents, had the chance to develop an
inner dialog during their childhood and youth, and they have thereby been
able to develop thoughts and ideas. In some testimonies of child survivors,
revenge fantasies came to the surface and showed how thin the border is
between perpetrators and victims, especially if the strain is too great, as a
result of insufficient caregiving and of the lack of an empathetic listener
for the victim's rage and destructive thoughts. If a person cannot mourn,
is overwhelmed by the inconceivable losses of genocide, and furthermore
cannot wipe out horrifying memories, the ensuing rage may trigger an urge
to kill, as in the case of Jean, who was ultimately able to let his revenge
fantasies remain fantasies. Revenge fantasies serve to restore the inner
psychic balance, but they risk being transmitted to the next generation,
who receive the 'relay baton' of unresolved traumas. It is important to
create a containing environment for all kinds of thoughts and affects—for
the individual to be able to proceed with *generational linking*—in order to
reach a state where the victim feels free enough in relation to the past that
he or she can develop an image of what was experienced. Jean wants to
tell his family what he went through, and we can trust that when he does
so, he will use his mentalization skills, with his pain still very much inside
of himself, but nonetheless regulated.

Neuroscientific findings on affect regulation—the regulatory function
designed to help us keep our inner psychic balance and avoid loss of integrity and threat of death—resonate with this call for a support system and
with the role that affect regulation plays in the dynamics between trauma
linking and generational linking.

Notes

1 Interview, Kaplan, Kigali, January 2003.
2 Van der Hart, Nijenhuis, Steele, and Brows (2004) exhibit a remarkable lack of
  consensus regarding the concept of dissociation, and claim that a proper definition of dissociation should be based on neurobiology.
3 Interview Kaplan, Kigali, January 2003.

References

Acierno, R., Hernandez, M. A., Amstadter, A. B., Resnick, H. S., Steve, K., Muzzy, W., & Kilpatrick, D. (2010). Financial abuse and potential neglect in the United States: The national elder mistreatment study. *American Journal of Public Health, 100*, 292–297.

Allen, B. (2011). The use and abuse of attachment theory in clinical practice with maltreated children, part I: Diagnosis and assessment. *Trauma, Violence, & Abuse, 12*(1), 3–12.

Anzieu, D. (1989). *The skin ego*. New Haven, CT: Yale University Press.

Axline, V. (1964). *Dibs in search of self*. New York: Ballantine Books.

Bar-Tal, D. (2000). From intractable conflict through conflict resolution to reconciliation: Psychological analysis. *Political Psychology, 21*, 351–365.

Bateman, A. W., & Fonagy, P. (2004). *Psychotherapy of borderline personality disorder: Mentalization based treatment*. Oxford: Oxford University Press.

Bion, W. R. (1967). *Second thoughts: Selected papers on psychoanalysis*. London: Heinemann.

Böhm, T., & Kaplan, S. (2011). *Revenge: On the dynamics of a frightening urge and its taming*. London: Karnac Books.

Boulanger, G. (2008). Witnesses to reality: Working psychodynamically with survivors of terror. *Psychoanalytic Dialogues, 18*, 638–657.

Bowlby, J. (1969). *Attachment* (vol. 1 of: *Attachment and loss*). London: The Tavistock Institute of Humans Relations.

Breidenstine, A. S., Bailey, L. O., Zeanah, C. H., & Larrieu, J. A. (2011). Attachment and trauma in early childhood: A review. *Journal of Child & Adolescent Trauma, 4*(4), 274–290.

Briere, J., Kaltman, S., & Green, B. L. (2008). Accumulated childhood trauma and symptom complexity. *Journal of Traumatic Stress, 21*(2), 223–226.

Carlson, E. A. (1998). A prospective longitudinal study of attachment disorganization/disorientation. *Child Development, 4*, 1,107–1,128.

Carlson, V., Cicchetti, D., Barnett, D., & Braunwald, K. (1989). Disorganized/disoriented attachment relationships in maltreated infants. *Developmental Psychology, 25*(4), 525–531.

Cassidy, J., & Mohr, J. J. (2001). Unsolvable fear, trauma, and psychopathology: Theory, research, and clinical considerations related to disorganized attachment across the life span. *Clinical Psychology: Science and Practice, 8*(3), 275–298.

Cloitre, M., Stolbach, B. C., Herman, J. L., Van der Kolk, B., Pynoos, R., Wang, J., & Petkova, E. (2009). A developmental approach to complex PTSD: Childhood and adult cumulative trauma as predictors of symptom complexity. *Journal of Traumatic Stress, 22*(5), 399–408.

Damasio, A. R. (1999). *The feeling of what happens: Body and emotion in the making of consciousness*. London: Harcourt.

D'Andrea, W., Ford, J., Stolbach, B., Spinazzola, J., & Van der Kolk, B. A. (2012). Understanding interpersonal trauma in children: Why we need a developmentally appropriate trauma diagnosis. *American Journal of Orthopsychiatry, 82*(2), 187–200.

Dannlowski, U., Stuhrmann, A., Beutelmann, V., Zwanzger, P., Lenzen, T., Grotegerd, D., Domschke, K., Hohoff, C., Ohrmann, P., Bauer, J., Lindner, C., Postert, C., Konrad, C., Arolt, V., Heindel, W., Suslow, T., & Kugel, H. (2012). Limbic scars: Long-term consequences of childhood maltreatment revealed by functional and structural magnetic resonance imaging. *Biological Psychiatry, 71*(4), 286–293.

Davis, J. T. (2001). Revising psychoanalytic interpretations of the past: An examination of declarative and non-declarative memory process. *International Journal of Psychoanalysis, 82*, 449–462.

Dimitrijević, A., & Hamburger, A. (2016). Trauma. In B. J. Carducci (Ed.), *The Wiley encyclopedia of personality and individual differences.* New York: Wiley Blackwell.

Emde, R. N. (1999). Moving ahead: Integrating influences of affective processes for development and for psychoanalysis. *International Journal of Psychoanalysis, 80*, 317–339.

Fonagy, P. (2008). Psychoanalyse und Bindungstrauma unter neurobiologischen Aspekten. In M. Leuzinger-Bohleber, G. Roth, & A. Buchheim (Eds.), *Psychoanalyse, Neurobiologie, Trauma* (pp. 132–148). Stuttgart: Schattauer.

Fonagy, P. (2010). Attachment, trauma, and psychoanalysis: Where psychoanalysis meets neuroscience. In M. Leuzinger-Bohleber, J. Canestri, & M. Target (Eds.), *Early development and Its disturbances: Clinical, conceptual, and empirical research on ADHD and other psychopathologies and its epistemological reflections.* London: Karnac Books.

Fonagy, P., Gergely, G., Jurist, E. L., & Target, M. (2002). *Affect regulation, mentalization and the development of the self.* New York: Other Press.

Fonagy, P., & Target, M. (2007). Playing with reality IV: A theory of external reality rooted in intersubjectivity. *International Journal of Psychoanalysis, 88*, 917–937.

Ford, J. D. (2015). Complex PTSD: Research directions for nosology/assessment, treatment, and public health. *European Journal of Psychotraumatology, 6*: 10.27584. doi: 10.3402/ejpt.v6.27584.

Fraiberg, S., Adelson, E., & Shapiro, V. (1975). Ghosts in the nursery: A psychoanalytic approach to the problems of impaired infant–mother relationships. *Journal of the American Academy of Child Psychiatry, 14*(3), 387–422.

Freud, S. (2003). Mourning and melancholia. *Standard Edition, 14*, 237–258. (Original work published 1917)

Freud, S. (1955). Beyond the pleasure principle. *Standard Edition, 18*, 7–64. (Original work published 1920)

Freud, S. (1955). Group psychology and the analysis of the ego. *Standard Edition, 18*, 65–144. (Original work published 1921)

Gagnon, M., & Hersen, M. (2000). Unresolved childhood sexual abuse and older adults: Late-life vulnerabilities. *Journal of Clinical Geropsychology, 6*(3), 187–198.

Gobodo-Madikizela, P. (2013). Acting out and working through traumatic memory: Confronting the past in the South African context. In M. Linden & K. Rutkowski (Eds.), *Hurting memories and beneficial forgetting: Posttraumatic stress disorders, biographical developments, and social conflicts* (pp. 217–226). Newnes: Elsevier.

Hamburger, A. (1998). Traumnarrativ und Gedächtnis. In M. Koukkou, M. Leuzinger-Bohleber, W. Mertens (Eds.), *Erinnerung von Wirklichkeiten. Psychoanalyse und Neurowissenschaften im Dialog. Vol. 1: Bestandsaufnahme* (pp. 223–286). Stuttgart: Verlag Internationale Psychoanalyse.

Hamburger, A. (2017). Genocidal trauma. Individual and social consequences of the assault on the mental and physical life of a group. This volume, chapter 4.

Herman, J. L. (1992). *Trauma and recovery*. New York: Basic Books.

Igra, L. (2004). *Die dünne Haut zwischen Fürsorge und Grausamkeit*. Nierstein: IATROS Verlag.

Kaplan, S. (2006). Children in genocide: Extreme traumatization and the "affect-propeller." *International Journal of Psychoanalysis, 87*, 725–746.

Kaplan, S. (2008). *Children in genocide: Extreme traumatization and affect regulation*. London: International Psychoanalysis Library.

Kaplan, S. (2013). Child survivors of the 1994 Rwandan genocide and trauma-related affect. *Journal of Social Issues, 69*, 92–110.

Laub, D. (2017). Traumatic shutdown of narrative and symbolization: A failed empathy derivative. Implications for therapeutic interventions. This volume, chapter 3.

Laub, D., & Auerhahn, N. C. (1989). Failed empathy: A central theme in the survivor's Holocaust experience. *Psychoanalytic Psychology, 6*, 377–400.

Lebovici, S. (1988). Fantasmic interaction and intergenerational transmission. *Infant Mental Health Journal, 9*(1), 10–19.

Lindner, E. G. (2001). Humiliation and human rights: Mapping a minefield. *Human Rights Review, 2*, 46–63.

Lowell, A., Renk, K., & Adgate, A. H. (2014). The role of attachment in the relationship between child maltreatment and later emotional and behavioral functioning. *Child Abuse & Neglect, 38*(9), 1,436–1,449.

Main, M., & Weston, D. R. (1981). The quality of the toddler's relationship to mother and to father: Related to conflict behavior and the readiness to establish new relationships. *Child Development, 52*, 932–940.

Mamdani, M. (2001). *When victims become killers.* Princeton, NJ: Princeton University Press.

Marusak, H. A., Martin, K. R., Etkin, A., & Thomason, M. E. (2015). Childhood trauma exposure disrupts the automatic regulation of emotional processing. *Neuropsychopharmacology, 40*(5), 1,250–1,258.

Maschi, T., Baer, J., Morrissey, M.B., & Moreno, C. (2012). The aftermath of childhood trauma on late life mental and physical health: A review of the literature. *Traumatology, 19*(1), 49–64.

Morgan, C., & Fisher, H. (2007). Environment and schizophrenia: Environmental factors in schizophrenia: Childhood trauma—A critical review. *Schizophrenia Bulletin, 33*(1), 3–10.

Perry, B. D., Pollard, R., Blakely, T., Baker, W., & Vigilante, D. (1995). Childhood trauma, the neurobiology of adaptation and "use-dependent" development of the brain: How "states" become "traits." *Infant Mental Health Journal, 16*(4), 271–291.

Read, J., Os, J. V., Morrison, A. P., & Ross, C. A. (2005). Childhood trauma, psychosis and schizophrenia: A literature review with theoretical and clinical implications. *Acta Psychiatrica Scandinavica, 112*(5), 330–350.

Roth, S., Newman, E., Pelcovitz, D., Van der Kolk, B., & Mandel, F. S. (1997). Complex PTSD in victims exposed to sexual and physical abuse: Results from the DSM-IV field trial for posttraumatic stress disorder. *Journal of Traumatic Stress, 10*, 539–555.

Scaer, R. (2014). *The body bears the burden: Trauma, dissociation, and disease.* London and New York: Routledge.

Schore, A. N. (2003). *Affect dysregulation and disorders of the self.* New York and London: Norton.

Shengold, L. (1989). *Soul murder: The effects of childhood abuse and deprivation.* New Haven, CT: Yale University Press, 1989

Staub, E. (2011). *Overcoming evil: Genocide, violent conflict, and terrorism.* New York: Oxford University Press.

Stessman, J., Cohen, A., Hammerman-Rozenberg, R., Bursztyn, M., Azoulay, D., Maaravi, Y., & Jacobs, J. (2008). Holocaust survivors in old age: The Jerusalem Longitudinal Study. *Journal of the American Geriatrics Society, 56*, 470–477.

Streeck-Fischer, A. (2006). *Trauma und Entwicklung. Folgen früher Trauma-tisierungen in der Adoleszenz.* Stuttgart: Schattauer.

Terr, L. (1991). Childhood traumas: An outline and overview. *American Journal of Psychiatry, 148*, 10–20.

Tutté, J. C. (2004). The concept of pyschical trauma: A bridge in interdisciplinary space. *International Journal of Psychoanalysis, 85*, 897–921.

Van der Hart, O., Nijenhuis, E., Steele, K., & Brows, D. (2004). Trauma-related dissociation: Conceptual clarity lost and found. *Australian and New Zealand Journal of Psychiatry, 38*, 906–914.

Van der Kolk, B. A. (1993). Biological considerations about emotions, trauma, memory, and the brain. In S. L. Ablon, D. Brown, E. Khantzian, & J. E. Mack (Eds.), *Human feelings: Explorations in affect development and meaning* (pp. 221–240). Hillsdale, NJ: Analytic Press.

Van der Kolk, B. A. (2005). Developmental trauma disorder. *Psychiatric Annals, 35*(5), 401–408.

Van der Kolk, B. A., & Fisler, R. E. (1994). Childhood abuse and neglect and loss of self-regulation. *Bulletin of the Menninger Clinic, 58*, 145–168.

Van der Kolk, B. A., McFarlane, A. C., & Weisaeth, L. (1996). *Traumatic stress.* New York: Guilford.

Varvin, S. (2003). *Mental survival strategies after extreme traumatisation.* Copenhagen: Multivers Academic.

Winnicott, D. W. (1971). *Playing and reality.* London: Tavistock.

Wurmser, L. (1981). *The mask of shame.* Baltimore, MD, and London: Johns Hopkins University Press.

Zulueta, F. de (2006). *From pain to violence: The traumatic roots of destructiveness.* West Sussex: John Wiley & Sons Ltd.

Part II

Perspectives on testimony

Building on the psychoanalytic concepts of social trauma discussed in the first section of the book, the second part presents the major approach to social trauma taken in our work. It contains interdisciplinary approaches to testimony by Daniel Dayan, Sonja Knopp, and Andreas Hamburger. Dayan traces the representation of psychiatric patients back to Charcot, whose aim was to 'illustrate' a syndrome, a disciplinary origin which he juxtaposes to the video testimonies, whose nature is exploratory—not only of the symptom and its etiology, but also of the failure of the viewer to see and to hear. He explores the different levels of witnessing that are part of the testimonial process. Knopp examines the controversial question of whether and how subjective and distorted memories of survivors, recorded in the testimonial process, can serve as historical data. Hamburger opens a new psychoanalytically inspired pathway to a qualitative reconstruction of the testimonial process: a 'scenic-narrative microanalysis' based on reflecting the countertransference reaction of the researchers themselves. The emotional experience of the rating group parallels the significant transferential moments ('now moments') in the relation between survivor and interviewer. Thus, through the lens of scenic-narrative microanalysis, deeper layers and forms of relatedness in the traumatic reenactment are revealed.

This section is opened by Johanna Bodenstab's autobiographical essay, which after her premature death has been published in *Contemporary Psychoanalysis*. It is the testimony of a witness, who opened her beautiful mind to contain the incomprehensible.

To Johanna, in love and friendship, we have dedicated this book.

Chapter 7

The question of my German heritage

Johanna Bodenstab

I started working with video testimonies of survivors of the Shoah in 1995 and moved to the United States in 1997. The question of my German heritage and its connection to my research has always had a choking quality for me: It casts me, burdened by a heavy load of irrevocable guilt, on a quest for redemption, caught up in an impossible repair project that will never materialize. I must labor eternally under this burden like Sysiphus under the heavy weight of his stone, without any hope of ever completing the task at hand. This question seems to imply that the impossibility of change weighs me down: I will always be trapped in an underlying dichotomy of perpetrators and victims, held hostage by the undeniable guilt of the generation of Germans before me.

For a long time, I remained guarded by the fear that a perpetrator might be lurking in me, that my internal German Shepherd was just waiting to be unleashed. Today, I understand these worries as more of a counter-transference reaction, indicative of fears and deep unease my presence evoked among the Jews I encountered. I was channeling the uncomfortable conversation that should have happened between my parents, that is, with the generation of Germans directly involved in the Third Reich and World War II, and the survivors. My father once told me that during a business trip to New York in the 1970s, he was invited to the home of his Jewish business partner. The man had managed to escape from Germany in the trunk of a car to find refuge in Belgium, from where he made it to the United States. While our meeting gave him the pleasure to revive his once severed ties with the country of his birth, his children—as my father observed with a shrug—were much less welcoming. During the dinner, an elderly lady told my father that back in Germany she had received the ashes of her husband in the mail. He had been sent to a concentration camp where he was murdered. I asked my father: "And, what did you say to her?" My father answered: "You know, Johanna, there are moments when it is better to remain silent."

For many years, I have mourned the lost opportunity that this conversation would have provided. Could he not have asked the elderly lady at least a simple question like "When did this happen?" to let her know that he was willing to listen? I imagine his silence falling around that hospitable table, feeding the rage and the resentments of the second generation. My own disagreement with my father is, likewise, part of this twisted conversation that never happened. Many years went by before I could conceive of a response to the elderly lady, a response that would have broken my father's silence. So, the channeling went both ways: I was receiving messages for my parents as much as I had to find words for them. But did this conversation, which never happened, ever fuel my research? Hardly. That would have been horrible: For the rest of my life I would have had to prove to myself and to my Jewish friends or fellow researchers that I can do better than a German Shepherd.[1]

It is clear to me that the question of the connection between my German heritage and my interest in the Shoah taps into something quite primitive and invites reenactment. My research is pitched against this, trying to engage the primitive without getting caught up in it, while at the same time transcending it. Today there are undoubtedly terms of German–Jewish engagement that are more fluid and nuanced. The impulse my research follows is not to undo the Shoah but to think beyond it while fully acknowledging its primitive horrors. Maybe that is a specifically German approach: We created this terrible destruction; now let's see how we can live after it, how we can carry on in the face of it. Let's at least claim our responsibility for what comes afterwards. Don't let the Shoah have the last word.

I have always experienced my feelings of guilt and sense of shame as obstacles hindering my thought process and preventing me from fully unleashing my intellectual power when it comes to the Shoah. Rather, I remained stuck with a feeling of great uncertainty as to whether it is appropriate for me to speak my German mind; I have worried that my thoughts could be taken as provocations or even insults by survivors and their children. So, if anything, my German background has, at times, been paralytic. Today, as I look back, I feel very much like my father's daughter, clinging to a self-protective shell of silence. My greatest fear remains that I will be heard only as 'the German' when speaking about the Shoah.

What also seemed paralytic was my fear to feel the lingering rage that connected me back to the pain that some of the survivors and their offspring felt, even decades later. It was impossible to take refuge in the fact that I was born well after the end of World War II, in fact, in 1961, in the year the Berlin Wall was built. I had to unlearn my fear, which is foremost my parents' fear. Not only was there no closure, despite all the time that had passed since 1945, there was also something that remained raw and unredeemed, regardless of what was comfortable or preferable to a German. There was the envelope with the ashes still coming in the mail. Still begging for a reply: However, not by the addressee. But it was not only my parents' fear I channeled—I was also experiencing the fear of being persecuted, if only in my imagination: This fear is a fantasy of Jews wanting to get back at me. (Who could blame them?) It is the destructive rage of the Germans who came before me that revisits me as a Jewish gesture—a projective assault of imagined aggression and revenge. This fear, that beseeches me as if it were my own, is perhaps my deepest connection to the Jewish suffering the Germans inflicted.

It so happened that at conferences and discussion groups I found myself in the absolute minority. This was of course a consequence of my emigration. I had created an outpost for myself. I had stepped beyond the habitual discourse of my in-group. Over the past decade or so, this has dramatically changed: Nowadays there are many Germans vigorously contributing to the field and there is an ongoing academic dialog established regardless of the background or heritage of those researchers participating. But initially it was from a position of 'exile' that I realized that there was a fine line of division between me and the Jewish participants: They were grappling with their heritage, burdened by traumatic experience not even their own, sometimes surrounded by a timelessness as if their lives were caught in the past, as if they were living in a different time zone, viscerally connected to the generations of their murdered and surviving relatives. Despite all the discontinuity their heritage enveloped, it paradoxically suggested a continuity foreign to me. My own lineage was riddled with conflict and lack of connection. That is another aspect of my 'exile.' At the core of this complex confluence of discontinuity and continuity lies the most vexing question: How do we go on from here? What can we do with the Shoah given that we cannot step out of it, since it clings to us and makes it so difficult to find words? To me, this remains the biggest challenge: There is simply no other choice than to build our future on this trauma. There is no way around it. But how can this future be meaningful? Is there anything to be gleaned from the Shoah that can be helpful in opening future perspectives for us?

Watching video testimonies of survivors has involved me in an altogether different conversation. I increasingly experience these encounters as a special dialog: I had no say in the narrative flow of the testimonies, but I was touched and shaken, and learned to analyze my intense responses as reverberations of the emotional pain conveyed in the testimonies. It became my task to listen and allow that which I heard to stir my mind. The trauma transmitted in so many of the survivors' testimonies weighed too heavily to permit my involvement to become a playful act of my imagination. But I could allow the survivors' narratives to take root in me, where they might unfold with the help of a careful analysis of my countertransference reactions—unfold beyond the narrating 'I' of the survivor, struggling with and against her or his own traumatization. Insofar as the survivor testimonies are trauma narratives, they have to oscillate between knowing and not knowing (described so vividly by Laub & Auerhahn, 1993). But the question is not only how the narrating 'I' can survive the proximity of its ow trauma: The question is also how an experience that registered as fragmentation, as loss of structure, because it was an assault on the survivors' ability to relate to themselves, can be captured at all in a narrative that has to rely on a narrating 'I.' The dialog I refer to us ultimately an act of secondary witnessing (Felman, 1992). Such a project seems daring because it eradicates the dichotomy between Jews and German. It aligns us in an effort to understand and to be present.

However, the survivors are not simply telling stories of their survival, opening doors to empathy and knowledge for me that could never have been opened by my parents or my teachers. The survivors are deeply engaged in their lives after the Shoah. They moved on, despite the fact that their trauma never let go of them. But their trauma did not have the last word—through their firm will and best intentions. Among the survivors, I was among the living. If fact, the survivors and I were more alive than my parents: They knew their pain and had a story they were willing to share.

So, for me, it became important to measure the losses but also to acknowledge that the destruction my people plotted again the Jews ultimately failed. It could not fully succeed because the Jews under persecution did not comply. They wanted to live. As they were persecuted, the processes of life continued and emotional needs persisted. Against the German perspective of total destruction and genocide stands a perspective of survival, from an enormous effort to hold onto life as they knew it, despite the fact that they were surrounded by a world of massive persecution nullifying the meaning of their lives and denying that they were a living part of the world. There is tremendous human dignity and psychological strength in this refusal to admit that an absolute endpoint has been reached, a highly nuanced perspective that cannot be unified easily into a master narrative as created by previous generations of researchers. The perspective I am trying to describe opens as a murmur of divergent voices. Each voice coming for a different survivor needs to be heard because only the sum of voices can convey the force of the persecution and the tremendous emotional and psychological efforts to withstand it.

It matters a great deal to me that the narrative of the Shoah, such as the mother–daughter relationships during the Holocaust—the focus of my research—is a compromise of diverse experiences so that highly individualized stories emerge in an environment where a totalitarian impetus want us to believe that all individuality was extinguished and that the persecuted Jews were all the same. Thus, my stance is invested in the subjectivity and uniqueness of the divergent experiences of single survivors to restore humanity to their individual significance, thereby contradicting the declared program of genocide.

My discovery that the genocidal project failed remains exhilarating for me even today. It happened in 1996 on my first visit to Israel. It was my first evening in Tel Aviv, the city on the beach. Standing with my back to the Mediterranean, with the murmur of the waves behind me and the night sky above, I was taking in the sparkling city glowing in front of me. The relief that came with the realization that the German project to exterminate the Jews had failed was overwhelming. Until today, the beauty of that failure moves me deeply, although I am fully aware that we almost did succeed.

Note

1 Editor's Note: "German Shepherd" here is used by the author as a metaphor for the dogs used to attack Jews in the camps.

References

Felman, S. (1992). Education and crisis, or the vicissitudes of teaching. In S. Felman & D. Laub, *Testimony: Crises of witnessing in literature. psychoanalysis and history* (pp. 1–56). New York: Routledge.

Laub, D. & Auerhahn, N. (1993). Knowing and not knowing massive psychic trauma: Forms of traumatic memory. *International Journal of Psychoanalysis, 74*, 287–302.

Chapter 8

Visible witness

Watching the footprints of trauma

Daniel Dayan

To Sol

Listening to a witness offering testimony invites a displacement of attention from the storyteller to the story told. What occurs here might be the
exact opposite. This chapter discusses four videos of Shoah survivors
recorded by Dori Laub and his colleagues at the Fortunoff archive. These
videos offer a powerful illustration of the psychic impact of severe traumas. While accepting the need to bear witness, certain survivors explicitly or implicitly relent to do so. Their testimonies are paradoxically
characterized by denial concerning the aggressions they were submitted
to and by generalized doubt as to the very reality of the events they witnessed. An unsettling combination of memories and delusion condemns
survivors' accounts to become illustrations of psychic collapse.

In two of the videos, survivors are interviewed on an individual basis.
This is the case for Israeli survivors Rafi and Shmuel, who were filmed at
the Beer Yaakov Psychiatric Hospital. In two other videos, groups of two
survivors appear side by side.

The testimonies we hear are peculiar. They are tentative testimonies,
hesitant testimonies, interrupted testimonies, mistaken testimonies, and,
sometimes, silent testimonies. The situations witnessed seem obscure, contradictory, incoherent. Often, videos are less about witnessing than about a
failure to bear witness. Familiarity with the psychoanalytic study of major
traumas might illuminate certain aspects of the videos. Yet one does not
need to be a psychiatrist in order to understand their import. These videos
are not meant to offer illustrations of some dogma. If such videos exist,
perhaps it is precisely in order to be read in a number of ways, some of
which are yet to be found.

This chapter is an attempt at 'ekphrasis': My reading of video images will systematically rely on other images (documentaries, fiction films, paintings). Such images will, I hope, provide me with a descriptive vocabulary. Whenever words are missing, I shall use these other images as relays towards description.

Videos and visibility

The videos I saw could be displayed as 'art' (as 'installations'), or put on stage, as 'theater.' But it makes more sense to situate them in reference to a tradition of medical or psychiatric displays, a tradition which would include many of those to whom Oliver Sacks referred when he spoke of the "literary psychiatrists" of nineteenth-century France: Clérambault, Moreau de Tours, and, first of all, Charcot.

While Charcot still relied on a type of scenography, already illustrated in the paintings of Rembrandt, the videos of Laub—like the films of Rouch—seem to mobilize an original dramaturgy. Describing this dramaturgy is one of this chapter's main ambitions. How determined is it by the choice of a given medium? And what sort of visibility does it involve? Is it a visibility that illustrates? A visibility that interrogates? A visibility that invites meditation?

At the time of Charcot's presentations at the Salpêtrière, visibility was meant to stress the accuracy of what was being shown. Visibility was backed by knowledge. It provided 'illustrations,' demonstrations. Yet, there is another form of visibility, also associated with science, that calls for interrogation, for scrutiny, for confirmation or rejection. One may show a situation and make a claim about its relevance, but such a claim is neither exclusive nor final. One rapidly realizes that the Fortunoff videos are far removed from any sort of 'illustrative' visibility. Their visibility is that of questions.

Pathos and unpathos

Think of Rouch's (1955) famous documentary on possession ceremonies in Africa. *The Mad Masters* was so paroxystic that it gave birth to a classic of modern theater: Jean Genet's *Les Nègres*. In contrast, the tonality of Laub's videos is one of bleak despair. On the face of it, the videos look like banal job interviews interspersed with long moments of silence. But their appearance of banality does not withstand a second viewing.

In the first projection one would probably miss the poignancy of what is being said. But each new viewing would add a new layer of horror. Here is an example provided by the double interview of two survivors: a mother (Rosalie) and her daughter (Jolly). The interview starts in a peaceful setting. The two women are recalling very old facts. But these very old facts concern an infanticide. A Nazi doctor killed a newborn baby in their presence, by plunging him into a pail of water. A second viewing reveals an additional layer of cruelty: "Here goes little Moses," said the doctor, after killing the baby. This sinister joke refers to Exodus, and to the slaughter of all first borns. It also refers to Moses as savior of the Jews. It further refers to Moses as a baby saved by the Nile's water. Baby Moses is sarcastically drowned in the water meant to save him. A further viewing reveals that the infanticide was not merely witnessed. One of the survivors was forced to take part in it.

What I am proposing here is not an analysis of this video. Johanna Bodenstab has beautifully conducted such an analysis, highlighting the erasure of Rosalie's role by her daughter Jolly, telling us what such an erasure meant. My point here is to stress what hides underneath the smooth surface of 'unpathos.' I also wish to stress that this 'unpathos' is often worse than the horror it conceals. Horror does not reside in the stories themselves, but in their telling by an apparently calm, composed speaker; in their telling by an erased speaker.

Monstration, unwitnessing, validation

This chapter is organized into three parts. The first looks at the videos as forms of 'monstration,' contrasting the display of survivors to earlier scenographies in the history of medical displays.

Focussing on the situations in which survivors are interviewed individually, the second part of this chapter relies on a general theory of 'recognition' to discuss what I would call the 'unwitnessing' of Shoah survivors.

The final part of this chapter looks at the 'validating' gestures performed by interviewers who are at once analysts, fellow survivors, and managers of a memory institution.

The displayed witness

Visibility comes in many forms. According to the philosopher Jean-Luc Marion (2004), a phenomenological distinction should be made between "what is seen" and "what appears." "What is seen" merely concerns objects, or objectified realities. "What appears," on the contrary, is endowed with a dimension of activity, of agency. Appearing calls for a temporality that excludes anticipation. Appearing occurs when new and unanticipated realities enter the world. When appearing takes place, that which appears does not obey established categories. It escapes pre-vision.

The antonym of appearing—its radical opposite—is what I would call 'monstration.' Monstration presupposes knowledge. 'Monstrators' already know what they intend to show. In a way, the very fact of monstration— the very intentionality of display—leaves very little room, or no room at all, for the possibility of appearing. Monstration characterizes a whole tradition of medical displays.

Charcot and the model of theater

A life-size painting by Brouillet depicts Charcot discussing a hysterical patient—'Blanche'—during a clinical lecture. Blanche has fainted and is being held by a young doctor. The lesson is taking place in a packed classroom. Charcot is talking to the audience. He looks at the listeners. He does not look at Blanche.

In Charcot's time, the display of patients was meant as a confirmation of a thesis. Presentations at the Salpêtrière were classes offering young psychiatrists an initiation into the symptoms of a given illness. They were lectures aimed at a scientific public and meant to demonstrate the existence of a given syndrome, as well as the accuracy of the diagnosis by which this syndrome was identified. Like Rembrandt's 'anatomy lesson,' in which the cadaver is flanked by a textbook, psychiatric presentations combined the display of patients with a lesson.

Charcot's presentations were not only dogmatic but theatrical. Charcot offered a show in which he induced patients to produce symptoms. Patients were led to a classroom. Assistants were ready to set them into motion. What occurred was predictable. It was a 'hysterical' outburst. Of course, hysteria was only a moment in a process conceived as a preamble to inducing recollection. Yet this preamble offered a powerful dramatic performance. Photographs taken at the Salpêtrière give a sense of "the amazing theatricality of the hysterical body" (Huberman, 1970). Like theater in Artaud's view, Charcot's stage was subordinated to a preestablished set of meanings.[1]

Temporal economies of attention

The Fortunoff videos depart radically from this theatrical model. Those in charge talk *to* and not *about* the survivors they show. Were it not for the presence of a camera (and cameraman), the interviews would be reminiscent of a face-to-face therapy session. The interviewers ask questions. They do so for the sake of those they are interviewing. No public is in attendance.[2] On one side of a table are the interviewees, who sit with a curtain as a backdrop. On the other side are the interviewers. Survivors are filmed continuously, usually in medium close-up. The camera never leaves their face while questions are asked. Interviewers turn their back to the camera and remain generally invisible. We know of their presence from the questions they ask and from the gaze and behavior of the interviewees. Yet a public is involved.

Archiving, virtual publics, future meanings

Theater addresses an attending public. The public of videos is an absent, virtual public. The video machinery is part of a composite medium. Combining recording, archive, and seminar, this medium commands a specific *temporal economy of attention*. It addresses contemporary publics, but also future publics. Today's public brings together a scientific audience (the audience of medical institutions, the audience of trauma studies) and a Jewish audience to whom the Fortunoff videos provide a powerful argument against negationism. Yet, the very existence of an archive creates the possibility of reaching many other publics. What is recorded is something the interviewers theoretically know about, but the nature of which is ambiguous and the occurrence of which is uncertain. There is an excess, a supplement to what these interviewers are aware of displaying. What might future publics seek or find in the archived documents? The survivors' performances are submitted to a 'framing.' Yet the videos are constantly open to the possibility of revealing much more than what was originally anticipated. What is being transmitted is an invitation to future definitions.[3]

Being shown in seminars will further accentuate a dialogism already inscribed in the recorded interviews themselves. In contrast to what often occurs in journalism, the Fortunoff interviews avoid suppressing the questions asked. On the contrary, the soundtrack monitors both the performance of survivors and that of their interviewers. It records their proddings, disagreements, parapraxes, and slips of the tongue. Soundtracks display countertransference in action. Future publics will be able to monitor this countertransference, as if they were fellow analysts involved in 'supervision.'[4]

Regard and disregard

Besides dialogism, virtual publics, and the possible emergence of unanticipated micro-events, the Fortunoff videos are characterized by a gesture that clearly sets them apart from other sorts of medical displays. This gesture is one of regard.

Dr Nicolaes Tulp is displaying the muscles of a cadaver's left arm to medical students. Attendants focus their attention on Dr Tulp and not on the naked, grayish cadaver. In fact, this cadaver has a name (Adrian Adriaanse). He has a story (he was probably a convict). Adrian's life, name, and story are ignored. To Dr Tulp and his listeners, Adrian is little more than a forearm. To this day, Rembrandt's painting lesson is known by the surgeon's name (Kofman, 1995).

Offering another type of medical display, Rouch's film *The Mad Masters* is about the power of trance. The young Africans it shows are 'possessed.' Their behaviors strike the viewer as repulsive, and many commentators initially reject the film as 'offensive to Africans.' Yet Rouch's approach is in fact respectful. The young men filmed in trance are also filmed when the trance is over. They are now poised, smiling young men, in full control of how they look. Rouch's approach to 'the mad masters' differs radically from Rembrandt's display of Adrian, and from the shows of nineteenth-century 'alienists.' His approach is one of 'de-othering.' Those deemed different are brought closer *and* they are filmed as subjects. Like Rouch's documentary the Fortunoff videos are characterized by what the doctors in Rembrandt's famous painting dramatically lack: regard.

The survivor as unwitness

Reluctant witnessing

Here are two severely traumatized survivors. Both have volunteered to bear witness and are quite conscious of how they appear. Shmuel is a ruddy, toothless fellow of 76 years. Framed by short hair, Rafi's handsome face is almost that of an ascetic. Both have dressed up for the occasion: Shmuel wears an ironed blue shirt, a dark blue sweater. His cheeks are freshly shaven. He wears a cap, perhaps to hide his baldness, perhaps to shield his face. He also wears large untinted glasses.

Both survivors keep regulating their own visibility, 'editing' their appearance. Caps, visors, and glasses serve as so many stage props or curtains shielding the survivors from the interviewers' gaze. Sometimes they lean back in their chairs. Sometimes they move forward. Sometimes an inclination of the head succeeds in masking their eyes. These gestures are attempts at maintaining dignity. They also serve the purpose of 'unwitnessing.' Survivors often respond to questions with a blank stare. The dramaturgy of the videos is one of interruptions, of silences. The story that reaches us is not that of a traumatic event (which remains out of reach), but that of its erasure. The videos are meant to be recording factual testimonies. But these testimonies only become testimonies once one realizes that what counts in them is their un-factuality. They are testimonies by virtue not of what they say, but of what they avoid saying. A non-performance becomes the actual subject of the videos. Testimonies address not a situation, but a condition.

Narrative aphasia

There is a method to the silence of survivors. Shmuel ben Meir is asked about specific events. His answers speak of context, circumstances. Events are replaced by progressive evocations. Individuals are replaced by general categories (the Ukrainians, the Romanians, the father, the brother, etc.). The first-person pronoun, 'I,' is replaced by 'We,' or by 'One.' Rafi Rakovsky similarly transforms every specific situation into a general category: This war was like any other war; the military occupation was quite ordinary; loneliness is the same for all orphans. Events and actions dissolve into regularities. Nothing stands out. A narrative aphasia puts an end to the very possibility of differentiating persons, situations, and events.

Yet a few events survive. These are lucky events. A Nazi officer releases Shmuel, thereby saving his life. A fellow soldier saves his life once again by shielding him from a volley of bullets. Narrative aphasia is selective. Shmuel and Rafi do sometimes express pain, shame, resentment, and despair. But these intense feelings are not expressed in regard to the Shoah. Shmuel comes alive when he speaks of his adult life spent in Israel, after fighting the war of independence. The story of this life is a bitter sequence of failures: no job, no home, no wife, and none of the compensations he sought (political career or the ability to learn languages). Rafi's adult life also accumulates failures: losing girlfriends, losing the major parts he used to play to other actors, being reduced to playing small parts, being offered no parts at all. These are all still open wounds, but when it comes to the traumatisms of childhood indifference prevails. Survivors are perhaps disappointed at what they would perceive as an excessive interest in their childhood (and in History), as opposed to an insufficient interest in their adult life. They perhaps mean to be heard as who they are and not as whatever happened to them.

Events and speech events

In fact, the Fortunoff videos involve two sorts of events: (1) reported events, events that occurred during the Shoah; and (2) speech events through which the reported events are discussed. The videos are ostensibly about the former. They are actually about the latter. As in analysis, or in Lanzmann's film *Shoah*, the dramaturgy of the videos focusses on speech events. Reported events are mostly used to endow the process of speaking with visibility. The ostensible plot concerns past events. The actual plot is the process by which the narrative of such events is made impossible. Trauma here is not what the narrative is about. It is what makes the narrative impossible.

There are two senses of the word 'witness' in English. A witness is a person, someone who offers testimony. A witness is also a text, the content of a testimony. In the Fortunoff videos, many witnesses start as persons (they are introduced, named, and situated), but soon they become texts. Events are not what witnesses tell us about, but rather what has imprinted itself on their bodies, faces, gestures, silences. Each survivor has become an archeological remnant, a footprint.

Recognition

An overarching theme connects the dramaturgies of the different videos and provides their moral context. In reference to the work of Axel Honneth (1996), I woud call it 'recognition.'

Recognition is closely imbricated with visibility. Central to Honneth's thinking is the notion of 'social recognition' or 'regard,' a type of recognition whose absence often translates into 'social invisibility' and into a form of social death. Honneth stresses that Ralph Ellison's novel *The Invisible Man* is not about any literal form of invisibility, but about the refusal to acknowledge the existence of someone. Invisibility is a condemnation to nonexistence.

Of course, 'regard' is not the only existing form of 'recognition.' I can also recognize someone whom I already know or have met. Finding out who this someone is—finding the name that matches the face—is a cognitive exercise. 'Recognition' here tends to be synonymous with 'identification.' Yet recognition is not merely cognitive or ethical. It involves many other dimensions. Acknowledging a crime, recognizing a debt, pleading guilty: these are forms of recognition. In ancient Rome, a father used to pick up a baby and lift it off the ground. Such a gesture was codified. It meant: I 'recognize' this baby as my child.

Recognition directly concerns the question of witnessing. Whether or not Rafi or Shmuel, or Jolly 'recognize' what happened to them does not merely mean that they 'identify' certain facts. It also means that they relate to the experience of these facts, that they are capable of the type of acknowledgement that distinguishes witnessing from mere knowledge. I would refer in this case to an *existential* form of recognition. Witnessing is hardly reducible to propositional contents. Witnessing involves something else. Witnessing involves someone. Witnessing involves a mode of recognition that we tend to perceive only when it is lacking. Among all modes of recognition, this is perhaps the one that most needs to be accounted for, because—for all of us who are not psychiatrists—it is generally taken for granted.

Some survivors of a traumatic event may be left with an abstract sort of knowledge, with a 'dis-affected' knowledge. Some others are not even left with that much. What is impaired in them goes far beyond the possibility of an 'affective,' existential recognition. They have lost even the possibility of cognitive recognition. The knowledge of a particular event is not only dissociated from the affects that accompany it, but also blotted out altogether. As Laub has noted, the traumatic event did not 'register': it just disappeared from the mnesic archive. This eclipse of both affective and cognitive recognition may amount to a feeling of an erasure of the self. To survivors, this feeling is terrifying.

Avoiding subjectivation

In her study of the danger involved in the 'writing' of severe traumatic experiences, Rosenblum (2012) asks why so many survivors who mean to write about their own experience end up steering clear of their own history, avoiding 'autobiography' and practicing at best 'heterobiography.' Why do so many survivors end up discussing the traumas of others?

The danger such survivors are skirting is of course that of publicizing episodes of shame and guilt. But it goes deeper. Potential witnesses realize that the process of writing can hardly be controlled. There is no guarantee that the account of a trauma will remain confined to a 'cognitive' sort of recognition and not spill over into something much more fearsome. Instead of merely noting 'what occurred,' potential witnesses realize they are exposing themselves to the risk of a full-scale, and in fact *first-time* traumatic experience. They realize that one may end up dying, "not because one has lived, but because one has written" (Castillo, in Rosenblum, 2000, 82; Rosenblum, 2012).

An awareness of this sort of danger transpires on the faces of Rafi and Shmuel. Sometimes a perplexed expression gives the feeling they are about to answer the interviewer's questions, and then it fades away as if they had changed their mind. In spite of the interviewer's reassuring presence, the survivors seem to believe that bearing witness is like opening Pandora's box: Is Rafi really not remembering when he keeps saying that everything was just "ordinary," "commonplace," "like everything else," "like everybody else"? Or is he refusing to remember?

Chronicling entelechy

Recognition seems 'about to occur.' Will survivors address their 'extreme knowledge'? Will their narrative take another course? Will they maintain an obstinate silence? The possibility of recognition hovers over the situation. Laub's videos are about suspended recognition. To better understand this sort of suspense, let me refer to a situation which classicist Pascal Quignard (2014) discusses in reference to Ancient Greek painting, and which he calls by a scholarly name, 'entelecheia,' in reference to Aristotle's distinction between 'actuality' and 'potentiality.' For Quignard, entelecheia is the moment of potentiality that precedes action. It is the moment in which both action and inaction are still possible. We know, says Quignard, that Medea murdered her children, and so, of course, did the Greek painter who depicted her. But when that Greek painter painted the scene, he chose not to show Medea killing her children. Instead, he showed the children playing, and he showed Medea staring at them. Medea's gaze was thoughtful. Her sword was stored. She could still take another course of action. Medea was "like a storm when clouds start filling the sky" (Quignard, 2014, 29–30). Medea was like the possibility of a storm.

The Fortunoff videos allow us to catch similar moments of entelechy, moments of hesitation, of potentiality. Shmuel ben Meir is facing the camera. He has been asked a specific question. He sucks on his lip, passes his tongue over his missing teeth, lowers the visor of his cap. A struggle seems to go on inside him. Like the storm in Medea's sky, a narrative is on the verge of bursting. Will Shmuel speak or remain silent? Will he confront horror or dodge the question? Like Medea's painter (Timomachus), we (and the interviewers) already know that certain events did happen. What we are looking at is the drama of their being uttered or avoided.

This hesitation on the verge of the utterance is fleeting, almost invisible. Yet the videos manage to capture some of it. These videos invite us to change scale. The climax of their dramas takes a fraction of a second. We are far from Charcot's theatrical machinery of monstration; far from the convulsions produced at will by hysterical patients. Laub's dramaturgy is so subtle and so quick that recording it requires a microscope, or a seismograph. But, as Laub himself has put it, this video-seismograph is preceded by another one. The other seismograph is the interviewer himself, whose countertransference steers the nature and sequence of questions, organizes the progression from one question to the next. Both seismographs measure recognition.

The validating witness

As opposed to what might occur in other archives, the Fortunoff interviewers are analysts, theorists of trauma. Their sensitivity to countertransferential processes informs the questions they ask. These questions are more than questions. They are attempts at mending the fabric of torn memories, at reigniting denied resentment, at addressing situations that have been misperceived, or not perceived at all.

Survivors often erase the traces of crimes committed against them the way actual perpetrators might erase the traces of their own crimes. Rafi Rakovski systematically stops short of passing judgment on those who destroyed his life. His absence of reaction causes his interviewer to express irritation: "Why do you always say that everything, every situation, every person I ask you to describe is 'normal,' 'ordinary,' 'standard'?" Manifesting irritation might be spontaneous. It is also a therapeutic gesture: It invites the survivor to come to terms with his own resentment, to turn his destructiveness outside, rather than against himself.[5]

There is another therapeutic gesture that I would like to describe. I shall do so with reference to a recurring theme in Alfred Hitchcock's cinema. Characters in Hitchcock's films frequently face skepticism or hostility whenever they mention violent incidents they have witnessed. In the eyes of some of their listeners, such incidents never occurred. (An ornithologist in *The Birds* pronounces seagulls incapable of attacking humans.) To others, such events might have occurred, but were incorrectly interpreted. (The protagonist of *Rear Window* was 'wrong' in assuming that what he saw was an assassination.) Not only do third parties express skepticism, but witnesses themselves become hesitant and start doubting their own perceptions. In response to such doubts, Hitchock invented an interesting character: the 'validating witness,' the witness of the witness, the companion who double checks stories told by hesitant witnesses and comes to the rescue of disputed facts (see *The Lady Vanishes*).

Like Hichcock's perplexed characters, and even without being confronted with the scepticism of others, survivors are prone to doubt the reality of unbearable events. They are often ready to mistrust their own perceptions. This turns the Fortunoff interviewers into 'ambassadors of reality.' They are in charge of dispelling potential confusions between actual occurrences and fantasies. Confirming that certain events did occur, they become 'validating witnesses.'

Dialogic witnessing

They are not the only ones. In the double interviews I saw, fellow survivors acted towards each other like 'validating witnesses,' endorsing, or failing to endorse, other witnesses' testimonies.

Sometimes such validations ended in fiasco. Sometimes they were successful. Sometimes they were not even necessary. Validation had already taken place in the form of an ongoing conversation between memories. Dori Laub (2015) stresses the comforting dimension inherent in the existence of such conversations: "There was something very reassuring for me in experiencing the convergence of her and my testimony. I was not alone with my memories. But, in fact I had never been alone with my memories. I experienced my mother as always present with me" (p. 201).

A similar presence is described by Proust in the opening pages of *Du côté de Guermantes*. The death of Proust's grandmother meant the extinction of a gaze, the disappearance of a certain point of view on the world, the erasure of that vantage point he used to adopt when it came to judging or assessing people. Proust's grandmother was the one who validated his perceptions of people and situations. With the death of his grandmother, Proust became deprived of the inner dialog by which he compared his emerging perceptions to hers. He had to content himself with his own judgments.

Both Proust and Laub are describing a conversation. In Laub's (2015) version of this conversation, each partner may take the lead, at least for a while: "As long as my mother's testimony related events that preceded my own conscious memories, I could listen to it as if it were any other testimony of a Holocaust survivor. The moment she started talking of events of which I had my own clear and conscious memories, my listening changed . . . My own memories felt to me to be more immediate and more specific, and I often filled in the 'gaps' in her testimony" (pp. 200–201). Such differences in witnessing did not result in a rift. On the contrary, the memories turned out to complement each other: "These were now like composite memories I was hearing, constructed from her memories and from my own."

Yet 'double interviews' also call on memories that are not 'composite,' but exclude each other. One of them, which I have already mentioned, reveals a major dissonance between two narratives: those of a mother (Rosalie) and her daughter (Jolly) about the murder of a newborn baby (Bodenstab, 2015). The witnessing dissonance is too crucial to be ironed out. Yet it never takes the form of an open contradiction. Listening to her daughter's story, Rosalie multiplies signs of agreement. She keeps murmuring "Yes, Yes . . ." ("Yes, this was Kummel"). She keeps nodding, like a music professor approving the accuracy of a pupil's performance. All her gestures endorse her daughter's narrative. Then, suddenly, she overturns the narrative, by quietly adding that the baby was not drowned in a sink under a running faucet: the baby was plunged headfirst into a pail of boiling water which she had herself heated. Unless one listens very carefully to the words she pronounces, it all seems as if Rosalie were still validating the narrative she is in fact denouncing. What is transmitted here is a failure at constructing a shared memory of the event. The story offered is not that of a reciprocal validation. It is that of a consensual fiasco. Did validation occur at a later stage? Did Jolly hear the confession? Did she accept it? Did she rather prefer to keep her internal image of a protective mother (Bodenstab, 2015)?

The smile of Clara L.

Look, by contrast, at a case of successful validation. Dori Laub has joined his mother Clara Laub on the witnessing side of the camera. A relatively minor detail prompts him to contradict her story. Unlike what she asserts, the toy closet he found when returning home was not full of toys: "There were hardly any toys! . . . The closet looked to me to be empty!" Clara Laub is astonished but she does not protest. Instead, she turns towards her son. "You are right," she says with a delighted smile. This is a joyful smile, almost a triumphant smile. It means, of course, "I am proud of you." But it also means "You remember better than I did. I accept and share your recollection." This smile is an endorsement.

I found a ritualized equivalent of such an endorsement in a film by John Ford. *Stagecoach* is about a group of travelers embarking on a dangerous journey across the Arizona desert. The stagecoach passengers profoundly differ from each other by their ideologies, their ingrained prejudices, the values to which they subscribe. Yet their journey forces them to witness the same events. The film chronicles these events and carefully monitors the possible emergence of a consensus about how each event is perceived. Whenever such a consensus occurs, a recurring ritual celebrates it. Having watched an incident unfold, the passengers turn towards each other and exchange a long look. This exchange of gazes serves as a punctuation mark throughout the film. No word is pronounced. The exchange means, "Yes, I saw what you saw." It means, "I confirm what you saw." It means, "We live in the same world. Our points of view are exchangeable" (Dayan, 1977).

This exchange of gazes constructs a community of witnessing based on a reciprocal validation by passengers of what other passengers have witnessed.

The exchange of gazes ratifies the emergence of a collective point of view. It defines a shared reality.

Clara Laub's smile to Dori endorses his recollection of the toy closet. It also celebrates the emergence of a shared reality. Both Clara's smile and *Stagecoach*'s exchange of gazes are moments of validation.[6] Being composite is perhaps what characterizes all forms of social memory.

Let us return to traumatic events. Dori Laub and Johanna Bodenstab have highlighted the importance of 'collective witnessing': that of reinserting traumas within the domain of those realities that can be shared. Collective witnessing is a way of coming to terms with trauma, instead of condemning it to both invisibility and irruptive emergence. What is at stake in the Fortunoff videos is the possibility of attending the process through which extreme knowledge can be integrated, and, in a way, pacified.

Notes

1 Artaud makes a case for an autonomy of the stage. His 'theater of cruelty' is one that would escape the tyranny of the text and renounce any sort of 'illustrative' status.

2 Think, in contrast, to earlier medical displays. Rembrandt's *Anatomy Lesson* was a social event, open not only to students and doctors but also to the general public. Some of the spectators could pay to be included in the painting. Some others were allowed to attend upon payment of an entrance fee. The public was an essential aspect of the display.

3 Earlier commentators on the Fortunoff videos speak of a systematic avoidance of the artistic or aesthetic, or 'expressive' potential of the medium. I would rather suggest that the videos' systematic reliance on long, continuous shots does in fact obey an aesthetics. Of course, this aesthetics is not that of Eisenstein or Hitchcock. It is the very opposite of an aesthetics of 'monstration.' But it is an aesthetics that runs throughout the history of cinema as an alternative to its dominant, monstrative, version, and was theorized by André Bazin. Thus, in a way Laub is closer than Rouch—its inventor—to practicing 'cinema verité': Rouch's film *The Mad Masters* is heavily edited, and is steered by a very directive narration. In contrast, Laub does not narrate and does not edit. His videos allow things to "appear."

4 Amit Pinchevski (this volume, chapter 17) notes that witnessing, in the Fortunoff archives, involves three steps. The first step is the witnessing by survivors. The second witnessing is enacted by the interviewer as corroborative witness. The

third witnessing is that of the video recording machinery. I very much agree, noting however that the 'second' witnessing is an attempt at 'animating' the frozen witnessing of survivors, and that the 'third' witnessing is in fact the witnessing of future publics.

5 On this, see Laurent Danon Boileau (2014).

6 In *Stagecoach* (and in classical cinema in general), what spectators are invited to see is what those who ride on the stagecoach agree on having seen. In other words, throughout the film, in incident after incident, the spectator is invited to become an honorary member of a gazing community: to share a point of view that keeps being constructed as common. The film thus connects the problematics of transmission, collective memory, and that of the construction of factuality.

References

Bodenstab, J. (2015). Parapraxis in mother–daughter testimony: Unconscious fantasy and maternal function. *Contemporary Psychoanalysis, 51*(2), 219–228.

Clara L. (1993). Holocaust testimony (HVT-1850). Fortunoff Video Archive for Holocaust Testimonies. New Haven, CT: Yale University Library.

Danon-Boileau, L. (2014). L'écueil des bons sentiments. *Revue française de psychanalyse, 78*(5), 1,668–1,671.

Dayan, D. (1983). *Western graffiti: Jeux d'images et programmation du spectateur dans "La Chevauchée fantastique" de John Ford*. Paris: Clancier Guénaud.

Didi-Huberman, G. (2012). *Invention de l'hystérie: Charcot et l'iconographie photographique de la Salpêtrière*. Paris: Macula.

Felman, S., & Laub, D. (1992). *Testimony: Crises of witnessing in literature, psychoanalysis and history*. New York and London: Routledge.

Ford, J. (1939). *Stagecoach*. USA: Warner.

Hitchcock, A. (1938). *The Lady Vanishes*. Britain: Gaumont British.

Hitchcock, A. (1954). *Rear Window*. USA: Paramount.

Hitchcock, A. (1958). *Vertigo*. USA: Paramount and Hitchcock Productions.

Hitchcock, A. (1963). *The Birds*. USA: Universal.

Honneth, A. (1996). *The struggle for recognition: The moral grammar of social conflicts*. Cambridge, MA: MIT Press.

Honneth, A. (2007). *Disrespect: The normative foundations of critical theory*. Cambridge: Polity Press.

Kofman, S. (1995). La mort conjurée: Remarques sur la leçon d'anatomie du docteur Nicolas Tulp, 1632, Mauritshuis, La Haye. In A. Kyritsos (Ed.), Médecine et Arts Visuels [Special issue], *La part de l'œil, 11*, 41–45.

Laub, D. (2015). Listening to my mother's testimony. *Contemporary Psychoanalysis, 51*(2), 195–215.

Marion, J.-L. (2004). "Ce que nous voyons, ce qui apparaît," entretien à l'invitation de F. Soulages, 24 juin 2003. *Cahiers du collège iconique, 16.*

Pinchevski, A. (2012) The audiovisual unconscious: Media and trauma in the video archive for Holocaust testimonies. *Critical Inquiry, 39*(1), 142–147.

Quignard, P. (2014). *Sur l'image qui manque à nos jours.* Paris: Arléa.

Rosalie W., & Jolly Z. (1979). Holocaust testimony (HVT-34). Fortunoff Video Archive for Holocaust Testimonies. New Haven, CT: Yale University Library.

Rosenblum, R. (2000). And till the ghastly tale is told: Sarah Kofman, Primo Levi and the dangers of testimony. *European Judaism, 33*(2), 81–103.

Rosenblum, R. (2010). Shoah et psychanalyse. *Psychanalyse internationale, 18,* 40–42.

Rosenblum, R. (2012). In more favourable circumstances: Ambassadors of the wound. In J. Secakz & T. Keve (Eds.), *Ferenczi Today.* London: Karnac.

Rouch, J. (1955). *Les Maîtres Fous (The Mad Masters).* France: Ethnofiction.

Videos

Shmuel Ben Meir: Interview conducted by Dori Laub and Osrit ben Ari. Beer Yaakov.

Rafi Rakovsky: Interview conducted by Dori Laub and Irit Felsen. Beer Yaakov.

Chapter 9

Reflections of voice and countenance in historiography

Methodological considerations on clinical video testimonies of traumatized Holocaust survivors in historical research

Sonja Knopp

Introduction

The video, which will be the focus of the following study, is of an interview with 76-year-old Shmuel B., led by psychiatrist and psychoanalyst Dori Laub and social worker Oshrit Ben Ari at the Beer Yaakov Mental Health Center in Israel in 2003. The interview, mainly played out between the two men, was documented as part of a psychiatric study on trauma research. Today, it is part of Yale's *Fortunoff Video Archive for Holocaust Testimonies*. At the time of the interview, Shmuel B. had been—apart from a few brief respites—hospitalized for nearly 50 years. He was diagnosed as chronic schizophrenic. Due to this diagnosis, the consequences he suffered from massive psychic trauma, stemming from childhood experiences during World War II and the Holocaust in his home region Bessarabia, went unnoticed for years.

The interview targets Shmuel B.'s memories of the so-called forgotten Holocaust: the persecution and murder of at least 250,000 Romanian and Ukrainian Jews on Romanian-ruled territory between 1941 and 1944 (Ioanid, 2004, 77f.; Benz, 2009, 30). Because the interview is conducted on video it documents not only the dialogical testimony given by an aged survivor to his interlocutors, but a testimony that infuses his entire figure. He testifies not only in words, but with his whole body, with voice and countenance, connecting his experiences of persecution as a boy with their persistence in the lifelong trauma brought upon this man.

In his description of the Paul Klee painting *Angelus Novus*, Walter Benjamin gives a perspective on history that inspired historians to focus on social aspects of experience in various historical contexts. As Benjamin puts it, "With his eyes staring, his mouth open and his face turned towards the past, the angel is fixated on a catastrophe, which touches the angel through wreckage that is hurled in front of his feet" (Benjamin, 1974/2003, Thesis IX). Video testimony from Holocaust survivors are like those wreckages: sources dredged up from historical disaster. They come with a moral claim of being received, and, as Saul Friedländer framed it, they are "a constant source of bewilderment—a bewilderment that arises on the first confrontation with the Shoah from the depth of one's own immediate understanding of the world, which determines the perception of what is 'normal' and what remains 'incredible': a reaction that occurs before knowledge arrives to suppress it" (Friedländer, 2007b, 26–27). With the term "bewilderment," Friedländer points to the ambivalent position of the historian between "the (mostly involuntary) smugness of scholarly detachment and 'objectivity'" on the one hand, and a position of exposing yourself to the voices and what they talk about, that is, a position of personal concern, on the other (Friedländer, 2007a, xxv–xxvi). With Benjamin and Friedländer in mind, and the idea of integrating the voices of the muted into historical narratives, this examination will reflect on historiographical methods of analysis and interpretations of video testimony from Holocaust survivors.

This chapter will reflect upon historico-philosophical questions in regards to violent experience, will try to formulate a definition of those experiences and identify the impact of these definitions upon historiographical investigation. Next, it will forge a bridge to trauma concepts in psychoanalysis, and put forth the question "How can historiography benefit from psychoanalytic contributions to the Holocaust testimony debate?" Finally, I will try to find out what historiography can contribute, in particular, to a broader understanding of video testimony from survivors of genocidal events, and why it makes sense for historiography to concern itself with the video testimony of survivors.

The witness in the center of the picture

Video testimonies from Holocaust survivors as we know them, the camera focused on the survivor, the interviewer often invisible, with little movement, put the testifying person in the center (cf. Knopp, Schulze, & Eusterschulte, 2016; Dayan, 2017). All other aspects of this complex source seem to be arranged around this dominating figure. Unusually for the historian, the information is not written but audible and visible, it is experiential.

Hence, the nature of the video testimony itself already suggests that it is not merely about objective and cognitive content. If it were only about the factual content of the witnesses' utterances, a written record would simply be able to replace the video testimony (Young, 1992, 245–246; Liebsch, 2016, 56). The bottom line is in the act of witnessing itself, which is documented and furthermore continued in the video. As the philosopher Burkhard Liebsch (2016) puts it:

> Certainly, it shatters *what* witnesses of a devastating, disastrous destruction policy and genocidal practices have to say. But it is precisely the incarnate presence of the witnesses, who survived this violence, although its devastating shadow has fallen upon them, what the secondary witnesses affects here, from which they have to assume even that they would have probably not survived it; even more: it is to survive basically by anyone, if it is true, what is witnessed: that the violence in question meant nothing less than the radical disaster of any human world. (p. 56; trans. S.K.)

The witness, indeed the center of video testimony, also reminds me of a particular perception of historical understanding, highlighted by philosophers like Benjamin (1974/2003), Liebsch (1999), and Ricœur (2004). In the evidence of the personal appearance of the testifying survivor, the historical subject can be identified as a history-stricken human being, susceptible (to attacks), vulnerable, and mortal, reminding us that history is always the history of mortals. Shmuel B. is an old man in a hospital. His being old and being a patient emphasize his vulnerability. His frequent smiling, his black cap, set at a rakish angle, and his somewhat bulky body seem to disguise his brittleness. But his glance, the sound of his voice and his body language, as well as his repeated assuring that nothing ever happened, speak volumes.

Video testimony as a historical source shows the survivor as author of his or her testimony, and as a historical subject at the same time. The person we are looking at and listening to is both, past and present, a remembered past in the present. But there is a difficulty in defining the author of the testimony, which lies in the evolution and interpretation of memory, as, especially when it comes to trauma, it is "not a single-persons-phenomenon" (Hamburger, 2017). The testimony is not just shaped by the witness but also by the listener, the interviewer, and furthermore, by the later recipient(s) of this testimony. This kind of historical source unfolds while being read, while being interpreted.

Experiences of disaster, trauma, and testimony

In the following passages the issue of experiences will be broached, at whose core lies an increased kind of violence, which does not only injure, but also destroys (Liebsch, 2016, 43). These experiences refer to forms of negativity like pain and distress, and they take on the perspective of the suffering. "That means . . . that in order to understand violence, the perspective of suffering should be taken into account as fundamental and may neither be overlooked nor subordinated" (Delhom, 2003, 63–64). But in the video testimony the violence is invisible at first glance (Liebsch, 2016) and it is only through the course of the testimonial process that it manifests itself between the people involved, and initiates a collapse of communication and social bond. Referring to Merleau-Ponty's *Phenomenology of Perception* (1945/2012), Grüny (2003, 81) describes this collapse as a kind of "lesson" taught by the actions of a torturer.

> The "Lesson" consists precisely in this detachment from all respects of everyday life, in the destruction of the "living communication with the world," within which a sense of elementary physicality right through to verbal communication can take place. This staging of senselessness as sense, as one might call it, is a materialization, a total access and a fleshing out into an embodiment (*Verfleischlichung*) at the extreme limits of experience and the social. It forms the core of the logic of torture. (ibid.; transl. S. K.)

Experiences of brute force compromise the integrity and identity of a person and subsequently the ability to transmit and tell, to testify; they compromise the "authority," the "authorship" of a person, and they mark a "crisis of witnessing" (Felman & Laub, 1992). What Grüny describes here recalls the explorations of Laub about the trauma phenomenon, insisting on the termination of dialog between the tormentor and the victim in the outcome of violence; the relentless proceedings of the torturer in spite of the victim's plea for life (Laub, 2016, 102). Using the video testimony of Leon S. (1980) as an example, the witness remembers his handicapped grandmother asking his cousin for help to get into the train for deportation. One of the German soldiers who understood Polish answered "Yes, I will help," and took his gun and shot her. Leon describes a jarring lack of humanity. A defenseless woman asks for help and the help is expressed by a killing action. This testimony shows precisely what Grüny and Laub mean when they describe the violence of torture and trauma with the fundamental destruction of communication and the loss of an inner resonating other (the "internal Thou"; Laub, 2016). The collapse of interhuman communication and verbal representation correlates with the materialization and embodiment of violent experience.

From birth, every human being is exposed to the harshness of the world and is at the mercy of a care taking person. With regard to an ontological state of said exposure, experience can be generally considered as preempting self and challenging the subsequent answers, enabling a person to perceive what has happened to them. From this perspective, experience has a temporal structure and requires a responsive subject; it indicates an empathic dimension and turns out to be closely related to the attendance of a resonating other. This idea of experience is based on a concept of interpersonal approachability and responsiveness, and constitutes the human being as ethical subject, as responsible for the other. This responsibility in turn is given by the other and enables one to live an ethical life, actively involved in an interhuman social bond; it adds an ethical sense to human subjectivity and life (Liebsch, 2014, 43). Although, as Liebsch notes elsewhere (Liebsch, 2014, 31; 2016, 44), this idea clearly contradicts the self-image of enlightened Western civilizations, which—on the basis of a strong and self-determined individual—promotes social progress and freedom from pain and distress. Therefore, human subjectivity and experience appear linked to the idea of the other. And the idea of responsive subjectivity in temporally structured process of experiencing goes hand in hand with conceptions of witnessing and testimony. Experiences, however, are overwhelming, and testimony threatens to break down, when the responsive subject fails, when no answer can be given, and the person finds herself helpless (cf. Liebsch, 2014, 45).

When it comes to experiences of disastrous violence and their representations, should one not distinguish between different witnesses and processes of witnessing? Can a person bear witness to her own experiences of suffered violence? The act of witnessing is compromised until a testimony from secondary witnesses is made. The primary witness is then accredited and the testimony authenticated, while at the same time the suffering of this primary witness is vouched for externally. In the idea of secondary and tertiary witnessing, these matters are addressed exactly. The famous Celan poem "Aschenglorie" ("Ash glory"; 1967/2005) results in referring to the demands on secondary and tertiary witnessing, as well as to the ideas on the claim of the other, and the resulting responsibility for the other thereby implied, to ethical subjectivity and finally to the task of witnessing the truth of human experience.

Memory, affect, and mourning in the face of traumatic experience

When experiences of violence are categorized as traumatic and as such come heavily weighted, one of the central aspects to deal with is affect. Aleida Assmann has argued convincingly that affect and symbols function as sta-bilizers of memory (Assmann, 1998). We remember biographical situations layered with strong emotions particularly well. The ability to remember autobiographical situations increases with the power of affect that is related to it. We remember moments in our life as extraordinary because they were (emotionally) extraordinary. But once the emotion is too strong or unbear-able, the experience is felt on a physical level. The overwhelming presence of corporeal experience precludes memory and divides it into individual splinters whose connection is hard to reconstruct. By affect and dissociation, this phenomenon of trauma has a destabilizing effect on memories.

> If the affect exceeds a conducive measure and turns into an excess, then it does not stabilize memories but smashes them. This is the case with trauma, which makes the body directly to an imprinting surface and it deprives the experience of the linguistic and interpretive pro-cessing of it. Trauma, that is the impossibility of narration. Trauma and symbol are in mutual exclusivity opposite; physical force and con-structive sense seem to be the extremes between which our memories move. (Assmann, 1998, 151; trans. S.K.)

With regards to experiences of violence, the most important affect is angst against a background of absolute powerlessness. Furthermore, the impact of affect on memory reverberates in Ricœur's dictum of "the living experience of the injury that happens to you in the process of history-making" (Ricœur, 2002, 41; trans. S. K.). "Living experience" implicitly refers to emotions at the core of human memories. For the carrier of the memory, the direct corporeal, bodily, and sensual emotion that comes along with memories—feelings of anxiety, relief, anger, happiness, contentment, and so on—is indisputable. It immediately affects the understanding of what is the authenticity (truthfulness) of memories. "The application of this living reference to the past is also of historical value" (Assmann, 1998, 141; trans. S. K.).

The way Shmuel B. is talking, his bodily expressions, the fragmentation of his narrative, his ways of reacting to the interviewer, the interpersonal dynamics during the interview, all of this has been described as trauma-related, and identified as psychic trauma. It is another representation of vulnerability, it tells us of another time: a person who was part of history shows great hurt. Trauma first marks tangibility (*Affizierbarkeit*), and second, it highlights the absence of a meaningful other.

Mourning and trauma both circulate around the absence of a self-constituting other. Both are reactions and reflections to a severe loss that includes parts of identity and that cannot be realigned. The trauma-reaction fails in processing loss and reintegrating it into a reorganized self. The experience of loss seems to reserve the absence of the other in an empty space. No resonance, no reverberation can fill this vacancy. No integration of self-identity is possible; on the contrary, the vacancy seems to corrode the texture of identity.

Mourning, however, is understood as a creative and productive way of coping with loss, of working it through until, finally, it can be assimilated into the self-consciousness. The loss and the absence are confined, as if with a fence, which makes it less threatening to the self. But, and this is what makes the concept of mourning so interesting in this context, mourning recognizes and accepts the loss and the absence of the other. Mourning neither ignores nor suppresses the existential loss and the absence; on the contrary, it actively concentrates on it in order to reintegrate it into meaningful self-perception. Concerning video testimony from Holocaust survivors as sources of historical research, it may therefore be beneficial to think of "historical thinking as *Trauerarbeit*," as historian Jörn Rüsen suggested (Rüsen, 2005, 147; see also Rüsen, 2001). A manifestation of mourning may be the need to collect video testimonies from Holocaust survivors as archival artifacts, in order to preserve their memories and perpetuate the survivor's memory. The survivor in turn represents those who have died, in the sense that he or she was supposed to have died like the others. I therefore stick with the idea that history that deals with survivors deals equally with mourning (Liebsch, 2006).

The talk of trauma in survivors' testimonies emphasizes the medical and psychological aspects in the testimony. In contrast to psychoanalytic and psychological discourses, historians justifiably urge caution not to pathologize and medicalize the witnesses (Brunner, 2012). On the other hand, signs of trauma should not be marginalized and shifted outside historians' research responsibilities (Trezise, 2008, 2013). This approach would miss the opportunity to realize that manifestations of trauma also belong to the linguistic signs and symbols, and non-verbal representations that need to be decrypted and interpreted. Although it is sometimes helpful not to use terms that overload the subject, to avoid big concepts, where a little goes a long way, in the case of Shmuel B. it makes sense to use the trauma concept, even from a historian's point of view. This acknowledges the fact that Shmuel B. was a patient in a hospital at the time of the interview, that he had been diagnosed as mentally ill, and it acknowledges that this "medical landscape" shapes the source in several ways. As it turns out, Holocaust survivors in psychiatric institutions in Israel have their own, rather upsetting, history of marginalization (Zalashik, 2012, 2017). Furthermore, it is worthwhile recognizing the moments of loss and absence, which can be marked in the manifestations of trauma in this video testimony.

Witnessing witnessing in historiography

The identification of (invisible) violence in video testimony from Holocaust survivors comes with a task to observe, to construe, and finally to describe violence *as* violence, to make it visible and to articulate it. The work of the historian in the face of video testimony is, in this sense, a visual and conceptual illustration of invisible violence through historically informed interpretations of the interview passages, which articulate and make discernible manifestations of violence in the testimony (Liebsch, 2016, 45–46; Laub, 2017b).

The concepts of historiography and history raise theoretical issues concerning methods and analytical instruments. In other words, how can historians read sources of loss and destruction, sources of trauma? If testimony of traumatized survivors is about moments and experiences of destruction, "the deconstruction of all reference points . . . of total estrangement, of absolute aloneness with regard to all the ties that, up to that point, were familiar" (Davoine & Gaudillière, 2004, xxviii), how is it to be described? Moments excised from history are actualized in the present in survivor testimony, in moments of bearing witness.

As this investigation is focused on the experiences of one particular witness Shmuel B., a microscopic view of "thick descriptions" (Geertz, 1973), of concrete situations appears to make sense. A microscopic approach, a combination of close description and reflection can contribute language that helps illustrate, sometimes for the first time, what the witness is struggling with (Grüny, 2003).

At this point I feel it important to mention the alleged unrepresentability and voicelessness in view of the Shoah in relation to video testimonies (Lyotard, 1983/1988). Important though it is to acknowledge that, contrary to the topic of unrepresentability, tens of thousands of survivors, as well as already many of those who did not survive, have created testimonials, which include an infinite variety of descriptions of human experience. As with more than 100,000 testimonies kept in (video) archives worldwide, a tremendous effort has been made to ultimately counteract the perpetrators' initial intention to silence their victims and prevent witnessing.

The testimonies of the survivors of the Shoah involve at least two epistemological levels. Regarded as a historical source, the historian must question the verifiable data in order to reconstruct actual facts of the past. At this level, the testimony of Shmuel B. contains a wealth of information and makes it possible to trace on a micro-historical level the histories of persecution and extermination of Jews in Bessarabia and Transnistria between 1941 and 1944, and furthermore, a history of migration and integration into the newly built State of Israel of Romanian-Jewish survivors in the decades following World War II (Knopp, 2016). It is part of the process of accreditation and verification to correlate the testimony with other sources and review its information content critically. This level of analysis and interpretation is based on the assumption that some of the memories of the witness, as set out in the testimony, refer to verifiable historical events, that is, that they are credible by the standards of historical knowledge extraction.

A second dimension of the understanding of testimony, in turn, refers to the portion of memory that is valid, albeit seemingly independent of external verification, although some in the area of oral-history research (and myself) would disagree. Ricœur has discussed the concept of trust based on the questions regarding modes of representation in historiography (Ricœur, 2002, 13). He powerfully argues for the idea that in the case of contemporary witnesses—contrary to the usual critical-hermeneutic work practice of historians—the witness, in the first instance, must be met with confidence. In video testimony work with Holocaust survivors, historians must process empathically and intersubjectively and create a situation of interpersonal trust, whilst maintaining the ability to process and examine critically in equal measures (Assmann, 1998, 142).

What makes dealing with verbal memory in testimonies so difficult for historians, among others, is essentially the complex relationship between memory and evidence. The question of the reliability of memories must differentiate between the cognitive levels of memory; between truth and veracity, between externally verifiable biographical facts and the subjectively experienced world of perception. The second (subjective) level of memories concerns the relationship that the witnesses maintain with their, potentially traumatic, past. But does this concept work at all? Is there not an "objective, empirically verified world of experience" (Assmann, 1998, 141; trans. S. K.)? What is important to hold on to is that memories do not (only) relate to the structure of an outer reality, but also to the structure of an inner reality, the world of experience.

Historiographical investigation of video testimonies from Holocaust survivors can draw on methodical resources of oral-history research. Referring to Lutz Niethammer, a prominent representative of German oral-history research, Assmann points out three crucial aspects concerning analysis of commemorative sources. Firstly, striking discrepancies between strong emphasis or specific attention to detail in the witnesses' narrative on the one hand and the concrete situation of testimony (situational framing) on the other hand, indicate spontaneous and authentic, albeit encapsulated, commemorative content. Secondly, oral-history research relies on the assumption that everyday life lingers in the memory through routine and repetition. For lack of thematization and interpretation, it remains in a state of latency, which keeps memory from alteration. Thirdly, and in stark contrast, the strong shaping of memory indicates subsequent conversions through later processing of experiences and adaption to common modes and structures of understanding. For oral-history research, the reliability and trustworthiness of memory is immediately interrelated with its state of preservation. Also for historians, those memories that are most viable are those which are least consciously affected and which are stabilized throughout their affective impact and state of latency (Assmann, 1998, 142).

In this context, it should be noted that the mental suffering of the witness does not constitute a criterion for the exclusion of evidence in the testimony. That the witness at the time of the interview had been a patient in a psychiatric facility in Israel for decades, allows presumptions about his mental state, and its relationship to the past. However, a categorization with respect to his credibility is neither possible nor sensible. Stigmatization must also not be turned into an overevaluation of disease and a generalization of the victim status. Davoine and Gaudillère even emphasize that "madness" can be considered as a form of social bond in an extreme situation, "in which the breakdown of all reference points gives rise to links outside the norm" (Gaudillère & Davoine, 2004, xxii). Patients—like Shmuel B.—as they explain elsewhere, "teach us that this absence of boundaries is the source of their ability to bear witness to the stories that have been erased from history, the history of breakdowns in the social link, whose disaster they reveal at the price of their own identity" (Gaudillère & Davoine, 2004, xxi–xxii). Liebsch has also emphasized the close connection of suffering to pathology. The pathological would be imagined as a more or less profound impairment of a vital and rational normality. This normality seems therefore to owe neither suffering nor even the pathological the slightest thing (Liebsch, 2014, 31). Furthermore, Jens Brockmeier underlines the productive power that is inherent in the narratives of the traumatized and opposes a characterization of these narratives as mere deficit. He calls also for a critical appreciation of what is at first glance usually perceived as deficient trauma narratives and encourages a break away from conventional notions of narrative structures (Brockmeier, 2008; Brockmeier & Medved, 2010).

Holocaust testimony and negativity

The testimony of Shmuel B. is unforgiving and irreconcilable, desolate, and challenging with respect to all common categories that are usually discussed in regard to survivor testimony, like narration, listening, or survivor status. It is almost unbearable. It gives no comfort. Narration, reverberation, and communication constantly dry up and fail (Laub, 2017a). There is loneliness and desolation, there is disaster and calamity imprinted on the mind (Blanchot, 1980). For the historian, the testimony barely gives the opportunity to palliate or colour the landscapes of genocidal experience that occur in the narratives. Listening to Shmuel B.'s testimony feels like there is nothing left, like it is always ending. As distinguishable from many other testimonies of Holocaust survivors the Shmuel B. testimony is not about survival; it is about loss, death, unbearable misery; it is about the insufferableness of becoming a witness of mass violence, about total collapse and despair. The testimony, in its fragmentation and mirrored shards of memory, is in a shattered state, in a form of devastation. It is not just the words or their meanings that explain or represent devastation; it is the form of the testimony itself.

In recognition of disastrous testimony Liebsch reasons: "Perhaps pain and violence are generally discredited unjustly and are still misunderstood in this way as communicative possibilities of injured life which must continually struggle for its precarious, never definitively secured *livability* and thereby often experiences itself as *dependent on pain and violence*" (Liebsch, 2014, 12; trans. S. K.). Thus, testimonies teach us the fractured subtleties of "injured life," and of death, as he posits:

> In a mass death, the victims are not only "uncounted," but also *uncountable*; not because so many perished without a witness, without leaving a trace, or because one would have to count individual death ad nauseum, but because only the vessel perished. The death of every other cannot be summed up. Each other "died a different death," found Timothy Snyder. And this difference can't be shown by any life account or mortality rate table. Everyone perishes *in another way*. Everyone also perishes *as another*. This gives us no deeper insight into comparative research on violence and related statistics, but only *the testified and narrated death of others as others*. And this death . . . in turn will be brought close to us only thanks to the witness of others who make us in turn to witnesses, in order to transfer in this way their testimony historically. (Liebsch, 2016, 47; transl. S. K.)

Conclusions

The importance of contemporary witnesses was long minimized in historical science. Only few researchers such as Reinhart Koselleck (2003) revalued contemporary witnesses and their testimonies for the study of history in a systematic way, while philosopher Paul Ricœur (1998) laid the theoretical foundations for history in the "era of the witness" (Wieviorka, 2006). What then is the significance of these interviews with survivors of the Shoah for the science of history, especially if they are as convoluted as the Shmuel B. testimony? The analytical and interpretative work of the historian can be described as a dialogical function in relation to the testimony. In this form, it contributes to a historical understanding in genocidal violence that—without these interpretive articulations—would often remain invisible. The importance of testimonies for the study of history is again on two levels: firstly, a broader recognition, understanding and comprehension of historical violence, as tacit violence often eludes even the work of scientific comprehension; second, the positioning of historical science as a socially relevant and key discipline for the recognition and processing of socially effective collective experiences of violence.

Given the virtually monumental number of archived testimonies, is it sensible to focus on one single testimony? This approach is certainly reminiscent of the psychoanalytical practice of case studies. But bringing a more contextual impact, I agree with Johanna Bodenstab (2015, 19–20), who chose to study the "singularity of individual life stories" in contrast to the unification and victimization of Jews during the Holocaust. In the appreciation of the single testimony, the claim is virtually expressed to accord each victim a dignity that threatens to disappear without a trace in statistical body counts (Liebsch, 2016, 47). Besides which, the study of the single testimony allows an in-depth interdisciplinary dialog and collective interpretation (Knopp, Schulze, & Eusterschulte, 2016). As such, this approach contributes to the observation of Felman (1992, 41) that testimonies from Holocaust survivors have a historical, a clinical, and a poetical dimension; therefore, all of those three dimensions need to be regarded in order to grasp the complexity of testimony of trauma.

References

Assmann, A. (1998). Stabilisatoren der Erinnerung: Affekt, Symbol, Trauma. In J. Rüsen & J. Straub (Eds.), *Die dunkle Spur der Vergangenheit. Psychoanalytische Zugänge zum Geschichtsbewusstsein* (pp. 131–152). Frankfurt am Main: Suhrkamp.

Benjamin, W. (2003). On the concept of history. In H. Eiland & M. W. Jennings (Eds.), *Selected Writings: 1938–1940*, Vol. 4 (E. Jephcott et al., Trans.). Cambridge MA: The Belknap Press of Harvard University Press. (Original work published 1974)

Benz, W. (2009). Rumänien und der Holocaust. In W. Benz & B. Mihok (Eds.), *Holocaust an der Peripherie. Judenpolitik und Judenmord in Rumänien und Transnistrien 1940–1944* (pp. 11–30). Berlin: Metropol.

Blanchot, M. (1980). *L'Ecriture du désastre*. Paris: Gallimard.

Bodenstab, J. (2015). *Dramen der Verlorenheit: Mutter-Tochter-Beziehungen in der Shoah. Zur Rezeption und zur narrativen Gestalt traumatischer Erfahrungen in Videozeugnissen*. Göttingen: Vandenhoeck & Ruprecht.

Brockmeier, J. (2008). Language, experience, and the "traumatic gap": How to talk about 9/11? In L. C. Hyvén & J. Brockmeier (Eds.), *Health, illness, and culture: Broken narratives* (pp. 16–35). New York: Routledge.

Brockmeier, J., & Medved, M. (2010). Weird stories: Brain, mind, and self. In M. Hyvärinen, L.-C. Hydén, M. Saarenheimo, & M. Tamboukou (Eds.), *Beyond narrative coherence* (pp. 17–32). Amsterdam and Philadelphia, PA: John Benjamins.

Brunner, J. (2012). Medikalisierte Zeugenschaft. Trauma, Institutionen, Nachträglichkeit. In M. Sabrow & N. Frei (Eds.), *Die Geburt des Zeitzeugen nach 1945* (pp. 93–110). Göttingen: Wallstein.

Celan, P. (2005). *Paul Celan: Selections* (Pierre Joris, Trans.) (pp. 104–105). Berkeley, CA: University of California Press. (Original work published 1967)

Davoine, F., & Gaudillère, J.-M. (2004). *History beyond trauma: Whereof one cannot speak, thereof one cannot stay silent*. New York: Other Press.

Dayan, D. (2017). Visible witness: Watching the footprints of trauma. This volume, chapter 8.

Delhom, P. (2003). Erlittene Gewalt verstehen. In B. Liebsch & D. Mensink (Eds.), *Gewalt Verstehen* (pp. 59–77). Berlin: Akademie.

Felman, S. (1992). Education and crisis, or the vicissitutes of teaching. In S. Felman & D. Laub (Eds.), *Testimony: Crises of witnessing in literature, psychoanalysis, and history* (pp. 1–56). New York: Routledge.

Felman, S., & Laub, D. (1992). *Testimony: Crises of witnessing in literature, psychoanalysis, and history*. New York: Routledge.

Friedländer, S. (2007a). *The years of extermination: Nazi Germany and the Jews 1939–1945*, Vol. 2. London: HarperCollins.

Friedländer, S. (2007b). *Den Holocaust beschreiben: Auf dem Weg zu einer integrierten Geschichte*. Göttingen: Wallstein.

Geertz, C. (1973). Thick description: Toward an interpretive theory of culture. In *The Interpretation of cultures: Selected essays* (pp. 3–30). New York: Basic Books,.

Grüny, C. (2003). Zur Logik der Folter. In B. Liebsch & D. Mensink (Eds.), *Gewalt verstehen* (pp. 79–115). Berlin: Akademie.

Hamburger, A. (2017). Refracted attunement, affective resonance: Scenic-narrative microanalysis of entangled presence in a Holocaust survivor's testimony. This volume, chapter 21.

Ioanid, R. (2000). *The Holocaust in Romania: The destruction of Jews and Gypsies under the Antonescu Regime, 1940–1944*. Chicago: Ivan R. Dee.

Knopp, S., Schulze, S., & Eusterschulte, A. (Eds.) (2016). *Videographierte Zeugenschaft: Geisteswissenschaften im Dialog mit dem Zeugen.* Weilerswist: Velbrück Wissenschaft.

Koselleck, R. (2003). *Zeitschichten. Studien zur Historik.* Frankfurt am Main: Suhrkamp.

Laub, D. (2016). Re-establishing the internal "Thou" in Testimony of Trauma. In S. Knopp, S. Schulze, & A. Eusterschulte (Eds.), *Videographierte Zeugenschaft: Geisteswissenschaften im Dialog mit dem Zeugen.* Weilerswist: Velbrück Wissenschaft.

Laub, D. (2017a). Introduction to this volume.

Laub, D. (2017b). Discussion of Bodenstab, Knopp, and Hamburger. This volume, chapter 22.

Leon S. (1980). *Video recording of Leon S.* Holocaust Video Testimony HVT-45. Fortunoff Video Archive. Yale University, New Haven, CT.

Liebsch, B. (1999). *Geschichte als Antwort und Versprechen.* Freiburg and Munich: Alber.

Liebsch, B. (2006). *Revisionen der Trauer. In philosophischen, geschichtlichen, psychoanalytischen und ästhetischen Perspektiven.* Weilerswist: Velbrück Wissenschaft.

Liebsch, B. (2014). *Verletztes Leben. Studien zur Affirmation von Schmerz und Gewalt im gegenwärtigen Denken* (*Graue Reihe* 63). Zug, Schweiz: Die Graue Edition.

Liebsch, B. (2016). Unsichtbare Gewalt: Bezeugung, Aufzeichnung, Überlieferung und Techniken der Visualisierung. In S. Knopp, S. Schulze, & A. Eusterschulte (Eds.), *Videographierte Zeugenschaft: Geisteswissenschaften im Dialog mit dem Zeugen.* Weilerswist: Velbrück Wissenschaft.

Lyotard, J.-F. (1988). *The Differend: Phrases in dispute* (G. Van Den Abbeele, Trans.). Minneapolis: University of Minnesota Press. (Original work published 1983)

Merleau-Ponty, M. (2012). *Phenomenology of perception* (D. A. Landes, Trans.). New York: Routledge. (Original work published 1945)

Ricœur, P. (1998). *Das Rätsel der Vergangenheit. Erinnern—Vergessen—Verzeihen (Vortrag in Essen).* Göttingen: Wallstein.

Ricœur, P. (2002). *Geschichtsschreibung und Repräsentation der Vergangenheit.* Münster, Hamburg and London: Lit Verlag.

Ricœur, P. (2004). *Memory, history, forgetting* (K. Blamey & D. Pellauer, Trans.). Chicago: University of Chicago Press. (Original work published 2000)

Rüsen, J. (2001). *Zerbrechende Zeit: Über den Sinn der Geschichte.* Cologne and Weimar: Böhlau.

Rüsen, J. (2005). *History: narration—interpretation—orientation* (*Making sense of history*, Vol. 2). New York, Oxford: Berghahn Books.

Trezise, T. (2008). Between history and psychoanalysis: A case study in the reception of Holocaust survivor testimony. *History & Memory, 20*(1), 7–47.

Trezise, T. (2013). *Witnessing witnessing: On the reception of Holocaust survivor testimony*. New York: Fordham University Press.

Wieviorka, A. (2006). *The era of the witness* (J. Stark, Trans.). Ithaca, NY: Cornell University Press. (Original work published 2002)

Young, J. E. (1992). Video- und Filmzeugnisse des Holocaust. Die Dokumentierung des Zeugnisses. In J. E. Young (Ed.), *Beschreiben des Holocaust. Darstellung und Folgen der Interpretation* (pp. 243–265). Frankfurt am Main: Suhrkamp.

Zalashik, R. (2012). *Das unselige Erbe. Die Geschichte der Psychiatrie in Palästina und Israel*. Frankfurt am Main and New York: Campus.

Zalashik, R. (2017). The psychiatrically hospitalized survivors in Israel: A historical overview. This volume, chapter 11.

Chapter 10

Scenic-narrative microanalysis

Controlled psychoanalytic assessment of session videos or transcripts as a transparent qualitative research instrument[1]

Andreas Hamburger

The method described in this chapter builds upon psychoanalytic understanding, but nevertheless tries to meet the justified claims of both analytic and non-analytic scholars to transparency and efforts for validation. Its three constituents—the scenic, the narrative, and the microanalytic approach—will be discussed in the following sections, as well as the specific nature of video data. The basic element of the method is 'scenic understanding,' which has been the gold standard and core of clinical experience in relational psychoanalysis for about seven decades now, and has widely replaced a one-body psychological, top-down interpretation in psychoanalytic practice. The narrative element of the method reflects the fact that human mental life is situated in interaction as well as in time, thus formed by and actively forming narrative processes. A case example presented in this volume (Hamburger, 2017b) may illustrate the method's application in an interview of a Holocaust survivor, showing the importance of understanding the breakdown of the narrative function in the survivor's mental life in relation to the unconscious response of the interacting listener. Third, the microanalytic aspect of the approach connects it to some recent developments in qualitative research, where detailed analysis of selected paradigmatic sequences serves to indicate more subtle properties of the material than otherwise shown by data analyses conducted on a higher level of abstraction. Finally, the application of the method to videotaped interviews requires additional consideration.

Elements of scenic-narrative microanalysis

Psychoanalysis has been a pioneering discipline in the interpretation of human behavior and experience. It combines a detailed inspection of individual mental processes in hundreds of sessions following the detailed procedure of psychoanalytic technique. However, it has not been unanimously regarded as research, as the opacity of the psychoanalytic situation itself, usually poorly and selectively documented, has not really encouraged sceptics to follow the sometimes complicated and individualized clinical conclusions. Despite its lack of transparency and simplicity, however, these conclusions have widely inspired research on the processes and conditions of mental life, and have even divided it ideologically, serving as a shining example of single case research for its admirers or as a horrifying example of arbitrariness for its adversaries.

However, in the meantime, things have changed. The use of audio- and videography has improved the documentation of psychoanalytic sessions, and progress in qualitative research has provided the background for a closer assessment of the psychoanalytic experience. Scenic-narrative microanalysis (SNMA) is one way among others to enhance the transparency and reduce the arbitrariness of psychoanalytic interpretation, without disturbing the unfolding of the process itself. As a research approach based on re-analysis, scenic-narrative microanalysis does not (or minimally) interfere(s) with the analytic process, while still allowing for a detailed, transparent, and replicable research process.

Scenic understanding as a means of psychoanalytic research

Sigmund Freud's notion of the "inseparable bond between cure and research" (Freud, 1926/1959, 255) has sometimes been understood to mean that clinical experience itself was meant to replace confirmative research. Quite the opposite: Freud's methodological education in neuropathology enabled him to understand the psychoanalytic situation as a site of detailed observation, allowing for the interpolation of "connecting links" (Freud, 1917/1953, 387) that had to be confirmed by eliciting further associations and memories; and, as in his former profession of neuropathology, he expected that aggregations of such single case studies would lead, in the long run, to an overall theory. This form of aggregated single case studies is what Freud meant by "inseparable bond": only the psychoanalytic process provides the data and the individual explanation of the personal symptom—and only the additive process of comparative casuistics links these single case hypotheses to theories of a higher order (cf. Leuzinger-Bohleber & Fischmann, 2006; Jüttemann, 2009; Desmet et al., 2013).

Decades later, the psychoanalytic research paradigm had changed from the pathological to a more interactive understanding. One prominent example of the relational research paradigm in modern psychoanalysis is Georges Devereux' Book *From Anxiety to Method in the Behavioral Sciences* (1967), which developed the anthropological methodology of countertransference-based field research. Both Freud's and Devereux' strategies implied what we call today a mixed-method approach, but Devereux' approach is marked by a significant difference to Freud's in that it concentrates on the countertransference of the researcher as a leading and reliable data source. It parallels the concept of 'scenic understanding' as developed in the later Frankfurt School in Germany in the 1970s. Scenic-narrative microanalysis builds on these paradigms and reflects the fact that psychoanalysis has in the meanwhile developed even further towards intersubjective theory and practice (Kirshner, 2004, 2011), and it connects the paradigms to the methodology of qualitative and especially hermeneutic research approaches that have blossomed since this period (Lorenzer, 1970, 1986; Flick, 2009). However, qualitative research cannot simply incorporate the concept of countertransference; a broader basis, rooting in a relational or interpersonal approach to psychoanalysis is indispensable (Holmes, 2014).

Scenic-narrative microanalysis assumes as a principle that meaning itself, and not only in the field of human psychology, is a relational phe-nomenon. Behavior never has a significance 'in itself,' but is understood and responded to in a social context and environment. The same applies to the more intra-psychic levels of conscious, preconscious and even uncon-scious mental life. The child develops its representational world and the attunement and regulation of its needs and self-concepts in close contact with a surrounding environment, embedded in a cultural context.

Psychoanalysis in its new understanding has consequently become a relational mode of experience, its interpretations and findings being related to the interactive context of the consulting room. The former picture of the analyst as an expert for the reconstruction of drive vicissitudes has given way to the analyst as a present Meaningful Other, evenly exposed to expe-riences of defense and transference, but able to absorb and integrate them in a productive and helpful way, so as to become able to impart the fruits of his self-analytical process to the patient.[2]

The same is true for psychoanalytic researchers. Their work is never dis-engaged from its subject; the researcher is part of the same society, living the same defensive construction of the world as the social phenomenon he is trying to investigate. Psychoanalytic research in this sense is based on ongoing self-analysis, including the reflection on counter-transference processes, very much like clinical practice itself. Scenic microanalysis includes an important trait of psychoanalytic hermeneutic in-depth analysis: a detailed analysis of readers' reactions to the texts (i.e., 'reader transference'). However, in the re-assessment of psychoanalytic situations, interpretive processes take place on three levels:

1 The expert research team's reactions to the transcribed text and/or video.
2 The interviewer's reactions within the psychoanalytic situation, his interactions with the interviewee.
3 The account of the interviewee himself, representing his interpretation of the narrated experiences.

This method has been developed explicitly since 2005 in the context of the Yale video testimony study (Laub and others), building on former analyses of literary and dream narratives (Hamburger, 1998a, 1998b, 2003a, 2006a, 2006b). It builds upon a hermeneutic procedure guided by Lorenzer's (1986) "cultural analysis," which is based on a repeated oscillation between the positions of participant and reflecting psychoanalyst. In the participant position, the analyst introspectively observes his own transference as a recipient of the text; in the reflecting position, he connects this observed participation to the microstructure of the text. This hermeneutic method can be applied to transcripts of psychoanalytic sessions and interviews (Hamburger, 1998b, 2015). It draws specifically on the temporal dimension of the listening process (Hamburger, 2006b, 2009, 2013b).

Narrative analysis: temporality of the interpersonal mind

Scenic-narrative microanalysis is not only based, in principle, on mental data; since we are dealing with human mental life, these data are also narrative in structure.

The narrative approach, a paradigm shift in many fields of the human sciences, has been heatedly discussed in psychoanalysis (e.g., Spence, 1982; Mitchell, 1988; Ahumada, 1994; Govrin, 2006). It conceptualizes mental life as an ongoing process of narration. "The 'Ego' is the narrator, the 'Self' the protagonist of a narrative, constantly retold in a conscious and unconscious stream of phantasy" (Hamburger, 1998a, 229), and it corresponds to a trend in psychoanalysis to model mental life less as a physiological 'apparatus' and more as an aesthetic process. Mental life is in itself an interpretive process, and as such is to be described in terms of hermeneutics (cf. Hamburger, 1987, 305–348; 1998a).

In a social constructivist key, narrated meaning is produced in a constitutive "relational scenario" (Gergen, 1994). Therefore, to understand the narrative process means to reflect one's own listening position. The definition of the researcher as a listener reflecting his listening makes quite clear how closely the process of social research can be compared to the analytic process itself.

In this way, the concept of mental life as narrative leads to methodological consequences. If we adopt this viewpoint, mental life has to be regarded as basically dialogic and sequential, that is, meaningfully ordered in shared time. This has consequences for data analysis in scenic-narrative microanalysis. Rather than assessing characteristic psychological features of the speakers by additive item-sampling, a dynamic and dialogic approach aims at reconstructing the dynamic process of the dialog. In this respect, scenic-narrative microanalysis contradicts most methods of qualitative analysis in the field of clinical research, for instance CCCP (Luborsky & Crits-Christoph, 1990), which are based on additions of coded prominent traits of the material, and thus of the patient. This is extremely helpful for comparing diagnoses and therapy processes over time; it does not help, however, in reconstructing the microstructure of a single session.

Microanalysis: a detailed qualitative research strategy

Since the end of the 1960s, qualitative research strategies have gained enormous importance in the social and human sciences, especially in psychology, in comparison to the former predominance of quantitative approaches. 'Scientism,' having been the paradigm for some decades, with its demand for a unified science on the model of physics, had led to research methods in psychotherapy research inappropriate for (and thus hindering for some time) active research in psychoanalytic therapy (cf. Hamburger & Mertens, 2004). Modern qualitative social research has broadened into many different working areas and methodological approaches, such as

Conversation and Discourse Analysis (cf. Sidnell & Stivers, 2013). In previous psychoanalytically inspired narrative analyses (e.g., Gergen & Gergen 1986; Gergen, 1994; cf. Hamburger, 1998a, 1998b), the data were reconstructed as a subjective, biographical construct. Characteristics of the texts' unique identity—for example, turn-taking phenomena, breaks in the narrative, and signs of relatedness or interruptions in relatedness—are described and interpreted, using the introspective description of the interpreter's own countertransference reactions.

Video data: beyond the 'talking cure'

Like the analysis of a narrative text, the analysis of a video interview can be conducted by reflecting and explicating the listening or viewing process, thus providing a key to the comprehension and description of the interview process itself. However, video documentation differs in more than one way from audio-documented sessions.

Any kind of recording is of course an intervention in the psychoanalytic frame. It is like a leak, transcending the sheltering walls of the consulting room, transgressing the uniqueness and unrepeatability of the dyadic analytic situation. The presence of an anonymous Third as well as the fact that every moment of the session can be traced back in time alters the potential space and therefore the transferential frame of the session.

Moreover, video recording has some additional properties that differentiate it from audio recording. First, in addressing a camera eye, the interviewee turns to an audience in a different way than if speaking into a microphone. This may be due to the fact that in our present culture, images tend to become the reigning medium, and virtual images are received as a reality of their own. Thus, while the microphone is perceived more as a note-taking instrument of the interviewer, the camera seems to dominate the scene in such a way as to make the interviewer into a moderator, mediating the contact between the interviewee and an imagined audience. Second, in video more than in audio documentation, facial expressions and gestural display are part of the testimony, drawing the attention away from the message to the medium, from intended content to unintentional affective communication. This additional source of information may enrich the testimony, but on the other hand may also thin it out. The illusion of presence—like the 'cinematographic illusion' of the audience as a part of the scene being shown, generally inherent in media communication—may impede the awareness of the only real presence existing in the testimony, which is the mutuality in the interview as it is taking place. The more the interviewer takes on the role of moderator, serving the illusion of unmediated contact through the camera, the less personal is his contact to the survivor. Scenic-narrative microanalysis as a re-analysis of such an actual, documented situation therefore has to remain conscious that its approach is (literally) mediated.

Application of scenic-narrative microanalysis

In the following section, the discrete steps of the scenic-narrative microanalysis process will be defined (for further illustration, cf. the case example of Shmuel B. in Hamburger, 2017b).

Steps and procedures

In the frame of the Yale video testimony study, SNMA was carried out in six discrete steps, as described in the chapter on the case example already mentioned (Hamburger, 2017b). These steps would have to be adapted to varying research contexts. The combination with parallel Grounded Theory, for example, is not essential for SNMA, since it was chosen for convergent validation of the method while SNMA was in development. Further development of the method, however, is a continuing task. The manual is undergoing continual revision. What is essential, however, is to include in any individualized SNMA research design the adequate integration of psychoanalytic competence, preferably on both the levels of data generation and data analysis. SNMA was designed as a method of re-analysis of psychoanalytically conducted testimonial interviews, and itself relies on the psychoanalytic competence of extracting significant moments of meeting when they emerge.

To formulate it more generally, the systematic steps in applying SNMA are:

1 Referring to meaningful data, usually in the form of interviews or sessions, where a kind of listening prevails that facilitates the emergence of moments of meeting (Stern, 2004). To allow for a microanalytic approach, this material must be documented on video or audio and then transcribed.

2 Identifying and commenting on such 'now moments' and/or moments of meeting by at least three independent raters schooled for this task either

by clinical psychoanalytic training or other specialized preparation. The moments identified are to be assigned to one or two consecutive phrases.

3 Discussing the sentences that have been unanimously marked by all raters in one moderated consensus conference for each analyzed interview. The discussion compares and evaluates the individual reasons for qualifying them as a now or meeting moment, and reflects the differences in interpretation, as well as the group dynamics of the consensus conference as an indicator of the underlying unconscious relational structure. The conference agrees on a final statement, which also incudes dissenting opinions, on the underlying interpersonal re-enactment scene apparent in the material through discussion of the selected passages.

4 Conclusive discussion of the entire material by the main researcher considering the statements of the raters, the raters' discussion agreement, the dynamics of the consensus discussion, and re-contextualizing the chosen passages in the broader context of the material.

Scenic-narrative microanalysis in survivor research

The manifest verbal content of the video testimonies discussed in this book is but one source leading to an understanding of their message. Other sources of data must be included: the complex interrelationships between the survivors' past traumatic experience, the characteristics of the interview 'scene,' and the survivors' recurrent patterns of interpersonal interaction.

Although the individual experiences of chronically psychiatrically hospitalized survivors of the Shoah are only transformed into narrative identity through being recounted, many of the individuals who gave these testimonies were either unable to speak about the massive traumata that they had experienced, or were searching for words as if groping in the darkness, unable to bring the fragments of their disintegrated life experience into a recognizable sequence of narration. A narrative analysis of the interview texts addresses and illustrates the modes of representation used by the survivors. Breaks in the narrative, retraction of statements, contradictions, silences, and refusals are most valuable and are telling para-verbal signals.

These signals are not just data provided by the survivor as an object of investigation. Memory is not storage within an individual mind, but a shared, ongoing, reconstructive process—and thus the symbolization process can be affected by interactional factors, including the establishment and maintaining of symbolic capacity in development and social interaction. When testimony is given, recollection is not just hampered by 'individual' forgetfulness or fragmentation on the part of the survivor, and the interviewer's psychoanalytic capacity is not just a kind of archaeological instrument to dig out the buried memories from the ruins of the survivor's mental life: instead, an ongoing, mutual process is in process (Laub & Felman, 1992; Laub, 2005).

Social traumatic experience is often hidden from consciousness. Individually, there is repression, denial, or splitting at work. As a social, systemic process, however, which is more than the sum of its parts, it is a vicious circle. The individual may be ashamed, anxious, and emotionally overburdened by recollections, which may lead to repression or splitting-off on their part. Such a process of defensive splitting is exacerbated in a social environment where another individual is similarly afflicted by such feelings—if perhaps for different reasons. It is hard to speak about the experience of deportation and be heard if the interlocutor has had the same bitter fate. Many have survived in silence, and passed on the silence to their children and grandchildren. It is also unlikely that one will be heard if the dialog partner's (or his parents', relatives', friends', teachers', leaders') participation in the events was on the other side of history.

In the testimonial process explored in this volume, we have documented material illustrating the specificity of the hampered dialog on genocidal trauma, and we have had the opportunity to describe the obstacles as being not only in the bruised memory of the survivor, but also in the emotional reactions of the witnesses: the interviewers and ourselves in the rating group. Detecting, repeating, unfolding, and eventually naming these obstacles is therefore what we can do.

In our own experience as witnesses to the testimony, we have relived the powerful emotional processes triggered by it, leading to symptoms such as distortion and denial, requiring continuous self-analytic reflection and research in order to overcome the conspiracy of silence.

Quality criteria of scenic-narrative microanalysis

Scenic-narrative microanalysis is part of a qualitative research strategy in the sense outlined above, matching both of the following requirements: (1) the development of a method for the collection of meaningful clinical data; and (2) the degree of transparency and explicitness required for interdisciplinary dialog, as well as for future testing of hypotheses. The kind of data it operates on and the findings it provides reflect the relational nature of human mental life and the narrative structure of its development. SNMA manifests its own qualitative version of (3) reliability; and (4) validity.

Meaningful clinical data

The material of scenic-narrative microanalysis is not, as in many other qualitative research strategies, any sort of cultural artefact or 'mentefact,' that takes the form of interviews, texts, films, and so on. Scenic-narrative microanalysis aims at re-analyzing documented psychoanalytic sessions, interviews, or testimonies. The video testimony interviews that were under consideration in its first applications had been conducted by a psychoanalytic researcher and constitute in and of themselves a psychoanalytic experience (Laub & Felman, 1992; Laub, 2005). Consequently, one source for the meaningfulness of the results is the meaningfulness of its input material (which is not at all 'raw' material, but in its essence a highly differentiated interpretive process).

However, the procedure proposed here as scenic-narrative microanalysis could also be applied to material originating outside of the psychoanalytic consulting room. The material it is applied to should be 'meaningful,' as the method's claim is to extract important moments of unconscious correspondences and encounters. Following the principles of Lorenzer's (1986) "Cultural Analysis," the method here uses exisiting records of human interaction to unfold and explicate an unconscious layer of hitherto uncommunicated meanings, implicitly contained in these records. The method does not aim at diagnosing the patient or the interviewee, but is directed towards reconstruction of the unconscious transference relation visible in the documented interaction. In order to address this interaction, it uses a core psychoanalytic method: the systematic assessment of the relationship between the researcher himself and the research object. Thus, the focus of the inquiry is not upon the patient-participant or the interviewer, but has shifted to the researcher's own introspective perception of his mental changes while interacting analytically with the material. The observation and reflection of this self-change is at the core of the psychoanalytic method in the clinical context (Lorenzer, 1970) as well as the cultural-analytic research method (Lorenzer, 1986). Only after completion of this inner hermeneutic circle can inferences be made on its significance for the patient's or interviewee's mental situation—or in the case of cultural analysis, on the unconscious significance of the cultural artefact, which of course is not just a matter of personal mental life, but of shared meanings and cultural codes (for further discussion and literature, cf. Hamburger, 2013a; Hamburger & Leube-Sonnleitner, 2014).

Transparency and explicitness as approximation of scientific objectivity

The scientific transparency and explicitness required for interdisciplinary dialog are provided by several measures in scenic-narrative microanalysis: the raw data of the session are audio- and/or videotaped, and the first psychoanalytic assessments of the material are provided by independent raters and documented in comments written in the margins of the transcripts. The discussions during consensus sessions are recorded on tape. All documents are merged, with marginal comments and segments of the consensus session transcript assigned to the relevant lines of the original interview (this procedure is supported by a qualitative research tool, atlas.ti). The selection of significant moments for further interpretation follows a defined procedure. In the final step of interpretation, all elements have to be taken into account.

Reliability

Since scenic-narrative microanalysis introduces among its quality control features the independent assessment of the material by expert raters, the issue of inter-rater-reliability comes up. It is not as crucial as in psychodiagnostic models, where the overall objectivity of the procedure is based on control of subjective assessment bias, as proven by high correlations between raters. In scenic narrative microanalysis, the independent rating does not aim at approaching a virtual 'true value.' Quite the contrary: it opens a dialogic space for individual perspectives on the material. Since the rating is neither a numeric process nor a coding within a given thesaurus, the inter-rater-reliability cannot be calculated. Moreover, the narrative structure of the material forbids the addition of values over time (cf. above), so it would be hard to correlate the ratings. Qualitative ratings of narrative transferential processes are not even made on a nominal scale (as they are not assigned defined codes or labels), ruling out any mathematical operations (even addition).

However, when working with the material, it can be seen that raters show a remarkable inter-rater-reliability in identifying significant moments, even if they interpret them in different ways. Aside from this tendency to 'find' the same turning points in the material with great accuracy, they also show a certain variance in designating other passages of some significance, where they individually perceive important shifts in the transference relationship.

These restrictions regarding the concept of reliability are reflected in the method by a very limited counting of similarities between the ratings. Only in the first step of identifying significant passages of the text does the inclusion of text passages in the consensus session follow the criterion of concurring assessments. The second step—the discussion of these selected passages in the consensus session—does not aim at equalizing the diversity of interpretations, but at reflecting their span and entering into an open discourse.

Validity

Eventually, we have to ask ourselves whether this whole procure yields any valid result at all—to put it dryly in the formula of test diagnostics, whether it accurately measures what it purports to measure. However, we have to keep in mind that we are not pursuing test diagnostics. Scenic-narrative microanalysis molds psychoanalytic experience into a procedure that allows for maximal transparency and explicitness of the process, while preserving its specific quality. It is evidently less objective than formalized diagnostic tools, but it is expected to produce individualized, rich, and even surprising insights into a process which is defined as a narrative, relational entity.

Scenic microanalysis elucidates the significant resonances found between the experience of the researcher witnessing the video and the experience in the interview 'scene.' Ultimately, this analytic approach leads to hypotheses about resonant interactions in the interviewee's life. This criterion of resonance reflects what clinical psychoanalysts are familiar with as the 'Menninger Triangle,' inferring the validity of a psychoanalytic interpretation by its embracement of (1) transference, (2) symptom, and (3) the biography of the patient.

Conclusion

In the wide methodological range of qualitative studies, psychoanalytic social research is but one paradigm amongst others. This paradigm, though well respected by qualitative researchers because of its closeness to one of the most fruitful research paradigms of the previous century (and sometimes even idealized because of the psychoanalytic researchers' unique possibility to access their subjects), now seems to be receding in the academic community, mainly due to declining research and publication options. It therefore should be re-introduced into this discourse, with close contact being kept to psychoanalytic clinical experience and theoretical development.

In these ways, modern approaches to psychoanalytic research rely on the professional skills of psychoanalysts to generate analyzable, meaningful data, for example, in the field of psychotherapy research by catamnesia interviews and qualitative evaluation (Leuzinger-Bohleber, Stuhr, Rüger, & Beutel, 2002; Leuzinger-Bohleber & Fischmann, 2006).

Psychoanalytic qualitative research is an inductive process that moves from the ground level of gathered data to the formulation of hypotheses. It is not concerned with testing previously formulated hypotheses, as would be necessary to meet Popper's falsificationist model, but is rather aimed at generating hypotheses that emanate from the controlled research process itself (Sandler, Dreher, & Drews, 1991; Hinshelwood, 2013). Only in a second step can these hypotheses be submitted to quantitative analysis and more objective testing procedures. If research aims at generating meaningful and non-arbitrary results, the two strategies mentioned above have to work hand in hand. This is the case at least in some advanced fields, for example, in the co-operation of clinical psychoanalysts and empirically oriented researchers in infant research, as well as in psychotherapy and trauma research. Scenic-narrative microanalysis of video testimony data is one contribution to emerging activities in qualitative psychoanalytic research.

Notes

1 This research was supported by IPA RAB and performed in the frame of the Yale video testimony study group, in close cooperation with Dori Laub, Yale University Medical School, and Marianne Leuzinger-Bohleber, Sigmund-Freud-Institut, Frankfurt am Main, Germany. I thank my Kassel doctoral

candidate Pascal Heberlein, as well as Saskia Wessel, Sabine Nüsser, and Sarah Katharine Schmidt, who wrote their masters' theses on the project, furthermore the Rating Groups in Munich and Frankfurt am Main: Tamara Fischmann, Hella Goldfein, Kurt Grünberg, Salek Kutschinski, Friedrich Markert, Lilian Otscheret-Tschebiner, and Naomi Silberner-Becker. Parts of this chapter were presented at the 2010 Sandler Research Conference, Frankfurt am Main; 11th ISPS-US Meeting, November 2010, Stockbridge, USA; 2013 IPA Prague Congress Panel: "Manifestations of extreme traumatization in the testimonial narration of hospitalized and non-hospitalized Holocaust survivors" (chair: Dori Laub).

2 This position has been described in detail in several former papers; cf. Hamburger 1998a, 2010, 2013a, 2013b.

References

Ahumada, J. L. (1994). Interpretation and creationism. *International Journal of Psychoanalysis, 75*, 695–707.

Desmet, M., Meganck, R., Seybert, S., Willemsen, J., Van Camp, I., Geerardyn, F., Declercq, F., Inslegers, R., Trenson, E., Vanheule, S., Kirschner, L., Schindler, S., & Kächele, H. (2013). Psychoanalytic single cases published in ISI-ranked journals: The construction of an online archive. *Psychotherapy and Psychosomatics 82*, 120–121.

Devereux, G. (1967). *From anxiety to method in the behavioral sciences*. Berlin: de Gruyter Mouton.

Flick, U. (2009). *An introduction to qualitative research*. New York: Sage.

Freud, S. (1953). Introductory lectures on psycho-analysis. *Standard Edition, 16*, 241–463. (Original work published 1917)

Freud, S. (1959). The question of lay analysis. *Standard Edition, 20*, 177–258. (Original work published 1926)

Gergen, K. J. (1994). Mind, text, and society: Self-memory in social context. In U. Neisser & R. Fivush (Eds.), *The remembering self* (pp. 78–104). Cambridge: Cambridge University Press.

Gergen, K. J., & Gergen, M. M. (1986). Narrative form and the construction of psychological science. In T. R. Sarbin (Ed.), *Narrative psychology: The storied nature of human conduct* (pp. 152–173). New York, Westport and London: Praeger.

Govrin, A. (2006). The dilemma of contemporary psychoanalysis: Toward a "knowing" post-postmodernism. *Journal of the American Psychoanalytic Association, 54*, 507–535.

Hamburger, A. (1987). *Der Kindertraum und die Psychoanalyse. Ein Beitrag zur Metapsychologie des Traums*. Regensburg: Roderer.

Hamburger, A. (1998a). Traumnarrativ und Gedächtnis. In M. Koukkou, M. Leuzinger-Bohleber, & W. Mertens (Eds.), *Erinnerung von Wirklichkeiten. Psychoanalyse und Neurowissenschaften im Dialog. Bd. 1: Bestandsaufnahme* (pp. 223–286). Stuttgart: Verlag Internationale Psychoanalyse.

Hamburger, A. (1998b). Solo mit Dame. Traumgeschichten einer Psychoanalyse. In M. Leuzinger-Bohleber, W. Mertens, & M. Koukkou (Eds.), *Erinnerung von Wirklichkeiten: Psychoanalyse und Neurowissenschaften im Dialog. Bd. 2: Folgerungen für die psychoanalytische Praxis* (pp. 96–127). Stuttgart: Verlag Internationale Psychoanalyse.

Hamburger, A. (2003a). Erinnerter Abschied. Zur psychoanalytischen Interpretation des Trakl-Epitaphs von Else Lasker-Schüler nebst Anmerkungen zum Übertragungsangebot der Lyrik. In W. Mauser & J. Pfeiffer (Eds.), *Trauer* (pp. 185–226). Würzburg: Königshausen & Neumann.

Hamburger, A. (2006a). "Setzt ein Krug, und schreibt dabei: Dem Amte wohlbekannt." Lachen in Heinrich von Kleists "Zerbrochnem Krug. " In W. Mauser & J. Pfeiffer (Eds.), *Lachen* (pp. 133–175). Würzburg: Königshausen & Neumann.

Hamburger, A. (2006b). Traum und Zeit. Traumerzählungen als Elemente der Spannungsdramaturgie. *Forum der Psychoanalyse, 22*(1), 23–43.

Hamburger, A. (2009). Zeitfenster: für eine Metapsychologie der Gegenwart. *Forum der Psychoanalyse, 25*(3), 199–218.

Hamburger, A. (2010). Traumspiegel: Gegenübertragungsträume in der Beziehungsanalyse. In H. Hierdeis (Ed.), *Der Gegenübertragungstraum in der psychoanalytischen Theorie und Praxis* (pp. 23–50). Göttingen: Vandenhoeck & Ruprecht.

Hamburger, A. (2013a). Arbeit in der Tiefe: Vorüberlegungen zu einer skeptischen Kulturanalyse. In H. Hierdeis (Ed.), *Psychoanalytische Skepsis* (pp. 123–183). Göttingen: Vandenhoeck & Ruprecht.

Hamburger, A. (2013b). Via Regia und zurück: Traumerzählungen und ihre Resonanz. In J. Bernhard, B. Unruh, & S. Walz-Pawlita (Eds.), *Der Traum* (pp. 123–143). Giessen: Psychosozial-Verlag.

Hamburger, A. (2015). Refracted attunement, affective resonance: Scenic-narrative microanalysis of entangled presences in a Holocaust survivor's video testimony. *Contemporary Psychoanalysis, 51*(2), 239–257.

Hamburger, A. (2017a). Genocidal trauma: Individual and social consequences of the assault on the mental and physical life of a group. This volume, chapter 4.

Hamburger, A. (2017b). Refracted attunement, affective resonance. Scenic-Narrative Micro-Analysis of entangled presence in a Holocaust survivor's testimony. This volume, chapter 21.

Hamburger, A., & Leube-Sonnleitner, K. (2014). Wie im Kino: Zur Filmanalyse in der Gruppe. Methodologie der psychoanalytischen Filminterpretation anhand von Lars von Triers "Melancholia." In R. Zwiebel & D. Blothner (Eds.), *Melancholia: Wege zur psychoanalytischen Interpretation des Films* (pp. 72–109). Göttingen: Vandenhoek & Ruprecht.

Hamburger, A., & Mertens, W. (2004). Review of the book *"Forschen und Heilen" in der Psychoanalyse. International Journal of Psycho-Analysis, 85*(2), 535–565.

Hinshelwood, R. D. (2013). *Research on the couch: Single-case studies, subjectivity and psychoanalytic knowledge.* London: Routledge.

Holmes, J. (2014). Countertransference in qualitative research: A critical appraisal. *Qualitative Research, 14*(2), 166–183.

Jüttemann, G. (Ed.) (2009). *Komparative Kasuistik: Die psychologische Analyse spezifischer Entwicklungsphänomene.* Lengerich, Berlin: Pabst.

Kirshner, L. A. (2004). *Having a life: Self-pathology after Lacan.* Hilsdale, NJ: The Analytic Press, Inc.

Kirshner, L. A. (Ed.) (2011). *Between Winnicott and Lacan: A clinical engagement.* New York and London: Taylor & Francis.

Laub, D. (2005). From speechlessness to narrative: The cases of Holocaust historians and of psychiatrically hospitalized survivors. *Literature and Medicine, 24*(2), 253–265.

Laub, D., & Felman, S. (1992). *Testimony: Crisis of witnessing in literature, psychoanalysis, and history.* New York: Routledge.

Leuzinger-Bohleber, M., & Fischmann, T. (2006). What is conceptual research in psychoanalysis? *International Journal of Psychoanalysis, 87*, 1,355–1,386.

Leuzinger-Bohleber, M., Stuhr, U., Rüger, B., & Beutel, M. (2002). Psychoanalytische Forschung und die Pluralität der Wissenschaften: Einige kritische Anmerkungen illustriert am Beispiel einer repräsentativen, multiperspektivischen Katamnesestudie von Psychoanalysen und psychoanalytischen Langzeitbehandlungen. *Bulletin Psychoanalyse in Europa, 56*, 194–220.

Lorenzer, A. (1970). *Sprachzerstörung und Rekonstruktion: Vorarbeiten zu einer Metatheorie der Psychoanalyse.* Frankfurt am Main: Suhrkamp.

Lorenzer, A. (1986). Tiefenhermeneutische Kulturanalyse. In H.-D. König, A. Lorenzer, H. Lüdde, S. Nagbol, U. Prokop, G. Schmid Noerr, & A. Eggert (Eds.), *Kultur-Analysen: Psychoanalytische Studien zur Kultur* (pp. 11–98). Frankfurt am Main: Fischer.

Luborsky, L., & Crits-Christoph, P. (1990). *Understanding transference: The core conflictual relationship theme method.* Washington, DC: American Psychological Association.

Mitchell, S.A. (1988). *Relational concepts in psychoanalysis: An integration.* Cambridge, MA: Harvard University Press.

Sandler J., Dreher, A.U., & Drews, S. (1991). An approach to conceptual research in psychoanalysis illustrated by a consideration of psychic trauma. *International Review of Psychoanalysis, 18*, 133–141.

Sidnell, J., & Stivers, T. (Eds.) (2013). *The handbook of conversation analysis.* Chichester: Wiley-Blackwell.

Spence, D. P. (1982). *Narrative truth and historical truth.* New York: Norton.

Stern, D. (2004). *The present moment in psychotherapy and everyday life.* New York and London: Norton & Company.

Part III

Exploration in the social void

The Israel video testimony project

Part III, "Exploration in the social void: the Israel video testimony project," reports on the specific case study at the center of this book. The public in Israel was shocked when it learned in the 1990s that a high number of chronically hospitalized patients in psychiatric institutions, most of them diagnosed as schizophrenic, were Holocaust survivors, whose persecution history had not quite been acknowledged and included in their diagnosis and treatment. Subsequently, these patients were transferred from the substandard institutions they were found in to specialized homes for Holocaust survivors. Some of them who were able to communicate gave their video testimonies to Dori Laub and his colleagues. Rakefet Zalashik contributes her historical research on the fate of the psychiatrically hospitalized Holocaust survivors in Israel. In their separate chapters Laub and Felsen give a detailed chronological account of the evolution of the project, its conception, planning, fundraising, implementation, and aftermath—culminating in the depositing of about two thirds of the tapes at the Yale University Sterling Memorial Library. Rael Strous, director of research in the hospital when this study was carried out, summarizes the clinical outcomes of the study, as evidenced by extensive psychological testing. Baruch Greenwald, the director of the 'Survivor unit,' reports on his experience working psychotherapeutically with this patient population and on his observation of changes that occurred in patients and in staff, during and after the video testimony project. Laub and Felsen in their joint chapter address the testimonies from a depth-psychology perspective. Deficit and defense are elaborated on and the "voids of memory" that punctuated the testimonies are demonstrated, as are the strategies survivors employ to cope with them. The final contribution is by Pinchevski, who elaborates on how these texts constitute "counter testimonies" and how they jointly form a "counter archive."

Chapter 11

The psychiatrically hospitalized survivors in Israel

A historical overview

Rakefet Zalashik

In the 1950s, mental problems among survivors in Israel were explained by migration difficulties. Ben Ami Finkelstein presented a case of a female survivor from Lithuania, diagnosed as a paranoid schizophrenic, to show "the impact of immigration on the character of a person who tends toward insanity." The patient survived concentration camps working as a nurse. After the liberation, she married her perished girlfriend's husband and left for Australia. "However the patient . . . wished to immigrate to Israel. This wish derived from the Zionist ideals she had gotten in the youth movement" (Finkelstein, 1952, 124). In the first months in Israel, she lived with her husband's friends, who had also known his first wife and very often spoke about her and the children that perished. This caused her great suffering. At her new job, the patient felt that she was being monitored. At the hospital, she was very irritated and expressed her desire to commit suicide (Finkelstein, 1952, 124). Finkelstein referred to the patient's war experience only in two sentences. He claimed that what had caused the outbreak was migration to Israel and the gap between reality and the patient's youthful dreams. The patient's biography, as well as her and her husband's traumatic pasts, were almost ignored in Finkelstein's analysis.

A common claim was that survivors in Israel suffered from mental problems less than survivors in other countries. Mark Dvorjetski argued that the psychic complexes which survivors suffer from on arrival in Israel disappear when they become rooted in the country. This is because of "the process of reintegration of the personality," which characterizes the survivors in Israel, who had "returned to normal life, restoring the right to housing, to work and to health" (Dvorjetski, 1955, 65). Nevertheless, he called for more study of the pathology of the Holocaust and recommended that admission forms to psychiatric facilities indicate whether the patient was a survivor. This regulation, made in 1964, was not fully applied; to this day, there is no exact data on hospitalized survivors.

The first article on mentally ill survivors as a distinct group was published in 1956 by Greda Barag (1956). As a psychoanalyst, she focused on her patients' childhoods and argued that they were disappointed by the 'oedipal object' and did not reach identification with the parent of the same sex, presenting three cases of survivors who suffered from fainting. She explained: "All the three got ill when they started normal life, where physical existence was secured. However, they were disappointed from their environment . . . Their behavior [fainting R.Z.] served as an expression of their will to scare their surroundings or to punish it, or at least to get its attention" (Barag, 1956, 229). However, Barag, like other local psychiatrists believed that "Jews were more resistant . . . than any other race" (Barag, 1956, 229).

The impact of German restitution

According to the German Federal Law for Compensating Victims of Nazi Persecution (1953), (former) German citizens or residents were eligible to submit claims of damage caused by the Nazi regime. Israeli psychiatrists submitted medical opinions for claims against Germany, as well as for a disability pension from the Israeli authorities. In 1953, Kurt Blumenthal discussed "compensation neurosis," where he warned that the social situation in Israel "created a special neurotic readiness . . . Too much social aid and a valueless assistance that comes from excessive pity can only help increase compensation neuroses" (Blumenthal, 1953, 177). Additionally, and more specifically, Blumenthal explained: "Let us consider the special situation among our trauma neurotics. They lack professional education because of war . . . Very often there is no connection between their work and personality. It is no wonder then that this situation inspires a neurosis that one might more easily get the 'prize'" (Blumenthal, 1953, 177). Also Julius Baumatz, the director of the mental health station in Jerusalem, warned in 1959 of compensation neurosis. For him, survivors who come to get a medical opinion regarding mental problems have to be suspected for simulation, exaggeration or attempts to get compensated for pre-war mental damage (Baumatz, 1960, 148).

In contrast, Louis Levinger in his article on compensation in *Der Nervenarzt* (Levinger, 1962, 75) declared that he hardly ever encountered cases of compensation neurosis in Israel. The life of survivors in Israel was not fertile ground for the development of such a neurosis. They had been rehabilitated before the claims against Germany thanks to the Israeli absorption system that gave them housing, work, and education. Even those who wanted compensation because of compensation neurosis were not in his view swindlers, but individuals who suffered from a real neurosis (Hermann, 1955, 44–45; Chodoff, 1963, 327).

Israeli psychiatry from the 1960s

In 1961 Leo Eitinger, the Czech-Norwegian Jewish survivor psychiatrist, came to Israel to conduct a study on the prolonged psychic effects of concentration camps (Eitinger, 1964, 183). His stay contributed to local understanding of trauma among survivors.[1] Eitinger carried out a comparative study together with Zvi Winnik and T. Nathan on camp survivors and patients who had been in the Soviet Union during the war (Nathan, Eitinger, & Winnik, 1964, 56–58). The results proved that concentration camp survivors' syndrome is a distinct clinical entity.

Treating Holocaust survivors presented a conflict. On the one hand, the psychiatrist strove to neutralize the trauma, to enable the survivor to have a normal life. On the other hand, the therapist had to deal with the survivor's need to remember and be acknowledged as a victim. Ruth Yaffe presented four categories of survivors' reaction to trauma: people who did not want to forget the past, people who wished to forget but failed, people who seemed able to suppress the past but had mental problems, and people who had succeeded in forgetting (Yaffe, 1962). Hypermnesia (Niederland, 1961) was one of the sources of conflict in the interaction between the therapists of survivors. Of the fourth category—survivors who succeeded in forgetting their past—Yaffe (1962) wrote: "This reaction is considered to be the healthiest, and it is the reaction of most of the survivors. Nevertheless, we assume that this forgetfulness, by suppressing traumatic memories from consciousness, carries with it the reduction of the personality" (p. 128). She believed that the Holocaust damaged all survivors. The outbreak of mental problems was a result of a secondary crisis, which a healthy personality could overcome.

The 1960s also witnessed the Eichmann trial, which had a minor impact on the treatment of clinical survivors. The number of publications on the topic did not increase. Nevertheless, the studies carried out tended to be more focused and deeper than the previous ones, trying to examine the prolonged impact of trauma on the survivors. In 1963, Hillel Klein, Julius Zellermayer, and Joel Shanan published a study on patients from the outpatient clinic in order to see if there was a difference between survivors and others. The study showed that in the first group, which had high rates of physical and psychological complaints, there were many cases of anxiety and withdrawal from social life. Dividing the types of trauma into concentration camps and ghettos, hiding, labor camps and partisans, the psychiatrists found that the severest cases of psychotic syndromes were more common among patients who belonged to the two first groups (Klein, Zellermayer, & Shanan, 1963, 340).

From denial to recognition? The 1970s until today

In the first decades after the establishment of Israel, the focus of psychiatric research was upon clinical survivors, but from the end of the 1970s, there was a gradual shift to the study of 'healthy' survivors who led 'normal' lives. Some of the studies showed that the 'healthy' group suffered from a high level of symptoms, stress, and other mental problems, even 40 years after the end of the war (Robinson et al., 1990, 312–313). Other studies showed that the state of the survivors was better than expected, and that in many cases their ability to deal with stress situations was better than that found in the general population (Kahana, Harel, & Kahana, 1988, 413–429). On the other hand, Dov Shmotkin and Jacob Lomranz, who studied the subjective well-being of survivors in Israel, argued that the subjective well-being of the various sub-groups of survivors did not allow for the evaluation of the impact of the trauma on the survivors through the years (Shmotkin & Lomranz, 1998).

Since the end of the 1970s, but even more so since the 1980s, a process of differentiation between the various survivors has emerged: there is a growing interest in child survivors and the so-called second generation, as well as in the impact of aging on survivors. Aging survivors raised a new layer of relationships between Israeli society in general and the psychiatry of the Holocaust in particular. In this period, the psycho-geriatric framework became the common paradigm, which emphasized the new needs and problems of aging individuals who were traumatized (Arie & Shushan, 1989, 287).

The question of war, stress, and the Holocaust was also a theme among Israeli psychiatrists, who examined PTSD among 'second generation' soldiers, and the resilience of survivors during the first Gulf War and terror attacks (Solomon, Zahava, Kotler, & Mikulincer, 1988; Yehuda, Schmeidler, Giller, Siever, & Binder-Brynes, 2014; Yehuda, Schmeidler, Wainberg, Binder-Brynes, & Duvdevani, 2014; Alexandrowicz, 1973, 385–392; Gay, Fuchs, & Blittner, 1974).

Nevertheless, despite diverse research activity on survivors in Israel, the treatment of mentally ill Holocaust survivors did not undergo a change until the 1990s. A series of events created new circumstances which brought the issue to the fore and led to the summation of the Bazak Investigation Committee, which examined the harsh conditions of 1,000 hospitalized survivors in psychiatric facilities (Nadav & Zalashik, 2007, 145–163).

Is Israeli psychiatry unique?

In terms of content, the psychiatric literature that deals with mental damage as a result of the Holocaust can be divided into three central phases. In the first—during World War II and up to the beginning of the 1950s—most research focused on what was called "the pathology of deportation," the mental changes of victims during imprisonment and immediately after liberation. Some of these studies were written by survivor psychiatrists or by the medical staff who escorted the liberating forces (Bettelheim, 1943, 417–452; Bondy, 1943, 453–475; Niremberski, 1946, 60–74; Friedman, 1949, 601–605). In the second phase, from the beginning of the 1950s up to the mid-1950s, the emphasis was on mental changes among displaced people and their readjustment to their homeland or country of immigration (Arnold, 1954, 96–98; Bakis, 1955, 76–88; Murphy, 1955, 58–63; Harmsen, 1958). From the mid-1950s until the end of the 1960s, the discussion focused on the mental problems discovered after liberation, which were seen as the late impact of persecution. In June 1954, an international medical conference took place in Copenhagen which focused on the physical damage of persecution and imprisonment and their late impact.[2] In 1966, a workshop was carried out at Wayne University on the late implications of massive psychic trauma (Krystal, 1968). In any case, the discussion during this period partly addressed the specific issue of restitution from Germany (Chodoff, 1963, 323; Eitinger, 1964, 23).

From a medical perspective, the psychiatric literature is organized on three axes: the subject of research, nosology, and aetiology. The subject of research immediately after World War II consisted of the concentration camps' survivors. Later, it was extended to survivors who had not been prisoners in concentration camps, and today it also includes the children and grandchildren who were born to Holocaust survivors. From the nosological perspective, in the first decade of the State of Israel the discussion focused on physical diseases, and later medical attention was also given to psychosomatic and mental diseases. These two axes were reflected in newly coined terms such as the 'survivor syndrome,' and the 'Concentration Camp syndrome.' With regard to aetiology, and in the first years after the war common opinion stated that health damage to survivors was the outcome of malnutrition and injuries resulting from slave labor and beatings. The search was for organic damage, especially to the brain and the nervous system. When no pathological evidence was found, the patient was not diagnosed as sick (Eitinger, 1964, 771; Nathan, Eitinger, & Winnik, 1964). Only later did the medical profession come to understand that the living conditions during the Holocaust entailed extreme stress factors, and therefore that the lack of pathological evidence did not indicate a lack of physical and mental damage. The acknowledgment that the Holocaust was not over for the survivors after the liberation, and that it had left 'psychic scars' became accepted only during the 1960s.

The comparison between Israeli and European psychiatric attitudes toward Holocaust survivors indicates three main differences. First, the psychiatric research outside of Israel began straight after the war and thus preceded Israeli psychiatric efforts (Minkowski, 1946, 104; Dreyfus-Moreau, 1952, 207–211; Helweg-Larsen et al., 1952; Targowla, 1955, 31–34; Bastiaans, 1957). Part of the immediate interest in the survivors derived from the issue of compensation (Targowla, 1955, 30; Eitinger, 1964, 771).

A second difference between the Israeli and European cases emerges from an analysis of the different research periods. Israeli psychiatry dealt with the problems of survivors only after they had arrived in the country, and focused on their adjustment difficulties. Thus, the first phase literature, which examined the psychic changes of survivors during imprisonment and shortly after liberation, has no Israeli parallel. The only Israeli physician who dealt with the pathology of deportation was Mark Dvorjetski, who touched only slightly on the psychiatric aspect.

Third, in contrast to the scientific activity in Europe, and even after the arrival of survivors in Israel, there was no psychiatric study of the survivors' condition. The first psychiatric research in Israel only began in the 1960s (Klein, Nathan, Eitinger, & Winnik, 1964, 47–80). Moreover, there is also a lack of a discussion on the issue of compensation for mental damage in the Israel psychiatric discourse. The debates about trauma and compensation that took place in Germany hardly had an echo in Israeli psychiatry, even though Israeli psychiatrists also wrote medical opinions for claims against German and Israeli authorities (Venzlaff, 1958; Matussek, 1961, 540; von Bayer, 1961; Bayer, Häfner, & Kisker, 1963, 1964).

Nevertheless, there are also similarities between psychiatry in Israel and in other countries in this period, as well as in their attitude toward survivors. First of all, many psychiatrists were affected by stigmas given to Holocaust survivors. They argued that the stories told by the survivors were exaggerated, generally demonstrating ambivalence about the guilty feeling survivors had for having stayed alive. Indeed some therapists thought that some of their patients could have behaved differently in order to rescue their relatives, or argued that the feelings of guilt were in fact the shame of an unconsciousness death-wish towards their parents, which had been realized. Most psychiatrists believed that Holocaust survivors tended to complain in order to obtain higher compensation (Danieli, 1981, 27). Secondly, not dealing, or hardly dealing, with the patient's past during World War II was not unique to Israel. In psychiatric hospitals in Europe and the United States, one can find medical files in which patients' experiences in the Holocaust were summarized in a single laconic sentence, "the patient is a concentration camp survivor" (Danieli, 1981, 27). This might have been because therapists in all the countries that absorbed survivors could not cope with the past of their patients and preferred to ignore it, even though it was essential to understanding the mental difficulties suffered by the patients.

Thirdly, and in all psychiatric literature that discusses mental problems of Holocaust survivors, there is a constant avoidance of expressions of feelings toward the subject of research, an attitude seen as scientific objectivity and neutrality (Danieli, 1981, 27).

Notes

1 Ulrich Venzlaff told me that the quality of medical evaluations written by Israeli psychiatrists for German compensations improved after Eitinger was in Israel and he believes it was thanks to him (personal communication, Göttingen, June 22, 2004).
2 The minutes of the conference were published a year later in an edited volume (Sichel, 1955).

References

Alexandrowicz, R. R. (1973). Children of concentration camp survivors. In E. Anthony & C. Koupernik (Eds.), *The child in his family* (Vol. 2, pp. 385–392). New York: Wiley.

Arie, N., & Ben-Shushan, D. (1989). Forty years later: Long-term consequences of massive traumatization as manifested by Holocaust survivors from the city and the Kibbutz. *Journal of Consulting and Clinical Psychology, 57*(2), 287–293.

Arnold, W. (1954). Flüchtlingsjugend und sittliche Reifung. *Integration, 1*, 96–98.

Bakis, E. (1955). DP-apathy. In H. B. M. Murphy (Eds.), *Flight and resettlement* (pp. 76–88). New York: Columbia University Press.

Barag, G. (1956). Late reaction among concentration camps survivors. *Harefuah, 40*, 211–212.

Bastiaans, J. (1957). *Psychosomatische Gevolgen Van Onderdrukking en Verzet.* Amsterdan: Noord-Hollandsche Uitgevers Maatschappij.

Baumatz, J. (1960). On problems of trauma neurosis. *Harefuah, 49*, 146–148.

Bayer, W., Häfner, H., & Kisker, K. (1963). "Wissenschaftliche Erkenntnis" oder "menschliche Wertung" der erlebnisreaktiven Schäden Verfolgter? *Nervenarzt, 34*, 120–123.

Bayer, W., Häfner, H., & Kisker, K. (1964). *Psychiatrie der Verfolgten: Psychopathologische und gutachtliche Erfahrungen an Opfern der nationalsozialistischen Verfolgung und vergleichbarer Extrembelastungen.* Berlin: Springer.

Bettelheim, B. (1943). Individual and mass behavior in extreme situations. *Journal of Abnormal Social Psychology, 38*, 417–452.

Blumenthal, K. (1953). The fostering of neuroses and means to prevent them. *Harefuah, 44*, 177–178.

Bondy, C. (1943). Problems of Internment camps. *Journal of Abnormal Social Psychology, 38*, 453–475.

Chodoff, P. (1963). Late effects of the concentration camp syndrome. *Archives of General Psychiatry, 8*, 323–333.

Danieli, Y. (1981). *Therapists' difficulties in treating survivors of the Nazi Holocaust and their children.* PhD dissertation, New York University, NY.

Dreyfus-Moreau, J. (1952). Etude structurale de deux cas de nervose concentrationnaire. *La Vie médicale. Evolution médicale et thérapeutique, 33*, 207–211.

Dvorjetski, M. (1955). The pathology of the Holocaust period and the pathological remains among Holocaust survivors. *Dapim Refui'Im, 15*, 60–67.

Eitinger, L. (1964). *Concentration camp survivors in Norway and Israel*. Oslo: Universitetsforlaget/Norwegian Research Council for Science and the Humanities.

Finkelstein, B. A. (1952). Mental diseases with a connection to immigration. *Harefua'h, 42*, 124–126.

Friedman, P. (1949). Some aspects of concentration camp psychology. *American Journal of Psychiatry, 105*, 601–605.

Gay, M., Fuchs, J., & Blittner, M. (1974). Characteristics of the offspring of Holocaust survivors in Israel. *Mental Health & Society, 1*(5–6), 302–312.

Harmsen, H. (1958). *Die Integration heimatloser Ausländer und nicht deutscher Flüchtlinge in Westdeutschland*. Augsburg: Hofmann.

Helweg-Larsen, P., Hoffmeyer, H., Kieler, J., Thaysen, E. H., Thygesen, J., Hertel, P., & Wulff, M. (1952). Famine disease in German concentration camps; complications and sequels, with special reference to tuberculosis, mental disorders and social consequences. *Acta Psychiatrica et Neurologica Scandinavica Supplementum, 83*, 1–460.

Hermann, K. (1955). Die psychischen Symptome des KZ-Syndroms: Versuch einer pathogenetischen Schätzung. In M. Michel (Ed.), *Gesundheitsschäden durch Verfolgung und Gefangenschaft und ihre Spätfolgen* (pp. 41–47). Frankfurt am Main: Roederberg.

Kahana, B., Harel, Z., & Kahana, E. (1988). Predictors of psychological well-being among survivors of the Holocaust. In J. Wilson & Z. Harel, *Human adaptation to extreme stress: From the Holocause to Vietnam* (pp. 171–192). New York: Plenum Press.

Klein, H., Nathan, T. S., Eitinger, L., & Winnik, H. Z. (1964). A psychiatric study of survivors of the Nazi Holocaust: A study in hospitalized patients. *The Israel Annals of Psychiatry and Related Disciplines, 2*, 47–80.

Klein, H., Zellermayer, J., & Shanan, J. (1963). Former concentration camp inmates on a psychiatric ward. *Archives of General Psychiatry, 8*(4), 334–342.

Krystal, H. (1968). *Massive psychic trauma*. New York: International University.

Levinger, L. (1962). Psychiatrische Untersuchung in Israel an 800 Fällen mit Gesundheitsschadenforderungen wegen Nazi-Verfolgung. *Nervenarzt, 33*, 75.

Matussek, P. (1961). Die Konzentrationslagerhaft als Belastungssituation. *Nervenarzt, 32*, 538–542.

Minkowski, E. (1946). L'Anesthesie affective. *Annuaires Medico-Psychologiques, 80*, 80–88.

Murphy, H. (1955). The camps. In H. B. M. Murphy (Ed.), *Flight and resettlement* (pp. 58–63). New York: Columbia University Press.

Nadav, D., & Zalashik, R. (2007). Recalling the survivors: Between memory and forgetfulness of hospitalized holocaust survivors in Israel. *Israel Studies, 12*(2), 145–163.

Nathan, T. S., Eitinger, L., & Winnik, H. (1964). A psychiatric study of survivors of the Nazi Holocaust: A study in hospital patients. *Israel Annals of Psychiatry and Related Disciplines, 2,* 56–58.

Niederland, W. (1961). The problem of the survivors. *Journal of the Hillside Hospital, 10,* 233–247.

Niremberski, M. (1946). Psychological investigation of a group of internees at Belsen camp. *Journal of Mental Science, 92,* 60–74.

Robinson, S., Rapaport, J., Durst, R., Rapaport, M., Rosca, P., Metzer, S., & Zilberman, L. (1990). The late effects of Nazi persecution among elderly Holocaust survivors. *Acta Psychiatrica Scandinavica, 82*(4), 311–315.

Shmotkin, D., & Lomranz, J. (1998). Subjective well-being among Holocaust survivors: An examination of overlooked differentiations. *Journal of Personality and Social Psychology, 75*(1), 141–155.

Sichel, M. (1955). *Gesundheitsschäden durch Verfolgung und Gefangenschaft und ihre Spätfolgen.* Frankfurt: Röderberg.

Solomon, Z. (1995). From denial to recognition: Attitudes toward Holocaust survivors from World War II to the present. *Journal of Traumatic Stress, 8*(2), 215–228.

Solomon, Z., Kotler M., & Mikulincer, M. (1988). Combat-related posttraumatic stress disorder among second-generation Holocaust survivors: Preliminary findings. *The American Journal of Psychiatry, 145*(7), 865–868.

Targowla, R. (1995). Die neuropsychischen Folgen der Deportation in deutsche Konzentrationslager. In M. Sichel (Ed.), *Gesundheitsschäden durch Verfolgung und Gefangenschaft und ihre Spätfolgen* (pp. 30–45). Frankfurt: Röderberg.

Venzlaff, U. (1958). *Die psychoreaktiven Störungen nach entschädigungspflichtigen Ereignissen (Die sogenannten Unfallneurosen).* Berlin: Springer.

von Bayer, W. (1961). Erlebnisbedingte Verfolgungsschäden. *Nervenarzt, 32,* 534–538.

Yaffe, R. (1962). The mental adjustment of the Nazi regime survivors after their immigration to Israel. *Dapim Refui'im, 21,* 127–130.

Yehuda, R., Schmeidler, J., Giller, E. L., Jr, Siever, L. J., & Binder-Brynes, K. (2014). Relationship between posttraumatic stress disorder characteristics of Holocaust survivors and their adult offspring. *American Journal of Psychiatry, 155*(6), 841–843.

Yehuda, R., Schmeidler, J., Wainberg, M., Binder-Brynes, K., & Duvdevani, T. (2014). Vulnerability to posttraumatic stress disorder in adult offspring of Holocaust survivors. *American Journal of Psychiatry, 155*(9), 1,163–1,171.

Chapter 12

The Israel project story

Dori Laub

I cannot remember exactly how it started. Sometime in the late 1990s, a relative who knew of my work with Holocaust video testimonies told me that the Israeli news channels were reporting on the large number of chronically hospitalized Holocaust survivors. When I viewed the videos he sent me, I felt like I had been struck by lightning. I'd been unknowingly waiting for these survivors, those hovering between having a voice and being mute. If extreme trauma exceeds the mind's ability to symbolize and to represent it, hospitalized survivors who had given up and had retreated into psychosis would exemplify this most strikingly. Their testimonies would demonstrate the destructive effects of extreme trauma. I felt moved by such a possibility. How could I not have realized it before?

My colleagues at Yale and fellow members of the Jewish community responded with unease. Logistical difficulties were only part of their concern. How could hospitalized patients give true consent? Were they capable of giving their testimonies? What was the use of this project? Could it harm them further? These questions foreshadowed what was to come.

The project started in 1996 with a conference held in Maaleh Hachamisha, near Jerusalem, with support from the Israeli Ministry of health. Dr Moti Mark, the Commissioner of Mental Health, spoke at the conference and endorsed the project. I brought in experts from Israel, the United States, and Germany for three inspiring days of exchanging ideas. Now it was time to act.

It took several years of struggle to find funding and a home for the project. Time and again I was sent away empty-handed, feeling like I had transgressed some boundary. It was more than a simple refusal. I had touched a raw nerve. The logical explanations didn't address the affect involved.

I eventually stopped speaking to colleagues and potential donors, and accepted that I was not going to be able to find support for the project. Almost as an afterthought, I submitted a grant proposal to the Claims Conference for $150,000. Irit Felsen, a clinical psychologist and the daughter of two Holocaust survivors, promised to help in obtaining the grant. About one year later, I was informed that a $30,000 grant had been approved. This amount eventually grew to $75,000, and the Yale Kempf Fund provided an additional $75,000 through the Institute for Social and Policy Studies (ISPS). The chairman of the psychiatry department, Stephen Bunny, MD, agreed to accept the grant and administer it.

I learned that a film, *The Last Journey into Silence*, based on interviews with three mothers and daughters, had been produced in a specific psychiatric facility in northern Israel housing Holocaust survivors. I contacted this hospital and a psychiatrist was assigned to coordinate the work with me. Lengthy debates followed. My Israeli counterpart advised me that I had to think of the project as "going on a safari"; that is, I had to first to raise a large budget so I could fund the salaries of all the personnel involved in the project for a period of three months. No such resources were at my disposal, but I kept hoping that we would find a more reasonable formula.

Our next step was to set up a planning meeting in Israel. The date was set and I booked my flight to Israel for September 13, 2001. Then September 11 happened. Air traffic to and from the United States stopped, and it was uncertain when it would resume. The psychiatrist at the Israeli institution called to ask me whether the meeting was going to take place as planned. I responded that I would be there. Indeed, on Friday, September 14, I found myself on the first El Al flight to leave JFK for Israel after the terrorist attack.

The meeting on September 16 was quite matter-of-fact. The director was not present, but the clinical staff were enthusiastic and accepted the responsibility of organizing and carrying out the project. We did not finalize the exact date on which it would begin. I was satisfied with what we had accomplished.

Three weeks after I returned to the United States, I received a letter from the hospital administration informing me that they were unable to participate in the video testimony project for lack of adequate resources. I was outraged. More than half a year had passed, and I was back to square one. Dr Zehava Salomon, the Dean of the Tel Aviv University School of Social

Work, introduced me to the directors of two hospitals—Beer-Yaakov and Lev-Hasharon—which had specialized 'survivor hostels' attached to them. We had a planning meeting on July 2, 2002, during which we made all the necessary decisions, including that of the starting date: October 28, 2002.

I established a close collaborative relationship with Dr Rael Strous, the director of research at one of the hospitals. He participated in every phase of planning and implementing the study. The project had been delayed by about one year.

Twenty-six video testimonies were obtained from hospitalized survivors housed in two facilities. Substantial psychological testing was administered in order to examine the impact that giving the testimony had. The study was carried out in two stages, five months apart, in 2002 and 2003. First came the 'experimental group,' whose members were tested before and after giving testimony. Second came the 'control group': survivors who were also tested in November to establish a baseline, and retested in April without having given testimony. After the control group gave testimony in 2002, both groups were once again re-tested.

In spite of a complex research design and the Iraq war, the study was carried out successfully. The commitment and enthusiasm of the clinical staff generated a momentum that overcame various difficulties. The survivors who volunteered very much wanted to give their testimony, and their caregivers were thrilled to hear it. Many of the latter, children of survivors themselves, harbored the wish to hear their own parents' stories, but didn't dare ask. That wish may have carried over into the interview project.

It was obvious that we had opened the door, but the road ahead was still very long.

Speaking in a different language

Taking a step backward and reflecting upon my sense of excitement and passion when I started this project, I realized that I had discovered an opening, an entry point, through which a decades-old, burdensome enigma could be addressed. Why wasn't this evident to everyone? If we took this step, we would be freed to move on. The clinical staff in the two hospitals shared this excitement. They needed no prodding, no convincing. The patients, too, had been waiting for this moment to come and were enthusiastic to give their testimony. I could see their struggle to find words, to put them together, to begin their story, and, most of all, to carry it forward.

They were very motivated and experienced an internal urgency. But they could not find in themselves the agency needed to formulate their story coherently. No spontaneous flow could be elicited. As interviewers, we had to repeatedly ask detailed questions to keep the testimony going. We continuously felt the survivors' demanding presence, their yearning to relate. We never felt at loss, disinterested, or fatigued.

Because of all the above, we were shocked when colleagues, institutions, and potential funders repeatedly turned us down. How could they be so oblivious? Were we speaking a different, incomprehensible language? Were we living in different worlds?

In reflecting about it later, we became increasingly convinced that countertransference resistance to knowing extreme trauma played a very important role in these refusals.

The most unacknowledged and forgotten group of Holocaust survivors, as the historian Rafeket Zalashik (2017) has documented, were those who were psychiatrically hospitalized. A routine census in the 1990s put their number at close to 900; most of them had been hospitalized for decades. This number did not take into account the thousands who must have died before then, simply because they were older. These survivors were the undeniable evidence, the ultimate proof, of the horrendous emotional devastation wrought by the Holocaust, which directly affected a large portion of Israeli society and, indirectly, Jews all over the world. To recognize their existence was, for many, to begin to acknowledge its shadow in themselves.

Furthermore, to witness extreme traumatization, as is true for all Holocaust testimonies, is tantamount to reliving it. At its core, such reliving is ahistorical. It does away with place and time. It all happens in the here and now. Accompanying affects are immediate, intense, and unregulated. It can evoke a cauldron of images, fragments of events, voids, and feelings of sheer terror and bottomless loss. All these may exceed one's capacity to symbolize, find words, and build narrative. Even for the most willing listener, there can be a sense of overwhelming 'too muchness.' One can imagine oneself walking in a death march, but only for a brief moment, whereas the march itself was endless. One can imagine entering a gas chamber, but such fantasy has to be abruptly curtailed.

Powerful countertransference resistances, both feelings and enactments, are therefore the rule when it comes to knowing extreme traumatization. They range from complete erasure and denial, as in the case of the 'forgotten' hospitalized survivors, to sweeping countertransference parapraxes, such as an analyst 'not knowing' for more than a year and half of analytic work that her patient's family had the same Holocaust background as her own family.

I shall now present an example from my clinical practice: a patient, the son of a Holocaust survivor, who had escaped to the Soviet Union. He wondered whether psychosis was genetically transmitted in his family. He considered both his mother and his sister to be 'crazy,' although neither had been in psychiatric treatment. His mother, however, had a sister, 'Chanale,' who had been chronically hospitalized in a psychiatric institution in Israel, until she died in the 1970s or 1980s. All this had been revealed by a cousin about a year previously. His sister was so outraged that she had stopped speaking to their mother ever since. I asked the patient if his aunt, too, had helplessly witnessed the death of her mother—the patient's grandmother—of dysentery. He had earlier told me that his mother had. The patient responded that that was exactly what the cousin had said: both the patient's mother and his aunt were present at their mother's death, and the aunt had since suffered a mental breakdown. I told the patient, who had been in treatment with me for about a year, that this was the first time I had heard about it. He was quite surprised and a bit incredulous.

After the end of the session, I felt a certain unease. I decided to look up my notes on our first session. And there it was: his mother had had a sister, 'Chanale,' who had spent years, and eventually died, in a psychiatric institution in Israel. She had been one of the type of patients whose testimonies I took down decades later, and who are the centerpiece of this book. Yet when the patient told me about this aunt, I neither registered nor remembered it. How could I not have noticed it, when he first mentioned her existence? How could I have so thoroughly erased her from my own memory? Was not she herself, potentially, one of the group of patients whose testimonies I had pursued with such passion and against all odds? What psychological processes were operating in me, to lead to such an outcome?

It hence comes as no surprise that the Fortunoff video archive, which I cofounded, initially refused to archive these testimonies. The reasons given were lack of funding for this work, and that it was simply impossible to accept consent forms signed by psychiatrically hospitalized patients. Once again, I felt that I was encountering the 'refusal to know.' I kept the original videos in my basement for more than ten years, trying again and again to get them archived, until in January 2013 there was a complete reversal in attitude, and Yale's Sterling Memorial Library accepted the testimonies of the psychiatrically hospitalized Holocaust survivors as a special collection.

Failed empathy, on an individual and on a societal level, is ubiquitous when it comes to registering extreme traumatic experience. Every single genocide—the Armenian, the Cambodian, the Rwandan—remains essentially unknown and is ultimately forgotten. Information about the slaughter of the Tutsis was televised all over the world in real time, but it was not registered in such a way as to trigger an intervention that could have stopped it. Such intervention would require what could be called 'action knowledge,' that kind of human knowing that was typical of those resisters in World War II who took every risk possible in order to save the lives of those who were persecuted. It is only "real knowing" that leads to action, and it is only action that leads to "real knowing" (Hallie, 1994).

But even the Holocaust, in spite of an enormous amount of study and research, remains to a large extent unknown. We know close to nothing about what happened to the 600,000 Jews deported to and killed in Bełżec. Only two of them survived, and one was murdered in 1946, during the trial of a war criminal in Poland. The Polish emissary, Jan Karski, who visited Bełżec in 1943 disguised as an Estonian guard, reported what he saw to Churchill, Roosevelt, and other politicians, and published it in a book in 1946. Yet the information he transmitted found no substantive response.

The struggle against 'knowing' is not limited to genocidal trauma. Knowledge about child sexual abuse found its place in societal awareness only a few decades ago. In psychiatry, the diagnosis of PTSD was introduced only in 1980 (cf. Hamburger, 2017), while in psychoanalysis traumatic experience has until recently been subordinated to the "internal psychic reality," ever since Freud abandoned his "seduction theory" (cf. Bohleber, 2017). Multiple studies show that among the seriously mentally ill (SMI), over 90 percent have had a history of trauma, yet nothing has been undertaken to contextualize this finding (Kilcommons & Morrison, 2005).

Psychoanalytic reflection explains this countertransference resistance to knowing trauma. The listener or viewer momentarily identifies with the victim of extreme trauma, has an imaginary glimpse of his pain, and promptly disidentifies with him, fleeing from such terror, such pain, for the sake of self-protection. We believe there are additional, deeper layers to this 'not knowing.' The impact of extreme traumatic experience deactivates the processes of symbolization, integration, and affect regulation, making its registration in the psyche no longer possible. In its place, voids of experience and of memory are created, and trauma that was experienced, either directly or vicariously (through hearing about or seeing it), remains essentially unknown.

References

Bohleber, W. (2017). Treatment, trauma, and catastrophic reality: A double understanding of the "too much" experience and its implications for treatment. This volume, chapter 1.

Hallie, P. P. (1994). *Lest innocent blood be shed: The story of the village of Le Chambon and how goodness happened.* New York: Harper Collins.

Hamburger, A. (2017). Genocidal trauma: Individual and social consequences of the assault on the mental and physical life of a group. This volume, chapter 4.

Kilcommons, A. M. and Morrison, A. P. (2005) Relationships between trauma and psychosis: An exploration of cognitive and dissociative factors. *Acta Psychiatrica Scandinavica, 112*(5), 351–359.

Zalashik, R. (2017). The psychiatrically hospitalized survivors in Israel: A historical overview. This volume, chapter 11.

Chapter 13

The Israel story
My story

Irit Felsen

The idea—to interview Holocaust survivors who had spent decades chronically hospitalized in psychiatric institutions, diagnosed with schizophrenia—initially seemed 'crazy.' I thought about the chronically hospitalized schizophrenic patients I had come across during my years of training in psychiatric hospitals. Some were immersed in bizarre delusions, speaking an incomprehensible word salad; others appeared disconnected and apathetic, beyond reach. I remembered how empty the intersubjective field between us felt, despite my efforts to connect. How long, I wondered, would elderly chronic patients be able to talk? Would they say just a few words? Or would they ramble on about bizarre topics for hours? Would we be able to understand them, or would we be interpreting, and perhaps misinterpreting, their unintelligible words? To what extent was their illness related to the Holocaust?

After their decades of chronic schizophrenia, long years in psychiatric hospitals, and extended use of now outdated psychotropic medications, I expected the patients to look dilapidated and dazed. Unexpectedly, we entered a beautiful hostel recently built on the grounds of a psychiatric hospital, especially for the survivors. The place was clean and bright, and the people looked 'normal.'

I was surprised by the length of the testimony sessions and by the sustained effort the survivors made to communicate. Most surprising was the feeling one had in their presence. They did not seem disconnected or disorganized, as one might have expected. In fact, their very 'normalcy' amplified their tragedy. It seemed so unbearably sad that despite it, they had resigned themselves to living their lives in closed psychiatric institutions.

We began the process of taking the testimonies. It was remarkably normal, the way each interviewee walked in, greeted us, and sat down. The videographer set up the microphone; the interviewee waited politely.

There was a clear sense of a special event taking place, not just another medical or clinical interview. There was a TV camera and a professional cameraman; this was a solemn event the subjects seemed to feel honored by.

Then they spoke. Neither we nor the survivors hurried through the conversation. Our shared experience emerged hesitantly: out of the survivors' initially shy responses, the silences between them, and our comments, questions, and non-verbal encouragement. We, too, did not know how well our questions would be understood, accepted, and responded to. We, too, were somewhat hesitant and cautious, not sure what shape the interviews would take. After the first interview, it became clear that this 'crazy idea' was going to work. The first testimony took much longer than the hospital staff, who knew the patients well, had anticipated. I felt completely immersed in the mutual engagement that filled the room. The interviews that followed were similarly enrapturing. The survivors seemed intensely engaged and motivated to participate, even when they fell silent. Their silence felt dense, meaningful—not empty. It was important to notice its place in the narrative: what came just before it, what just after; to notice the body language that accompanied it, the facial mannerisms, the breathing. This silence often came when the survivor's story approached the most painful moments, the most terrible losses they had suffered.

Our familiarity with the language in which each survivor gave testimony, or with which their testimony was peppered, whether German, Hebrew, Polish, or Romanian, together with our knowledge of relevant historical facts, geographical details, cultural nuances, and even our ability to use shared humor, was paramount in animating what seemed like a frozen landscape in the survivors' testimonies. It established a sense of implicit knowing and shared belonging. It introduced us into their landscape as if we were somehow part of it, accompanying them in a place somewhat familiar to us, too. It helped jolt their memory and propel their stories forward.

I was in awe of the process and deeply moved. We were taking the testimonies of people who had retreated from the world decades ago. One of them had literally stopped speaking. Yet he, too, came to give his testimony.

As they told us about the war, about their parents and their homes; as they recounted their losses, and their struggles afterward when they came to Israel, these chronically hospitalized patients did not seem all that different from many other survivors who managed to live outside of mental institutions, despite the presence of some psychiatric symptoms.

I realized that, for me, the lines distinguishing these survivors from others I have known are blurry. The Holocaust survivors we interviewed did not resemble chronic schizophrenia patients. Their original symptoms were buried in charts that had disappeared over the years. Most of them did not display current psychotic symptoms, and many denied ever having them. Yet I did not doubt their disability. What they described was a loss of hope, a lost capacity to work, a lack of perceived support. I wondered what made it possible for other survivors I have known to remain functional, while these survivors so tragically could not.

Raised in Israel, I have known many Holocaust survivors. Some of them functioned marginally, some even manifested psychiatric symptoms. However, many of the survivors I knew growing up, as well as subsequently as a psychologist, functioned sufficiently well despite their symptoms. They worked and interacted with people appropriately enough to remain productive and to be part of a community. Some had families, even if their functioning within these families was impaired. For example, 'Henry,' the youngest of five siblings, survived the war with two brothers. He was fifteen years old when he came to America, where he learned watch repair. Henry married young and owned a jewelry store with his brother. He worked every day in the back room and barely interacted with the customers. At home, Henry just sat at the kitchen table in silence. His children reported that they never exchanged more than a sentence or two with their father.

One interviewee had a nephew, 'Tomer,' who came to meet us before his aunt's interview. Her story illustrated most concretely how blurry the distinction was between some of survivors I knew in childhood and our interviewees. Tomer's mother, Rivka, owned a flower shop not far from my childhood home. In the building where I lived, there was another flower shop, owned by Bluma. Rivka and Bluma were friendly with each other. Bluma, whose shop was right under my parents' apartment, was orphaned in childhood, came to Israel young and alone, and never married. She often suffered from terrible 'attacks,' including severe head and neck pain, accompanied by an agitated mental state. She would regularly talk to herself in the mirror, her conversation accompanied by odd mannerisms. People thought she was strange, and at times labile.

Tomer told me that when his aunt, Rivka's sister, our interviewee, came to Israel, she lived in a hostel for new immigrants and had a job. Some time later she became unable to work and moved into the small apartment where Tomer and his family lived. At some point afterward, his aunt was hospitalized. Since then, she had spent her life in psychiatric hospitals.

What made for the difference between Tomer's aunt, a chronic psychiatric patient, and Bluma? Tomer's aunt had a supportive and caring family, while Bluma did not. Yet despite her orphaned childhood, her lack of family support and her psychological and somatic symptoms, Bluma managed to keep her shop and apartment, and even helped the underprivileged flower-delivery boys she employed.

In those days in Jerusalem, there were many people like Bluma. Some survivors functioned well until suddenly they could not go on; this was often when they began to age. 'Mona' was the first chronically hospitalized Holocaust survivor I met as a young psychologist. She seemed completely 'normal': an elegant middle-aged woman who looked out of place in the run-down psychiatric hospital where she was a chronic patient. Mona was intelligent, appropriate, and pleasant, without any psychotic symptoms. Yet she had been in the hospital for several years, and would not leave. Prior to her hospitalization, Mona had had a long career at Yad Vashem, the museum commemorating the Holocaust. From a presentation about her case, I learned that Mona was a child survivor who had been hidden in the woods. She was saved by a Polish peasant who raped her repeatedly. Mona functioned well in society until she was near sixty, perhaps nearing retirement, when she was no longer able to continue to live in the world outside the hospital.

Other survivors showed uneven functioning across various domains. 'Yaro' was a lifelong friend of my parents; once, he assured me that the Holocaust had no impact on him. "After you walk over bodies for three days, you feel no different than if you were walking on stones," he said. He was jovial, fun-loving, the life of the party, a very successful businessman, and a generous philanthropist. Yet he hit his wife and beat his daughters severely on multiple occasions, kicked the milkman, and punched a uniformed policeman. When triggered, Yaro had no self-control. Recently, one of Yaro's daughters told me, "He was an evil man!" and the other stated, "He was a sick man."

Despite Yaro's joviality, I always sensed something disquieting. My parents would not think of Yaro as evil, though they knew of his violent outbursts. One of the positive things survivors provided for each other was an unspoken, non-judgmental understanding of things incomprehensible to others, things they did not condone but yet did not condemn.

They understood the damage and the consequences of the trauma that continued to haunt some of their fellow survivors years after the war. They saw both the 'crazy' and the positive in each other, and tried to help.

This implicit acceptance among survivors extended also to knowledge of terrible things that had happened during the Holocaust. Some survivors, like 'Korina,' harbored traumas so far outside normal human experience that they defy the ultimate concept of normality. Korina was my favorite 'aunt'—not really my aunt, but a very close friend of my parents. She had one grown son and enjoyed spending time with me; perhaps she thought of me as the daughter she never had. On occasions, fragments of her Holocaust experiences would surface briefly. I listened silently. These, I felt, were uniquely intimate moments.

Korina lived a comfortable, calm life, somewhat isolated socially, with a husband who adored her. At some point I learned that her previous husband, the father of her son, had committed suicide. It was implied that his suicide was related to his having been in the *Judenrat*, the supposedly self-governing Jewish body in the Ghetto, established by the Nazis. Korina was left a widow, with a young boy, in a new country. She later met 'Jacob,' whose wife and daughter had been killed in the Holocaust. Jacob adopted her son and became a devoted father to him. The son became a successful adult, both professionally and personally. One could conclude that Korina showed remarkable resilience in the face of repeated traumatic losses, maintained good functionality, remained symptom-free, and raised a successful son.

I later learned that during the Holocaust, Korina had had a child from her first marriage. They were in hiding with ten other people. At some point, the Nazis were very near. The other people feared that a crying baby might be heard and demanded that it be killed to save everyone else. The baby was smothered to death with a pillow. Korina lived with this trauma, the loss of her first husband, the suicide of her second husband, and the loss of her entire family of origin. Yet she showed no psychiatric symptoms, and was kind and loving.

Stories like Korina's were kept secret. However, witnesses sometimes revealed them. Fran described and revisited, in a documentary made by her cousin, the barn in which a Polish woman hid both their families, together with a physician and his family, for the duration of the war. One day, while in hiding, within earshot of the neighbors, five-year-old Fran began crying inconsolably. Everyone tried to quiet her, but she did not stop crying for three days. In desperation, they decided that the doctor would give her a lethal pill. Fran remembers being given that pill. She was supposed to die, and the Polish lady came up with a bag to dispose of the body. However, Fran woke up. Her pulse was very weak, but she was alive. And so she survived. Fran stated that her family was never "the same" after the war, that they were "broken." Nevertheless, after immigrating to the USA, they were able to work and reestablished their lives, without mental-health assistance. They did not succumb to mental illness.

What is normal in such extreme circumstances? How is an internal balance maintained between haunting trauma, and staying alive and functional in the present? What is the cost of such functionality? How fragile might such a balance be, and what are the conditions that support or disrupt it? What allows some people to remain connected to themselves and to others after such devastating experiences?

These are questions that must be asked in order to help current and future trauma survivors. Many of the survivors I have known, despite having endured horrific traumatic experiences, were not 'crazy.' Korina was not crazy. Fran, despite her difficulties with depressive mood, anxiety, and relationships, was not crazy either. One might have expected they would be, but they were not.

Those who grew up in Israel shortly after the war have personal memories of survivors in our daily lives. These survivors were our parents and their friends, the parents of our own childhood friends, shopkeepers and street vendors, neighbors, and people on the streets of Jerusalem or Tel Aviv. The hospitalized psychiatric patients we interviewed were more similar to the survivors I knew in childhood than to the chronic schizophrenic patients I met during my training. Some of our interviewees were much like the silent grocer, whose face was etched with constant pain and who seemed to function in a sad daze, or the toy-shop owner, who was often shrouded in a dark, explosive mood, or Bluma, with her bizarre mannerisms.

Had the hospitalized survivors been more obviously different from the others, it might have been easier to categorize them as 'crazy.' However, encountering the interviewees was all the more painful because they seemed so 'normal' in so many ways. It was tragic because they might have had businesses, a place in the community, and lived among us if had they received more support. They were not dead, like the six million; they were alive and had spent decades in neglected psychiatric institutions. They lost their lives in the Holocaust in a different way. Having met them, it was difficult not to wonder how much of their experience was unavoidable. There was a delicate balance between wellness and 'craziness' in the adaptation achieved by many after such extreme trauma as the Holocaust. A fine line separated some survivors who did not become psychiatric patients from those who did. Individual adaptation was multifaceted, consisting unevenly of aspects of more and less successful functioning. Individual survivors might have crossed over these fine lines in *either* direction at different times.

There were also highly resilient, functional, and exuberant survivors. Yet even they manifested dramatic psychological defenses to keep traumatic material from consciousness. My mother, the most realistic, down-to-earth, and resilient person I have ever known, told me matter-of-factly that she could not willfully call up the memory of her mother's face in her waking hours. She could only 'see' her in her dreams. Similarly, the father of my patient 'Jody' told her that he can remember himself standing next to his mother in the kitchen, as he had done many times, but he can only 'see' her hands kneading and cooking. He cannot 'lift' his view to include her face, much as he wants to. Such 'holes' in memories might have provided protection from intolerable pain, might have allowed forward movement perhaps not otherwise possible. Despite their persistence in nonconscious form, extremely important mental representations were barred from voluntary recall and lived experience. Such clearly stored yet inaccessible imprints raise questions about what else might have been 'cut off' to allow some to survive psychologically, and even thrive, while others became disconnected from their own narrative and from society. 'Deletions' of trauma-suffused mental content, observed even in highly functioning survivors, may have had a protective effect. As the hospitalized survivors show, however, such psychological erasures can also be potentially destructive.

This chapter has described my reactions to the hospitalized psychiatric patients as well as to survivors whom I have met in my personal and professional life. I suggest that processes of deletion, erasure, and the denial of extreme trauma might compose a continuous spectrum. The chronically hospitalized survivors we met represent the more extreme points on this range, with their tragic fate as the ultimate enactment and consequence of their own, and society's, attempt to cut off and not know extreme trauma.

Chapter 14

Video testimony of long-term hospitalized psychiatrically ill Holocaust survivors[1]

Rael Strous

It is well known that symptoms of PTSD may be long lasting. This is often true in the case of PTSD with an underlying context of a severe trauma, a human induced trauma, and a trauma involving children. Being a victim of experiences during the Holocaust would clearly qualify as such a trauma, especially since support structures such as family—which would have otherwise assisted in coping with trauma—were often unavailable. Symptomatology of PTSD, whether severe or mild, may often be chronic despite the passage of time. This has been reported to be true, especially with many victims of the Holocaust who often did not speak about their experiences immediately after having been exposed to trauma. While the reasons are numerous, they include loss of previous support structures, disbelief by many—with the accompanying difficulty of talking about it with those who did not experience the atrocities—and the general mood by some that one should "move on" and not focus on the past, no matter how distressing. Thus what Holocaust survivors experienced was often ignored, overtly or covertly, by health care providers, including those in the mental health community (Vigoda, 1996). For many patients in mental health contexts, and despite the obvious influence that traumatic experiences would have in any event played in their lives, and despite the importance in addressing them, no mention was made of these experiences in their health care files.

Thus, in order to explore whether addressing these issues would have any influence on the clinical state of individuals whose traumatic experiences lay in the distant past, we conducted a study exploring the value of the video testimony method, pioneered by a group of Chilean therapists (Cienfuegos & Monelli, 1983; Weine, Kulenovic, Pavkovic, & Gibbons, 1998). We considered the study and its potential findings important since at the time, and as far as we knew, no one had investigated the value of this method in connection with Holocaust survivor patients who had been chronically hospitalized with mental illness. This was by no means a small subpopulation, and in 1993 consisted of approximately 18 percent of the chronic psychiatric hospital population in Israel (Terno, Barak, Hadjez, Elizur, & Szor, 1998). We aimed to explore the value of the technique as a helpful clinical tool in order to address traumatic experiences resulting from the Holocaust, traumatic experiences that may not have been explored to the extent to which, perhaps, they should have. Most importantly, we knew that we had to ensure the safety of the patients and to monitor any effects, positive or negative, following the video testimony intervention. The results of the study have been published in the *American Journal of Psychiatry* (Strous et al., 2005) and are reproduced here in order to reflect findings within the context of a publication exploring and describing the larger phenomenon.

Study population

We recruited long-term psychiatric in-patients from two large academic state hospitals in Israel (Beer Yaakov and Lev Hasharon Mental Health Centers) over a period of approximately a year and a half (2002–2003). The initial sample consisted of 24 patients including ten females and fourteen males. All subjects at the time were hospitalized in specialized units catering to long-term hospitalized Holocaust survivors, who also happened to have severe mental illness. The age range was 60 to 85 (mean 71.9, SD 7.2). Countries of origin included Poland (seven patients), Romania (five patients), and Hungary (three patients), and France, Greece, Yugoslavia, Czech Republic, Russia, and Morocco (one patient each). Inclusion criteria included all subjects being classified as victims of Nazi persecution, as defined by the Conference on Jewish Claims Against Germany, Inc (Schwartz, 2014) (for example, in hiding, ghettos, concentration labor and death camps, and so forth), and who were at least three years old during the time of persecution, and who were, finally, willing and capable of telling a story, even if only in part. Anyone with signs of major intellectual impairment or severe psychosis that would interfere with effective video testimony was excluded from the study. It is important to state that the study was approved by the local Helsinki Committee Ethical Review Committee, as well as by the Yale Human Investigation Committee. All subjects and their legal guardians provided signed, informed consent, once the nature of the study and its potential risks and benefits had been fully explained. In addition, considering the clinical sensitivity of the study, consent was also obtained from the subject's designated clinician. Subjects were informed, obviously, that they had the right to end study participation at any time.

Study plan

All those participating in the study were evaluated with clinical ratings consisting of the Positive and Negative Syndrome Scale (PANSS) (Kay, Fiszbein, & Opler, 1987) and the Clinical Global Impression Scale (severity and improvement) (CGI-S, CGI-I) (Guy, 1976, 218–222). In addition, each subject was rated with the Clinician-Administered PTSD Scale, Form 2 (CAPS-2) (Blake, 1990), the Structured Interview for Disorders of Extreme Stress (SIDES) (Pelcovitz et al., 1997), and the Mini-Mental State Examination (MMSE) (Folstein, 1975). Following these initial clinical ratings, subjects were randomly allocated to one of two groups. One group immediately undertook the video testimony, with the other group serving as the control group, initially without the video testimony. Four months later both groups were again administered clinical ratings. Following this second round of clinical ratings, the second group now undertook the video testimony experience, followed by another round of clinical ratings which were again administered 4 months after the first video testimony of the second group had been taken (similarly to what the initial experimental group underwent). Throughout the duration of the study, all patients continued with their standard medication regimen and were scored by the same rater at each stage of the study. In order to prevent any untoward reactions as a result of study participation, all patients were monitored daily by clinical staff on the inpatient units.

The video testimony took place on the ward in a specially designated room, over a period of up to three hours. Depending of the patient's skill and level of cooperation, the testimony would consist of usually one, though every so often two interviews, which were then conducted in the patient's preferred language (Hebrew, Yiddish, German, or Polish). Patients were monitored closely on the ward by their treating psychiatrists for any deterioration or change in clinical status potentially occurring before, during, and after the testimony. Patients were encouraged to provide details of their experiences during and after the Holocaust period, including their reconnecting with family, if relevant, as well as any bereavement issues and treatment they may have undergone. Patients benefitted directly from the intervention, as after having conducted the interview, the two interviewers would discuss their observations with the clinical treating team, in addition to providing a clinical formulation for the staff's benefit after each interview had taken place (cf. Greenwald, 2017).

Findings of the study

Interestingly and somewhat unexpectedly, no differences were noted between pre- and post-interview PANSS sub- or total scores, CGI, or MMSE measures. This finding showed that the testimony had no effect on psychotic symptomatology, overall impression of the clinical state, as well as no effect on dementia symptoms and cognitive decline.

Clinical changes in symptomatology following testimony

Data from the CAPS-2 rating scale, which measures PTSD symptomatology, were analyzed according to DSM-IV criteria (at least one intrusion, three avoidance, and two hyperarousal items required for a diagnosis of PTSD). It is important to note that eight patients (38.1 percent) exhibited symptoms of PTSD at the time of the first interview. Following the testimony, this decreased to only four patients (19 percent) by the time of the second interview. Although only a subset of patients met the applicable criteria for PTSD, all patients did indicate some posttraumatic symptoms, which in many cases did improve following testimony.

In addition, there was a clear reduction in symptom severity of all three diagnostic clusters, especially avoidance severity. The severity scores are measured as the sum of frequency and intensity measures of the CAPS scale, with total severity score being the sum of the three diagnostic clusters. When frequency and intensity scores were analyzed separately, we noted a significant decrease in the intensity of all three diagnostic clusters, but decreased frequency was only observed in the avoidance cluster. Since the criteria for DSM-IV require functional impairment, this criterion was also analyzed (items 18 and 19 of CAPS-2 scale reflecting social and occupational functioning). Results indicated that there indeed was a decrease in impairment between the two interviews ($p=0.017$). We also analyzed the proportional change in total severity score (severity after/severity before interview) for each patient. Results indicated that six subjects showed no change, one subject an increase of symptoms, and all other subjects showed improvement, including nine patients demonstrating an improvement of 30 percent or more. The most significant change was seen on the intrusion cluster of symptoms, followed by avoidance and then the arousal cluster of symptoms. Further analysis with regression models indicated that higher avoidance score and low arousal scores predict greater reduction of total severity scores. We noted an inverse correlation between total CAPS-2 scores and total PANSS scores, both at baseline (r=−0.454, p=0.044) and at follow-up (r=−0.443, p=0.044), and a positive correlation between CGI-severity and total PANSS score at baseline (r=0.616, p=0.006) and follow-up (r=0.748, p<0.001).

For research purposes, we decided to classify responders to the video testimony as those patients with a proportional severity score indicating a reduction of 30 percent or more, and non-responders as those patients indicating a response of less than 30 percent. According to this tagging, 11 patients were responders and another 10 were non-responders.

Gender effects

As expected based on previous studies in the literature (Fullerton et al., 2001), female subjects exhibited higher prevalence of PTSD symptomatology (55.6 percent) compared to males (16.7 percent) (p=0.061). This distinction was also noted following the completion of the testimony with one follow-up: 33.3 percent of females and no male patient meeting PTSD criteria (p=0.031). No gender differences were observed on CGI-I, MMSE, and SIDES.

Discussion

Important findings from the study include the following:

1   Although we did not find any change in psychotic symptoms as a result on the testimony intervention, we did observe significant improvement in posttraumatic symptomatology. This improvement was noted especially with respect to avoidance symptoms.
2   Although a greater severity was noted in PTSD at initial evaluation in females, females tended to respond better following the video interview, indicating that the method may be especially useful in the management of females with long-standing PTSD.

3   The inverse correlation between PTSD symptomatology and overall psychotic state was clearly evident. While preliminary, it may be suggested that those with less severe psychosis are more open to ruminating on painful traumatic memories of the past. Alternatively, rejection or misrepresentation of reality may be adaptive in the face of severe trauma; thus, those with more severe psychotic symptoms may be protected in some way from the memories of trauma.

4   Video testimony has value in the management of Holocaust survivors with severe, chronic mental illness, similar to other subpopulations of victims of persecution and human rights violations. This study indicates that verbalizing what happened—even many years after the event or events—can assist in the reduction of posttraumatic symptoms and improve quality of life. In this manner, we maintain that the testimony approach can be cathartic and provide substance for therapeutic work. We have also previously noted that the video interview may encourage self-reflection and openness with fellow patients, family members, and health care providers. This in turn should lead to improved relationships with those around and, indirectly, an improvement in mood should result.

5   The constructive value of the video interview method appeared to be evident irrespective of the age of the patient at the time of exposure to the traumatic Holocaust event.

6   Since psychotic symptoms did not improve despite PTSD symptoms improving, it may be suggested that these patients did not suffer from PTSD with psychosis, but rather, in most cases, from schizophrenia. This in some way challenges some psychoanalytic theory which suggests that psychosis is a defensive response against intense internal traumatic experience (Freud, 1911/1958). However, it still may be that those with a tendency or diathesis to schizophrenia may be more vulnerable to suffering from full blown PTSD following exposure to severe stress, such as was experienced during the Holocaust (Seedat, Stein, Oosthuizen, Emsley, & Stein, 2003).

7   Many of the patients indicated signs of dementia as reflected in low mean MMSE scores. Some have proposed there may be exaggerated cognitive decline and certain memory disturbances in individuals with chronic PTSD symptomatology, as experienced after the Holocaust (Yehuda, Golier, Halligan, & Harvey, 2004). Whether this may have been a factor in the patients who participated in our study remains unknown.

8   There were no adverse events noted following the testimony interview. Thus while we may have expected some anxiety, sleep interference, and so forth, none of these concerns became an issue.

In summary, study observations suggest the important value that video testimony may have in the management of posttraumatic symptoms in those with long standing comorbid PTSD and psychiatric illness. This may even be the case 60 years after the event in question. It appeared that with testimony, patients feel less burdened by the weight of their experience, which may be associated with the knowledge that their story is now kept safe in another 'external place.' Conditions specific to the method of video testimony, including videotaping and archiving in a prestigious library, serving as a living memory of the event, may also have assisted in the success of the method. The method also assists the clinical treating staff in clinical reassessment of the patient, as well as in developing sensitivity to various special needs in the management and treatment of each patient.

Note

1   Revised version of Strous, R.D., Weiss, M., Felsen, I., Finkel, B., Melamed, Y., Bleich, A., Kotler, M., & Laub, D. (2005). Video testimony of long-term hospitalized psychiatrically ill Holocaust survivors. *American Journal of Psychiatry, 162*, 2,287–2289. Reprinted by permission of *The American Journal of Psychiatry* (copyright ©2005). American Psychiatric Association. All rights reserved. This study was supported by grants allocated by the Institute for Social and Policy Studies, Yale University and the Conference on Jewish Material Claims Against Germany, Inc.

References

Blake, D. (1990). *Clinician-administered PTSD scale: Form 2: One-week symptom status version.* Boston, MA and West Haven, CT: National Center for Posttraumatic Stress Disorder.

Cienfuegos, A. J., & Monelli, C. (1983). The testimony of political repression as a therapeutic instrument. *American Journal of Orthopsychiatry, 53*, 43–51.

Folstein, M. F. (1975). "Mini-mental state": A practical method for grading the cognitive state of patients for the clinician. *Journal of Psychiatric Research, 12*, 189–198.

Freud, S. (1958). Psycho-analytic notes on an autobiographical account of a case of paranoia (dementia paranoides). *Standard Edition, 12*, 1–82. (Original work published 1911)

Fullerton, C. S., Ursano, R. J., Epstein, R. S., Crowley, B., Vance, K., Kao, T. C., Dougall, A., & Baum, A. (2001). Gender differences in posttraumatic stress disorder after motor vehicle accidents. *American Journal of Psychiatry, 158*, 1,486–1,491.

Greenwald, B. N. (2017). The institutional experience: Patients and staff responding to the testimony project. This volume, chapter 15.

Guy, W. (1976). *ECDEU assessment manual for psychopharmacology*. US Dept Health, Education, and Welfare publication (ADM) (pp. 76–338). Rockville MD: National Institute of Mental Health.

Kay, S., Fiszbein, A., & Opler, L. A. (1987). The positive and negative syndrome scale for schizophrenia. *Schizophrenia Bulletin, 13*, 261–276.

Pelcovitz, D., van der Kolk, B., Roth, S., Mandel, F., Kaplan, S., & Resick, P. (1997). Development of a criteria set and a structured interview for disorders of extreme stress (SIDES). *Journal of Traumatic Stress, 10*, 3–16.

Schwartz, E. (2014). Holocaust survivors living in Israel: Data and characteristics. Retrieved December 2, 2016, from http://www.knesset.gov.il/mmm/data/pdf/me03361.pdf.

Seedat, S., Stein, M. B., Oosthuizen, P. P., Emsley, R. A., & Stein, D. J. (2003). Linking posttraumatic stress disorder and psychosis: A look at epidemiology, phenomenology, and treatment. *Journal of Nervous and Mental Disease, 191*, 675–681.

Strous, R. D., Weiss, M., Felsen, I., Finkel, B., Melamed, Y., Bleich, A., Kotler, M., & Laub, D. (2005). Video testimony of long-term hospitalized psychiatrically ill Holocaust survivors. *American Journal of Psychiatry, 162*, 2,287–2,294.

Terno, P., Barak, Y., Hadjez, J., Elizur, A., & Szor, H. (1998). Holocaust survivors hospitalized for life: The Israeli experience. *Comprehensive Psychiatry, 39*, 364–367.

Vigoda, R. (1996). Helping haunted souls of Holocaust. *The Philadelphia Inquirer*, 28 January, MC6.

Weine, S. M., Kulenovic, A. D., Pavkovic, I., & Gibbons, R. (1998). Testimony psychotherapy in Bosnian refugees: A pilot study. *American Journal of Psychiatry, 155*, 1,720–1,726.

Yehuda, R., Golier, J. A., Halligan, S. L., & Harvey, P. D. (2004). Learning and memory in Holocaust survivors with posttraumatic stress disorder. *Biological Psychiatry, 55*, 291–295.

Chapter 15

The institutional experience

Patients and staff responding to the testimony project

Baruch N. Greenwald

Introduction

It had long been suspected that Holocaust survivors were represented in Israeli psychiatric hospitals in disproportionate numbers. The findings of the Bazak Commission (Bazak, 1999) confirmed that among the then 5,000 long term psychiatric patients hospitalized, some 725 (14.5 percent!) could be identified as Holocaust survivors. At that time, many of them had been already hospitalized for 20 years or more and a few since the mid-twentieth century. Most of these patients were diagnosed with chronic schizophrenia and no special attention had been given to the historical circumstances related to their psychiatric symptoms and disabilities. The fact that these patients, like the 'healthy' Holocaust survivors, had not been given special attention suited the attitude of many Israelis back in the 1950s and 1960s who had no patience for the tragic narratives of these ex-ghetto residents, many of whom had chosen to remain in Europe even when options of immigration to pre-Israel Palestine were still open. Many felt that Israel should be about creating a 'new Jew' and images of masses being led to crematoriums were in contradiction to this image. Bronzed and muscled Jews would replace those European Jews who had proved themselves incapable of self-defense. The general public treated survivors with condescension. 'Why didn't you fight back?' they would often ask. 'Why did you go like sheep to the slaughter?' The first turning point toward a change of attitude began with the trial of the Nazi arch-criminal, Adolph Eichmann, in Jerusalem in 1961. The trial broke down the reluctance and opposition of many Israelis to approach the issues of what had actually taken place during the Holocaust due to the powerful impression left by the personal testimonies of over a hundred witnesses.

Many survivors, who had hesitated to tell their personal stories prior to the trial, were gradually more willing to share these narratives. Still, the stigmatized psychiatric patients were remote from the mainstream, and since the government-owned hospitals were becoming overcrowded in the 1960s, the Health Ministry adopted a policy of funding the stay of chronic patients in privately owned institutions.

The owners of these institutions, motivated by hopes of profit, sought to provide minimum care for minimum cost, and visits of government inspectors were not sufficient. The result was an atmosphere of institutionalization, with no incentive to seek rehabilitation programming or updating medications. This status quo went on for about three decades until the mental health reform program was proposed in the 1990s and a movement for de-institutionalization began affecting policy decisions of the Health Ministry officials. In 1993 when Dr Moti Mark was appointed national director of Mental Health Services, it was his own personal life experience as the son of a mother who was a Holocaust victim who had been hospitalized on and off since Dr Mark was four years old that motivated his efforts to influence the Ministry to build designated hostels for the psychiatric disabled survivors. Part of the funding was acquired from the Conference on Jewish Material Claims Against Germany, after the organization's director, the late Rabbi Dr Israel Miller, saw survivors being showered with an open water hose at one of the private institutions marked for closure. Rabbi Miller's decision to populate those designated hostels with mental health candidates from only the private institutions was altered after the author of this chapter visited him in his Jerusalem home in 2001 and told him about the plight of some of the patients in the government-owned institutions. Miller had been manipulated by certain Health Ministry Officials whose first priority was the de-institutionalization and closure of the private institutions, an issue of economic and not moral priorities. Miller, himself not a survivor, had been an American army military chaplain and his connection to the Holocaust was his meeting with survivors in the camps in 1945. After the war Miller rose to influential positions in the American Jewish leadership, culminating with his position as chairman of the Claims Conference. He immigrated from the US to Israel only in the late 1990s.

Three hostels for survivors were finally built and opened—Shaar Menashe in 1998, Beer Yaakov in 2000 and Lev Hasharon in 2001. At these hostels some of the more difficult cases were accepted and treated, mostly those who had no supporting family to care for them.

Populating the hostels

It was the author's job in 1999 to visit one of the institutions being closed (KG) and to try to recruit candidates and staff members for the hostel to be opening in Beer-Yaacov. We also visited another government funded private hospital (NM) whose officials were told to cooperate by allowing us to interview and recruit their survivors for the new hostel. NM was still actively struggling to remain open and functioning, while KG already was set to close its doors on December 31, 1999. The patients at KG were mostly confused and upset by the upcoming closure of their institution. Before the closure, we brought them to visit the structure at Beer Yaacov. We also chose about half of the staff of the new hostel from the KG nurses and orderlies. The group from KG were the first group of residents, and populated about a third of the hostel's beds. Now for the first time they were called 'residents,' not 'patients,' and were aware that their eligibility to live in the new facility was because they had been identified as survivors of the Holocaust. This identification given to them by the Health Ministry was not based on a meticulous investigation of their whereabouts during World War II, but only on the basis of their being born in countries dominated by the Nazis and their allies before 1945 and not leaving them before 1939. There was now a 'hierarchy' of survivors among victims of persecution who had not been evicted from their homes, ghetto-residents, children transported to England or rescued in monasteries, forced labor survivors, and the 'hard-core' concentration camp survivors.

Those candidates from NM were unique since they had chosen to leave their facility while it was still open and functioning (it was shut down about four years later). Even while the advantages of the new facility—with two residents per room, sparkling bathrooms, and spacious halls—were clear, in several cases it was only the intervention of family members (a son, a sibling) that convinced the patient to leave NM. In the case of Shmuel B., the subject of analysis in a previous chapter of this book, it was acquaintance and discussions with the author that helped him to decide to leave NM. Shmuel was impressed by the community-like approach of the staff and the added autonomy and independence which would be given to him at the hostel. The fact that Shmuel had had a positive experience living on a kibbutz before being hospitalized might have been relevant.

The testimony project

When Dr Dori Laub of Yale University sought to record the testimonies of psychiatrically disabled survivors the three new hostels were perfect grounds for the project. Two of the three mental health directors, Dr Avi Bleich of Lev Hasharon and Professor Moshe Kotler of Beer Yaacov, were quite willing and pleased to cooperate. For unclear reasons the director-ship at Shaar Menashe chose to shy away from the project. The bulk of the testimonies came from the Beer Yaacov facility—more than half of the 32 residents were active participants in the project, so it would be fair to say that the project had a very major influence on the atmosphere at the new facility during the years 2002–2005.

Since most of the patients had legal guardians and thus were tech-nically unable to consent independently to cooperate in the project, we had to approach the patients and their guardians as well. With only two exceptions all the patients approached agreed almost immediately. Mrs G. and Miss M., patients with a diagnosis of severe paranoid schizo-phrenia, refused and Mrs G. (Golda, who we will return to below) even seemed upset about what was going on—for example, because of the pres-ence of photographers and other strangers in the home. The process of attaining permission from the legal guardians was not easy, with many of them concerned about possible emotional damage to the interviewees. Those guardians who were close relatives of the patients were easier to convince once they realized the potential value of the taped testimony for them and for future generations. Some of the other guardians, who were either lawyers or worked for health NGOs, sought medical guarantees that were not easy to provide, but agreed in the end. They probably realized the broadness of the project that was to affect so many of the Home's residents as well as the historic and psychological value of the testimonies. Each filmed testimony session involved two interviewers and a video techni-cian. In most of the cases all three of these individuals were outsiders, not previously acquainted with the patients. Past experience with testi-monies has indicated that the victims' pre-existing transference feelings toward people in the interview may impede them from testifying freely and in an unencumbered fashion. The average video session lasted about

60 to 90 minutes (the testimony of Shmuel B. was a lengthy exception). The unedited films of the sessions became available to us about six weeks after the initial interviews. After the staff director had viewed the films, individual staff members were invited (with the patient's permission) to sit with the patient and view the testimony together. In two cases the patients objected at first, but later agreed after other patients had finished joint video sessions. The viewing event lasted for one or two sessions, depending on the length of the particular testimony. After the joint viewing, staff members discussed the content with the patient. As a result of these meetings, the staff felt enriched by learning about and vicariously re-experiencing the patient's life experiences. Consequently, a new and deeper bond was created between the staff and the patients, based on a mutual understanding of the tragic events that played such a major role in the patient's life and pathology. During the joint viewings it was surprising to discover that a number of patients could not identify themselves as the image giving the testimony on the screen. For example patients said: "Who is that?" or "How does she know about that? Who told her?" What possible explanations might there be for this phenomenon? Perhaps the patients had been somehow trapped in an encapsulated adolescence interrupted by the Holocaust, and hearing the recollection of those memories conflicted with their present views of themselves, as they had not been able to understand what had happened to themselves in the intervening years.

As previously mentioned, some of the staff members at the Survivor Home had been formerly employed at KG, the institute closed by the Health Ministry. It is quite interesting to note how these staff saw the effect of the testimony project on the patients some of the staff had known already for 10–15 years. At KG these patients had no special attention or privileges at the institution, and their awareness of an identity as survivors of the Holocaust was conspicuous only on the annual Holocaust Memorial Day (Yom Hashoah) in April, or on the day they received "renta"— a check from the German government. If stories about their experience during the Holocaust were told by some of these patients, it was only on Yom Hashoah. Fabian, a nurse's aide, remembers survivors talking about soap being made out of Jewish corpses. This is one of those myths that has never been verified historically, yet nonetheless the description 'soap' had become a nomenclature for those 'weakling' Jews who had gone like 'sheep to slaughter.' The testimony project turned the patients into celebrities overnight. The wretched souls were now international stars wooed by the Hebrew-speaking scholar from Yale University, Dr Dori Laub. Everyday at the Home now became Yom Hashoah. As part of the follow-up after the video sessions an art therapist (Ilana Reman) and a social worker (Oshrit Ben-Ari) held weekly sessions attended by about half of the residents, most of them participants in the testimony interviews. Part of these sessions included showing short excerpts from the video interviews and discussing their content. This was done in cooperation with those interviewees who, as already noted, had become "celebrities." It was an open group and even though a majority of the participants had been interviewed on video, these group settings fulfilled the need of those residents who had not agreed to be filmed but were nonetheless now very eager to tell their stories. A special case was Golda, who had refused to be interviewed, probably because she was trying so hard to avoid dealing with her past. Golda eventually found this setting to be a safe place to tell her story of how she chose not to escape from the German soldiers even when a friend offered her an opportunity to run. Instead she stood close to her mother who was cremated at Auschwitz. Golda 'survived.' The group listened carefully to Golda's story and now gave her the opportunity to share her story and ease a bit of her distress.

Testimonies of Hannah, Sarah, and David

At the time of writing this chapter, only Hannah is still alive of these three patients (Hannah, Sarah, and David are all pseudonyms). She is soon to be 88, in relatively good health, and living a quiet enclosed life in the Holocaust Survivor Home. Born in a village in eastern Romania, Hannah was the youngest child in a family of five siblings. Shortly after the war began, the family was forcibly uprooted and moved to Yasi. According to the 1930 census Jews were the second largest ethnic group in Yaşi with a population of 34,662 (some 34 percent) ("Yasi," in: *Yivo Encyclopedia of Jews in Eastern Europe*). Hannah remained in Yasi after the war, wed, bore a child, and divorced, all before immigrating to Israel in 1948. In Israel she lived with her sister and son, wed again, and divorced again after having a second son. She was already showing signs of so-called mental disease, and did not raise her second son. From information we have in her file, self-neglect and behavior described as unusual or bizarre preceded psychiatric hospitalizations. Diagnosed as having paranoid schizophrenia, she was in and out of hospitals until the Health Ministry authorized her permanent hospitalization at KG in 1980. Hannah was part of the group that moved to the Holocaust Survivor Home when KG was closed. Her testimony described her experience during the Russian bombing of Yasi, the mass murder of Jews in Yasi later, and particularly the 'death train' incident. The incidents took place from June 29 to July 6, 1941, and at least one third of the Jewish population were massacred in the pogrom itself or in its aftermath (Carp, 2000). Hannah describes thousands of Jews being forced onto overcrowded, sealed 'death trains' that drove slowly back and forth across the country in the hot summer weather until most of their passengers were killed by hyperthermia, thirst, or infection and bleeding. Hannah describes the Soviet bombing of Yasi, which, according to historical sources took place on June 26, 1941. Both the bombing and the mass murder were extremely traumatic experiences for Hannah. When the trains returned to Yasi filled with corpses, Hannah and her father were among those forced by the Germans to bury bodies. Hannah was 12 years old. The city's Jewish population had been accused of aiding the Soviets, and rumors were promoted among the general population that the Jews were anti-Romanian. On one hand, Jews were accused of signaling the Soviet aircraft and showing them where to bomb, yet, on the other hand Hannah's testimony describes a direct hit on her (Jewish) neighborhood. Asked in the interview about her dreams, Hannah replied: "I have dreams about it [World War II]. But then I realize that, thank God, we are here now, free. It's a great miracle. But they shouldn't throw us out of here as well. I think about it. Maybe they will close down this place and throw us out, who knows where! [Pause, then looking straight at Dr Laub, the interviewer.] Will they close this place?" Dr Laub: "No, never." (For this and more on the content of the testimonies, see Greenwald, Ben-Ari, Strous, & Laub, 2006.)

After viewing Hannah's testimony in its entirety, staff members found it to be easier to recognize the connection between Hannah's traumatic childhood and her suspicious behavior, lack of trust, self-neglect, inability to make independent decisions, and her ever-constant reconciliation. Hannah tends to define for herself a 'safe' territory, often standing or sitting close at the entrance to her room and leaving this 'safe' territory only to go the dining room for meals or when a staff member calls her for a specific activity. Before the taping of the testimonies it was known that Hannah never attended outings organized by the staff, including concerts, movies, or one-day trips. Following her testimony, a social work student worked very closely with Hannah to gain her trust and hopefully recruit her participation in the extra-curricular activities accompanied by the student. Success was only partial. Since the 'second intifada' was still exacting a toll of victims of terror in Israel at the time (2003–2005) and restaurants and other public gatherings were often chosen as targets, Hannah's hesitance about leaving the 'safe' territory of the Survivor Home could not be viewed as irrational. Hannah's lifetime history of being uprooted from place to place, mostly unwilling, and even the institutional changes forced upon her by the Ministry of Health make her last remarks in the testimony both genuine and sad: "Maybe they will . . . throw us out who knows where!"

Excerpts of Hannah's videotaped testimony have been shown, with her permission, at various conferences both in Israel and overseas. Despite the permission she gave us to show the testimony to professional audiences, she specifically asked that it not be shown to her sons, to save them from the painful content. However, when she realized the first time that we were taking the film with us to Canada, she uncharacteristically stormed into the Home Director's office urgently requesting that a copy of the film remain in Israel should her sons wish to view it after her demise. We calmed her, explaining that we had two copies of the film: one intended for the researchers and a second one, her copy, which has also remained in her hands at her request. We usually give the second copy to a guardian or family member after permission from the patient.

Sarah's personality and story differ from Hannah's, although she also suffered from extreme anxiety and was diagnosed as a paranoid schizophrenic. Sarah was born in Greece in 1927, the second of three daughters. When she was a year old her family left Greece when her father got a prestigious rabbinical position in Belgium. Shortly after the war broke out Sarah's father died from a sudden heart attack, which she attributed to his "heart-break" when he realized what was soon to happen. When the Nazis occupied Belgium and began to round up Jews for departure, their house was not on the list and they tried to remain there in hiding, paying a neighbor in cash and jewelry to bring them food, only to be eventually betrayed by children of other neighbors who told the police that there were still some Jews in that house. Sarah and her family had managed to evade the Nazis for two years before being sent to Auschwitz. Sarah remembers all the events clearly—even the Gestapo soldier who told her they would be drinking coffee before the transport. Instead of coffee, they were all huddled into an open cattle car for the three-day train ride to Auschwitz, where the three daughters were separated from the mother they never saw again. The three surviving sisters returned to Belgium after the war, and while attempting to immigrate to Palestine in 1947 they were arrested and held in a camp in Cyprus until they were allowed to immigrate a year later. Arriving in the newborn State of Israel, all three sisters settled on a kibbutz. Sarah describes the death of her older sister from pneumonia during the severe winter of 1950 (that winter snow accumulated in most of Israel, the only time in the twentieth century that it did so). The two remaining sisters married and left the kibbutz for city life. Sarah divorced, which according to her was a result of her fear of pregnancy and bearing children. At the age of 34 she first began to receive care in a psychiatric outpatient clinic. She was living with her younger sister, his husband, and their three children who she helped, cared for and became very attached to. Sarah was first hospitalized at the age of 41 in 1968. She had been having severe anxiety attacks but the official diagnosis was "schizophrenic reaction." She was in and out of several psychiatric hospitalsfor about three years before she was permanently hospitalized at KG. Like Hannah, Sarah was part of the first group of patients moved to the Holocaust Survivor Home when KG was closed. At KG Sarah confided her life story to nurse's aide Fabian—and was very close to her.

At the Holocaust Survivor Home, prior to the testimony project most of the staff had not been aware of Sarah's hiding during the war and her experiences thereafter. Sarah definitely had classic PTSD symptomology: avoidance, constant tension, and nightmares with flashbacks. Like Hannah, she rarely ventured outside the premises of the Home. On rare occasions when the staff convinced her to participate in outings, she was tense all the time, even screaming, for example, when the bus hit a bump, or if there were sudden noises. But on the premises of the Home, Sarah was an active participant in all activities. She sought to have a relationship with staff members that gave her a special status, had a tendency to criticize staff members who did not meet all her immediate requests, and developed a dependent, sometimes symbiotic, relationship with her roommate. The roommate, a younger woman who had been a small child at the end of the Holocaust, had grown up as an orphan, and interestingly some of her psychotic content was the delusion that Sarah was her mother. Sarah was not delusional or psychotic in the Home. We think that her 1968 diagnosis of having a "schizophrenic reaction" is dubious and wonder how her life might have changed had she been given more appropriate treatment in the community, with behavior therapy for anxiety, instead of being institutionalized for most of her life.

David, born in Czechoslovakia in 1934, was the younger of two siblings. We know that David began elementary school around 1940. It was reported that he had been an excellent pupil, very punctilious in his studies. The 'normal' life of the family was soon interrupted by the war and the Holocaust, as they survived only by hiding in underground bunkers for almost five years. Four years after the war (1949) the family immigrated to Israel, where David completed his high-school matriculation, as well as army duty. In the army he had disciplinary problems and was discharged before serving his full term of duty. His first psychiatric hospitalization was in 1957, two years after his discharge from the army. His complaints then included anxiety and somatic symptoms. Like Sarah, he was hospitalized "on and off" until he was permanently hospitalized at KG in 1965 at the age of 31. David also was also moved to the Holocaust Survivor's Home when KG closed. David was a very quiet man who never said more than two or three words. All we knew about him was from his file or from his elderly aunt (her deceased husband and David's father—many years deceased—had been brothers) who came to visit once every two weeks. At first he refused to be interviewed for the testimony project; however, soon he suddenly said: "okay, let's do it." He said little and most of the interview consisted of the interviewer speaking, to which he agreed or disagreed. David had no real memories of those years spent in the bunkers, only of asking his mother: "Why are we here?" He could not remember what she answered. When asked whether he felt terror all that time his answer was "Probably." His facial and body expressions did speak of terror and sadness, yet he refused to acknowledge that he felt something. David was one of the only residents of the Home who was almost constantly silent, yet he was prone to violent outbursts if and when he felt his private space had been violated (e.g. if someone sat on 'his' chair in the lobby). David also viewed his testimony video together with staff members but had no verbal reactions to the film. Apparently, no one knew David had been suffering and he died unexpectedly four months after his testimony, of massive, undiagnosed lung cancer.

Conclusions

Three survivor homes were built and populated under the auspices of the Ministry of Health. The facility at Shaar Menashe did not participate in the testimony project, and the involvement of Lev Hasharon was minute in comparison to Beer Yaacov. What we witnessed at Beer Yaacov was a renewed vitality that took hold and transformed the relations between staff and patients into an intimate adventure to a lost past. New bonds were forming, not only between staff and patients, but amongst the patients themselves as well. A better knowledge of the past had an enormous impact. Realizing that as a result of the Holocaust trauma, the individual's very sense of self was often erased, we took steps to restore that self, by enabling more self-expression and encouraging empowerment.

References

Bazak, Y. (1999). The findings of the public committee of inquiry into the situation of the psychiatrically ill patients hospitalized in Israeli psychiatric facilities. (Hebrew, available from the Israeli Ministry of Health.)

Carp, M. (2000). *Holocaust in Romania: Facts and documents on the annihilation of Romania's Jews 1940–1944*. Safety Harbor: Simon Publications.

Greenwald, B., Ben-Ari,O., Strous, R.D., & Laub, D. (2006). Psychiatry, testimony, and Shoah: Reconstructing the narratives of the muted. In G. Rosenberg & A. Weisman (Eds.), *International social health care policy, programs, and studies* (pp. 199–214). New York: Haworth Press.

Yivo Encyclopedia of Jews in Eastern Europe. www.yivoencyclopedia.org. Last accessed August 14, 2015.

Chapter 16

Traumatic psychosis

Narrative forms of the muted witness

Dori Laub and Irit Felsen

Through a series of newspaper articles that appeared in the Israeli press in the 1990s, I learned that there were large numbers of Holocaust survivors dispersed among various Israeli hospitals without recorded histories. The rumor was that a ship bearing 1,500 psychiatric patients—the last inmates of displaced persons camps in Germany that the government wanted to close—had arrived in Israel about a decade after the war. By special agreement, the German government compensated Israel for their treatment.

After Yehuda Bauer, the renowned historian and Holocaust scholar, confirmed that such a ship had indeed arrived, I decided to take testimonies from these patient-survivors. I wondered whether their psychological impairment was related to the phenomenon of *having no history*—and whether the testimonial event, the process of telling one's story of persecution and suffering to a totally present listening companion, could address this deficit. I had been impressed by the power of testimony to bring into relief the internal landscapes of survivors—their experience of themselves, of history, and of the world they lived in. I had also been impressed by the possibilities opened up by capturing such testimonies on video. However, none of the video testimonies that I had collected up to that point included psychotic survivors like those just mentioned.

Surveys conducted in the 1990s showed that amongst the approximately 5,000 long-term psychiatric inpatients in Israel in 1999, a surprisingly disproportionate 725 were Holocaust survivors (Bazak, 1999). A review of these cases showed that these patients had not been treated as a unique group, and that the trauma-related aspect of their illnesses had been neglected in their decades-long treatment. The medical-psychiatric establishment in Israel, very much like society at large, was not ready to address the extremity of the traumatization that these survivors had experienced and its impact on their lives (Dasberg, 1991; Stern, 2000; Davidovitch & Zalashik, 2007).

Most were diagnosed as having chronic schizophrenia. Their charts often included their date and place of birth (say, Poland, 1924) and the year of their immigration to Israel (1948), as if nothing had happened in between. Many of their treating psychiatrists now insist that these patients have been incorrectly diagnosed as schizophrenic, noting that they do not respond to traditional treatment, including antipsychotic medication (Cahn, 1995; Rees, 2002). Could they have avoided lengthy if not lifelong psychiatric hospitalizations had they been able, or enabled by their caregivers and society at large, to share more openly their histories of severe persecution? As it was, these gruesome and traumatic experiences remained enclosed within them, split off from conscious awareness.

The findings I write of here are drawn from the video testimony study of 26 of these chronically hospitalized Holocaust survivors. Some have been hospitalized since World War II. These patients represent the 'extreme' on the spectrum of speechlessness and silence. Nevertheless, once asked, they were very willing to give testimony.

The giving of Holocaust testimony, as we have come to know it, is an event in which two partners must be involved. One is the survivor or 'witness' who is asked to remember and who must then struggle with unwanted memories and inner barriers to remembering and expressing what he or she is able to recall. The other is the listener-companion on that journey into remembrance. Under optimal conditions, the latter's primary role is to be intensely present and actively listening, picking up on subtle hints and cues, such as hesitancies that impede the narrative flow, or gaps all too evident in it. Keeping a timeline, with a list of questions about dates and places, protects the narrative frame. Under such conditions, the listener experiences a myriad of countertransference feelings, which serve as a valuable source of information.

In interviews with this special group of survivors, we were attempting to probe the *limits of testimony* in those who are believed to have given up on communicating and to have withdrawn into their private psychotic world. In my opinion, their psychotic silence is *not* schizophrenia but rather an extreme case of the speechlessness of trauma that afflicts victims, witnesses, and those who attempt to chronicle that trauma (Laub, 2005).

Close scrutiny of personal experiences of massive violence, destruction, and betrayal—experiences that are commonplace in times of war—reveals that when they exceed a certain threshold, they remain outside conscious awareness. When an experience assumes the proportion of 'the extreme,' the human capability to perceive, register, know, transmit, record, and remember—even to see the whole 'Gestalt'—is largely impaired. In her paper "Life within death," Tarantelli (2003) explains this phenomenon using the metaphor of an explosion, which "disintegrates whatever is in its epicenter. It cannot be perceived or experienced or thought for there is nothing left to do so . . . Hence the narration of this state from within is impossible" (pp. 916–918).

What we encounter in such an explosion's aftermath are nonmentalized fragments frozen in time. Such fragments consist of words that have concretized and become things, detached forms, bizarre dreams, neologisms, and, above all, repeated idiosyncratic enactments. These can be understood as gestures representing Lacan's "return of the Real," Sullivan's "dreadful not me," or Bion's "nameless dread" (Davoine & Gaudillière, 2004, 27). For the clinical observer it is as though there persists a gallery of petrified images of terror waiting to be set in motion again, so as to enter narrative and history, be assimilated and forgotten, and thus release the patient from captivity.

Yet the events frozen into these images of terror can never be told and contextualized as history, because they mark the breakdown of social order and of all reference points (Davoine & Gaudillière, 2004). They congeal into a world where any form of otherness is murderous (LaMothe, 1999, 2002). During the experience of massive external trauma, such as facing the executioner who ignores all pleas for life and relentlessly proceeds, the internal empathic dyad ceases to exist. If there is no longer an internal 'thou' with whom dialog can take place, the processes of symbolization, associative remembering, and narrativization come to a complete halt. Temporality, identity, and self are no longer experienced as continuous; this results in a withdrawal from experiencing both external and internal life. An abject state of paralyzing objectlessness ensues; when extreme, it can lead to psychogenic death—the Muselmanner state, in which not a trace of thought remains. This is a world without memory, in which all history is dead—and very much like the inner world of the hospitalized Holocaust survivors.

In the aftermath of trauma, life continues in a pseudo-normality that is often insensitive to the survivor's suffering. Families and societies move on, and trauma survivors who protest and investigate the 'obscure' through psychosis are consigned to the fringe of life. Yet their symptoms are an attempt to break the grip of silence, distortion, and oblivion: theirs is a "normal craziness that bears witness to a normality that is crazy, trivialized, dehistoricized and condemned" (Davoine & Gaudillière, 2004, 148).

The giving of video testimonies was preceded by extensive psychological testing, including symptom scales for psychosis and PTSD, as well as the Rorschach; these tests were repeated five months after the interviews had concluded. What is noteworthy is that in the testing conducted after the interview, the scores of trauma-induced symptoms (in particular the avoidance symptom cluster of PTSD) had been reduced by close to 30 percent. A control group of survivors who had not given testimony showed no decrease in such posttraumatic symptoms after a five-month interval. After this control group also gave testimony, the same positive results were observed (Strous et al., 2005). These findings suggest that the process of creating a narrative with an empathic listener, even for so short a time (as compared with long-term psychotherapy) did, in fact, make a difference in the quality of these patients' lives. Sadly, they also suggest how much more might have been possible had there been listeners able and willing to bear witness to their testimony earlier.

At one hospital I was told by the clinical staff that 20 percent of the patients were silent. They walk around, watch TV, smoke, then unexpectedly walk away. Watching their facial expressions, one can see their ongoing struggle. When they do attempt to say something, their voice may come out as barely audible, or as a scream, a moan, or a sigh. Even in the testimonies of survivors who do talk, there is a struggle, a parsimony, and a restraint bordering on erasure. In all that relates to the Holocaust, many deny memories or simply use code words and phrases like "It was awful, you know," or "What is there to talk about?" Such moments can also be particularly intense, with fragments of memory coming back, being uttered, and then quickly withdrawing again. It is as though survivors experience themselves on the brink of an abyss.

With hospitalized survivors, keeping the box of traumatic memories so tightly closed impressed me as evidence of a certain strength, not of fragility. They were desperately attempting to cobble together fragments of the shattered self into a semblance of cohesion, in the form of a rigid traumatic organization (a "beta screen" in Bion's [1962/2007] terminology). Their battle was "for mastery over the deadly inner object" (Tarantelli, 2003, 915); that is, over emotions which, in Matte-Blanco's terminology, are "of an intensity which is felt as tending towards the infinite" (quoted by Tarantelli, 2003, 919). The psychic disintegration resulting from this unsuccessful struggle leads to an inner objectlessness: an all-encompassing, absolute void leaving no space for life.

Why, for some patients, did the traumatic experience, the deadly inner object, remain split off, yet enclosed and contained, while for others it eclipsed life and became its all-devouring center? Non-psychotic survivors suffered, too: about 50 percent of Holocaust survivors examined in one study (Yehuda, Schmeidler, Giller, Siever, & Binder-Brynes, 1998) qualified for the diagnosis of PTSD. A meta-analysis (Barel, Van IJzendoorn, Sagi-Schwartz, & Bakermans-Kranenburg, 2010) has shown that PTSD symptoms in Holocaust survivors persist even after 60 years, and these might become aggravated with old age (Brodsky, Shnoor, Sharon, King, & Be'er, 2010). By and large, however, Holocaust survivors lead 'normal' social, familial, and vocational lives. Their traumatic experiences have been—often by conscious decision—kept walled off, in a parallel life. Posttraumatic distress increased in life situations that resonated with survivors' traumatic experience (Robinson et al., 1994; Solomon & Prager, 1992), but they were mostly able to regain functionality. For many, giving testimony, public speaking, writing, or making art allowed for some degree of integration of these traumatic memories.

There is widespread consensus that people feel better after opening up and talking (Pennebaker, 1993, 1997; Pennebaker & Seagal, 1999). Empirical evidence suggests that revisiting trauma by speaking or writing has many benefits, including global improvement in physical health, improvements in specific physical measures of health, and reduction of psychological distress (Baikie & Wilhelm, 2005; Konig, 2011). Disclosing traumas also changes self-perception, resulting in a more resilient self-concept (Hemenover, 2003). Various studies have observed positive results after victims of political violence in particular have testified about their traumatic experiences (Cienfuegos, 1983; Agger & Jensen, 1990; Laub, 1995; Weine, Kulenovic, Pavkovic, & Gibbons, 1998; Van Dijk, Schoutrop, & Spinhoven, 2003).

The mechanisms that confer health benefits are complex. Several possible explanations have been offered, especially for the benefits of expressive writing; these include emotional catharsis, the facilitation of a coherent narrative, and prolonged exposure (Baikie & Wilhelm, 2005). Particularly relevant in this context is the proposition that "adapting to traumatic experiences involves either intra- or interpersonal verbal behavior with an actual or imagined audience whereby an individual constructs a more coherent narrative of the experience and, thus, a more adaptive and verbally accessible memory" (Burke & Bradley, 2006, 142). Yet the conditions under which trauma disclosure occurs are important in determining outcomes (Littrell, 2009).

The case of the psychotic survivors differs from the success stories recorded in much of this literature. Keilson's (1979) study of child survivors shows that the life experience following the trauma (the third traumatic sequence) is decisive in clinical outcomes. For whatever reason, the psychotic survivors in Israeli hospitals were never able to find or rebuild the relational space in which life could resume. They had been either too damaged, were too alone, or both. The decades they spent in psychiatric institutions, treated for schizophrenia and often living in subhuman conditions, made a favorable outcome even less likely.

The videotapes of the chronically hospitalized survivors revealed a common thread: *erasure*. It is unclear to what extent this erasure emanates from an absence of the experience of trauma, which prevented the creation of a memory, and to what from an experience that has been suppressed, repressed, and ultimately completely forgotten because of the affective storm its remembrance threatens to create. While I suspect a mixture of both, I am increasingly convinced of the former—that, indeed, *the experience never consciously took place.*

The difference between psychotic and non-psychotic survivors is largely captured by the nature of their testimony. In the testimony of non-psychotic patients, the survivor begins to remember, and memories—both cognitive and affective—exponentially increase. What are at first vague remnants or residues blossom before our eyes, many decades later, into knowledge. With survivors who have been chronically hospitalized for psychotic illness, this process does not take place. The latent remains mostly latent, almost willfully so, as far as verbal narrative is concerned; and yet survivors were more than willing to talk, with interviews continuing for more than an hour or two without interruption.

Frequently I felt a strong positive transference, a determined working alliance. Still, a wide spectrum of phenomena manifested the patients' holding back. To begin with, there was the ease with which survivors claimed, "I have forgotten." It was as though when turning their gaze inward toward a certain experience, they would shrink away and abruptly withdraw in horror from what they had glimpsed. Then, they would return to look at it again, this time apparently seeing nothing, and an impersonal general statement would follow. Other survivors would ask at such moments, "Can we stop now?" A brief crying spell sometimes followed. Occasionally, on subsequent questioning, they would recount what they had claimed to have forgotten.

'Sarah,' whose detailed history we knew from her chart, claimed to have forgotten almost everything we asked her about; she was only willing to make general statements about how bad it was, and to call down eternal curses upon Hitler. Another common mechanism of holding back and erasure was displayed by 'Shimon,' who professed to consider life during the Holocaust quite ordinary, so that there was nothing to tell: "In war, people die, so what is there to talk about? My parents, my siblings, everybody died. To this day it remains unimportant." Horrific events, like waking up to find one's father dead in the adjacent bunk, were recounted without affect. When asked how he felt about that, this survivor responded, "We were too abnormal to have feelings."

Another strategy was ambiguity. One mostly silent survivor, 'Avner,' answered every question with "Maybe yes, maybe no," "Perhaps," "Obviously," or "It's all the same, so what's the point?" Nevertheless, he insisted on precision when it came to other details. His mother was the only one who came to visit him in the hospital when she was alive, and she alone now visits him in his dreams. Only with her did he ever have long intimate conversations. No, he was not depressed: "It was only horror that continued and continues."

Other testimonies evidenced more acute restlessness and storminess, as if the traumatic experiences were contemporaneous with the interview. Sometimes, survivors could directly relate their agitation to the atrocities they had experienced. At other times, the inner turmoil was quickly transformed into a psychotic symptom, a compensatory grandiosity, or paranoid persecutory delusions. With still other survivors, we could see that their horror was without words, a visible affective state completely void of memory and experience. Occasionally, a substitute for experience— a screen memory—filled the void. 'Ora' claimed never to have seen a German soldier because she spent all of World War II in Kazakhstan, thousands of kilometers from her native town. Then, the memory of one single day unexpectedly emerged—a Sunday, the day the Germans entered her town and executed her bedridden father and many other Jews. Her mother and two brothers tried to flee and were apprehended and shot. When I asked whether that had happened on the day her father was murdered, she responded, "No, it was a few days later." She claimed that her Lithuanian neighbors had told her about the killing of her family when she came back in 1953, after the war. Certain details in her account, however, seemed to suggest that she might have been an eyewitness to these events.

Another survivor, 'Yair,' claimed to have fled with his parents from Rovno to safety in Kiev, in the Ukraine—despite the fact that it was under Nazi occupation. He had no memories or words, but his eyes expressed an abysmal horror. As he tried to speak, he experienced an intense headache. I ventured the reconstruction that his flight to safety *had not taken place*; that the horrors of his experience had obliterated his memories. He agreed to that. When specifically asked whether he would have consented to the interview had he known what it entailed, Yair said no—but added that the interview did good "for his soul."

An accomplished theater actor, 'Gideon' presented himself as cultivating a state of mental "equanimity." This was his motto, and he enacted it in his interview. Even when he spoke of a Partisan revolt in which he had participated, it was with complete, affectless equanimity. When asked directly, he confirmed that he had felt happy about his participation, and sad when the Germans returned. However, there was no sad affect to be felt. It was as though Gideon had achieved a certain inner balance in which he could accept his past and current life, a balance he did not want disturbed. I respected that wish, and refrained from asking about his left hand, which he had almost severed in one of his suicide attempts. My communication with Gideon felt very close and very distant. It was gripping. There was something aesthetically appealing about him. His testimony was quite internally consistent and coherent. At the same time, I felt held at arm's length, as if gently and protectively pushed away. He had accepted all that had happened; there was nothing more to say. His testimony felt like the 'empty circle,' the vacuous core rendered by a gifted artist for an attuned audience to experience. He had thought it all through, was cognizant of his role, and embodied it in his testimony, almost to perfection. He had captured the predicament of the survivor who cannot and does not want to face his inner abject loss.

Emotionally intense, yet never remote or unreachable, the psychotic survivors displayed a marked absence of casualness, triviality, or small talk. They seemed profoundly and intensely preoccupied with something one could not surmise. Despite their readiness for engagement, their mutedness was tangible and accompanied by fathomless terror. One could sense the relentless struggle to break out of it. Their narratives contained discrete, vivid, yet discontinuous shards from the distant shores of memory. It was as though what they remembered was unexpected and surprising to them. Their narratives were fragmented, lacking shape or control. There was a remarkable absence of movement and layering, as if everything took place within a single time-frame. There was no branching out in these narratives, and neither was there evidence of associative elaborations or deepening. Continuous and smooth psychic movement was limited; instead, the narrative proceeded by fits and starts, with a certain spasmodic quality. The concrete seemed to be pervasive, with an accompanying impoverishment of mental representations, symbols, and metaphors. One could sense an absence of agency, especially where integration of the narrative was concerned. The interviewers' questions and a certain internal compulsion in the survivor were what drove the narrative on. It was not a process of unfolding and growth driven by an inner core.

For testimony to occur, there need to be both more intact ego functions *and* love objects in the internal and external life of the survivor. For the hospitalized survivors, despite their determination to see it through, and the fact that the interviewer was drawn in, giving testimony was a struggle to begin with. The interviewer had to be much more active and lead the way by offering himself as an authentic new object, totally present and engaged in the mutual endeavor to come to know. The interviewer had to be in the place of the trauma *ahead of the survivor*, patiently waiting there for the latter to arrive. Occasionally, the immediacy of the survivor's terror and agitation needed to be dealt with through reassurance. Sometimes a question had to be asked several times, and in differing forms, for a hitherto 'forgotten' answer to emerge. It was only through these highly differentiated engagements that a personalized signature, the survivor's 'individual take' on his life experiences during and after his Holocaust trauma, could be made explicit.

Mostly, what survivors gave was not a coherent story but only fragments, often very affect-laden, requiring interviewers to serve as holding containers for such fragments to come together. We were the ones who constructed their narrative and told it back to them. They listened very attentively, vehemently agreed or disagreed with what we said, and thus participated in the collaborative construction of their narratives.

Transference manifestations were limited in scope and undifferentiated. The sexual or erotic, sibling rivalry, and oedipal guilt were mostly absent.

What was paramount was a pervasive, intense, and mostly nonverbalized yearning to reconnect. As I revisited the video testimonies in order to write this chapter, I was repeatedly impressed by the depth of our involvement, by the inexhaustible patience and persistence of both survivors and interviewers in the wrenching struggle, and by the profound intimacy of moments of authentic contact.

My own countertransference feelings varied. Most prominent were: a sense of the immense effort involved in dislodging events and feelings from a receding past; the acute pain and despair involved in facing such events and the survivor's life as a whole; the profound sadness that accompanied each such confrontation and that was continuously present, even when confrontation did not consciously take place; the painful yearning to find the lost ones, or at least (re)connect with someone who would make things 'whole' again; the desperate attempt to find a compromise, a mental place or space in which one could experience 'acceptance' of one's life; the relative relief or peace that comes with it, and the tenacity with which one must cling to it; and, lastly, the safety, momentary richness, and homecoming experienced when such acceptance is understood and respected by an empathic listener, in all its ramifications.

I often felt that I never wanted to leave them—or, at the very least, that I wanted to make absolutely certain that what they experienced in the testimony would be indelible, absolutely their own, and prey neither to forgetfulness nor erasure.

From my feelings of tenderness and protectiveness for the survivors I interviewed, I glean that I wanted to fulfill a wish, a deep yearning they harbored. I felt I was being welcomed to a long-awaited reunion. I felt moved, drawn into the intensity of that welcome, and also into the pain of loneliness and loss. I found myself wanting to stay and comfort them, yet unable to comfort enough. At the same time, I felt neither burdened nor encumbered. I experienced an immense feeling of respect and admiration for the people I spoke to, sometimes one of love. I wanted to cherish the moment, the seriousness of the encounter, and our shared focus.

The other side of the coin is my own terror when I try to approach their terror: my urge to flee from it, to look at something else. This was also the case when writing this chapter—it was an ongoing struggle not to close in and close up. Interestingly, when I rewatch the interviews, I do not feel afraid. It is because *they* are present—with me. I feel I have in them the companion without whom it would be a disaster to cross over into the void.

I do not experience such fear with non-psychotic patients. They are protected from their internal voids; they have sealed them off, and are not dangerous to me. I do not face in them the abyss of my own fragmentation.

My response to the mutedness of the psychotic survivors was to speak a lot. My speech rhythm and tone of voice functioned as a holding matrix; survivors listened intently, picking up on a story I was not fully articulating. I asked for and offered contact. Implicitly I told them: "I know what you are about, what you are afraid of, because I was there, too. I will try to protect you."

Into that matrix of speech emerged the survivors' fragmented and broken speech. Sometimes it was monosyllabic. Frequently it wasn't put into words—yet we, the listeners, could experience it. It was as though, on the edge of knowledge and on the border of silence, shapes began to appear, shapes that we were mutually beholding. These continued to evolve; they fell into place and formed a narrative.

Testimonies of sufferers from traumatic psychosis are very different from those of non-psychotic survivors. The volume of words is ten to twenty times smaller. In non-psychotic survivors, speech evolves and awakens their interest in themselves, leading to self-reflection, imaginativeness, free associations, elaborations, and branching out. All of these phenomena seem markedly diminished in the testimonies of psychotic survivors. Their narratives seem frozen. There is no sense of agency: the psychotic survivor hardly uses the pronoun 'I,' despite remaining engaged and committed to the conversation, terrified and struggling throughout.

The driving force behind these testimonies is the interest, commitment, and total presence of the interviewer. The survivor seems to be drifting through an interior landscape colonized by extreme otherness—emotions split off and are experienced as alien. Frequently, his responses include only affect-laden, wordless experiences of pain and loss. Occasionally, a disconnected fragment of a memory emerges. Yet these fragments do not gel into a whole. Like his life, the patient's story remains static and fragmented.

Both the witness and the interviewer experienced a pervasive, nearly paralyzing cautiousness about not stepping into the abyss. The positive transference and countertransference, however, made each feel as if the other had been waiting, making the testimonial event a homecoming of sorts. The relibidinization of the dead object allowed for resumption of movement, albeit a tremulous one. The interviewer's bountiful speech, freely associating with what he perceived in the survivor and in himself, provided the safe holding space for the survivor to glimpse at the abyss, retreat in horror, then come back again, giving his own form to what he glimpsed.

For Gideon, the actor, it was the equanimity he displayed. For Shimon, it was the ordinariness of all that happened: "In war, people die"; there was nothing unusual to mourn about a bad life. For Ora, it had all happened far away: she was safe in Kazakhstan, except for the memory of that particular Sunday. For Yair, who could hardly speak, it was his timely escape from the Nazis—from Rovno to Kiev, which was "safe." For Sarah, it was "I do not remember," and the stoic statement: "When you don't have what you want, you want what you have." For Avner, it was ambiguity: "Maybe it was this way, or maybe it was that way. What difference does it make? It's a waste of time." What the various strategies had in common was their outcome: a state of acceptance, of resignation. In my countertransference feelings, I felt unburdened and unencumbered. Nothing more was wanted from me, and I was free to leave.

I believe the same processes were set in motion in the clinical staff of the hospital, who eagerly watched the tapes. Many were themselves children of Holocaust survivors. Freed from silent guilt and from a daunting sense of obligation, they could be more present to the survivors in their care.

The video testimony project thus came to be a partially successful intervention in starting the process of the survivors' reintegration into their own history and into the social milieu of the hospital where they were living. The robust 30 percent improvement in PTSD scores (most pronounced in the withdrawal symptom cluster) five months after the testimony was given is just one measure reflecting this change.

References

Agger, J., & Jensen, S. B. (1990). Testimony as ritual and evidence in psychotherapy for political refugees. *Journal of Traumatic Stress, 3*(1), 115–130.

Baikie, K. A., & Wilhelm, K. (2005). Emotional and physical health benefits of expressive writing. *Advances in Psychiatric Treatment, 11*(5), 338–346.

Barel, E., Van IJzendoorn, M. H., Sagi-Schwartz, A., & Bakermans-Kranenburg, M. J. (2010). Surviving the Holocaust: A meta-analysis of the long-term sequelae of a genocide. *Psychological Bulletin, 136*(5), 677–698.

Bazak, Y. (1999). *Principles of the general guardian (apotropos) regarding care in the community for mentally ill survivors of the Holocaust.* Jerusalem: Ministry of Justice.

Bion, W. (2007). A theory of thinking. In *Second thoughts: Selected papers on psychoanalysis* (pp. 110–119). London: H. Karnac. (Original work published 1962)

Brodsky, J., Shnoor, Y., Sharon, A., King, Y., & Be'er, S. (2010). *Holocaust survivors in Israel: Population estimates, demographic, health and social characteristics, and needs.* Jerusalem: Meyers JDC Brookdale Institute.

Burke, P. A., & Bradley, R. G. (2006). Language use in imagined dialogue and narrative disclosures of trauma. *Journal of Traumatic Stress, 19*(1), 141–146.

Cahn, D. (1995). Holocaust survivors mistreated. *Associated Press*, November 26.

Cienfuegos, A. J., & Monell, C. (1983). The testimony of political repression as a therapeutic instrument. *American Journal of Orthopsychiatry, 53*(1), 43–51.

Dasberg, H. (1991). Why we were silent: An Israeli psychiatrist speaks to Germans on psychic pain and past persecution. *The Israel Journal of Psychiatry and Related Sciences, 28*(2), 29–38.

Davidovitch, N., & Zalashik, R. (2007). Recalling the survivors: Between memory and forgetfulness of hospitalized Holocaust survivors in Israel. *Israel Studies, 12*(2), 145–163.

Davoine, F., & Gaudillière, J.-M. (2004). *History Beyond Trauma* (S. Fairfield, Trans.). New York: Other Press.

Hemenover, S. H. (2003). The good, the bad, and the healthy: Impacts of emotional disclosure of trauma on resilient self-concept and psychological distress. *Personality and Social Psychology Bulletin, 29*(10), 1,236–1,244.

Keilson, H. (1979). *Sequentielle Traumatisierung bei Kindern: Untersuchung zum Schicksal jüdischer Kriegswaisen.* Stuttgart: Ferdinand Enke Verlag.

Konig, A. (2011). *Disclosure and health: Enhancing the benefits of trauma writing through response training.* PhD dissertation, Virginia Commonwealth University, Richmond, VA.

LaMothe, R. (1999). The absence of cure: The core of malignant trauma and symbolization. *Journal of Interpersonal Violence, 14*(11), 1,193–1,210

LaMothe, R. (2002). "Where art thou?" Defensive dissociation and fragments of annihilated faith. *Pastoral Psychology, 50*(3), 173–189.

Laub, D. (1995). Truth and testimony: The process and the struggle. In C. Caruth (Ed.), *Trauma: Explorations in memory* (pp. 61–75). Baltimore, MD: Johns Hopkins.

Laub, D. (2005). From speechlessness to narrative: The cases of Holocaust historians and of psychiatrically hospitalized survivors. *Literature and Medicine, 24*(2), 253–265.

Littrell, J. (2009). Expression of emotion: When it causes trauma and when it helps. *Journal of Evidence-Based Social Work, 6*(3), 300–320.

Pennebaker, J. W. (1993). Putting stress into words: Health, linguistic, and therapeutic implications. *Behavioral Research and Therapy, 31*(6), 539–548.

Pennebaker, J. W. (1997). *Opening up the healing power of expressing emotions.* New York: Guilford Press.

Pennebaker, J. W., & Seagal, J. D. (1999). Forming a story: The health benefits of narrative. *Journal of Clinical Psychology, 55*, 1,243–1,254.

Rees, M. (2002). Surviving the past. *Time*, January 14.

Robinson S., Hemmendinger, J., Natanel, R., Rapaport, M., Zilberman, K., & Gal, A. (1994). Retraumatization of Holocaust survivors during the Gulf War and SCUD missile attacks on Israel. *British Journal of Medical Psychology, 67*(4), 353–362.

Solomon Z., & Prager, E. (1992). Elderly Israeli Holocaust survivors during the Persian Gulf War: A study of psychological distress. *American Journal of Psychiatry, 149*(12), 1,707–1,710.

Stern, J. (2000). The Eichmann trial and its influence on psychiatry and psychology. *Theoretical Inquiries in Law, 1*(2), 393–428.

Strous, R. D., Weiss, M., Felsen, I., Finkel, B., Melamed, Y., Bleich, A., Kotler, M., & Laub, D. (2005). Video testimony of long-term hospitalized psychiatrically ill Holocaust survivors. *American Journal of Psychiatry, 162*(12), 2,287–2,294.

Tarantelli, C. B. (2003). Life within death: Towards a metapsychology of catastrophic psychic trauma. *The International Journal of Psychoanalyis, 84*(4), 915–928.

Van Dijk, J. A., Schoutrop, M. J., & Spinhoven, P. (2003). Testimony therapy: Treatment method for traumatized victims of organized violence. *American Journal of Psychotherapy, 57*(3), 361–373.

Weine, S. M., Kulenovic, A. D., Pavkovic, I., & Gibbons, R. (1998). Testimony psychotherapy in Bosnian refugees: A pilot study. *American Journal of Psychiatry, 155*(12), 1,720–1,726.

Yehuda, R., Schmeidler, J., Giller, E. L., Jr., Siever, L. J., & Binder-Brynes, K. (1998). Relationship between posttraumatic stress disorder characteristics of Holocaust survivors and their adult offspring. *American Journal of Psychiatry, 155*(6), 841–843.

Chapter 17

Counter-testimony, counter-archive

Amit Pinchevski

For the last fifteen years, Dori Laub has been recording the testimonies of chronically hospitalized Holocaust survivors in Israeli psychiatric institutions. This project is a late extension of another project Laub had initiated in the 1970s: the Holocaust Survivors Film Project, later to become the Fortunoff Video Archive for Holocaust Testimonies at Yale University. It is hard to imagine contemporary memory of the Holocaust without the prevalence of what Geoffrey Hartman (1996) aptly termed "videotestimony." This distinctive genre, which could be described as a cross between a television interview, oral history, and a psychoanalytic session, is now almost synonymous with Holocaust testimony itself. The Yale archive was also the context of a seminal book, *Testimony: Crises of Witnessing in Literature, Psychoanalysis and History* (1992), coauthored by Laub and Shoshana Felman, which founded a new discourse of trauma and testimony. In the following, I want to suggest that the recent project dedicated to the testimonies of hospitalized survivors is nothing short of a radical revision of the widely recognized type of testimony produced by the Yale project. Laub's engagement with these previously misdiagnosed victims of war throws a new light not only on Holocaust testimony but also on his lifelong work on the subject. The full consequences of this project become clear when employing a perspective never considered by Laub himself, but one that is nevertheless fundamental to his entire testimony project: the technical media at the base of videotestimony.

Employing a media perspective to testimony involves a Gestalt shift: what is background becomes foreground, and what is taken for granted is precisely what demands explication. Such is the audiovisual media technology that makes the production of survivors' testimonies possible: the presence of the video camera, the receptivity of videotape recording, and the archiving and dissemination potential that audiovisual technology affords. Despite the focus on technology, this is hardly a 'technical' matter: the audiovisual media apparatus is the condition of possibility—the media a priori—of both the object and the genre identified as Holocaust testimony. Precisely because embedded in the scene of testimony, media are never mentioned as such; like the background, they are what allow other things to show up. Yet the media of witnessing interestingly crop up by way of metaphors: displaced from their original technical function, they are conjured up to describe the inner workings, or unworkings, of human memory. Consider Laub's seminal essay in *Testimony* (1992) on the vicissitudes of listening, which begins with the memorable phrase: "A record that has yet to be made." Whether the reference is to the mind or to the videotape remains constructively vague. He then describes trauma as situation in which "the observing and recording mechanisms of the human mind are temporarily knocked out, malfunction" (the failure to record traumatic memory is a recurring theme in Laub's writing). The listener is portrayed as "the blank screen on which the event comes to be inscribed for the first time" (p. 57). Metaphors such as 'records' and 'screens' are key markers of the "audiovisual unconscious" of Laub's trauma and testimony discourse (Pinchevski, 2012).

Audiovisual media go deep into the structure of testimony. Laub describes the listener as performing a maieutic function: midwifing the emergence of a narrative whose telling has been impeded by the pains of survival. The listener comes to partake in bearing witness by acting as a restorative addressee—as a Thou in Martin Buber's terms—thereby making testimony a profoundly dyadic process. But there is another witness to the witnessing process: the video camera bearing witness to the listener's bearing witness to the witness. If the listener, as second witness, facilitates the testimony of the first, the audiovisual technology, as the third witness on scene, is what facilitates the entire process of witnessing. Indeed, it is for the sake of recording that the testimony dyad came together in the first place. It is the television screen that literally inscribes the event of witnessing for the first time. The camera acts as a surrogate audience for the survivor, providing the potential of numerous addressees. Hartman describes the Yale archive as constituting "a provisional 'affective community' for the survivor" (Hartman & Ballengee, 2001, 220). The profound meaning of this phrase becomes evident when considering audiovisual media as the enabling platform for a remembering community.

The third witness provided by media is therefore integral to the witnessing scene. As opposed to confidential therapy, testimony is conceived from the outset as public speech *in potentia*. Rather than dyad, the testimonial process comprises of a triad. If the listener acts as the Buberian Thou, the camera and the recording device act as what Emmanuel Levinas called 'le tiers': the always already present third-party. Just as society begins with the presence of the third person, testimony commences with the attendance of media as third witness. Charles Sanders Peirce's (1931) concept of thirdness is instructive here: if firstness is the quality of feeling as distinct from of objective conditions, and if secondness is externality as experienced by means of resistance and reaction, thirdness is "the medium or connecting bond between the absolute first and last" (p. 170). Thirdness is what joins first and second, inside and outside, while remaining independent of both; hence, whatever involves mediation and representation involves thirdness. This tripartite scheme applies directly to the testimonial process: traumatic experience is firstness; the enabling of witnessing by the listener is secondness; and the media context of testimony is thirdness. Thirdness entails generality and publicness, the birth of style and convention, as well as the conditions for comparison and judgment. Thirdness is what makes testimony collective.

The video camera and the attendant recording device do not bear witness in the same way that human eyes and ears do. Capturing acoustic and optical effects of reality, they are unselective inscription devices: what they put on record are both intended and unintended expressions, the narrative together with the minute incidents accompanying its telling—the data and noise of testimony. The significance of the decision to use audiovisual technology—rather than transcription or voice recording—cannot be overstated. What this media choice enables is direct access to the survivor's "embodied voice" (Hartman, 1996, 117); that is, the speaker's distinctive cadence and tone together with the puncturing gaps, halts, parapraxes and silences that coincide with bearing witness. Audiovisual recording picks up these haphazard cues and allows for their replaying and analysis. Videography is thus the sine qua non for the study of the performing of trauma in testimony. In Lacanian terms, this technological mediation registers what is left outside the realms of both the Symbolic and the Imaginary, namely, the realm of the Real: "It forms the waste or residue that neither the mirror of the imaginary nor the grid of the symbolic can catch: The physiological accidents and stochastic disorder of bodies" (Kittler, 1999, 15–16). The audiovisual bears witness to the crisis of testimony by mediating the vacillations of narrative in giving an account of trauma.

These media considerations become ever more critical when it comes to videotaping hospitalized survivors. To begin with, in contrast to the Yale project, where filming was done in a studio on campus, the filming of hospitalized survivors is conducted in the psychiatric ward. Laub and his colleagues seek out and go to the survivors, rather than the survivors coming to them. This is a significant difference that places Laub in a long tradition of introducing cameras into the mental institution, which goes back to the nineteenth century and to figures such as Hugh W. Diamond in England and Jean-Martin Charcot at the Salpêtrière clinic in Paris (Gilman, 1976; Didi-Huberman, 2003). For Charcot, photography provided a means to get as close as possible to an objective description of mental pathology, serving simultaneously experimental, taxonomical and didactic functions (Didi-Huberman, 2003, 30). The tradition continued by other means in the 1960s and 70s with the introduction of closed-circuit television (CCTV) and videotape recording (VTR) into psychiatric training and treatment. Videotape proved valuable in allowing both therapist and patient to watch and analyze recorded sessions. Videotape replay supplied a feedback mechanism for the therapeutic process: "The use of video both compels the therapist to see more of what goes on nonverbally than he had previously realized and demands of him an increasing alertness to the nonverbal signs and communication which are ever present" (Berger, 1970, 144). Audiovisual media opened up a non-symbolic channel into the manifest reality of mental pathology, realizing an unbounded interpretative potential of numerous reproducible moments of psychological behavior.

The videotaping of hospitalized survivors shares some of the characteristics of traditional videotape techniques in psychiatry. The introduction of cameras into the ward, the integration of recording into the session, and the attention to nonverbal and paraverbal expressions are among the obvious similarities. In some cases there were even shared viewings with survivors, in a similar vein to the aforementioned techno-therapeutic feedback mechanism (Greenwald, Ben-Ari, Strous, & Laub, 2006). However, there are profound differences that set Laub's project apart from previous psychiatric use of videotape. First of all, the ultimate goal of interviewing and recording survivors is not strictly therapeutic: recorded sessions are not part of individual treatment program intended for the betterment of emotional well-being. Nor are they produced as a diagnostic tool for the sole use of the psychiatric profession. The potential audience envisioned is much broader. Psychotherapy is what opens the door for Laub but not what keeps him there. The camera is employed as a redemptive rather than a surveying medium. The confidentiality of the session is breached—from the outset—in favor of public exposure (whether or not with the survivors' conscious consent is to be debated). Laub's combination of media and psychiatry diverges from that of his predecessors in that what is at stake for him are historical and moral concerns more than merely clinical ones.

These concerns, however, are not always easily discernible. Consider the case of Yehiel Dinur, the writer known by the pen name Katzetnik. His memorable testimony at the 1961 Eichmann trial, during which he termed Auschwitz "the other planet" before collapsing on the stand, was a defining moment in Holocaust memory in Israel (Bartov, 2000; Felman, 2002; Pinchevski & Liebes, 2010). But Katzetnik performed another, less known, testimony. In 1976 he underwent a series of LSD treatment sessions conducted by Dutch psychiatrist Jan Bastiaans at Leiden University, in the course of which he was recorded while in trance. After each session the two met to listen to and analyze the tapes. Bastiaans's use of tape-recording is akin to the psychiatric use of videotape as a feedback device. Transcripts of the recordings comprise the bulk of Katzetnik's book *Shiviti* (1989) where he renounces the cosmological separateness of Auschwitz: "Wherever there is humankind there is Auschwitz" (p. 111). In the book Katzetnik reports that the treatment cured his nightmares and contributed to a fundamental shift in his approach to past events. This case represents a situation where therapy and testimony coalesce, with recording technology partaking in the recovery of traumatic memory. And yet, there is a crucial difference: in Katzetnik's case, recording is subordinate to therapeutic concerns—the dedicated audience is doctor and patient with little, if any, intention of addressing a wider public (Katzetnik's book was written only a decade later). The project of hospitalized survivors rests on the opposite premise: if for Bastiaans testimony is at the service of psychiatry, for Laub psychiatry is at the service of testimony. It is not therapy per se that Laub seeks; or better, a different sense of therapy is sought: not that of the individual survivor but of testimony itself. And since testimony is never only personal or individual, its remedy requires the availability of both second and third witnesses.

It is worth lingering for a moment on the use of 'testimony' in recorded interviews with hospitalized survivors for it is far from obvious. It does not take more than a few viewings to see that the interviews collected in mental hospitals are very different from those recorded at Yale; so different, in fact, that one could even question whether these are testimonies at all. It is for this reason that the equivalence of testimony between 'the Israel video testimony project' and 'the Yale testimony project' is nothing less than dramatic. For what this suggests is a profoundly revisionist, if not revolutionary, understanding of testimony. If the spasmodic narratives of hospitalized survivors are on a par with the articulate narratives of the so-called normative survivors, if the two join to form a unified category, then the result is a thoroughly unsettled notion of testimony—and of the effect of trauma upon it.

It would be hard to find a better demonstration of the disparity between the two testimonial projects than the exemplary cases of Menachem S.'s testimony for the Yale project and Rafi Rakovsky's for the Israeli project. The former is the subject of Laub's extended discussion in *Testimony* (1992, 75–92), and a widely cited example of the vicissitudes of witnessing; the latter is at the heart of Laub's current preoccupation and a subject of recent discoveries. Menachem S. is a child survivor who became a doctor and a high-ranking officer in the Israeli army; Rakovsky, also a child survivor, was briefly an actor at Habima national theater before hospitalizing himself in a psychiatric institution, where he remained until his death. (It is not surprising that Laub, a child survivor himself, has found interest in these two cases.) Menachem S.'s edited testimony can be seen online on the Fortunoff Video Archive webpage (HVT-8063)[1]; until recently Rakovsky's testimony, together with two and a half scores of the project's testimonies, was kept in Laub's basement. Menachem S.'s testimony is eloquent and self-reflexive, copiously containing the seeds of Laub's analysis of it: an astonishing story of survival and triumph, which is also the story of the persistence of trauma despite the survivor's remarkable achievements. Watching this videotestimony, the viewer accompanies the survivor as he unfolds an account of coming to grips with traumatic memory. Watching Rakovsky's testimony, on the other hand, is an entirely different experience.

The frame is of Rakovsky in medium close-up; his voice is slightly muffled due to the distance from the microphone. The picture is grainy; an on screen timecode adds to the rawness of the image. What immediately stands out is the amount of turn-taking during the interview: the interviewers seem to do most of the talking while Rakovsky's answers rarely exceed a couple of sentences. This makes for a strangely acousmatic experience for the viewer, hearing Laub's and his colleague Irit Felsen's voices without ever seeing them. In stark contrast to Menachem S.'s gripping testimony, following the narrative here is an excruciating task; perhaps narrative is not the appropriate word. If it were not for the interviewers' empathic but persistent questioning even these fragments would not have been enunciated. Rakovsky sits with his head tilted back, looking at the interviewers obliquely. A recurring chewing-like tic hinders his already slurred speech. From the fragments arises a sketchy story: prewar childhood in Czechoslovakia; separation from parents at the age of 8; hiding in a monastery while concealing his Jewish identity; reuniting with his mother after the war, who later remarries; immigrating to Israel at 15 with a group of Zionist activists; working on a Kibbutz; a few years of marriage followed by divorce; a short career as a stage actor; and more or less continuous hospitalization since the late 1960s. Whenever Laub asks him about his feelings having had to endure such agonizing experiences, Rakovsky's repeated reply is in Hebrew: "*shivion nefesh*," "equanimity." Rakovsky's acting career draws the attention of the interviewers, who proceed to probe the mindset that allowed him to play the role of many different characters. "It comes by itself" is his reply. But a recently published short memoire by the late Habima actor, Misha Ashrov, sheds some light on the parts left dark in the testimony.[2]

It is a Saturday night a few hours before the play "The Deputy" is about to start in Jerusalem (*Der Stellvertreter* by Rolf Hochhuth deals with the Catholic church's denial of the fate of the Jews during the war). The cast is waiting on a bus for the understudy playing Pope Pius XII: Rafi Rakovsky. They finally head out to his apartment, where they find him in total disarray, lying on the floor naked, laughing inexplicably, spouting obscenities. On the way back they come by another actor who knows the part and is willing to take over. A few days later they receive a phone call from Rakovsky's psychiatrist informing them that he had hanged himself. The story is striking, even if its accuracy is questionable. It is hard to miss the melodramatic element of an actor, who as a child had been hiding in a monastery during the war, and years later—when about to play the part of Pius XII being accused of ignoring the Jewish Holocaust—fatally breaks down. Remarkably, none of this comes up in Rakovsky's recorded testimony. No less striking is the fabricated ending: whether invented or based on rumors, the suicide of the psychotic survivor provides a climactic closure to the story, denoting what would seem as an inevitable fate—or perhaps a wish fulfillment on the part of the narrator.

Obviously Laub did not know about the details presented in the story when interviewing Rakovsky. Had he known would it have changed the course of the interview? Would such knowledge have served his listening to Rakovsky? Knowledge has a precarious status for the listener: knowing about the witness or the event told might hinder listening. As Laub claims in *Testimony*, "it might be useful, sometimes, not to know too much" (1992, 61). In the case of hospitalized survivors, who are long-time psychiatric patients, the precariousness of knowledge is even more acute. When watching Rakovsky's testimony a certain suspicion arises: maybe he is acting all along? At one point he even says something to that effect. The question is never stated but is nevertheless felt, certainly by the viewer—and arguably also by the interviewers. All testimonies are plagued by factual errors and inconsistencies, but here it is the witness who raises the suspicion. Doubting a Holocaust survivor is a difficult feeling to bear, almost sacrilegious. While the viewer is left to deal with such feelings within the context of viewing, if the interviewer happens to feel that way the entire interview would be affected. That the witness might be acting, knowingly or unknowingly, must have crossed Laub and Feltsen's minds. Other testimonies in this project might also raise suspicion as to reliability of the witness. Maybe they are too sick to remember? Maybe the long hospitalization muddled their memory? None of the testimonies of hospitalized survivors is free from such questioning. Their condition as psychiatric patients inevitably plays into their believability as witnesses—and into the way both interviewers and viewers relate to them.

What, then, is the significance of the Israel video testimony project to the entire testimony and trauma discourse? What insights can the testimony of those "on the far end of the continuum of witnessing," as Laub puts it in the Introduction to this collection, offer to the understanding of Holocaust testimony in general? The clinical contribution, which may well be considerable, is beyond the scope of the present discussion. But insofar as the media perspective is concerned, the project bears critical import. This lies not strictly in what survivors say about their experiences (which were not expected to be more horrendous that those of 'normative' survivors), but rather in the consequences the project entails. As with the Yale project more than 30 years ago, testimony requires an empathic listener, a second witness to facilitate the survivor's bearing witness to traumatic experiences. In a time when numerous 'normative' Holocaust testimonies are being collected and widely disseminated, there are still, shockingly, Holocaust survivors who are not granted listening—who are denied the status of witness because they are deemed as having nothing to say. The Israel testimony project attempts to correct this wrong, even if belatedly, by providing a holding environment for listening to these testimonies, jumbled and spasmodic as they are.

The consequences of thirdness, the media context of this project, are no less crucial. Audiovisual recording proved essential in detecting the distinctive 'trauma signature,' as Laub puts it in his introductory essay, marking these spasmodic narratives. Seeking such a trauma signature has been a dominant theme in the analysis of the testimonies recorded at Yale (see Langer, 1991)—a 'signature' unattainable, to be sure, without the unselective technical inscription of audiovisual recording (Pinchevski, 2012). As Laub affirms, retroactive inspection of recordings from the Israel testimony project reveals a markedly different kind of parapraxis when compared to the Yale testimonies, and hence an entirely different manner by which trauma comes to inscribe itself audiovisually. But what it also reveals is a phenomenal amount of unconscious countertransference, of redirected responses toward the hospitalized survivors. Here we arrive at one of the most provocative issues of this project.

Listening to traumatic experiences no doubt entails the risk of counter-transference. Understood from a media perspective, countertransference could manifest itself as identification, especially when it comes to the more communicatively compelling testimonies; indeed, this was the subject of a recent criticism leveled against Laub's earlier work (Trezise, 2008).[3] It could also manifest itself as resistance, which is precisely the case with the Israel project, according to Laub. Countertransference is not limited to secondness but extends to thirdness—to the media-enabled conditions for social recognition. The testimonies of hospitalized survivors may well be described as the counter model of the publically accepted and documented testimonial genre. They are the counter-testimony of the popular Holocaust testimony. As such, they are bound to be rejected, as they unsettle the pre-vailing sense of what Holocaust testimony should look like. Questions about believability as raised in Rakovsky's testimony are one example of such resistance. Countertransference might take the more general form of public avoidance or dismissal, as was the case until recently.

Yet the distinctive considerations of countertransference associated with counter-testimony have implications not only for this relatively small collection but to testimony in general. Counter-testimony puts the widely established variety of testimony in a new light. It is as though Laub brings his recent project to bear on his earlier one, as a commentary on the existing testimony and trauma discourse to which he himself had been a key contributor. As if he was saying: notwithstanding previous discussions on the crisis of testimony, this is the true face of massive trauma, this is the ultimate crisis of testimony. Bringing forth this new type of testimony is epideictic in the literal sense: it declares by showing, asserts by indicating; it demands public attention and recognition. The lesson it sends is of the twofold problem of countertransference: identification with the conventional 'normative' testimony on the one hand, and resistance to the 'abnormal,' nonconforming testimony on the other. Calling attention to the risks of countertransference, both of the second and third witnesses, is arguably the underlying motivation behind the entire project.

With each of these testimonies constituting counter-testimony, combined together they form a counter-archive. As mentioned, the videotapes recorded in Israel had been initially denied deposit, and until recently were kept in Laub's basement. Here resistance takes a most concrete, material form: exclusion from the archive, from the kind of testimonies worthy of archiving—indeed, exclusion from thirdness. The basement archive is in this sense the counter-archive to the Yale archive: inaccessible and unwanted, just like the testimonies it holds. After a long postponement, the testimonies have finally been admitted into the Yale archive. And yet, does the recent admittance mean the assimilation of the counter-archive into the archive? Will the counter-archive retain its exception to the rule of the archive? These questions go to the very essence and meaning of the archive.

As Jacques Derrida (1996) argued, the archive, every archive, is both conservative and revolutionary: it preserves and safeguards but at the same time it institutes the conditions for archiving, the rule of the archivable. The archive does not simply store but shapes the very things it so stores. The Yale archive is no different: it was devised with the explicit intention of archiving something beyond the strictly factual, historical dimensions of loss and survival. The result was an archive of trauma, literally: the archiving of the attempts and failures of narrative in giving voice to trauma. Videography captured the audiovisual effects of the witnessing performed by survivors, thereby giving expression to the performing of trauma. With the admission of the counter-archive into Yale's depository, the archive expands to incorporate a most fatal strand of trauma: not just interrupting and puncturing narrative, but altogether damaging the possibility of its telling. The archive now stores "the far end of the continuum of witnessing," the point where testimony practically recedes from narrative structure. At the far end lie neither recovery nor redemption, only the incapacitating power of trauma.

Laub's revisionary impulse can now be seen as exemplary of what Derrida (1996) called "archive fever," a veritable *mal d'archive*:

> It is never to rest, interminably, from searching for the archive right where it slips away. It is to run after the archive, even if there's too much of it, right where something in it anarchives itself. It is to have a compulsive, repetitive, and nostalgic desire for the archive, an irrepressible desire to return to the origin, a homesickness, a nostalgia for the return of the most archaic place of absolute commencement. (p. 91)

Archiving trauma suggests a special case of archive fever whereby what evades proper registration in the mind—trauma—is sought through audiovisual traces on tape. In seeking the archive despite the archive, despite the impossibility of complete archiving, Laub exhibits symptoms of archive fever: the cofounder of the Yale archive, the father of video testimony, is the one to introduce the counter-archive into the archive. The archive is thus undone from within by the drive to archive. And the deeper the glimpse into the depth of trauma, the more trauma "anarchives" itself, skirts its registration.

The future of Holocaust testimony is no doubt tied to digital technologies and the affordances they offer. Accessibility, searchability, and shareability are likely to be the matching properties of audiovisual testimony, like any other online audiovisual data. Digital media invite new opportunities for, as well as new challenges to Holocaust remembrance (Presler, 2015). Thus, one project uses cutting-edge technology to produce a 3D hologram of a survivor, coupled with a voice-recognition algorithm to simulate a conversation with the audience.[4] Clearly, the media context of testimony, the technology allowing for thirdness, has gone a long way since the video camera and videotape. Attending to the testimonies of hospitalized survivors ends a latency period that included both the first and second generations to the Holocaust, reaching well into the third. And the media context of the third generation is new media and hyper-media. The cultural logic of digital media might not bode well for these patently uncommunicative testimonies: they are unlikely to be posted on a Holocaust related website; they are too few and too scarce to provide adequate material for data mining or metadata indexing. Yet precisely for this reason, the testimonies of hospitalized survivors illustrate most starkly the challenge facing future mediation of Holocaust testimony: the growing accessibility of media on the one hand, and the persistent inac-cessibility of trauma on the other. What hangs in the balance is the shape of Holocaust testimony to come.

Notes

1 The video is available on YouTube at: https://www.youtube.com/watch?v=UbBqOibdIfU.
2 http://www.haaretz.co.il/short-story/.premium-1.2619482.
3 What this criticism misses is that every empathic listening involves some degree of countertransference, which could then be processed through interaction. See Laub's rejoinder (2009). This debate could be described as a clash between secondness and thirdness: Laub's personal memory of the testimonies as an interviewer vis-à-vis Trezise's retrospective analysis of videotaped testimonies.
4 http://ict.usc.edu/prototypes/new-dimensions-in-testimony/.

References

Bartov, O. (2000). *Mirrors of destruction: War, genocide, and modern identity.* Oxford: Oxford University Press.

Berger, M. M. (1970). The use of videotape in private practice. In M. Berger (Ed.), *Videotape techniques in psychiatric training and treatment.* New York: Brunner/Mazel.

Derrida, J. (1996). *Archive fever: A Freudian impression.* Chicago: University of Chicago Press.

Didi-Huberman, G. (2003). *Invention of hysteria: Charcot and the photographic iconography of the Salpêtrière.* Cambridge, MA: MIT Press.

Felman, S. (2002). *The juridical unconscious: Trials and traumas in the twentieth century.* Cambridge, MA: Harvard University Press.

Felman, S., & Laub, D. (1992). *Testimony: Crises of witnessing in literature, psychoanalysis, and history.* New York: Taylor & Francis.

Gilman, S. L., (1976). *The face of madness: Hugh W. Diamond and the origin of psychiatric photography*. New York: Brunner/Mazel.

Greenwald, B., Ben-Ari, O., Strous, R. D., & Laub, D. (2006). Psychiatry, testimony, and Shoah: Reconstructing the narratives of the muted. *Social work in health care, 43*(2–3), 199–214.

Hartman, G. (1996). *The longest shadow: In the aftermath of the Holocaust*. Bloomington, IN: Indiana University Press.

Hartman, G., & Ballengee, J. (2001). Witnessing video testimony: An interview with Geoffrey Hartman. *The Yale Journal of Criticism, 14*(1), 217–232.

Katzetnik. (1989). *Shivitti: A vision* (E. De-Nur, Trans.). New York: Harper & Row.

Kittler, F. A. (1999). *Gramophone, film, typewriter* (G. Winthrop-Young & M. Wutz, Trans.). Stanford, CA: Stanford University Press.

Langer, L. (1991). *Holocaust testimonies: The ruins of memory*. New Haven, CT: Yale University Press.

Laub, D. (1992). Bearing witness or the vicissitudes of listening. In S. Felmand & D. Laub, *Testimony: Crises of witnessing in literature, psychoanalysis, and history* (pp. 57–74). New York: Taylor & Francis.

Laub, D. (1992). An event without a witness: Truth, testimony and survival. In S. Felmand & D. Laub, *Testimony: Crises of witnessing in literature, psychoanalysis, and history* (pp. 75–92). New York: Taylor & Francis.

Laub, D. (2009). On Holocaust testimony and its "reception" within its own frame, as a process in its own right: A response to "Between history and psychoanalysis" by Thomas Trezise. *History & Memory, 21*(1), 127–150.

Peirce, C. S. (1931). *Collected philosophical papers*, Vol. 1. Cambridge, MA: Harvard University Press.

Pinchevski, A. (2012). The audiovisual unconscious: Media and trauma in the video archive for Holocaust testimonies. *Critical Inquiry, 39*(1), 142–166.

Pinchevski, A., & Liebes, T. (2010). Severed voices: Radio and the mediation of trauma in the Eichmann trial. *Public Culture, 22*(2), 265–291.

Presler, T. (2015). The ethics of the algorithm: Close and distant listening to the Shoah Foundation Visual History Archive. In C. Fogu & W. Kansteiner (Eds.), *History unlimited: Probing the ethics of Holocaust culture*. Cambridge, MA: Harvard University Press.

Trezise, T. (2008). Between history and psychoanalysis: A case study in the reception of Holocaust survivor testimony. *History & Memory, 20*(1), 7–47.

Part IV

Manifestations of extreme traumatization in the testimonial narration of hospitalized and non-hospitalized Holocaust survivors

Two case studies

In Part IV, the reader will find the clinical core of the book, where detailed analyses of two testimony excerpts will be presented and compared. It consists of the 'Prague panel,' originally presented at the 48th International Psychoanalytic Congress, at which a psychoanalytic scholar, a practicing psychoanalyst, and a historian discussed two testimony excerpts, one from a hospitalized survivor, the other from a mother and a daughter who lived a regular life. The impact of trauma on narrative is examined, particularly in the areas of parapraxes and countertransference phenomena. The close and relational psychoanalytic interpretation of the testimonial process uncovers an otherwise invisible, although powerful process of transmitting the fragmented memory of genocidal traumatic experience to the listener, who unequivocally shifts his conscious and unconscious attention to the survivor, in order to witness his reenacting narrative, to document it, and to pass it on to his readers.

Chapter 18

Introduction[1]

Dori Laub

The Holocaust was an event and an experience that annihilated the *good object* (humanity, God, the intimate other) in the internal world, and in individual and collective representation. In its wake, experiencing, remembering, and imagining were severely compromised, if not abolished. In the absence of a protective parental shield, the processes of symbolization, mental representation, and narrativization came to a halt at the nadir of the extreme traumatization. A breakdown of intrapersonal and interpersonal communication ensued. Defensive processes, mobilized to address the catastrophe, were set in motion. What emerged were the 'shards of memory': composites of fragmented experience and of those defensive operations that attempted to contain them. It is through closely examining these shards of memory, this phenomenology of destruction, that we can get a better understanding of the damage that occurred, and begin to look for ways of addressing it. We can also come to see the way traumatic memory attempts to restore the lost good object, even as this memory attests to the continual destruction of that object.

This study necessitates close-up readings of survivors' testimony. These close-ups highlight the prevalence of parapraxes, which demarcate communicative breakdowns. Such breakdowns occur on an intrapersonal level when affects and experiences cannot be symbolized. They also occur on an interpersonal/intersubjective level: among survivors who jointly testify to an event, *and* between survivors and the interviewers who listen to their testimony. To illuminate this phenomenon, we have selected moments from two video testimonies, and subjected them to close reading. Bodenstab, Knopp, and Hamburger approach these testimonies through careful readings that integrate psychoanalytic and historical perspectives. Throughout, the phenomenon of 'parapraxes of memory' is most noteworthy when it occurs on an interpersonal level, when both survivors and interviewers 'mishear' each other. The force of this 'mishearing' infuses the process of witnessing, and points to the role of countertransference in the trauma discourse. Here, countertransference feelings and enactments emerge as the most informative database for the impact of traumatic experience, that can otherwise not be symbolized, consciously experienced and verbally conveyed.

The testimony

Even the most shattered narratives of Holocaust survivors powerfully speak to the horrors of their traumatization. We will present and discuss two video testimony excerpts. The first testimony is that of a mother and daughter who survived a concentration camp together, and then led adaptive lives after their persecution. In the second excerpt, the testimony is from a man who had been psychiatrically hospitalized since shortly after the war. There are marked differences in the intensity of their flashbacks, reliving versus retelling, their ability to exit the memory, to maintain a distanced perspective, and/or the narrative flow. The hospitalized survivor speaks in brief sentences in response to questions driven primarily by the interviewer's countertransference. The mother and daughter who lived adaptive lives are able to deepen and expand the testimonial discourse without much help from their interviewers. In both cases, the viewers of these video excerpts are inevitably taken aback by the disruptions of the narrative flow in both testimonies. These disruptions signal the encounter with particularly difficult and affect-laden traumatic memories. Such an encounter is evident for the survivors who struggle to form their narratives. But it also becomes evident for their interviewers, struggling to stay empathically connected with their interviewees.

In phenomenological terms, both testimonies have the same trauma signifiers in common: Perhaps the most tangible signifiers are the parapraxes that occur as part of the narrative act in both testimonies, albeit in different ways. In the joint mother–daughter testimony, the narrative of the traumatic moment—the murder of a newborn by the camp *Komandant*—proceeds smoothly. Both survivors describe the horrible scene with feelings and with presence of mind. However, neither their interviewers, nor the survivors themselves, notice that the survivors produce two differing versions of the same event and, therefore, a narrative incongruence. This oblivion in all the participants glaringly exposes the formidable defensive function of this incongruity. The not-noticing of the interviewers represents a countertransference response. It is as though a sudden process of massive all-enveloping repression occurs, that is concomitant with a full and detailed articulation of the traumatic experience.

In the testimony of the hospitalized survivor, the parapraxes are mostly countertransference phenomena, originating in the interviewer rather than in the survivor. The interviewer is thrown off balance by the fragmented, chaotic narrative. The parapraxes produced by the interviewer are replete with meaning. They are in response to what he imagines the survivor's traumatic experience to be, although this trauma cannot fully be formulated consciously or unconsciously by the survivor him- or herself. In the survivor, the traumatic memory exists only as split off chaotic fragments permeated by intense affect—primarily terror and unbearable grief.

The testimonies keep a record not only of the experience of the survivors but also of their interviewers' struggle to absorb their narratives. This dialog, focused on the traumatic experience, opens another layer of conflict experienced by the researcher working with video testimonies and, ultimately, a more nuanced understanding of the trauma signatures become manifest in the course of the testimonial intervention.

Note

1 First published in *Contemporary Psychoanalysis*, 51(2) (2015). Reprinted by permission of Taylor & Francis, LLC and the William Alanson White Institute of Psychiatry, Psychoanalysis, and Psychology, and the William Alanson White Psychoanalytic Society, www.wawhite.org.

Chapter 19

Parapraxis in mother–daughter testimony
Unconscious fantasy and maternal function[1]

Johanna Bodenstab

This chapter examines a moment of narrative dissonance in the joint testimony of a mother (Rosalie W.) and a daughter (Jolly Z.) who survived the Holocaust together. In the context of an extremely traumatic scene—namely an infanticide both women witnessed while they were held in Eidelstedt, a concentration camp in Hamburg—the common thread of their narrative is lost and contradictory memories emerge.

Although this unraveling of a shared perspective is understood as a clear indication of the trauma encapsulated in the survivors' narratives, the testimony is not simply maimed by experience and the difficulty representing the impact of the murder on the mother–daughter relationship. The testimony becomes a creative process that creates a montage of memory fragments, revealing horrors much larger than what the narrative of both survivors can explicitly cover: The contradiction between mother and daughter is really a condensation of two murders that occurred in Eidelstedt.

At the same time, the testimony is shaped by the daughter's attempt to preserve her good internal object despite the brutal onslaught of external reality. She creates a 'posttraumatic screen memory' that allows her to forget a situation in which her real mother could not provide any protection. In a complex weave of knowing and not-knowing, her narrative negotiates both the threatening loss of her mother relationship and the need for an internal object that allows for relatedness. Although the presence of the real mother at the scene speaks to the collapse of the maternal position in the face of trauma, the daughter's narrative forms scar tissue in an attempt to maintain relatedness, regardless of the trauma suffered.

Jolly Z. (JZ):	There is another incident in speaking about Hamburg. When we got in the ghetto. Some women were pregnant without realizing it, young women. There was a beautiful woman among us. And she was pregnant.
Rosalie W. (RW):	I know.
JZ:	By the time we got to Hamburg, she was already in her fourth, fifth, sixth month, and so on. And believe it or not, she was the hardest working person, even with her pregnancy. Maybe this life within herself gave her this courage to go on and wanting to give birth to her child. And the SS let her stay with us because he saw she's a good worker, so there was no reason to do something. And when the day of delivery was approaching, he actually made us prepare a little box for the baby. And my mother worked there in the kitchen. He asked her to prepare hot water. There was a prisoner doctor woman who assisted with the birth and I stayed in the next room. I was afraid to see a delivery. I was young. I never saw a delivery. And suddenly I heard the baby cry. And the SS brought out the baby and there was a sink. (Close to tears.) And I stood there with the little box, hoping he'd put the baby in. He took the baby under the sink faucet and drowned it. And he said: "Here you go, little Moses."
RW:	Yeah.
JZ:	And he drowned the little baby there.
RW:	Yeah. The head. In the hot water.
JZ:	And the woman went to work in two days.
RW:	And the baby. I maked [sic] it good hot [the water; JB]. I was sure they have to clean the baby.
JZ:	"Little Moses."
RW:	And he tooked [sic] the baby "Little Moses" down with the head in the hot water.

JZ:	He said: "Here you go, little Moses, down the river." Something like this, in German. And he drowned the little baby.
RW:	Yeah. Yeah. This was Kümmel.[2]
JZ:	Yah.
(Both fall silent.)	
Interviewer:	How did the woman get pregnant? I thought the men and the women were separated.
JZ:	She came in the ghetto pregnant.
RW:	She was [pregnant; JB] in the beginning.
JZ:	Or she might have even gotten pregnant in the ghetto. Now, the ghetto was in May. We were taken to Auschwitz in May. So if you figure out nine months—that takes us to what? December? Or January? (01:02:43– 01:05:50)

Narrative dissonance

The excerpt just presented is taken from the video testimony of Rosalie W. and Jolly Z., recorded in 1979 and now in the holdings of the Fortunoff Video Archive for Holocaust Testimonies at Yale University. The two women are mother and daughter and survived together. They were deported to Auschwitz in May 1944 as Hungarian Jews, and then sent as slave laborers to Hamburg during the summer of that year to be liberated eventually in Bergen-Belsen in April 1945. At the time of the recording, Jolly (the daughter) was 52 and Rosalie (the mother) was 78. The infanticide they relate in their testimony occurred around Jolly's 18th birthday and when her mother was 43. At the time of the recording, a role reversal had occurred between mother and daughter: Jolly was in charge of the narrative, providing structure, chronology, and historical context while supporting Rosalie's narrative efforts and functioning as her interpreter when her mother's English failed.

The narrative that unfolds between the two survivors is elaborate and brimming with nuance and detailed perceptions. Even the account of the crime seems vivid, despite the horror witnessed, and charged with intense drama and complex emotion. And yet, although the narrative is so well organized around the murder of a newborn baby, it also disintegrates in this context for it branches out into separate narrative perspectives.

Rosalie and Jolly contradict each other: Although the daughter relates that Kümmel drowned the baby under the running water of a faucet, the mother indicates that Kümmel drowned the baby in the hot water that he had previously ordered her to prepare.

There is no resolution of this contradiction in the testimony—mother and daughter go on record with entirely different recollections of the scene of the infanticide. Although it is safe to assume that although both women were eyewitnesses of a crime, their testimony would not stand in court. But from a psychoanalytic point of view, the disparity of their voices can be understood as an integral part of the narrative. I will argue that the separateness that occurs between mother and daughter, the narrative dissonance they produce, marks a moment of crisis in their relationship and that this crisis resonates with and stems from a traumatic experience.

Historical context of the murder/condensation

In the absence of any further clarification of this narrative dissonance by neither the two survivors nor their interviewers throughout the entire testimony, I suggest we favor Rosalie's account for the simple reason that she voluntarily puts herself in such close proximity to the murder committed by Kümmel. The only explanation for her narrative self-exposure is that she is telling the truth. She is, in fact, trying to justify why she heated the water that subsequently served as Kümmel's murder weapon. And although 'truth' is not a psychoanalytic category, 'guilt feelings' are. Rosalie is responding to her daughter's account with a memory of her own. Although she is listening to Jolly, she seems to lose touch with her daughter's narrative to the extent that she does not realize that she is contradicting Jolly.

To understand the dissonance between both survivors better, it is helpful to review the historical background of their situation. In 1980, Walther Kümmel, the former commander of Eidelstedt, a satellite camp of Neuengamme in Hamburg, was put on trial for the murder of two babies born in that camp during the winter 1944–1945. On the basis of my research, there can be no doubt that Kümmel used both killing methods described by Rosalie and Jolly—there is testimony by other witnesses to both the running faucet and the warm water. This means that, although on first sight it seems as if mother and daughter are splitting one murder into contradicting accounts, the historical evidence reveals their testimony as a condensation with two murders lumped into the same situation.

The narrative is therefore not simply coming apart in a representation of the traumatic impact of the murder, but is at the same time coming together—in a montage, as it were—arranging fragments of memory to reveal horrors much larger than what the testimony can explicitly cover. Together, Rosalie and Jolly carry the knowledge of two infanticides. In the moment of the narrative dissonance, the testimony becomes transparent for what the narrative effort tries to manage or contain: At the core of Rosalie's and Jolly's narrative lies a disproportionate horror, and although each of their sentences is a huge accomplishment of symbolization, their testimony equally speaks to a latent horror that goes without saying. I would argue that what connects mother and daughter in the context of the two murders in Eidelstedt is not their relationship, but the horror of what they witnessed in that camp.

In the light of this finding, what are we to make of Jolly's version of the infanticide she witnessed together with her mother? In her narrative, the running faucet functions as a screen, which allows the daughter to relate the scene of the crime while erasing her mother's unintended complicity from it. It seems that Jolly can testify to the murder only in the absence of Rosalie's participation. The Fortunoff Video Archive has two individual testimonies of Jolly Z. In both of them, the daughter consistently remembers the water in which the baby was drowned as running from a faucet. It is really only in and through the presence of Rosalie that this screen is torn and the mother's involuntary involvement in the murder can surface.

The mother in mind/traumatic loss

I shall return to the importance of the screen Jolly creates in the context of the infanticide shortly, but I would first like to comment on the meaning of the pregnancy for the daughter. Jolly's testimony makes it obvious that the pregnant woman was her hero. I want to suggest, however, that her victorious maternity implies a desperate effort on the part of the expecting mother not to stand out among the other inmates: Despite her pregnancy, she had to prove herself as a good worker to give the SS "no reason to do something." In other words, the pregnant woman was fighting for her life. In Jolly's mind, however, the pregnant woman was encouraged by "this life within herself" and fighting for her child. I understand this representation as a construction in an adolescent's mind of a strong mother figure, invested with the power of Jolly's good internal mother. It is striking that, in the retrospection of her testimony, the survivor manages to uphold this construct despite what happened immediately after the birth. During the interview, the figure of the victorious mother continues to bring Jolly visible pleasure. Although the infanticide represented a horrible loss, clearly, in her mind, not all is lost.

The pregnant women became the focal point of Jolly's projections: She also projected the encouragement that she herself felt through the pregnancy onto her fellow inmate. In other words, in the context of the pregnancy, Jolly's emotional reality could take root in external reality, despite the camp. Jolly could psychologically relate to the reality of the pregnancy. She came back into herself in the presence of the expecting mother. Maybe the expected baby was exciting and stimulating—stirring life within Jolly—because it opened a mental space for imagination and possibility.

This emotional link between the pregnancy and Jolly's mind had to make a radical difference in the environment of the camp where "the simple assumption of life is destroyed (so that) being alive is no longer natural"— in an environment that otherwise was so unreal in its extreme violence that it became hard for a person exposed to such reality to distinguish whether she lived through a terrifying fantasy or actual reality (Tarantelli, 2003, 925). This blurring of the spheres of emotional and external reality represents a fundamental loss of structure described as "psychic equivalence" (Boulanger, 2007) or "disarticulation" (Tarantelli, 2003). For Jolly, the pregnancy seems to have maintained or restored not only familiarity to the external reality but also meaning as a sphere shared with others that defined the limits of her inner world. Tarantelli reminds us that one's sense of being in the world is radically challenged whenever this habitual order of inside and outside is violated. When we think of the pregnancy as a structuring event for Jolly's mind we begin to grasp the magnitude of the loss implied by Kümmel's crime.

The pregnancy ultimately could not undo the "indifferent reality" (Boulanger, 2007) of the camp. Rather, it implied a seductive danger in an environment that did nothing to sustain those exposed to it. In the context of the birth, both mother and daughter were detached from the forceful grip of the camp's reality, entangled instead in a reemerging normality, all of a sudden imaginable, despite the camp. Even the threatening camp commander became part of this 'normalization' and was transformed into a caring paternal figure by both women.

Thus, not only young Jolly, but even the more experienced Rosalie was taken by surprise when Kümmel drowned the baby. The murder represents not only a complex symbolic loss, but also a profound disillusionment. Although the brutality of the camp prevailed as the absolute and ultimate framework of reality, Rosalie and Jolly had to reexperience the disarticulation of their existence: They were yet again reduced to prisoners in a concentration camp, with no meaning in the world and no part in the future.

Scar tissue: trauma and repression

But the joint testimony does not only speak to fundamental losses both women suffered. Another shared dimension of their experience is their paralysis in the face of the murder. This stands out particularly in Rosalie's case: Throughout the entire testimony she comes across as highly determined to deal with dangerous situations and to fight for her daughter's life. Only in the context of the infanticide is she caught off guard, unable to do anything to save the newborn. Thus, Jolly witnessed not only Kümmel's deed, but also the undoing of her mother. I would argue that, as a traumatic event, the infanticide had its immediate impact on the mother–daughter relationship of both women.

The crime must have come as a shock for Rosalie, who could grasp what had happened only 'post mortem,' that is, when it was too late already. This rupture of perception is caused by "the lack of preparedness to take in a stimulus that comes too quickly" (Caruth, 1996, 62). Here, the problem is that the threat is only realized when it is too late already. "The shock of the mind's relation to the threat of death is thus not the direct experience of the threat, but precisely the missing of this experience, the fact, that, not being experienced in time, it has not yet been fully known" (p. 62).

This is particularly grave in Rosalie's case, because her "being too late" implies the loss of her presence as a mother. Even if we must assume that, realistically speaking, she could have done nothing to save the newborn's life, Rosalie's grasping the situation too late also means that she could not spare her daughter the sight of the murder. For Jolly, this double eclipse of the maternal position, both vis-à-vis the baby and vis-à-vis herself, radically put into question the emotional safety of the relationship with her mother; for Rosalie, this eclipse undermined her confidence in her emotional strength as a mother. After Kümmel had killed the baby, the safety of the maternal position was highly questionable. Keeping in mind what

Auerhahn and Laub (1998, 361–365) noted, that trauma concretizes the destruction of the introjected mother, the psychic impact of the loss of a position of caring or empathy must be considered as devastating.

In the context of this observation, the utter importance of Jolly's narrative screen fully reveals itself: The daughter manages to contain this devastating impact in her testimony by omitting her mother from her narrative. On the one hand, Rosalie has gone missing from the scene, leaving her daughter to witness Kümmel's crime all by herself. On the other hand, she has vanished from the scene so that her involuntary contribution to the murder is erased from the testimony as if it never happened. Jolly's narrative records a loss of relationship and, at the same time, denies the connection between mother and murder. Her testimony is not simply affected or affected by the traumatic situation it refers to; it also carefully excises the real mother from the scene in an attempt at repairing the damage done to the introjected mother by the witnessed scene.

Of course, I do not suggest that these are conscious manipulations of a narrator in full command of her story. Rather, I think what comes to the fore here, in the context of an underlying traumatic experience, is a narrative weave of knowing and not-knowing as described by Laub and Auerhahn (1993): "Ways in which we attempt to know or not to know are major organizers of personality" (p. 288) with defense mechanisms helping to maintain and stabilize psychic structure. "The knowledge of trauma is fiercely defended against" (p. 288), because such knowledge may lead to dissociation threatening the ego, which is trying to master its trauma with a loss of structure. In relating to the trauma of the infanticide, Jolly cannot know the full extent to which her mother was at the scene because Rosalie's physical presence was linked with a threatening object loss for Jolly.

The narrative weave of knowing and not-knowing marks a scar in the connective tissue of Jolly's relationship to Rosalie: Regardless of the traumatic reality of her camp experience, the daughter is trying to maintain and/or repair the connection with mother. I would argue that this attempt is at the core of her condensation. The fact that the mother prepared the water in which the camp commander drowned the baby obviously stirred fears in the daughter so intense that she had to repress it. Jolly is constructing a scene of the murder that screens off the damage that her relationship to Rosalie suffered in the context of Kümmel's crime. In addition, she upholds the figure of a victorious mother who carries her child to term and is not present at its murder. Only in the joint testimony does Rosalie's account make Jolly's narrative construct transparent and cast light on the daughter's defendedness.

Jolly could maintain mother as good inner object because she succeeded in repressing her shock about her real mother. Hers is not an act of "primal repression," as postulated by Cohen and Kinston (1984) in the context of trauma to describe the loss of psychic structure and the lack of memory in the psyche of a traumatized subject but—on the contrary— an act of self-preservation, helping Jolly to not surrender psychically to the brutal external reality of the camp. She tried to salvage her maternal object from destruction to maintain herself within a complex relational structure. Her repression was aimed at maintaining a relational matrix (and herself within it), despite the onslaught of external reality and the dissociative forces of trauma. By separating her real mother from her internal representation of her mother, Jolly managed to diminish the full impact of her trauma. It is indeed possible for the ego to split in response to a trauma, to defend against psychic fragmentation: Whereas one part absorbs what is happening, the other part tries to isolate itself from what is happening, in order not to lose its connection to life and to the other. In addition, the second part tries to maintain its ability to integrate experience and to organize experience in a meaningful way (Auerhahn & Laub, 1998, 362). In Jolly's case, the splitting of the ego coincides with a separation of the good internal object and the real mother. This means that Rosalie can remain present to her daughter in her psychoemotional meaning, despite her eclipse as a caring mother during the scene of the murder. The running faucet becomes a "posttraumatic screen memory" (p. 362) blurring the original scene and its horrors. Repression must be understood in the context of Jolly's attempt at preserving the continuity of the relational matrix as the core of her psychic structure.

Conclusion

I suggest readers consider Jolly's testimony as narrative 'scar tissue': It is informed both by traumatic loss and by the survivor's ability to regain and/or maintain psychic structure, enabling her to organize her experience and to construct a highly complex narrative. The scar also speaks to a tear in the relation between mother and daughter that did occur in the face of the infanticide they jointly witnessed, as well as to the daughter's ability to outgrow this tear. Rupture and continuity go hand-in-hand in this testimony. Whereas Rosalie's eclipse is erased, a victorious mother figure is upheld. The intricate weave of knowing and not-knowing in Jolly's testimony becomes transparent only in the presence of Rosalie. However, the trauma of the infanticide is also reenacted—neither of the interviewers catches the narrative dissonance Rosalie and Jolly produce: Thus, the traumatic loss of structure of the original experience also continues.

Notes

1 First published as Parapraxis in Mother–daughter testimony: Unconscious fantasy and maternal function, *Contemporary Psychoanalysis, 51*(2) (2015). Reprinted by permission of Taylor & Francis, LLC.
2 The camp commandant.

References

Auerhahn, N., & Laub, D. (1998). The primal scene of atrocity: The dynamic interplay between knowledge and fantasy of the Holocaust in children of survivors. *Psychoanalytic Psychology, 15*, 360–377.

Boulanger, G. (2007). *Wounded by reality: Understanding and treating adult onset trauma.* Mahwah, NJ: Analytic Press.

Caruth, C. (1996). *Unclaimed experience: Trauma, narrative, and history.* Baltimore, MD: Johns Hopkins University Press.

Cohen, J., & Kinston, W. (1984). Repression theory: A new look at the cornerstone. *International Journal of Psychoanalysis, 65*, 411–422.

Laub, D., & Auerhahn, N. (1993). Knowing and not knowing massive psychic trauma: Forms of traumatic memory. *International Journal of Psychoanalysis, 74*, 287–302.

Tarantelli, C. B. (2003). Life within death: Towards a metapsychology of catastrophic psychic trauma. *International Journal of Psychoanalysis, 84*, 915–928.

Chapter 20

Narrative fissures, historical context

When traumatic memory is compromised[1]

Sonja Knopp

Introduction

Historiography labels the presentation of historical events. It is the linguistic communication of historical insight and, as such, historiography is a part of history as an academic discipline. Its method is historical criticism, and it aims to ascertain the essential meaning of a source from its original historical context. Furthermore, historiographical work attempts to reconstruct the historical situation of the source's author, as well as that of its interviewer. The original historical context of Shmuel's testimony, which will be addressed later in this article, includes, first, Bessarabia and Transnistria during World War II; second, the interview setting with Dori Laub, Oshrit Ben Ari, and Shmuel B., a Holocaust survivor and patient of the Israeli psychiatric institution of Be'er Jacov, in April 2003. In connection with the article of Andreas Hamburger, who focuses on the interview setting from a psychoanalytical perspective, here I will focus on a reconstruction of the perpetration and extermination of Jews in Romanian Bessarabia and Transnistria between 1941 and 1944. Contradictions to the accepted understanding of this historical event will become apparent in the Shmuel testimony. The testimony will also demonstrate how manifestations of trauma in Holocaust survivor testimonies give shape to a historical past of mass violence and its representations (i.e., source material, such as testimonies and archival documents).

Historiography is not a healing discipline in terms of trauma suffering, but it can contribute to the understanding of traumatic testimonies from Holocaust survivors and, conversely, these testimonies can help us to improve our historical understanding of the Holocaust.

There are three characteristics that unite historians and testimonies: (1) the internal pressure of the survivor to transmit his or her story meets with the historian's aim to reflect on and form societal representations of the past; (2) the story that is 'out there' refers to history, and is the essential precondition of testimony—and it is here that the traumatic situation can be situated—but is also subject to analysis and interpretation; and (3) the presence of a listener who receives the testimony opens toward the historian as a subsequent listener. Historiography, in this respect, can further develop testimony with analysis of events outside their historical time frame on the one hand, and empathy and remembrance on the other. In this sense, historiography can assume the role of preceding the dialog of the testimonial process on a societal level and convey the struggles of trauma from the individual to society as well as draw the two together. In a broader sense, the cage of trauma-induced isolation can be burst open through historiography.

Survivor testimonies can be considered as narrative-structured representations of—as well as commentaries on—experiences of the past. But what do we ask for when we consider testimonial narratives of traumatized and hospitalized Holocaust survivors, whose narratives are deeply fragmented and who frequently fall into silence?

A narrative is a modal and temporal structuring of a progression of incidents. However, for a traumatized person, the situation continues to persist internally far beyond the original incident. Thus, in order to recount the experience, the traumatized must shift from being the victim of trauma to being the distanced narrator of a past event. Because this is an impossible shift for the traumatized to make, their reconstructions often have fissures so large that narratives are hardly distinguishable. This is the case in Shmuel's testimony.

The singularity of the video testimony stems from a focus on the survivor's process of coming to terms with his or her experience. We see and listen to the weight of bearing witness directly. Hence, it is not only the narratives that help us understand the testimony, but also the narrative fissures, which, in many ways, shed light on the most crucial aspects of testimony. I will focus on both the narrative and nonnarrative aspects, on their relation to each other, and on their implications regarding the historiography of the Holocaust.

Narrative fissure 1: violence inflicted by Romanian authorities and civilians against the Jews in Bessarabia

In this excerpt, it is striking that the survivor, Shmuel B., maintains that the Romanians were not abusive. Moreover, he justifies abusive behavior from "some of the soldiers" as being due to their own lack of means. Despite repeated inquiries from the interviewer, Shmuel continues to deny Romanian abuse until he finally admits: "I do not complain of them because the Jews made fun of them and then revenge came." The term "revenge" indicates that the guilt for crimes perpetrated against the Jews is displaced from the non-Jewish Romanians to the Romanian Jews themselves, a process that Andreas Hamburger has called "guilt inversion."

Thus, the historical setting described in the interview excerpt reveals another perspective on the relationship between Jews and non-Jews in Bessarabia, Romania, at that time. The witness refers to the period between July 1941—when Hotin, his hometown, was occupied and demolished by the Romanian and German militaries—and November 1941, when the last convoys of Jews were deported from transit camps in Bessarabia to Transnistria, which lies on the other side of the Dniester River. Because Bessarabia was a part of the Russian Empire until the end of World War I, and part of Romania, a country bordering Ukraine, from 1918 on, Shmuel grew up in a multiethnic region in which Romanian, Russian, and Ukrainian Jews and non-Jews lived together peacefully.

But prior to the Romanian and German aggression against the Soviet Union in June 1941, the Romanian government had begun to push anti-Semitic legislation and anti-Jewish actions, leading to an explosion of atrocities and thousands of Jewish casualties, especially in Bessarabia and northern Bukovina. Both in the Romanian army and the Romanian gen-darmerie, leading officials incited their forces to propagate anti-Semitism and anti-Jewish cruelty. In the period between the withdrawal of Soviet troops from Bessarabia and Bukovina and the installation of a Romanian civil administration (within the first two weeks of July 1941), a wave of massacres struck the Jewish populations. In this phase, tens of thousands of Jews were killed by the Romanian army, the Romanian gendarmerie, the German Einsatzgruppe D, the German Wehrmacht, and local civilians. After the countless massacres of the Jewish population in various cities in northern Bukovina and Romania, the Romanian army and gendarmerie deported the remaining Jews in these regions to Transnistria. Gendarmerie General Ion Topor defined the procedures in his order from September 7, 1941: "The territorial station gendarmes help to cleanse the land [i.e., of Jews] and bury the dead with the help of locals; The way to han-dle those who do not submit? (ALEXIANU)[2]; Do not take them through customs. Those who loot will be executed" (Ioanid, 2001, 78). In other words, deportations were meant to "cleanse the land," deaths were taken into account, and Jews who disobeyed were executed. A deportee from Hotin, like Shmuel, was on the last convoy from Secureni (a transit camp leading from Bessarabia to Transnistria), and remembers:

> We were told that the sick who could not leave the camp would be executed. It was impossible to describe how people, consumed with typhoid fever, dragged themselves through the mud or mothers carried agonizing babies in their arms. Throughout the journey, we learned that the convoy before us had been robbed and partially eliminated by the escort. Our numbers diminished as we were forced, day and night, through hills, valleys, and swamps, under the rain and during the first frost of the fall. On the road we abandoned everything we had because we were so exhausted that we could not carry any luggage. At the Dniester, before entering Atachi, we were told under threat of execution, to hand over all identification papers and documents. (Carp, 1947, 88, as cited in Ioanid, 2001, 83)

Besides Romanian soldiers and gendarmes, Jews also had to fear Romanian and Ukrainian civilians who looted, raped, and killed them by hand or with agricultural equipment in the villages and along the deportation routes. The environment in which the Jewish communities had evolved had turned hostile on them. Historians Andrej Angrick (2003) and Jean Ancel (2011) emphasize that the brutal actions against the Jews in Bessarabia were dictated mainly by Romania. Yet, just the troops from the German Einsatzgruppe D killed at least 4,425 Jews between Hotin and Yampol in the summer and fall of 1941 (Ioanid, 2000). As historian Radu Ioanid (2000) summarizes, when the Germans and Romanians entered Bessarabia and Bukovina that summer, they found about 220,000 Jews who did not flee with the Soviet forces. Between 123,000 and 145,000 Jews arrived in Transnistria alive, indicating that at least 75,000 Jews died in Bessarabia and Bukovina in the massacres, deportations, and transit camps between July and November 1941. It was during this time that General Voiculescu proclaimed that the "Jewish question" in Bessarabia was "solved" and that the Bessarabian ground was "cleansed" of all Jews (Frilling, Ioanid, & Ionescu 2004, 131–137). Based on these historical findings, it can be assumed that Shmuel experienced or witnessed Romanian abuse. His denial and justification of Romanian behavior toward Jews can only be attributed to trauma, and knowing this gives insight into the trauma testimony.

Narrative fissure 2: in the Transnistrian ghetto: the death of the parents in Murafa and Djurin

Another narrative fissure in the Shmuel testimony occurs in the context of experiences in Transnistria, more precisely in the ghettos of Djurin and Murafa. He and his family arrived there no later than mid-November 1941, but more likely in September or early October. Whereas his mother and sister were sent to Murafa, he, his brother, and his father were sent to Djurin. In a direct example of narrative fissure, Shmuel overlooks the death of his mother in his testimony, forcing the interviewer to insist upon its discussion. In response, Shmuel says: "There was a hospital and the big sister took care of her. It was impossible to, then my dad and me had to get to the funeral." He skips the actual event of her death and arrives directly at her funeral, which he and his father could not attend. Shmuel's words "it was impossible to" likely refer to what he said a moment before: his mother had an infection in her leg and could not access antibiotics. In the end, he leaves the completion of his recollection to the listener and the listener's imagination.

Shmuel points out that his parents died within one month of each other, and because his father is listed as deceased on March 7, 1942 on a death roll of the Djurin ghetto, we can date the death of his mother back to early February of the same year (Shitnovitzer, 1974). At that time, in Murafa and Djurin, a ferocious typhus epidemic spread among the deportees, especially among those from Bessarabia (Carp, 2000; Ofer, 2009). The extremely high number of casualties due to typhus was the result of a lack of medication and health care in the ghettos. It was part of the controlled undersupply of the Jews in Transnistria. With the exception of some guards, the Romanian administration left the deportees to their own resources. But in what condition were those who arrived in Transnistria and what resources did they have? "Many deportees who had escaped from other places or from convoys," says historian Sarah Rosen (2010),

> also flowed into Murafa, among them deportees from Bessarabia, northern Bucovina and Cernauti. These deportees were frequently exposed to abuse from Romanian farmers, soldiers, and gendarmes during their

wanderings. Many of them were miserable and destitute, and all had experienced trauma, having lost their homes, all their possessions and in many cases their loved ones. Their testimonies reveal that, when they reached Murafa, they had almost no clothes, were half-starved, and were in a desperate physical and mental condition. (p. 162)

This implies that the Jews who were deported to Transnistrian ghettos such as Murafa and Djurin were destined to die there. They did not receive food, water, medical care, accommodation, or clothing. They had to organize everything themselves with the little means they had. And many of them had no means, this being the case for Shmuel's family. When Shmuel says that he slept with his father in the synagogue, it indicates that they were unable to find a place among the local Jews of the town as others did. In his chronicle about the ghetto, Wolf Rosenstock (1989), a survivor of Djurin, wrote that the synagogue was a place for those who had nothing and who were exposed to death first-hand. Furthermore, at the end of December 1941, extremely low temperatures accelerated the death toll in the ghettos, and a harsh wind from the surrounding steppe arose. Shmuel refers to these difficult weather conditions when he emphasized the "terrible snow storm" that prevented him and his father from getting to his mother's funeral. A survivor from Cimpuling, Bukovina, Mirjam Korber describes the route from Djurin to Murafa in her diary: "The road goes through wide fields reaching to the horizon without anything that could provide protection against cold or storm" (Korber, 1993, 65). When Shmuel's mother died, the family had already spent at least three months in the ghettos. Their physical and mental conditions were critical. His father would pass away soon after, and the day before he did, Shmuel mentions that he was no longer able to find food or had nothing left to barter in exchange for food. His sister would die one month after his father; the members of the family had been pushed to their limits or were already gone. Considering these extreme circumstances, a snowstorm became a question of life and death.

As mentioned above, the synagogue of Djurin was a gathering place for Jews in the most miserable situations, and this is where Shmuel's father died. Accordingly, death rates were likely highest there. The Jewish council of Djurin, an organization of rabbis and others who cared for the dying, created a type of religious welfare for those in the synagogue.[3] This is likely what Shmuel is referring to when he points out that his father "died a Hasidic death," although this comment makes it sound as though he is trying to give solace to the listener or to himself. The document, which lists Shmuel's father's date of death, indicates that he was 51 years old and died of myocarditis. However, as he died in the night and without a death investigation, it is impossible to say whether he died of a heart attack, as Shmuel supposes later in the testimony. His heart might have failed after months of stress due to the lack of food and protection against the winter weather and the death of his wife. Shmuel witnessed both the gradual physical and mental deterioration of his father and his eventual death, lying next to him and trying to wake him up. "Dad took it to heart," Shmuel notes in regard to his mother's death and the family's failure to bury her. Later in the testimony, Shmuel adds, "it affected him, he was devoted." The father fell silent and the son watched him grieve. Although he himself had lost his mother, he—"the youngest" and most helpless, as he emphasizes several times in the footage—became responsible for feeding himself and his father. As Shmuel does not mention the help of his brother or sister in his testimony, it becomes clear that, from his perspective, he was then, and still is, alone and isolated. The loneliness and isolation to which Shmuel testifies coincides with the historical situation of the Transnistrian ghettos, as it was a main goal of the Romanian government and administration to isolate the Jewish population, break their social cohesion, and force every individual into complete separation. From a historian's point of view, Shmuel's testimony demonstrates this through both the disruption of his family bonds as a consequence of the acts perpetrated against them and, beyond the individual level, the disruptions of communal and cultural bonds of the Jewish people in Bessarabia and Transnistria (e.g., the refusal to perform a ritual for the mother's funeral). There is no moment of farewell in Shmuel's testimony. Not for him and not for his father. Whether the Romanian authorities cared for a funeral according to the Hasidic canons is left open at this point. I assume they left it to the Jews themselves to care about their relatives. But considering the weather, I suppose it was difficult, maybe even impossible, to dig a grave in the frozen ground. Even if they could make it through the snowstorm, it is unclear if a "funeral" deserving of its name could have taken place. As a result, fundamental bonds in Jewish communal life, like the ritual burial of a mother, wife, and community member, were destroyed.

Although different in its narrative structure, there is cohesion between Shmuel's testimony and that of Jolly and Rosalie, a mother and daughter who survived a satellite camp in Neuengamme, as the two reveal another kind of narrative fissure due to a complete separation of both women from each other. As Johanna Bodenstab points out, their depictions of the murder of a baby by the SS lieutenant Kümmel show some inconsistencies, but neither woman corrects the version of the other. Although the narrative dissonance in this testimony is shaped by both trauma and historical constellations in the aftermath of the Shoah, the historian's perspective distinguishes between the National-Socialist aim to separate and isolate the persecuted Jews on the one hand, and the traumatic impact of these actions on the persecuted on the other—far beyond the end of the era, all the way to the end of their lives.

Conclusions

Such observations suggest that history has taken traumatic shape here. Testimonies like that of Shmuel reveal the traumatic structure of events in Holocaust history. Their analysis can hence contribute to a deeper understanding of the Holocaust, for example, in regard to the inner dynamics that conditioned the behavior of the Jews in camps and ghettos. Trauma structures in Holocaust history illuminate the destructive power of persecution and extermination unleashed by the perpetrators on every level of action. They allow for a focus upon the historical aspects that are difficult to seize in measures, but that are essential for the comprehension of the mechanisms of violence. Narrative fissures as manifestations of trauma in Holocaust survivor testimony create paradoxes, which refer to crucial situations and experiences in the witnesses' pasts. Trauma-induced characteristics of testimony, such as narrative fissures, demonstrate that it is not only the content but also the form of testimony that draws the picture of traumatic history.

Notes

1 First published as Narrative fissures, historical context: When traumatic memory is compromised, *Contemporary Psychoanalysis*, *51*(2), 2015. Reprinted by permission of Taylor & Francis, LLC.
2 'ALEXIANU' is code for the execution of Jews.
3 Rosenstock (1989) writes: "denn wer nichts zu bieten hatte, musste in die 'Schil' [Synagoge] gehen. Diese 'Schil' ist etwas Entsetzliches. Es ist fast eine Dschuriner Reproduktion des Mogilever 'Restaurants', dessen Erinnerung uns einen Schauder u¨ber den Ru¨cken laufen la¨sst" (p. 46) ("because whoever didn't have anything

to offer had to go to the 'Schil' [Synagogue]. The 'Schil' is something terrible. It is almost a Djurinian reproduction of the Mogilevian 'restaurant,' the memory of which runs a shiver down my spine.") The "Mogilevian Restaurant" refers to a terrible place in the Ghetto Mogilev, famous for its miserable living conditions.

References

Ancel, J. (2011). *The history of the Holocaust in Romania.* Jersualem: Yad Vashem.

Angrick, A. (2003). *Besatzungspolitik und Massenmord: Die Einsatzgruppe D in der südlichen Sowjetunion 1941–1943* (1st ed.). Hamburg: Hamburger Edition.

Carp, M. (1947). Cartea neagra: Suferintele Evreilor din România 1940–1944 [Black book of the suffering of the Jews in Romania 1940–1944], Vol. 3. Bucharest: Societatea nationala de editura si arte grafice Dacia Traiana.

Carp, M. (2000). *Holocaust in Romania: Facts and documents on the annihilation of Romania's Jews 1940–1944* (A. Simon, Ed.). Safety Harbor, FL: Simon Publications.

Frilling, T., Ioanid, R., & Ionescu, M. E. (2004). *Final report of the International Commission on the Holocaust in Romania.* Iasi, Romania: Polirom.

Ioanid, R. (2000). *The Holocaust in Romania: The destruction of Jews and Gypsies under the Antonescu regime, 1940–1944.* Chicago: Ivan R. Dee.

Ioanid, R. (2001). The deportation of the Jews to Transnistria. In M. Hausleitner, B. Mihok, & J. Wetzel (Eds.), *Rumänien und der Holocaust: Zu den Massenverbrechen in Transnistrien 1941–1944* (Nationalsozialistische Besatzungspolitik in Europa 1939–1945, Vol. 10, pp. 69–99). Berlin: Metropol.

Korber, M. (1993). *Deportiert: Jüdische Überlebensschicksale aus Rumänien 1941–1944: Ein Tagebuch* (E. Wiehn, Ed.). Konstanz: Hartung-Gorre Verlag.

Ofer, D. (2009). The ghettos in Transnistria and ghettos under German occupation in Eastern Europe: A comparative approach. In C. Dieckmann and B. Quinkert (Eds.), *Im Ghetto 1939–1945. Neue Forschungen zu Alltag und Umfeld* (Beiträge zur Geschichte des Nationalsozialismus, vol. 25, pp. 30–53). Göttingen: Wallstein Verlag.

Rosen, S. (2010). Surviving in Murafa ghetto: A case study of one ghetto in Transnistria. *Holocaust Studies, 16,* 157–176.

Rosenstock, W. (1989). Die Chronik von Dschurin: Aufzeichnungen aus einem rumänisch-deutschen Lager. *Dachauer Hefte: Studien und Dokumente zur Geschichte der Nationalsozialistischen Konzentrationslager, 5,* 40–86.

Shitnovitzer, S. (Ed.). (1974). *Sefer kehilat Hotin (Besarabyah)* [The book of the community of Khotin (Bessarabia)]. Tel Aviv: Khotin [Bessarabia] Society.

Refracted attunement, affective resonance

Scenic-narrative microanalysis of entangled presences in a Holocaust survivor's video testimony[1]

Andreas Hamburger

Scenic-narrative microanalysis and Shoah survivor research

The psychoanalytically inspired qualitative research approach of 'scenic-narrative microanalysis' is in line with a major methodological turn in psychotherapy research away from outcome and toward detailed process assessment. A similar change can be observed in the clinical research on social trauma over the last decades, which has turned to deepened qualitative process research on interactive aspects of trauma. Trauma is not a one-person phenomenon. It is experienced and reenacted in social situations, and one of its central symptoms is the loss of the communicative exchange with an internalized Other (Laub & Auerhahn, 1993). In social genocidal traumatizations, the resulting psychopathology is the outcome not just of the traumatic experience itself, but of the damage to the cultural and social "holding environment" as well. The "conspiracy of silence" (McKinney, 2007; Prince, 2009; Thomas, 2009; Delić et al., 2014), shared by the perpetrators as well as by the survivors, leads to a chronification of the traumatic experience of being alone with an overwhelming experience in an unsymbolized space. What da Rocha Barros and da Rocha Barros (2011) have described as an attack on the symbolic function by the traumatic experience corresponds to the distortion of the communicative space in social trauma.

The study presented here aims at reconstructing the reenactment of the traumatic experience in testimonies conducted with chronically psychiatrically hospitalized survivors of the Shoah, in the Yale video testimony study (Laub, 2005, 2015). Scenic-narrative microanalysis is methodologically rooted in hermeneutic depth analysis (Bereswill, Morgenroth, &

Redman, 2010). It is based on systematically reflecting the reader's reactions to the text (i.e., 'reader transference'). For the purposes of this study, we have used this technique to examine the interviewer's reactions within the testimonial situation, the interviewer's interactions with the participant, and the expert research team's reactions to the video testimonies. Scenic-narrative microanalysis elucidates the significant resonances to be found between the experiences of the researcher and the video data, as well as experiences in the interview 'scene' itself. This analytic approach eventually leads to hypotheses about resonant interactions in the patients' lives.

At stake in massive genocidal trauma is the process of narrativization of a life history—the transformation of the traumatic experiences into long-term memory through their recounting—as a consequence of the damage inflicted upon the holding environment. The survivors search for words as if they are groping in the darkness, unable to bring the fragments of their disintegrated life experiences into a recognizable sequence of narration. A systematic analysis of the testimonies demonstrates that narrative fragmentation (breaks, retraction of statements, contradictions, moments of silence, and refusals) form a second, desymbolized language: a pattern of destruction that communicates effectively with the interviewer who then reacts with communicative ruptures and parapraxes—a mutual enactment or "action dialogue," to adopt Klüwer's (2001) recoining of Schafer's (1976) term, that is observable even in the raters' assessments and discussions.

Findings of the study: the case example of Shmuel B.

Scenic-narrative microanalysis provides a formal analytic framework to decode the survivors' communications. The analysis of the video testimonies examined here is carried out in discrete steps:

1   From a total of 22 available transliterated video testimonies, a set of five representative tapes is selected.
2   The testimonies are analysed using a Grounded Theory approach[2] with regard to their inherent dialogic structure, but without introducing psychoanalytic expertise at this point.
3   Four independent psychoanalytic experts identify significant moments of unconscious matching ("now moments" or "moments of

meeting"; Boston Change Process Study Group, 2010) between the survivor and the interviewer(s), and then form hypotheses about the unconscious transference and countertransference as visible in the material. They use their own 'reader's transference' as an indicator to detect these significant moments. They comment on the related moments in the interview by writing marginal comments on the transcript itself, and eventually give a written conclusive comment on the whole interview.

4   After the conclusion of these individual expert ratings, the raters meet in a moderated 'consensus conference' in connection with each testimony in order to discuss their findings. This group session (or sessions—in the pilot case discussed here, for example, we needed four sessions to handle the material of one testimony) resembles a psychoanalytic casuistic seminar, where session transcripts are discussed, including the reflection of the seminar participants' emotional reactions and their dynamic interaction in the group. Testimony sequences are included in the group discussion, if chosen by a majority of raters. A written consensus for each testimony is then formulated by the moderator(s).

5   The documents of the expert rating process (marginal comments, conclusive comments, consensus formula) are then related to the Grounded Theory results (coded text properties, e.g., turn taking behavior, structuring interventions related to certain types of topics, characteristic forms of relatedness) and subsequently discussed in the applicable context.

6   A concluding line-by-line interpretation of turning points of the testimony allows a reconstruction of the scenic reenactment. A computer-assisted qualitative research tool (Atlas.ti) was used to assist in the lengthy processes of heuristic classification necessary in creating the indices.

The results of the detailed analysis of four video testimonies have been published as a doctoral thesis (Heberlein, 2015). As a first and preliminary example, however, the findings of a pilot study are presented here,[3] concentrating on one of the turning points.

The testimony of Shmuel B. was taken at the Holocaust Survivor Home, Beer Yaakov, Israel (cf. Greenwald, Ben-Ari, Strous, & Laub, 2006) by Dori Laub, then 66 years old, and 10 years younger than the survivor himself (a fact that will play a role in the following close reading of the interview). Laub himself grew up under similar threat and comparable persecution to Shmuel B. in Czernowitz, Romania, a town that is a close neighbor to Shmuel's home town of Chutin, Romania (Laub, 2015). The co-interviewer was a social worker at Beer Yaakov, Oshrit Ben Ari, who was once in continuous contact with Shmuel B. She (the co-interviewer) is a 'Sabra' (born in Israel). Because the interview was actively led by Dr Laub, Ms Ben Ari remained silent most of the time, inserting in a question only from time to time, and just once during the sequence discussed below.[4] The raters and the author (Hamburger, 2015) are all second-generation Holocaust survivors, each with a distinct history and background. This might have contributed to the extent of countertransference reactions in the raters' group—but, as later experiences in our study show, the countertransferential responsiveness to traumatic transference is not limited to personal involvement or experience.

We have chosen a five-minute clip from the testimony to show how the multilayered process of mutual reenactment takes place during the testimony. The segment was regarded as a turning point by all four raters and was therefore included in the consensus discussion. Raters' marginal notes, comments, and the topics of the consensus group regarding this turning point will be reported in the form of a line-by-line commentary of the testimony text, without omissions, in order to show the whole Gestalt of the dialog. Information from paraverbal or mimic material was occasionally used for the interpretation.

The segment (from 22:07 to 27:22 of the recorded testimony) is about Shmuel's report on deportation. It consists of three topics:

1 Guilt (22:07–24:04)
2 Merging biographies, mother's death (24:04–25:45)
3 Father's death (25:45–27:22).

Guilt (22:07–24:04)

The first topic of this segment starts when Dr Laub asked about the deportation, to which Shmuel reacted with an emotional onset of a narrative:

> *A:* Deportation, they threw us bread on the air, as dogs. In Ukrania they put me in a pigpen. But the Romanian did not abuse much generally. They were only in a certain area, in Moldavia. (22:07)

The survivor then turns the narrative to the Romanians, and expresses his conviction that they did not do any harm, neither to him nor in general. However, the interviewer insists on recalling memory images:

Q: But do you remember how they took you out from home, who came, were they peasants or workers? If there is no memory, then there is no memory.

A: I don't remember. But I do not complain of the Romanian, they did not abuse, did not abuse. Only some of the soldiers who did not have a sufficient childhood, so they envied the Jews, the Jews were their revenge. But only a few. (22:52)

The sequence displays an interview dyad occupied with complementary protection. Laub's offer "If there is no memory, then there is no memory" is a shelter for the patient's wish to protect the surrounding Romanian neighbors—which, in fact, is a reflex very often found in survivors of genocidal persecution. However, this sheltering attitude on the part of the interviewer does not keep him from further insisting—which indicates that although his attitude is protective and merciful, he nevertheless does not believe that what the survivor is saying is the historical truth (Knopp, 2016). He repeats his question several times, unimpressed by Shmuel's constant rejection:

Q: What did those Romanian do? What did you see?
A: When they arrived, Jews came and got organized in Ukrania, in Ukrania.
Q: Were there Romanian who abused, did you see the . . . ?
A: No, not much. (23:40)
Q: Do you remember something of such abuse?

This insisting takes the pragmatic form of a *presupposition*: the interviewer does not ask *whether* the Romanians had abused, he just asks *how* they abused. Thus, the proposition that they had committed something is turned into an implication. By performing this pragmatic speech act (cf. Stalnaker, 1999), Laub makes it very difficult for the interviewee to deny the question. In a court of law, such a questioning style would likely be characterised as being manipulative. At this point, the raters thought of this as something akin to a desperate search for historical truth buried in the fragmentary memory of the survivor. This persistent search then produced an answer, however, which was regarded as one of the main events of this segment:

> *A:* I do not complain of them because the Jews made fun of them and then revenge came.

All the raters reacted emotionally to this answer. The remarks in the transcript margins were: "Dori bringt gewisses Entsetzen zum Ausdruck = Ment.störung = kann es nicht vom Standpunkt des P sehen u. versuchen zu verstehen. Weil zu betroffen?" [Dori expresses a certain dismay = disturbed mentalization = can't see it from the patient's perspective and tries to understand, because too involved?] (Rater 4) or just "Ungläubiges Staunen" [unbelieving astonishment], "klar abweisend" [clearly dismissive] (Rater 2). In the consensus group session, a remarkable amount of debate erupted on the raters' own tendency to discharge this tension by blaming the interviewer for being rejecting. From this self-analytic movement in the group, it could be concluded that the constant inquiring of Dr Laub had disclosed an inner conviction of the interviewee, namely that the traumatic events had been caused by the victims. This guilt reversal is well known among traumatized patients. We find it in survivors of sexual abuse as well as in survivors of violence or ethnic persecution. To hear it stated in so frank a manner, however, is hard to endure. Furthermore, and since it is about genocidal trauma, the emotional reaction of an interviewer or a researcher, hearing a survivor overtly stating that the Jews were the party responsible for their own extinction, is probably more than we can bear with open consciousness; thus, we display an unconscious reaction, and resort to symptoms like impulsive rage or its opposite—dizziness and paralysis. From the reflection of these emotional reactions within the rater's group, it was inferred that the group was about to witness and partly repeat a countertransference reaction for and on behalf of the interviewer.

In the next turn, the interviewer gives in. He does not discuss or object to Shmuel's statement any more, but rather repeats Shmuel's words assertively, and leaves the country:

> *Q:* Revenge came. OK. So you arrived to Ukrania, to Transnisteria. Again, what was the name of the village?

After Laub's acquiescence of the guilt inversion, strong signs of drowsiness, even sleepiness were noticed in the rater's consensus group. As has been discussed thoroughly in clinical literature, drowsiness on the part of the analyst may be interpreted as a sign of defence against fusion (Brown, 1977), structural overburdening, and splitting (cf. Eshel, 2001; Zwiebel, 2010). If the analytic capacity is overburdened with the containment and the reflection of what has been projected into the analyst (using his own unconscious like piano keys, on which the intruding unconscious of the patient plays its sometimes unbearable cacophony), analysts may resort to a depressive downgrading of their vital functions.

Merging biographies, mother's death (24:04–25:45)

The interviewer in this testimony first tried to gain ground by asking for facts, but immediately afterward made some interesting mistakes. First, a hearing error, when he found difficulties in understanding the name of the village—which, as far as we can judge from the video, was clearly pronounced (for further information about the village, cf. Knopp, 2016):

A: Morava and Jorin. Morava and Jorin *[zɔɹin]*. (24:04)
Q: Morava and Julin *[zulin]*.
A: Jorin *[zɔɹin]*.
Q: Jorin *[zɔɹin]*. And what did you see when you arrived the new place? You are a seven-year-old child.

The raters observed an impressive degree of paramnesia on the part of Dr Laub in the last sentence. Given the survivor's age and the year of his deportation (repeatedly mentioned in the interview), Shmuel was already 14 by the time of the deportation. Commenting this error, one member of the rating group offered some external information obtained from the Yale University Fortunoff Video Archive site about the personal biography of the interviewer.

"Dori Laub was born in Czernowitz, Romania in 1937. With his parents, he was deported to Transnistria in 1942. His father disappeared during a German raid prior to liberation by the Soviets."[5] Thus, the person in the room who was a young child when deportation came was not Shmuel, but the interviewer himself, Dr Laub. The rating group dedicated considerable discussion time to this error in age, and to the similarities between both main participants of the interview. The unconscious moment here was interpreted as a partial fusion or merging of biographies, due to a counteridentification with a temporary loss of reality control. In any setting other than a psychoanalytic one, such a moment of confusion would be regarded as a lack of objectivity. From the viewpoint of the 'scenic' reenactment, however, we understand it as a communicative event. The interviewer is dragged into the fissures of the interviewee's mental life through the latter's fragmented narrative, thereafter forcing the interviewer himself to fill in the resulting gaps with entries from his own inner life.

This temporary mental fusion or merger is known to occur in clinical psychoanalysis when primary process material is enacted. Human communication is rooted in basic experiences of somatic and mental interaction, and the symbolic structure of mental life is shaped in protosymbolic interactions and mentalization processes (cf. Stern, 1986; Fonagy, Gergely, Jurist, & Target, 2004). Regressive situations in the psychoanalytic process, where these basic forms of interaction are repeated and enacted, may be experienced by both participants as a loss of boundaries.

Shmuel doesn't show any reaction to this error (which he must have noticed). He just says:

A: I was with dad, sister, and brother. (24:25)

The interpretation of this rejoinder leads to the conjecture that in his sudden mentioning of his father and family, Shmuel unconsciously reacts to the interviewer's implicit recall of the loss of his own father. Shmuel might have unconsciously noticed that his counterpart did experience a change in his inner status. Mentioning the little boy brought an affect-loaded memory into the dialog, which Shmuel naturally linked to this memory. He offered, analytically spoken, a father–son relatedness: "I was with dad," which, in the unconscious presence of the testimony, might mean "I am with dad," and, if we explicate the affective meaning of this notion, might mean something like: "I feel you are moved when you think of a little boy being with his dad, and therefore I feel moved too, as if I were this little boy, and you were my dad." In the light of this reconstruction of an emerging father transference, it is most surprising that the interviewer suddenly changes the subject:

Q: And mom?

The rating group understood this as a defensive shift. The father transference might have become too dense, given its intensity as a result of
the extent of fusion. However, the effective moment is hard to reconstruct, even if we take the information from the video into consideration.
Shmuel's face remains without a sign of emotion. And again, he does not
really object. His answer is evasive, but at the same time displays a moving, childlike intimacy. Referring to a social group in which he is "the
youngest," he implies his relatedness to both his parents and his siblings.
The interviewer, instead of accepting this offered intimacy, again insists
on the mother, urging the interviewee to touch upon a memory which he
was perhaps not quite willing to articulate:

A: We were together, they took care of me, I was the youngest, they
      took care of me. (24:32)
Q: You don't mention mom.
A: Mom died in Morva.

Once again, the interviewer's insistence and his failure to connect to
the offered transference ("I was the youngest") was regarded as a part of the
unconscious scene. In an earlier part of the interview, the notion of being the
youngest had already assumed significance: the interviewer had actively and
repeatedly asked for an even younger sibling—and it eventually turned out
that Shmuel had, in fact, a younger sister whom he had not yet mentioned.
She had died as a baby before the war (cf. testimony Shmuel B., 00:01:40).
This embedded scene, which the survivor alludes to by introducing himself as "the youngest," points to a close dyadic relatedness underpinning the
unfolding scene. Following the further unfolding of this new layer of relatedness, we observe that Laub again turns to facts and suffers from parapraxes:

Q: Where?
A: In Morva, in the hospital.
Q: Before?
A: She had an infection in the leg.
Q: That is, mom died before you were taken to Transnisteria.
A: In Transnisteria. (24:52)

The intrusion of the dead mother into the analytic space first leads to
another avoidance, expressed by a hearing error ("where?"), by paramnesia

("before?") as well as by a fact-bound approach. After first coping with his shock, however, the interviewer returns to his more accessible attitude and asks an opening question:

Q: How did it happen?
A: She was ill. She had an infection in the leg and there were no antibiotics. (25:02)
Q: Right, was there a hospital?
A: There was a hospital and the oldest sister took care of her. It was impossible to, then my dad and me had to get to the funeral. It was on winter, a very strong storm, we had to walk 12 km. But there was a terrible snow storm. We couldn't and came back. We didn't get to the funeral. (25:08)

This short sequence shows again the thin ice upon which the unconscious relatedness of the two participants are dancing. After the first very short onset of a narrative by the survivor, the interviewer is again afflicted by a loss of his short term memory: Understood at the denotative level, "Was there a hospital?" is an unnecessary question, as the hospital had been mentioned about 15 seconds earlier. But the "third ear" does not confine itself to the denotative level. Arguing that these kinds of short term paramnesias are part and parcel of the unconscious scene, we hypothesize that in the shared inner world of the dialog partners, this question could possibly be read as meaning something like:

> I almost cannot endure the thought that you, as a boy who in my inner life is a seven-year-old boy of the same age as I was when I lost my father in the deportation, should also have lost your mother, and that there was no help against it, not even a hospital, as the hospital you mentioned is not one I could remember for 15 seconds under the emotional pressure of this mental image. So please let me ask again, and hopefully it is the case that I did not understand you at all, and that your mother did not die at all.

This or a comparable process might have reigned inside the interviewer, while the survivor continues to answer, his answer evolving into the first longer narrative passage of the interview. He tells a story. It is a terrible story, because it recalls one of the deepest injuries a faithful Jew can suffer: he and his father, the only surviving relatives present at the time, were not able to attend the funeral of his mother. What is established in the transferential scene in this moment was characterized by the rater's group as an "inner storm," shared by both the survivor and the interviewer, mentally immersed in the impossibility to reach and attend the burial of the mother, and the feelings connected with it. We see that the interviewer reacts to Shmuel's last sentence in a most impressed manner. He repeats, in deep compassion with the gruesome experience: father and son struggling through the snow storm, until they understood that they could not resist its force, that they had to accept they would not make it to the funeral, and that they had to turn back. And this repetition is met with another blow:

Q: You didn't get to mom's funeral?
A: Dad took it to heart, he died within a month as well. (25:42)

Father's death (25:45–27:22)

Dr Laub reacts to this second blow with something that the raters experienced as a resumption of his holding capacity (Winnicott, 1986; Ogden, 2004). Taking in the disturbing fact that after the defeat against the storm Shmuel's father had died as well, he now answers in a different way. He puts an open question to Shmuel, encouraging him to share the experience, and he accompanies him throughout his story with mirroring and containing remarks:

Q: How did it happen?
A: In the synagogue, in the synagogue. We slept together.
Q: In the synagogue. (25:51)
A: They put us in the synagogue.
Q: All the Jews.
A: Not all the Jews, only those who had no place. Some hid among the village families. (25:59)
Q: I understand, some found a place.
A: With the Jews. (26:09)

The raters noted impressions like "er lächelt traurig!" [he smiles sadly] or "Verlust, Verlassensein vs. 'did take care of me'" [loss, being abandoned vs. 'did take care of me'] (Rater 1) or "vorsichtige Spiegelung" [cautious mirroring] (Rater 4). In the rating group's discussion this kind of "togetherness" was experienced as a quasi-maternal holding. It is only slowly that the interviewer tries to broaden the narrative by asking deeper questions, and by respectfully helping the old man—who is now close to the memory of the death of his father—in such a way as to allow him to find words for what he experienced. The relatedness in the following sequence was felt as being likewise direct and intensively close:

> *Q:* And what did you do in the synagogue, where did you sleep on?
> *A:* They built beds out of planks. (26:17)
> *Q:* Out of planks. And describe what happened to dad.
> *A:* He died in bed. He sent me for food and I couldn't walk, I had no energy. In the morning he was dead, they tried to wake him up and died. (26:27)
> *Q:* And you slept right next to him.
> *A:* I slept right next to him.

Echoing the last question, Shmuel seems to vocalize his transferential closeness to a father figure, who holds his unsymbolized grief, but also helps him to further verbalize his memory. We may assume that Shmuel's capacity to mourn the loss of both his parents was blocked by the socially traumatic circumstances of their death, and that this mourning process had never since been revived due to his later, similarly traumatic life and hospitalization history. Thus, the scenic relatedness in the testimony could be understood as a father–son relationship, acting as a dyadic container (Bion, 1962).

A traumatically shattered inner life history cannot, however, dwell safely in such a container. The next rupture was due to come. This time it troubled the raters' group. In the close and intimate moment where both men held the emerging memory of the death of Shmuel's father, an element of 'knowing' was incorporated ("a Hassidic death"), which was seemingly understood as a moment of being together. However, as a close reading of the next sequence will show, including the discussion it triggered in the group, this moment of knowing caused significant cognitive dissonance in the rating group:

> *Q:* Do you remember how did you wake up that morning?
> *A:* I woke up as usual. Nobody knew he had died, they tried to wake him up. He died a Hasidic death [or as a Hasidic/in Hassidic garb].

Q: Hasidic death, he was dressed up?
A: Yes.

This element of the "Hasidic death" brought up a considerable discussion in the rating group. Some understood it as a kind of self-soothing (Rater 1), while other fantasies reached out so far as to imagine that the father, mortally wounded by the death of his wife and his failure to bury her, had dressed up purposefully and had laid himself down to commit suicide ("Dieser Vater ist gestorben aus Sehnsucht nach der Mutter" [this father died from longing for the mother] (Rater 4). This fantasy is, as the historical investigation shows, far from realistic (cf. Knopp, 2016). Reflecting it as an unconsciously triggered group fantasy, we can understand that the inner world of the raters had been seized by suicidal impulses, indicating a severe split in the transferential scene and presumably in the inner world of the survivor—perhaps due to his unconscious accusations and guilt feelings as a child when both of his parents had died and left him alone. In the consensus session, this was pointed out, referring to a later moment in the testimony, when Shmuel turns the recalling of the parents' death into a memory of being protected ("I was protected, I was protected. The family protected me," 31:00): "dass er vielleicht sich schuldig fühlt, aber trotzdem verleugnen muss das er vollkommen verlassen ist, und deshalb sagt, die haben mich ja beschützt. Er ist total ungeschützt" [that he might feel guilty, but has to deny that he feels absolutely abandoned, and therefore says the family protected me. He is absolutely unprotected] (Rater 1).

The sequence ends with a shift on the level of the interview setting. For the second time in the interview, the (female) co-interviewer, Oshrit Ben Ari, breaks her silence. On the first occasion when she had spoken up, her intervention had not really been seized upon by the two men; now, when they had established a maternal-holding connection (Winnicott, 1986), her intervention was more appreciated. The rating group felt that at this point of the scene, the female triangulation could be supported by the men:

Q: [Oshrit]: Did you try to wake him up? (27:12)
A: Yes.
Q: And do you recall what you thought then?
A: God, no. We envied the dead. (27:22)

This palpable splitting off of grief could have provoked another projective identification, and in consequence, another round of re-enactment in the interview as observed before. And maybe such a scenic reenactment could have opened another door to Shmuel's memory. But this time, the main interviewer does not enter the action dialog. Taking over the paternal function, he decides to stop the established regression by turning to the factual level:

> *Q:* What year was this in?
> *A:* '41, '42.

Discussion: what can scenic-narrative microanalysis tell us about manifestations of extreme traumatization in testimonial narration of Holocaust survivors?

Attacks on linking and the symbolic function

As da Rocha Barros and da Rocha Barros (2011) have pointed out, the attacks on the symbolic function can cut off a person from the ability to feel and to convey his or her feelings. However, the victimization of the whole group cuts the individual's reparative abilities in relation to his or her group's identity. Individuals under persecution find a container in the uncontaminated social environment, for example, the family, relatives, peers. When whole social groups, like the Jews in the Shoah, are at stake, the identity they award to their members turns into a negative one.

Laub (2015) reminds us of the effect of genocidal trauma on symbolic functioning and the tendency of interactive repetition, eventually leading to the denial of social trauma. The psychoanalytic theory of symbol formation has undergone notable changes (cf. Hamburger, 2005): Object relations theory and structural linguistics led to extended definitions of the symbol. Today, relational psychoanalysis links symbolic functioning to a mutual enactment in the developmental matrix (Stern, 1986) as well as in the consulting room. Thus, trauma is not stored in a one-body memory of the survivor; it is inscribed in the mutual enactment between the survivor and the interviewer as well as between the videotaped testimony and the rating group.

Repetition in multiple layers

Freud understood that psychoanalysis is the communication from unconscious to unconscious. However, he conceptualized it as a one-way-process (Freud, 1912/1958, 150–151). The further development of psychoanalytic theory and technique has led to a broadening of this approach. The unconscious relatedness between analyst and analysand is a two-way process; this mutual relatedness prevails not only in the analytic situation, but also in development of psychic functioning itself. The psyche is not a "mental apparatus," wherein memories are "stored," but is, more precisely, an interface of the shared process of meaning (Hamburger, 1998). This concept of mental life corresponds to relational approaches in psychoanalysis, as well as to the concept of a "narrative unconscious" (cf. Frie, 2012; Hamburger, 1998). Memory is "part and parcel of the social and temporal coordinates when and where remembering occurs . . . of the developmental process that implicates a person in his or her own past, and that constitutes the person's self in relation to the surrounding social world" (Prager, 1998, 177). Testimony is not just hampered by 'individual' forgetting or fragmenting, and the interviewer's psychoanalytic capacity is not just a kind of archaeological instrument—they are mutual processes.

In the testimonial process explored here, we have documented material about the specificity of the hampered dialog on genocidal trauma, and we have described the obstacles as residing in not only the injured memory of the survivor, but also the emotional reactions of the witnesses: the interviewers and ourselves in the rating group. These results are consistent with what has been reported in historical research on witnessing (Baer, 2000). Detecting, repeating, unfolding, and eventually naming these obstacles is what we can do.

In our own experience as witnesses to the testimony, we have relived the powerful emotional processes triggered by it, leading to symptoms like distortion and denial, which require continuous self-analytic reflection and inner searching to overcome the conspiracy of silence, including our own inevitable participation in this conspiracy, despite all our good intentions. To accept the challenge of witnessing in a psychoanalytic way means to accept and reflect upon our countertransferential entanglement in witnessing the video testimonies—as the interviewers did in the original process of witnessing the survivors' testimonies— in a way that helps mentalize or narrativize the fragmented life histories of the survivors. The testimonial process itself had a healing aspect for the survivors (Strous et al., 2005), whose parental containment had been destroyed by the genocidal trauma of the Shoah, and was then symbolically restored through the reenactment in the process of the testimony, as traced in the close reading of a short sequence in this article. Moreover, the detailed acknowledgement of these entanglements is also a mentalizing process for our own present mental lives (cf. Hamburger, 2013). Reflecting upon the scars of social trauma in our own relatedness to the testimony—resulting in our proneness to denial, archaic fantasy, and repression—gives a voice to muted parts of our own mental lives as well. The survivors gave their testimonies not only to the 'third ear' of the interviewers, but also to the video camera, thus passing them on to us.

Notes

1 First published as Refracted attunement, affective resonance: Scenic-narrative microanalysis of entangled presence in a Holocaust survivor's testimony, *Contemporary Psychoanalysis, 51*(2) (2015). Reprinted by permission of Taylor & Francis, LLC. The study was conducted in cooperation with the Yale video testimony study group (Dori Laub) and the Sigmund Freud Institut Frankfurt am Main (Marianne Leuzinger-Bohleber), and funded by the IPA Research Advisory Board, grant no. 1290276.
2 Grounded Theory is a prominent methodological approach in the social sciences for the data-driven detection of inherent structures in a given data collection (see Glaser & Strauss, 1967/2012; Strauss & Corbin, 1996).
3 The text analysis, which follows the method of Grounded Theory (Strauss & Corbin, 1990) as carried out by Heberlein (2010) is not reported in this chapter, which concentrates on the psychoanalytic rating. Raters were Hella Goldfein, Salek Kutschinski, Lilian Otscheret, and Naomi Silberner-Becker; coding and integration of the scenic-narrative microanalysis Nüsser and Schmidt (2010); interpretation Hamburger (2010).
4 This triangular dynamics will be discussed in a forthcoming paper.
5 http://www.library.yale.edu/testimonies/about/founders/laub.html.

References

Baer, U. (2000). *Niemand zeugt für den Zeugen.* Frankfurt am Main: Suhrkamp.
Bereswill, M., Morgenroth, M., & Redman, P. (2010). Alfred Lorenzer and the depth-hermeneutic method. *Psychoanalysis, Culture & Society, 15,* 221–250.
Bion, W. R. (1962). *Learning from Experience.* London: Heinemann.

Boston Change Process Study Group (2010). *Change in psychotherapy: A unifying paradigm*. New York: W.W. Norton.

Brown, D. G. (1977). Drowsiness in the countertransference. *International Review of Psycho-Analysis, 4*, 481–492.

da Rocha Barros, E. M., & da Rocha Barros, E. L. (2011). Reflections on the clinical implications of symbolism. *International Journal of Psychoanalysis, 92*, 879–901.

Delić, A., Hasanović, M., Avdibegović, E., Dimitrijević, A., Hancheva, C., Scher, C., Stefanović-Stanojević, T., Streeck-Fischer, A., & Hamburger, A. (2014). Academic model of trauma healing in postwar societies. *Acta Medica Academica, 43*(1), 76–80.

Eshel, O. (2001). Whose sleep is it, anyway?: Or "night moves." *International Journal of Psychoanalysis, 82*, 545–562.

Fonagy, P., Gergely, G., Jurist, E. L., & Target, M. (2004). *Affect regulation, mentalization, and the development of the self.* London: Karnac Books.

Freud, S. (1958). Recommendations to physicians practising psycho-analysis. *Standard Edition, 12*, 109–120. (Original work published 1912)

Frie, R. (2012). On culture, history, and memory: Encountering the "narrative unconscious." *Contemporary Psychoanalysis, 48*, 329.

Glaser, B. G., & Strauss, A. L. (2012). *The discovery of grounded theory: Strategies for qualitative research.* Piscataway, NJ: Transaction Publishers. (Original work published 1967)

Greenwald, B., Ben-Ari, O., Strous, R., & Laub, D. (2006). Psychiatry, testimony, and Shoah: Reconstructing the narratives of the muted. In G. Rosenberg & A. Weissman (Eds.), *International social health care policy, programs, and studies* (pp. 199–214). Philadelphia, PA: The Haworth Press.

Hamburger, A. (1998). Traumnarrativ und Gedächtnis. In M. Koukkou, Martha, M. Leuzinger-Bohleber, & W. Mertens (Eds.), *Erinnerung von Wirklichkeiten. Psychoanalyse und Neurowissenschaften im Dialog. Bd. 1: Bestandsaufnahme* (pp. 223–286). Stuttgart: Verlag Internationale Psychoanalyse.

Hamburger, A. (2005). Linguistics and psychoanalysis. In S. Ross (Ed.), *The Edinburgh international encyclopaedia of psychoanalysis* (pp. 284–287). Edinburgh: Edinburgh University Press.

Hamburger, A. (2010). *Forgotten victims: Scenic analysis of video testimonies with hospitalized Holocaust survivors.* Paper presented at the Joseph Sandler Research Conference, Sigmund Freud Institute Frankfurt am Main.

Hamburger, A. (2013). Warum psychoanalytische Holocaustforschung nicht enden kann und soll. Einleitung zum Vortrag [von Kurt Grünberg und Friedrich Markert]. In C. E. Walker, H. Blaß, R. Paul, & M. Teising (Eds.), *Die Psychoanalytische Haltung: Ihre Bedeutung im Spannungsfeld innerer und äußerer Angriffe. Arbeitstagung der Deutschen Psychoanalytischen*

Vereinigung Bad Homburg, 21. Bis 24. November 2012 (pp. 261–265). Berlin: Deutsche Psychoanalytische Vereinigung.

Hamburger, A. (2015). Roots in Jewish and Christian soil: A portrait of the Holocaust researcher as an involved person. *Contemporary Psychoanalysis, 51*(2), 289–295.

Heberlein, P. (2010). *Mikroanalyse eines Videozeugnisses eines hospitalisierten Holocaustüberlebenden: Entwicklung einer Grounded Theory.* Masters thesis, University of Kassel, Germany.

Heberlein, P. (2015). *Zerstörte Lebensgeschichten: Mikroanalyse von Interviews chronisch hospitalisierter Holocaustüberlebender.* Hamburg: Verlag Dr. Kovacs.

Klüwer, R. (2001). Szene, Handlungsdialog (Enactment) und Verstehen. In W. Bohleber & S. Drews (Eds.), *Die Gegenwart der Psychoanalyse: die Psychoanalyse der Gegenwart* (pp. 347–357). Stuttgart: Klett-Cotta.

Knopp, S. (2017). Narrative fissures, historical context: When traumatic memory is compromised. This volume, chapter 20.

Laub, D. (2005). From speechlessness to narrative: The cases of Holocaust historians and of psychiatrically hospitalized survivors. *Literature and Medicine, 24*(2), 253–265.

Laub, D. (2015). Listening to my mother's testimony. *Contemporary Psychoanalysis, 51*(2), 195–215.

Laub, D., & Auerhahn, N. C. (1993). Knowing and not knowing massive psychic trauma: Forms of traumatic memory. *International Journal of Psychoanalysis, 74*, 287–302.

McKinney, K. (2007). Breaking the conspiracy of silence: Testimony, traumatic memory, and psychotherapy with survivors of political violence. *Ethos, 35*(3), 265–299.

Nüsser, S., & Schmidt, S. K. (2010). *Szenisch-narrative Mikroanalyse eines Videozeugnisses eines hospitalisierten Holocaustüberlebenden.* Master's thesis, University of Kassel, Germany.

Ogden, T. H. (2004). On holding and containing, being and dreaming. *International Journal of Psychoanalysis, 85*, 1,349–1,364.

Prager, J. (1998). *Presenting the past: Psychoanalysis and the sociology of misremembering.* Cambridge, MA: Harvard University Press.

Prince, R. (2009). The self in pain: The paradox of memory. The paradox of testimony. *American Journal of Psychoanalysis, 69*, 279–290.

Schafer, R. (1976). Emotion in the language of action. *Psychological Issues, 9*(4), 106–133.

Stalnaker, R. (1999). *Context and content.* Oxford: Oxford University Press.

Stern, D. N. (1986). *The interpersonal world of the infant: A view from psychoanalysis and developmental psychology.* New York: Basic Books.

Strauss, A. L., & Corbin, J. (1990). *Basics of qualitative research: Grounded theory procedures and techniques*. Thousand Oaks, CA: Sage.

Strous, R. D., Weiss, M., Felsen, I., Finkel, B., Melamed, Y., Bleich, A., Kotler, M., & Laub, D. (2005). Video testimony of long-term hospitalized psychiatrically ill Holocaust survivors. *American Journal of Psychiatry, 162*(12), 2,287–2,294.

Thomas, N. K. (2009). Which horse do you ride? Trauma from a relational perspective. Discussion of Prince's "The self in pain: The paradox of memory. The paradox of testimony." *American Journal of Psychoanalysis, 69*, 298–303.

Winnicott, D. W. (1986). *Holding and interpretation: Fragment of an analysis*. London: Karnac Books.

Zwiebel, R. (2010). *Der Schlaf des Analytikers. Die Müdigkeitsreaktion in der Gegenübertragung*. (3rd ed.) Stuttgart: Klett-Cotta.

Chapter 22

Discussion of Bodenstab, Knopp, and Hamburger[1]

Dori Laub

It is important to highlight how the interdisciplinary contributions in this Part enrich our understanding of the impact extreme traumatization has on the testimonial narrative. Sonja Knopp's chapter illustrates how the traumatic imprint that permeates Holocaust testimony informs history through its content, through its form, and through the corporeal information it contains—far exceeding what the written document can convey. This is all the more evident when the traumatic rupture is irreparable, as in Shmuel's testimony, creating so-called 'fissures.'

The scenic-narrative microanalytic approach, presented by Andreas Hamburger, applies a relational analysis to a severely trauma-fragmented narrative by demonstrating how transference, countertransference, and parapraxes are in minute-to-minute dialog with each other in order to fill the traumatic gaps of what had not been symbolized, and therefore unnarrated. This approach unequivocally underscores the profound damage to psychic structure and function, and to boundaries that are the backdrop for the survivor's fractured narratives.

Finally the chapter by Dr Johanna Bodenstab demonstrates the psychoanalytic listening to a mother–daughter interaction in an extremely traumatic moment—the joint witnessing of the unexpected murder of a newborn baby. The narrative evolves and is structured and layered. Feelings are experienced and expressed. The psychoanalytic interpretation of the formidable parapraxis that occurs in it, allows for the elucidation of the impact the witnessed event had on the mother–daughter relationship and on each of their self representations.

II

Comparing the two testimonial excerpts—the one by Shmuel, the other by Jolly—it is apparent that the proximity of traumatic memories affects them both. There are, however, marked differences between the two.

When we read Jolly's testimony it is as though we ourselves are present at the scene of the narration. It is as if we are watching the events unfolding, most likely, as she herself is watching them on her own memory screen. She is present to herself as well as to us. Events follow one another. She has created the mental space that contains this unbroken chain. There is curiosity, suspense, terror, helplessness, and grief. We are drawn in, are almost swept away, and become part of the experience, very much as she is while telling it. The visual and the affective are major components of this event. This is a full-bodied narrative, with agency, driven from inside.

It is very different when we watch Shmuel's narration. There is no continuity of the visual. There are only blips that remain static. They are forcefully hurled at us. This only happens after we have dredged them up and created the mental space for their containment. They are also laden with affect, mostly terror. The visual is actually almost absent and so is the color. It is as if he is reading about what he experiences in a very small print, in gray. There is no echo, no resonance to his reading. This is likely what Shmuel himself sees and experiences on his fragmented mental memory screen. We join him in watching what he watches. Memories come in jolts. No process of narration has been set in motion. There is no subject that holds it together, no agency that carries it forward. Each fragment is rich in information, but there is an intense, continuous push and pull, a tentative approach, and a terrified flight from the memory fragment. This is in itself testimony to the quality of Shmuel's retrieved memories.

The statements Shmuel makes are not open ended. They imply a certain finality and do not telegraph that something is still to come ("we envied the dead"). They are deliverd in a flat sound, without an echo. It is as if he has nothing in him that can respond to, amplify, or reverberate with this sound. There can be no further associations or reflections. It leaves an empty space that is closed. Unless someone intervenes it will remain that way. Yet such intervention is neither expected nor invited. Shmuel's statements are not meant to be part of a dialog.

It is interesting to observe the metaphors Shmuel uses. It is as though he cannot find the right descriptor for what he wants to say—so he invents a new one. The Romanian soldiers' "insufficient childhoods," father's dying in a "Hasidic garb," his growing up in an "intimate town," are examples of such metaphors. They are very saturated with meaning and one can understand what Shmuel is trying to say. However, the words he chooses are somewhat idiosyncratic and suggest a neologistic tendency. Moreover, when asked to elaborate and free associate to them he cannot do so, and falls silent.

Finally, there is a remarkable difference between Jolly and Shmuel's testimonies, in the way they deal with the perpetrator and with atrocities. Jolly pinpoints the murderer—the camp commandant—and describes the murder. In Shmuel's testimony, the human perpetrator is nowhere to be found. He insists that Romanian soldiers did not abuse Jews and claims not to have witnessed even a single act of such abuse. It is only in the "terrible snowstorm," a phenomenon of nature, that we notice the presence of powerful destructive forces. In Shmuel's internal landscape, there seems to be no space for the atrocities perpetrated by human beings.

III

In terms of psychodynamics, what the two testimonies have in common is the failure of the mothering function in the Holocaust. Jolly describes the murder of a baby whose life no mother could save, although all the women inmates present were eagerly waiting to give of themselves to take care of it. Shmuel, the 'youngest' and most cared for child in the family, ends up completely alone, having to fend for himself in the concentration camp.

In terms of phenomenology, the two testimonies share trauma signifiers. As already noted, the most tangible signifiers are the parapraxes. The presenters of both testimonies have highlighted them. However, the parapraxes are quite different from each other. In Shmuel's testimony they are mostly countertransference phenomena ("paramnesias," as Hamburger calls them). That sounds like a misattunement, a listening instrument that has been thrown off balance by the fragmented, chaotic nature of the narrative flow or by the 'guilt inversion' discussed above. In terms of psychoanalysis, they are replete with meaning, as Hamburger so impressively demonstrates, but they are not directly in response to Shmuel's trauma as an abandoned and bereaved child in the Holocaust. That trauma is not fully formulated consciously or unconsciously. It is neither woven into a narrative nor have defenses been erected that can contain it and ameliorate its impact. Therefore, there are no defenses to undo. This may explain the absence of parapraxes in the patient. The traumatic memory exists as split-off, chaotic fragments permeated by intense affects—primarily terror and unbearable loss. These memory fragments exert a continuous pressure, which if not held in abeyance may totally flood and obliterate the patient's life experience. This is what the patient spends most of his psychic energy on.

Jolly's parapraxes are of a completely different nature. Although the narrative of the traumatic moment—the murder of the baby—proceeds smoothly, and mother and daughter describe it with feelings and with presence of mind, no one involved notices the incongruence of the two stories. It becomes invisible. Yet this very invisibility glaringly exposes the formidable defensive function of that incongruity. Furthermore, the countertransference response of the interviewers is that they do not notice it either.

Note

1 First published as Discussion of Bodenstab, Knopp, and Hamburger, *Contemporary Psychoanalysis, 51*(2) (2015). Reprinted by permission of Taylor & Francis, LLC and the William Alanson White Institute of Psychiatry, Psychoanalysis, and Psychology, and the William Alanson White Psychoanalytic Society, www.wawhite.org.

PART V

Conclusions

Chapter 23

Unwanted memory
An open-ended conclusion

Dori Laub and Andreas Hamburger

Extreme traumatic experience is at the center of this book. As a gravity center, it resembles more a black hole than a solid object. What genocide leaves behind is a void in individual and collective memory. Although the book consists of a series of essays, each of which can also stand on its own and can be read separately, there is a shared point of reference: The authors oppose the notion of 'unspeakability' of the Holocaust, their respecting of silence notwithstanding. If survivors find it hard to verbalize their experience and transform it into a coherent narrative, if they have ever so often met deafness when they tried to talk, then the authors of this book agree on one point: silence is the beginning, not the end. It is a challenge. Unwanted memories, memories no one desires to tell or to hear, are the stuff that mental history is made of. The boundaries of traumatic silence still encroach on collective identities. Listening to the individual survivor, and becoming fully aware of one's own willingness as well as reluctance to listen is what we can do to break through these invisible, inaudible boundaries.

Each chapter in this book starts from the notion of severe social trauma, thinking through the topic from the angle it has chosen, and coming full circle back to the question of the book. They originate from different perspectives and disciplines, yet all relate to aspects of extreme traumatic experience. The different authors emphatically state their arguments in their specific, disciplinary voice. This springs from the need to counteract traumatic erasure and the psychological mechanisms it sets in motion. Differing though the chapters are, this need is something they share.

Part I begins by covering theoretical and clinical considerations (Bohleber, 2017; Laub, 2017a; Davoine & Gaudillière, 2017; Kaplan & Hamburger, 2017). Hamburger's contribution makes a foray into the social sphere (Hamburger, 2017a). Numerous clinical vignettes round out the picture. Part II examines testimony and offers new methodological approaches to its study and research (Bodenstab, 2017a; Dayan, 2017; Hamburger, 2017b; Knopp, 2017). Part III offers historical contextualization, description, and partial analysis of a video testimony study of Holocaust survivors hospitalized in psychiatric institutions in Israel; its authors are the professionals who planned, initiated, and carried out this study (Felsen, 2017; Greenwald, 2017; Laub, 2017b; Strous, 2017). The part concludes with a challenging article by a media scholar (Pinchevski, 2017) describing the interviews with these psychiatric patients in terms of "counter-testimony." Part IV consists of the comparison of two video excerpts, one from a mother and daughter who lived a regular life after surviving a labor camp together (Bodenstab, 2017b); the other from a survivor who spent close to five decades in a psychiatric hospital (Hamburger, 2017c). Together, the mother and daughter witnessed the murder of a newborn by the camp commandant. The differing nature of the parapraxes in the two testimonies is discussed in detail (Laub, 2017c). We want to emphasize that in addressing the difficulties survivors have in speaking about extreme trauma, we do not imply that they lived a broken life. Many survivors of concentration camps have successfully coped with their dreadful pasts and managed to live healthy lives. Children in the Rwandan genocide managed to find new attachments (Kaplan, 2008, 2013).

Where, given the work here presented, do we stand in relation to our original goal: to capture and examine the extreme traumatic experience? Have we gotten to the bottom of our pursuit? It is beginning to dawn on us that the very nature of the object of our inquiry may make its accomplishment impossible.

The various contributors to this volume, with their distinct and separate voices, form concentric circles around a core. That core is the phenomenon of extreme traumatization, which by its very nature eludes representation, articulation, and measurement. The different disciplinary approaches employed by the authors can only bring them so close to it, before they must abandon the pursuit. Ultimately, the core cannot be directly communicated, because it impacts the process of communication itself. Instead, most frequently, the transformational after-effects, the echoes and the debris that we find in its wake are what inform us about what happened. Similarly, the dimensions of that erasure are what inform us about the power of the traumatic impact. No methodology seems adequate to counterbalance and capture its destructiveness.

What extreme traumatization really does is highlight the limits in the human capacity to deal with 'reality.' This 'reality' includes questions about our temporary nature, our encounter with death, and other troubling aspects of life that we cannot grasp, think through, know, conceptualize, or remember. In order to go on, we live as if large sections of reality didn't exist. Everyday life in a highly complex and fast moving society is based on the capacity to split off signals of danger. We should not think of the immense space beneath us when we travel in an airplane, or the very narrow space between us when we come across another car on the road at high speed. But apart from this everyday splitting, which helps us handle our own technology, there are fields of unhealthy splittings, a 'dynamic' unconscious, as Freud would have put it. Here, it would be much better to know more about what is buried or drowned under the thin ice of consciousness we are walking on, lest those unwanted memories come back as revenants to haunt us. Here, it is unwanted history that causes the 'too muchness' that exceeds our capacity to absorb and digest, so we simply pay no attention to it. We tailor what we apprehend to our capacity for comprehending it intellectually and emotionally. The picture we paint in our minds is invariably composed of a plentitude of scotomata, yet we tell ourselves that it is complete and whole, and ferociously protect ourselves from knowing otherwise.

Just as in the case of dealing with death, where the human imagination, under the auspices of religion, has created the afterlife, so has that imagination created an imaginary mosaic of facts, voids, and plausible bridging explanations in order to represent reality to our mind. What is left out exceeds by far what is allowed into the mosaic; it consists of whatever challenges and puts into question our frame of reference and what we already know. In the Middle Ages, whoever dared to express that which was 'left out' could be burned at the stake; in modern times, we find other ways of obliterating unwanted information. Even if we register it cognitively, we remain deaf to it emotionally. No "action knowledge" (Hallie, 1994) comes into existence that can inform the decisions we make.

Traumatic experience pierces the psychological barriers erected to keep the 'left out' from our awareness. It eclipses modes of adaptation whose function is to keep the unknown out of reach. We come face-to-face with what we cannot fathom.

This book's various chapters examine breaches in the fabric of mental activity resulting from experiences of the extreme in outer reality.

As Cathy Caruth has helped us understand, that experience itself is recognized "one moment too late" (Caruth, 1996, 62) and only by noticing that it has been missed. To reconstruct it, one must draw upon one's imagination. The person to whom it is related must do the same. This also holds true for the listeners who follow, one after the other, as they attempt to carry forward the imagined reconstruction or representation of the experience of extreme traumatization. Explicating one's imagination may be the only way to grasp and register it. Yet to do so requires substantial effort, involving discipline and persistence. It amounts to bridging the gap, to undoing the breach that marked the original experience. In most cases, the imagination can only approximate the original 'missed experience.' That may suffice. Even if its contours remain blurry, the affect is unmistakably there.

The various contributors to this book have reached for the limits of what is currently known. The following are examples of limits that were reached.

Psychoanalytic theory was initially paralyzed in its encounter with traumatic memory. In its first theory of psychological trauma, it could only conceptualize it as a stimulus barrier having been breached, with the consequence of destroying the capacity for containment of the 'too-muchness' that kept gushing in. However, when psychoanalytic theory developed into an object relations approach, its concept of trauma changed accordingly. It was understood that a trauma is a damage not just to an apparatus, but also to a basic relatedness. The linkage and the flow of psychic life were no longer possible in the absence of libidinal ties to the object, which had been lost with the destruction of the internal 'thou.' In the mental life of the survivor of extreme trauma, the empathic dyad ceased to exist. With it ceased in-depth communication with oneself and the meaningful 'other.' Children were the most immediate victims of such psychological destruction. Extreme trauma stunted their emotional development. They were marked for life. Yet trauma also crossed boundaries between the individual and the collective, and between generations. The stable framework of time and place no longer existed. The appearance of historical trauma that afflicted the past and one's relations could occur at any place and any time. It even manifested itself as enactments of psychotic symptoms in patients belonging to later generations.

Inasmuch as the classical methodological approaches of history and psychoanalysis were no longer applicable, new qualitative assessment methods had to be created and applied to the gathering of data. The findings based on these new methodologies were, unsurprisingly, in line with the manifold ruptures in communication at the center of representations of extreme traumatic experience. These ruptures in themselves came to be markers of the traumatic experience. What replaced sensitive and meaningful human communication was a plethora of miscommunications, small and large: parapraxes, so to speak, of different orders of magnitude.

By using clinical material from analytic patients and quotations from Holocaust testimonies, this book implicitly highlights the relationship between these two differing trauma texts. While the first is created in the context of a therapeutic endeavor and the second in a testimonial context, the two nevertheless share many commonalities. The reason is that they both originate from the memory of extreme traumatic experience; both are therefore subject to its profound impact. Neither is created a priori as a complete narrative; rather, both consist of the rendition of fragments, saturated with sensory-motor percepts and bearing a high affective charge. Approaching them not only triggers defensive responses, but literally causes a profound disarticulation in the flow of mental life; it tears, so to speak, its very fabric. Turning attention to, and taking a systematic account of this torn fabric, or even the tornness of the fabric itself, is what Pinchevski (2017) calls the "counter-archive" of psychoanalytic testimony.

Turning one's attention to the traumatic experience elicits intense momentary pain, terror, or both—in patient and witness alike. The immediate reflexive response is to avert one's attention or gaze—in the direction of something else, or of nothing, by drawing a blank. Yet that momentary experience persists as a dull echo, accompanied by a pervasive unwillingness to return to it. Articulating these difficult fragments and weaving them into a narrative entails engaged and persistent emotional work.

Thinking through this question is a strenuous endeavor. One source of misdirection is that the answers seem all too evident, making it tempting to put them aside and not pursue the questions. This is very reminiscent of the conscious dream content. The images are so clear that one feels certain one will remember them, such that no effort needs to be put into recording them or reinforcing the memory. But when we start into the day, we often find it hard to recall what we thought to be so easily accessible—a reluctancy to and opaqueness of remembering, which is quite comparable to thinking of the Holocaust. To do so in either case is like working 'against' something. But what is it that we were trying to capture and get to the bottom of in this book? And why does it trigger such reluctance?

This book is about living life, being fully present to the blanks and scotomata, and about staying put in a place one doesn't want to be and can only remain in by holding at bay the pervasive impulse to flee. A great deal of discipline is needed to get at what is hidden in crevices, encrypted in blanks, and leaves affect traces at its periphery; these latter can range from a curious 'void of affect,' to blanks, to a sense of vague discomfort, to the suspicion that something is not quite right, to sheer terror at what is missing. All the above are accompanied by a pervasive reluctance to focus one's gaze on the blank and follow the thread of free associations to it. And yet, as awareness increases, doing so becomes less difficult.

This book attempts to strain our gaze at what we mostly cannot look at. In order to live our lives from one day to the next, we conceive of a reality that we feel capable of knowing. We believe that tomorrow will not be much different from today. We believe in the continuity of our 'self.' We believe that we can increasingly come to know the laws that govern our habitat and thereby master them and move ahead. Scientific and technological advances have indeed proven us right, in the last two centuries in particular. Predictability seemed to hold the upper hand and allowed us to put randomness out of our mind. Our sense of safety and tranquility benefited greatly.

The price we pay in order to hold on to this highly valued experience of stability is our disregard of all that does not fit into it. This disregard is multifaceted. Festinger (1957) observed it in the phenomena he named "cognitive dissonance." When we experience something that 'does not fit,' we respond with a whole range of affects. The most productive response is when we feel surprise. That is when we might try to change our 'schema'— the mental construct we have built to represent what we believe reality is—to incorporate the inconsistency we have just discovered. More often, we experience annoyance and a lingering sense of discomfort. We may have it wrong, yet we turn away from that discomfort to something else, something more familiar. The discomfort may remain with us and eventually become linked to a sense of helplessness, in that we really do not know how to resolve the inconsistency. We may invent a belief system that helps us live with it, much as the idea of the afterlife serves to address the awesomely unsettling question of death. When the inconsistency is too major and too threatening, it may be traumatizing enough to put the whole mental apparatus out of commission, so that what is threatening is not even noticed. It is tempting to think of the resultant blank as a product of defensive operations, but the absence thus created is phenomenologically closer to an 'erasure' than a repression.

When finally forced to take account of the discomfort, the mind does not 'recognize' it, but rather treats it as something never seen before. Despite being in full view, the incongruity remains unnoticed. Total denial works concurrently in a retrograde and an anterograde fashion; it always takes us by complete surprise. The media brought the Rwandan genocide and the Nazi death camps to the center of our attention. We were slow in drawing the lines between the dots that brought the genocidal project into relief. It contradicted twentieth-century belief in human progress.

It feels like such a effort to keep one's gaze focussed on what refuses to be seen, to hold on to the threads that lead us straight ahead. The thought of letting go of them, feels like such relief. Perhaps it is like what Donald Moss said (personal communication September 24, 2015): "we are dealing here with the ubiquity of an impulse to obliterate, that this stirred up by the threat of too muchness."

When re-reading the book, we notice that there is still the presence of the void. It seems that, on many issues, we have not gone far enough, not been thorough enough, not thought matters through to a sufficient extent, such that we might explicate them in finer detail. Despite all our efforts, we could not hold on to the thread long enough, and we prematurely let go of it.

Looking inward, we are aware of a certain ennui, as well as of an anxiety that we had set our goals too high, too far beyond what we could accomplish. It feels like the thread that we picked up simply vanished and came to nothing. Perhaps this is yet another manifestation of the countertransference resistance that impeded not only our work but also our ability to take stock of it.

However, with all our shortcomings we tried to navigate our way through the clouds of uncertainty, accompanying the dread that radiates from the black hole of the Holocaust. We tried to listen to the precise words and voids of the survivors. We did so in the hope that accepting unwanted memories might help them find some rest. 'Minding the gaps,' mentalizing the voids of the narrative, means giving voice to the unspoken, and adding the orphaned biographies to the many others, who have been successfully told and listened to.

References

Bodenstab, J. (2017a). The question of my German heritage. This volume, chapter 7.

Bodenstab, Johanna (2017b). Parapraxis in mother–daughter testimony: Unconscious fantasy and maternal function. This volume, chapter 19.

Bohleber, W. (2017). Treatment, trauma, and catastrophic reality: A double understanding of the "too much" experience and its implications for treatment. This volume, chapter 1.

Caruth, C. (1996). *Unclaimed experience: Trauma, narrative, and history*. Baltimore, MD: Johns Hopkins University Press.

Davoine, F., & Gaudillière, J.-M. (2017). The psychoanalysis of psychosis at the crossroads of individual stories and of history. This volume, chapter 5.

Dayan, D. (2017). Visible witness: Watching the footprints of trauma. This volume, chapter 8.

Felsen, I. (2017). The Israel story: My story. This volume, chapter 13.

Festinger, L. (1957). *A theory of cognitive dissonance*. Stanford, CA: Stanford University Press.

Greenwald, B. (2017). The institutional experience: Patients and staff responding to the testimony project. This volume, chapter 15.

Hallie, P. P. (1994). *Lest innocent blood be shed: The village of Le Chambon and how goodness happened*. New York: Harper Collins.

Hamburger, A. (2017a). Genocidal trauma: Individual and social consequences of assault on the mental and physical life of a group. This volume, chapter 4.

Hamburger, Andreas (2017b). Scenic-narrative microanalysis: Controlled psychoanalytic assessment of session videos or transcripts as a transparent qualitative research instrument. This volume, chapter 10.

Hamburger, Andreas (2017c). Refracted attunement, affective resonance: Scenic-narrative microanalysis of entangled presences in a Holocaust survivor's video testimony. This volume, chapter 21.

Kaplan, S. (2008). *Children in genocide: Extreme traumatization and affect regulation*. London: International Psychoanalysis Library.

Kaplan, S. (2013). Child survivors of the 1994 Rwandan genocide and trauma-related affect. *Journal of Social Issues, 69*, 92–110.

Kaplan, S., & Hamburger, A. (2017). The developmental psychology of social trauma and violence: The case of the Rwandan genocide. This volume, chapter 6.

Knopp, Sonja (2017). Narrative fissures, historical context: When traumatic memory is compromised. This volume, chapter 20.

Laub, D. (2017a). Traumatic shutdown of narrative and symbolization: A failed empathy derivative. Implications for therapeutic interventions. This volume, chapter 3.

Laub, D. (2017b). The Israel project story. This volume, chapter 12.

Pinschevski, A. (2017). Counter-testimony, counter-archive. This volume, chapter 17.

Strous, R. (2017). Video testimony of long-term hospitalized psychiatrically ill Holocaust survivors. This volume, chapter 14.

Chapter 24

Epilogue

Donald Moss

Yesterday, a dove flew into the glass wall of the back of our house. Stunned, it fell to the ground like a rock. It lay there, absolutely immobile. I thought it was dead. Like its chest, its wide-open beak was still. I touched it and it moved, but purposelessly, like any irritated living tissue might. I watched it closely, certain it was about to die.

Fifteen minutes later, though—fifteen perfectly still minutes later—the bird started to move, just a bit. Its wings flapped, just a little, as though for the last time. Flight seemed absolutely impossible. Now, I didn't know what to do. A wounded bird poses a more difficult problem than a dead one.

And then, suddenly, with no transition, the bird simply flew away, looking like an intact functional bird. I was amazed.

I now imagine this intact bird trying to report to other birds what it had undergone. The bird would have no capacity to explain itself, no way to conceptualize glass, no way to describe colliding with an invisible object. No matter what it might remember, it could transmit none of it—no warning, no narrative, no image. Its experience, though profound, would be useless.

Although the bird might always be burdened with both the memory and the urgency to tell, it would be even more burdened by its own incapacity to represent what it somehow remembers.

I, the only witness, know that a glass wall intervened in the life of a flying bird. I know the bird almost died. But what I know is also useless.

Maybe the bird knows a sequence: flight, collision, silence, stillness, and flight—nothing more, nothing less.

I know there will be more glass walls, awaiting this bird and all the others—glass walls everywhere—unpredictable, inexplicable.

I can place the event in time— it happened then, I'm remembering it now; it will happen again. The bird can do none of that. The collision lives timelessly and permanently inside the bird.

I imagine the bird's fractured efforts at giving 'testimony' to other birds. He will fail. None of them will know what he means, what he has undergone.

This may seem small and trivial but it is neither. Reading this book is akin to witnessing the bird. I am now more open, aware that at any moment not only the bird but all of us can crash into glass, or that glass can crash into us—unpredicted, unseen, incomprehensible, and uncomprehended.

Glass is both imperceptible and violent. We must tread carefully and anxiously, all of us—birds and humans alike. No one can adequately warn us, even though we can both witness the collision and perceive the fractured efforts of the wounded to tell us what remains of what they have known.

Index

abandonment 20, 23, 54, 67; by God 54
acceptance 237–9; implicit 205–6
accreditation 158
action knowledge 200
acute stress disorder 25
adaptive life themes 37
Adelson, E. 109
aesthetics 147, 170, 235
aetiology 190
affect: affective blackout of the present
   60; invading affects 106–7; memory,
   mourning and 155–7
affect regulation 107–8, 115–16, 117, 118
affect storms 60–1
aging survivors 188
Alexander, J.C. 71
Allen, J. 23
Amati, S. 26
ambiguity 79, 137, 234
ambivalence 191; of the historian 151
Amery, J. 51, 53
Amir, M. 76
Anatomy Lesson (Rembrandt) 136,
   138, 147
Ancel, J. 273
Andrews, B. 77–8
Angelus Novus (Klee) 150–1
Angrick, A. 273
annihilation 53, 82
anxiety 20–2, 73, 78, 107–9, 112, 156,
   215, 224–6; annihilation anxiety 20,
   75; fragmentation anxiety 42; signal
   anxiety 109
Anzieu, D. 111
aphasia, narrative 139–40
appearing 136
Appy, G. 39–40
archive fever 251

archiving 137–8, 250–1; counter-archive
   183, 242–53
arousal 26, 107; hyperarousal 212–13
'Aschenglorie' ('Ash Glory') (Celan) 155
Ashrov, M. 248–9
Assmann, A. 155, 156, 159
attachment 50, 78, 81, 108–10, 115–18,
   306; and trauma 23, 108–9
attributions 71–2
audiovisual media technology 242–53
Auerhahn, N. 52, 53, 62, 267
Auschwitz 55, 56, 224–5, 246, 262;
   uprising 3
automatic anxiety 21–2
Avner 234, 239

Badri, A. 77
Bastiaans, J. 246
Bakermans-Kranenburg, M.J. 76–7
Balint, M. 22
Barag, G. 186
Baranger, M. 21–2
Baranger, W. 21–2
Barel, E. 76–7
Bauer, Y. 228
Baumatz, J. 186
Bazak Investigation Committee 189, 217
Becker, A. 96
Beer Yaacov hostel 218–27
Belgium 224
Belzec 200
Ben-Ari, O. 222, 282, 291
Ben Meir, Shmuel *see* Shmuel's testimony
Benjamin, W. 150–1
Bergen-Belsen 262
Bessarabia 150, 158, 270, 271–4
bewilderment 34, 151
Birds, The 144

Blank, A.S. 33
Bleich, A. 220
blind spots 43–7, 62
Bluma 204–5, 207
Blumenthal, K. 186
Bodenstab, J. 162; German heritage 127–32
Boder, D. 9
Bohleber, W. 73
Böhm, T. 110
borrowed time 53–4
Boulanger, G. 265
Breslau, N. 75
Brewin, C.R. 77–8
Brockmeier, J. 160
Bukovina 272, 273
Bunny, S. 196

Carter, S. 76
Caruth, C. 3, 48, 70–1, 266, 308
catastrophe theory 101
Celan, P. 155
celebrities 221–2
Chanale 199
Charcot, J.-M. 125, 134, 136–7, 245
children: developmental psychology of social trauma and violence 18, 104–23; of Holocaust survivors 37–8, 40, 41, 45–6, 58; sexual abuse of 200
classification of posttraumatic disorders 67–70, 105–6
Clérambault, L.-N. 134
clinical outcomes 183, 209–16
clinical ratings 211, 231
closed-circuit television (CCTV) 245
cognitive dissonance 310–11
Cohen, J. 268
collective memory 29–30
collective witnessing 147
communicative breakdowns 6–8, 153–4, 257
compensation 191
compensation neurosis 186–7
complex posttraumatic stress disorder (CPTSD) 67–8, 69, 106
concentration camps 13, 34–6, 52, 187, 263–8, 300, 311; survivors rejected by German psychiatry 83; survivors' syndrome 187, 190
Conference on Jewish Material Claims Against Germany (Claims Conference) 196, 210, 218

conspiracy of silence 29–30, 279
constructions (memory) 28, 48, 61
constructivist approach 70–3
control group 197, 211, 231
conversation and discourse analysis 170–1
Copenhagen conference on the physical damage of persecution and imprisonment and their late impact 189
counter-archive 183, 242–53
counter-testimonies 183, 242–53
countertransference 249–50, 258; interviewer's in testimony-taking 237
countertransference-based field research 168
countertransference blindness 43–7, 62
countertransference resistance 13–14, 198–201, 250
Crutzen, R. 77
cultural analysis 169, 175–6
cultural trauma 71, 72
cumulative trauma 75
Czechoslovakia 226

Da Rocha Barros, E.L. 74, 279, 292
Da Rocha Barros, E.M. 74, 279, 292
Darfur 77
David 226
Davoine, F. 160
dead mother complex 51, 63, 79
death 161; escape from 93; fear of 20, 58; Hasidic 275–6, 290–1; infanticide see infanticide; longing for 51, 291; mass 161; psychic 98, 230; of Shmuel's father 274, 275–6, 289–92; of Shmuel's mother 274, 287–9; threat of 48, 53, 66, 100, 118, 266
death trains 223
defense mechanisms 33
de-institutionalization 218
Delhom, P. 153
delusions 95–8
dementia 214
denial 2, 174, 198–9, 208, 311
deportations: from Romania 272–3, 273–4, 282–92; pathology of deportation 189
'Deputy, The' (Hochhuth) 248
Derrida, J. 251, 252
desolation 54–6
development-based model of cumulative trauma 75
developmental trauma 105–10
Devereux, G. 168

dialogic witnessing 144–6
Diamond, H.W. 245
digital technology 251–3
DiMauro, J. 76
Dinur, Y. (Katzetnik) 246
disarticulation 265–6
disasters, man-made 29–30, 69–70
disclosure, benefits of 232–3
Disorders of Extreme Stress Not Otherwise
   Specified (DESNOS) 69, 105–6
disorganized attachment style 108
displaced people 189
disregard 138
dissociation 24–5, 112, 118, 174, 268
dissonance: cognitive 310–11; narrative
   145–6, 260–9
Djurin ghetto 274–6
dose-response model 75
drowsiness 285
DSM definitions of traumatic stress 66–7
Du côté de Guermantes (Proust) 145
Dvorjetski, M. 185–6, 190–1

Ehring, T. 76
Eichmann trial 187, 217, 246
Eidelstedt 260–2, 263, 264
Eissler, K.R. 83
Eitinger, L. 187
Ellison, R. 141
empathy, failed 17, 23, 50, 51–9, 200, 230
entelechy 142–3
envy 116
equanimity 235
erasure 7–8, 208, 233–4
ethnic persecution 29, 76, 111, 284
evidence, memory and 159–60
exchange of gazes 146–7, 148
execution fantasies 53–4
'exile' 129
existential recognition 141
expectancy 102
experiences of disaster, trauma and
   testimony 153–7
experimental group 197, 211
explicitness 174, 176
Eyerman, R. 71
Ezrahi, S.D. 54

failed empathy 17, 23, 50, 51–9, 200, 230
fantasies 25; execution fantasies 53–4;
   revenge fantasies 112–14, 117
father 58; death of Shmuel's father 274,
   275–6, 289–92

Fawzi, M.H. 75
Fawzi, M.M. 75
fear 237–8
Felman, S. 3, 162, 242
Ferenczi, S. 22
Festinger, L. 310
Finkelstein, B.A. 185
fissures, narrative 270–8
flashbacks 28, 107
Folk, J.B. 76
Ford, J. 146
forgotten Holocaust 150
Fortunoff video archive 150, 199–200,
   242, 247, 250–1
forward psychiatry 92, 102
fragments of memory 32, 34–5, 41, 230,
   236; failed empathy and fragmentation
   51–9
Fraiberg, S. 109
Fran 206–7
France: armistice celebrations 96; German
   occupation 96, 97
French Resistance 94
Freud, S. 19, 99, 117, 293; inseparable
   bond between cure and research 167–8;
   mourning 114; oceanic feeling 11;
   psycho-economic model of trauma
   21–2; symbolization 49–50
Friedländer, S. 151
fugue states 32, 33–4
functioning Holocaust survivors 203–8
Future of Holocaust Testimonies panel 3–4
future publics 137–8, 147–8

Gaudillère, J.-M. 160
gazes, exchange of 146–7, 148
gender effects 213
generational collapse 111
generational linking 112, 118
genocidal trauma 17–18, 66–91; specificity
   of 110–12
genocide denial 2
German heritage 127–32
Germany 191, 228; failure of the
   genocidal project 131; Federal Law
   for Compensating Victims of Nazi
   Persecution 186; German psychiatry's
   rejection of concentration camp
   survivors 83; occupation of France 96,
   97; restitution 186–7
Gideon 235, 239
Giesen, B. 71
Golda 220, 222

good internal object 11, 50–1; destroyed 26, 63
'good Nazi' 55–6
Green, A. 51, 63, 79
grounded theory 280, 294
group identity 72
Grüny, C. 153–4
guardians 220
Guez, J. 25
guilt 29, 30, 128, 191; Shmuel's testimony 272, 282–5
guilt inversion 272, 284–5

Hamburger, A. 3, 152, 272, 298
Hannah 222–4
Hartman, G. 242, 243
Hasanovic, M. 77
Hasidic death 275–6, 290–1
Heins, M. 76
helplessness 22
Henry 204
Herman, J.L. 105
hermeneutic in-depth analysis 169
Hilger, Y. 77
historicization 24–9
historiography 3, 270–1; methodological considerations on video testimony 125, 150–65; witnessing witnessing 157–60
Hitchcock, A. 144
Hochhuth, R. 248
holding back 233–4
holding environment 57, 62
Holocaust Memorial Day (Yom Hashoah) 221
Honneth, A. 140–1
hospitalized Holocaust survivors 5–6, 183, 198, 228–9; audiovisual technology and testimonies from 242–53; clinical outcomes of the video testimony method 183, 209–16; comparison with functioning Holocaust survivors 203–8; historical overview 185–94; impact of German restitution 186–7; institutional experience 183, 217–27; Israeli psychiatry 83, 187–91; see also Israel video testimony project
hostels for Holocaust survivors 218–27
Hotin 272–3
house burning 93
humiliation 113, 115–16
Hutus 110–11
hypermentalizing 110

identification 249–50
imagery 39–40, 41
imagination 308
immediacy 102
immigration 189
implicit acceptance 205–6
individual memory 29–30
individual trauma vs social trauma 17–18, 75–83
infanticide 206; mother–daughter testimony 135, 145–6, 258, 260–9, 277
injured life 161
inseparable bond between cure and research 167
institutional experience 183, 217–27
institutional rejection 82–3
integration 24–9, 60
intergenerational trauma transmission 9, 108–9, 308
internal good object 11; destroyed 26, 50–1, 63
internal other, loss of the link to 17, 51–9
International Psychoanalytic Congress of 2015 3–4
interpersonal parapraxes 6–7
inter-rater reliability 175, 176–7
intimate relationship 58, 59
intrapersonal parapraxes 6–7
intrusions of traumatic memories 28
invading affects 106–7
Invisible Man, The (Ellison) 141
Ioanid, R. 273
isolation 23, 54–6
Israel 158, 217; hospitalized Holocaust survivors see hospitalized Holocaust survivors; Israeli psychiatry 83, 187–91; uniqueness of Israeli psychiatry 189–91
Israel video testimony project 183; chronology of the project 195–201; clinical outcomes 183, 209–16; counter-testimonies and counter-archive 183, 242–53; funding 196; hostels' involvement 220–2; mother–daughter testimony see mother–daughter testimony; process of taking testimonies 197, 202–3, 220–1; Shmuel's testimony see Shmuel's testimony; traumatic psychosis and narrative forms 183, 228–41; see also hospitalized Holocaust survivors

Japanese POW camps 46
Jean 113, 117

Jewish Council of Djurin 275
Jolly 135, 145–6, 260–9, 276–7;
    importance of the woman's pregnancy
    to 264–6; testimony compared with
    Shmuel's testimony 298–301
Judenrat 206

Kaplan, S. 79, 105, 110, 111–12
Kaplan, Z. 76
Karski, J. 200
Kashdan, T.B. 76
Katzetnik (Y.Dinur) 246
Keilson, H. 233
Kiev 235
Kinston, W. 268
Kira, I.A. 75
Kirshner, L. 50, 61
Klee, P. 150–1
Klein, H. 55, 188
Klein, M. 49
knowledge/knowing: action knowledge
    200; forms of traumatic memory 17,
    32–42; not knowing 32, 33, 199–201,
    267; real 200
Kohut, H. 73
Korber, M. 275
Korina 206, 207
Koselleck, R. 161
Kotler, M. 76, 220
Kravic, N. 77
Kümmel, W. 261–2, 263, 265–6, 267, 277

Lacan, J. 99
LaCapra, D. 3–4
Lady Vanishes, The 144
Last Journey into Silence, The 196
late impact of persecution 189
Laub, Clara 146–7
Laub, D. 3, 52, 53, 62, 242, 247, 250,
    267; communicative breakdown 153–4;
    dialogic witnessing 145; genocidal
    trauma 74, 292; interview with Shmuel
    281–92; joint interview with his mother
    146–7; listening 243
leadership, destructive 116–17
Leon 38–9, 153–4
Lev Hasharon hostel 218–20, 227
Levi, P. 52
Levinger, L. 186–7
Liebsch, B. 152, 153, 154, 160, 161
life themes 32, 37–8, 41
linking: attacks on 292; generational
    linking 112, 118; trauma linking 112

listening 49, 115, 243, 249
living experience of the injury 155–6
Lomranz, J. 188
loneliness 23, 54–6
Lorenzer, A. 169, 175
loss, traumatic 264–6
LSD treatment 246
Luthra, R. 76

Maaleh Hachamisha conference of
    1996 195
Mad Masters, The 134, 138, 147
Maercker, A. 68
Main, M. 108
man-made traumatizations 29–30, 69–70
Marion, J.-L. 136
Mark, M. 195, 218
marriage 59
McFarlane, A. 48, 107
meaningful clinical data 174, 175–6
Medea 143
memory 173–4, 293; affect, mourning and
    155–7; collective and individual 29–30;
    compromised 270–8; developmental
    trauma 106–8; erased 7–8, 208,
    233–4; and evidence 159–60; forms
    of traumatic memory 17, 32–42;
    fragments of *see* fragments of memory;
    reconstruction, historicization and
    mental integration of traumatic
    memories 24–9; unwanted memories
    305–15
Menachem 247
Menninger Triangle 177
mentalization 80–2, 115; developmental
    trauma 109–10
merging biographies 285–9
metaphors 32, 39–40, 41, 299
microanalysis 166, 170–1; scenic-narrative
    microanalysis *see* scenic-narrative
    microanalysis
Miller, I. 218
Moeller, S. 77
Mom, J.M. 21–2
Mona 205
monstration 135, 136–8
Moore, R. 48–9, 61
Moreau, J.-J. (Moreau de Tours) 134
Moss, D. 311
mother 57–8; dead mother complex 51,
    63, 79; death of Shmuel's mother 274,
    287–9; failure of the mothering function
    300; Jolly's mother figure 264–5

mother–daughter testimony 135, 145–6, 258–9, 260–9, 276–7, 298; comparison with Shmuel's testimony 298–301
mourning 114; memory, affect and 155–7
Mucci, C. 3
Müller, H.H. 77
Murafa ghetto 274–5
Muselmanner state 230

narrative 10, 11; failure of the narrating function 81–2; narrative forms of psychotic sufferers 183, 228–41; overpowering narratives 32, 36–7; traumatic shutdown 17, 43–65; witnessed narratives 32, 38–9
narrative analysis 166, 169–70; scenic-narrative microanalysis *see* scenic-narrative microanalysis
narrative aphasia 139–40
narrative dissonance 145–6, 260–9
narrative fissures 270–8
narrative 'scar tissue' 266–9
Nathan, T.S. 187
naturalism 71–2
Nazi ideology 52
Nedeljkovic, J. 78
negative life themes 37–8
negativity 160–1
Neugebauer, R. 77
neutrality 60–1, 191
Niethammer, L. 159
nosology 190
not knowing 32, 33, 199–201, 267
not repressed unconscious 99–100

object deficit theory 17, 43–65
object-relations theory 308; model of trauma 22–4
objectivity 176, 191
objectlessness 230, 231–2
oceanic feeling 11
Ora 234–5, 239
oral-history-research 159
ordinariness 234
Ornstein, A. 3, 73
overpowering narratives 32, 36–7

Pajevic, I. 77
Pankow, G. 92
paramnesia 287–8
parapraxes 6–8, 257–8; comparison of Jolly's and Shmuel's testimonies 300–1;

mother–daughter testimony 258–9, 260–9; Shmuel testimony 259, 285–6
pathology of deportation 189
pathos 134–5
Peirce, C.S. 244
perforation 79, 111
perpetrators, in testimonies 300
persecuting object 26
Peskin, H. 62
photography 245
picrine 38
pogrom 93, 95
posttraumatic screen memories 26, 260, 264, 267–8
posttraumatic stress disorder (PTSD) 19, 25, 46–7, 200, 209, 212, 214; classification of posttraumatic stress disorders 67–70, 105–6; epidemiological and clinical data 75–7
potentiality 142–3
Prague Panel 255
pregnancy 109, 264–6
presupposition 283
pretend play 81
Priebe, S. 78
primal repression 268
Proust, M. 145
proximity 102
psychic equivalence 265–6
psychoanalysis 308; models of trauma 20–4; of psychosis 18, 92–103; testimonies and 9–12
psycho-economic models of trauma 21–2, 23–4
psychological testing 211, 231
psychosis: psychoanalysis of 18, 92–103; testimonies of sufferers from traumatic psychosis 183, 228–41
pure trauma 22

Quack, D. 76
qualitative research strategies 170–1
Quignard, P. 142–3

Rafi 139–40, 142, 144, 247–8
rage 129
Rakovsky, Rafi 139–40, 142, 144, 247–8
rape 80
Real, the 99
real knowing 200
Rear Window 144
recognition 140–1, 142–3; social (regard) 138, 141

reconciliation 114–17
reconstruction 24–9, 41, 60, 61
reflective functioning 80–1, 114–15
refusal to know 199–201
regard 138, 141
rejection, institutional 82–3
relational view 73
reliability 175, 176–7
reluctant witnessing 138–9
Reman, I. 222
Rembrandt van Rijn 136, 138, 147
reparation 114–17
repetition: compulsions 21, 28; in multiple
    layers 293–4
reported events 140
repression 174, 266–8; primal 268
research, psychiatric 190
resignation 239
resistance to countertransference 13–14,
    198–201, 250
resonance 177
responsive subjectivity 154
restitution, German 186–7
restoration 114–17
revenge 105, 112–17; acts 113–14; fantasies
    112–14, 117; spiral 113–17, 118
Ricoeur, P. 155, 158, 161
ritual double 98
Rivka 204
Rizzuto, A.M. 49
Romania 158, 222–3, 276, 282–3;
    forgotten Holocaust 150; Jews in
    Transnistria 158, 270, 272, 273,
    274–7, 287; violence against the Jews in
    Bessarabia 150, 158, 270, 271–4
Rosalie 135, 145–6, 260–9, 276–7
Rosen, S. 274–5
Rosenblum, R. 142
Rosenstock, W. 275
Rouch, J. 134, 138, 147
Rüsen, J. 156
Russia 30
Rwandan genocide 18, 77, 200, 311;
    developmental psychology 104, 109,
    110–12, 113, 117

Sacks, O. 134
'safe' territory 223–4
Sagi-Schwartz, A. 76–7
Salmon, T. 102
Salomon, Z. 196–7
Salpêtrière presentations 134, 136–7

Sarah 224–6, 234, 239
'scar tissue', narrative 266–9
scenic-narrative microanalysis
    (SNMA) 125, 166–82, 279–97, 298;
    application to video interview data
    172–4; contribution to knowledge
    about manifestations of extreme
    traumatization 292–4; elements of
    166–71; quality criteria 174–7; of
    Shmuel's testimony 280–92; steps and
    procedures 172–3; in survivor research
    173–4, 279–80
scenic understanding 166; as a means of
    psychoanalytic research 167–9
schizophrenia 214, 217, 229
Schore, A.N. 109
scientism 170
screen memories 26, 260, 264, 267–8
second generation 188, 189; children
    of Holocaust survivors 37–8, 40, 41,
    45–6, 58
secondary witnessing 130, 154–5, 249
Secureni 273
Segal, H. 49
self 169–70; loss of 53
self-discipline 36
self-object 62
sexual abuse 19, 200
sexual violence 67
Shaar Menashe hostel 218–20, 227
shame 113, 115–16, 128
Shanan, J. 188
Shapiro, V. 109
shards of memory see fragments of
    memory
Shimon 234, 239
Shmotkin, D. 188
Shmuel's testimony 150–65, 219–20,
    258–9, 298; comparison with Jolly's
    testimony 298–301; death of his father
    274, 275–6, 289–92; death of his mother
    274, 287–9; guilt 272, 282–5; merging
    biographies 285–9; narrative fissures
    270–8; scenic-narrative microanalysis
    280–92; unwitnessing 138–40, 142,
    143; violence against the Jews in
    Bessarabia 150, 158, 270, 271–4
Siegel, D. 25
silence 128; conspiracy of 29–30, 279;
    testimonies from muted witnesses
    228–41
simplicity 102

Smelser, N.J. 71
Snyder, T. 100
soap from corpses myth 221
social recognition (regard) 138, 141
social trauma 70–84; developmental
    psychology 18, 104–23; individual
    trauma vs 17–18, 75–83
Sophie's Choice (Styron) 36
space creation 111–12
spectrum of traumatic memories 17, 32–42
speech events 140
Sperling, W. 77
splitting 24–5, 112, 118, 174, 268
Srebrenica 77
Stagecoach 146–7, 148
Stalinist terror 30
Stefanovic-Stanojevic, T. 78
Strous, R. 69, 197, 231
structure, loss of 56–9
Styron, W. 36
subjectivation, avoiding 142
subjectivization of trauma 73
substitutes 58–9
survival 131
survivor syndrome 190
symbolic functioning: attacks on 292;
    breakdown of 73–4; traumatic shutdown
    17, 43–65
symptom reduction 212–13, 213–14, 231
synagogue of Djurin 275–6, 289–90
Sztompka, P. 71

Tarantelli, C.B. 230, 265
temporal economies of attention 137
temporal standstill 26
temporality of the interpersonal mind
    169–70
tertiary witnessing 155, 243–4
testimonies: Israel video testimony project
    see Israel video testimony project;
    and pychoanalysis 9–12; testimonial
    impulse 311–12
text, witness as 140
theatricality 136–7
therapeutic alliance 62
therapon 98, 100
therapy with survivors 59–62, 69, 99–101
Theresienstadt 62
thirdness 244, 249
Thom, R. 101
Tomer's aunt 204–5
'too muchness' 198, 311

Topor, I. 272
training analysis 43–7, 62
trance 138
transference 98–9, 101, 102, 236–7;
    phenomena 32, 35–6
Transnistria 158, 270, 272, 273,
    274–7, 287
transparency 174, 176
trauma: attachment 23, 108–9;
    countertransference resistance
    13–14, 198–201, 250; cultural 71,
    72; cumulative 75; defining 66–7;
    developmental 105–10; genocidal see
    genocidal trauma; healing 73; history
    of psychiatry and psychoanalysis
    and 17, 19–31; memory, affect
    and mourning 155–7; nature of the
    traumatic experience 47–8; notions of
    70–5; psychoanalytic models 20–4;
    pure 22; and repression 266–8; social
    see social trauma
trauma linking 112
trauma signature 249
trauma signifiers 258–9, 300
traumatic shutdown 17, 43–65, 78–9
Trezise, T. 3, 4, 157, 250
trust 158–9
Tulp, N. 138
Tutsis 110–11, 200
Tutté, J.C. 106
typhus epidemic 274

Ukrainian Jews 150
unconscious, not repressed 99–100
uniqueness: of the Holocaust 3–5; of
    hospitalized Holocaust survivors'
    testimonies 8–9; of Israeli psychiatry
    189–91
unpathos 134–5
unspeakability of the Holocaust 3–5
unwanted memories 305–15
unwitnessing 135, 138–43
Utzon-Frank, N. 76

Valentine, J.D. 77–8
validation 135, 143–7
validity 175, 177
Van IJzendoorn, .M.H. 76–7
Van den Borne, H.W. 77
Van der Kolk, B. 48, 105–6, 107, 115
Varvin, S. 79
verification 158

video recording: audiovisual technology 242–53; data 171–2; and visibility 134; visible witnessing 125, 133–49

video testimony method, value of 183, 209–16

video testimony project *see* Israel video testimony project

Vietnam veterans 33

violence, and revenge 112–17

virtual publics 137–8

visibility 134; videos and 134; visible witness 125, 133–49

Vitek 94–5

Voiculescu, General 273

Weisaeth, L. 48, 107

Wiesel, E. 52, 54

Winnicott, D.W. 57

Winnik, H. 187

witnessed narratives 32, 38–9

witnessing 95, 98, 154–5, 293–4, 309, 314–15; audiovisual media and 242–53; centrality of the witness 151–3; collective 147; dialogic 144–6; displayed witness 136–8; and reliving trauma 198; reluctant 138–9; secondary 130, 154–5, 249; tertiary 155, 243–4; unwitnessing 135, 138–43; validating witness 135, 143–7; visible witness 125, 133–49; witnessing witnessing in historiography 157–60

Wittgenstein, L. 101

World War I 92, 102

Wurmser, L. 113

Yaffe, R. 187

Yair 235, 239

Yale Fortunoff archive 150, 199–200, 242, 247, 250–1

Yaro 205–6

Yasi 222–3

Yom Hashoah (Holocaust Memorial Day) 221

Yom Kippur War 45–6, 95

Zalashik, R. 198

Zellermayer, J. 188

Zulueta, F. de 114